AF538972

ENCYCLOPAEDIA OF COMPUTER SOFTWARE TECHNOLOGY

ENCYCLOPAEDIA OF COMPUTER SOFTWARE TECHNOLOGY

[Volume –Three]

Editor-in-Chief
Ajay Kumar

INSTITUTE FOR SUSTAINABLE DEVELOPMENT
LUCKNOW
&
ANMOL PUBLICATIONS PVT. LTD.
NEW DELHI - 110 002 (INDIA)

ANMOL PUBLICATIONS PVT. LTD.
4374/4B, Ansari Road, Daryaganj
New Delhi - 110 002
Ph.: 3261597, 3278000
Visit us at: www.anmolbooks.com

Encyclopaedia of Computer Software Technology

First Edition, 2003

ISBN 81-261-1385-5 (Set)

PRINTED IN INDIA

Published by J.L. Kumar for Anmol Publications Pvt. Ltd., New Delhi and Printed at Mehra Offset Press, Delhi.

Contents

Vol. 3

Preface

Today, the term 'computer' is synonymous with digital computer, but until the 1960s, analog computers were popular. An analog computer relies on analogies between physical effects to make calculations. For example, the voltages in an analog computer may represent temperatures in a heat exchanger, capacitors may represent heat storage capacity, electrical currents may represent heat flow, and so forth. A digital computer, in contrast, deals with values as numerical digits. Because of their versatility, speed, and relatively low cost, digital computers have almost entirely replaced the analog variety.

Computer programs, the software that is becoming an ever-larger part of the computer system, are growing more and more complicated, requiring teams of programmes and years of effort to develop. As a consequence, a new subdiscipline, software engineering, has arisen. As the size and complexity of software has grown, the concept of reuse has become increasingly important in software engineering, since it is clear that extensive new software cannot be created cheaply and rapidly without incorporating existing program modules (subroutines, or pieces of computer code). Sophisticated techniques for testing software have therefore been designed. The need for better trained software engineers has led to the development of educational programs in separate program. The recommendation that software engineers, like other engineers, be licensed or certified is gaining increasing support, as is the momentum toward the accreditation of software engineering degree programs.

The lack of standardization and smooth interoperability in UNIX led Microsoft to develop Windows NT, an operating system that overcome these problems and also provided an integral GUI. From the outside, the system appears much the same as Windows 95 or a Macintosh system, with icons and a mouse. Internally it is quite different, structured so that it can serve in a hand-alone workstation or in a file server on a network, depending on the version of the product. The system also provides easy networking in a commercial environment; adding file servers or shared peripherals is a simple setup task that requires little more than physically interconnecting equipment and setting parameters in a menu.

Windows 95, MS-DOS, OS/2, and other common operating systems are then run as client processes under Windows NT, much in the same way CMS and MVS run under VM on IBM mainframes. A so-called hardware abstraction layer isolates the software from the details of the underlying hardware, giving Windows NT platform-independence. The operating system is therefore portable from one platform to another. Windows NT is used with the upper-end Intel microprocessors and DEC's Alpha chip, a microprocessor for the VAX computer, and will undoubtedly be transport to other platforms.

The present book in three volumes is welcome addition to the existing literature which is really encyclopaedic in nature. The entire information is gathered under twenty nine chapters followed by an exhaustive glossary and Index.

Finally, we will be failing in our duty if we do not acknowledge the kind of assistance we received from our colleagues at the Institute in completion of this volume. We are equally indebted to Shri J.L. Kumar, Managing Director, Anmol Publications Pvt. Ltd., New Delhi for publishing this manuscript in a very limited time.

—Editor-in-Chief

20

Software Documentation Tools

Learning Objectives

After completing this chapter, you will be able to:

- Appreciate the need for and nature of various techniques employed by systems analysts/programmers for software development.
- Distinguish between various symbols and conventions used for constructing flowcharts.
- Understand the basics of constructing flowcharts.
- Distinguish between the different types of flowcharts, and judge in what situation data flow diagrams (DFDs), can be a better alternative to flowcharts.
- Explain the techniques involved in the construction of limited entry and extended entry decision tables.
- Evaluate the respective advantages and limitations of decision tables and flowcharts.
- Discuss the technique of constructing decision trees.
- Explain the nature of methodology involved in writing pseudocode and how the latter is related to programming.

Overview

For the purposes of reorganising the massive raw data gathered for system design and programming and for facilitating comprehension of the complicated processes and procedures involved, software specialists commonly use the following tools:

- Flowcharts
- Data Flow Diagrams (DFDs)
- Pseudocode
- Decisions Tables
- Decisions Trees

Their description follows:

Flowcharts

Made up of standard symbols and interconnecting flow-lines (see Appendix A to this chapter for their description) a flowchart (also, called *block diagram*), is a tool used both by systems analysts and programmers in the planning phases of their work. The purpose is to graphically present the logical flow of data for the solution of the problem, defining as well the major phases of processing along with the various media to be used.

It is to be noted that flowcharts are sufficiently creative so that no two persons will draw them exactly alike.

While the flowcharting technique can be used for portraying, graphically, a variety of procedures, the flowcharts of special interest in the context of EDP are of the following kinds:

- Clerical procedure flowcharts
- Systems flowcharts
- Computer run flowcharts
- Program flowcharts

Clerical procedure flowcharts—These flowcharts depict, in sequence, the inputs, outputs and processes in clerical procedures. They may be drawn in alternative ways, depending on the aspects of the procedures to be emphasised. Their purpose is to highlight action (or absence of action) on decuments/files by persons, functions, departments, locations etc. The sequence flow is represented by means of continuous lines while reference to files is shown by dashed (broken) lines.

Figure 1 depicts a typical clerical procedure flowchart in respect of the commercial activity 'sales order processing'.

Systems flowcharts—A systems flowchart provides an outline of the sequence of events in a system, alongwith the department or function responsible for each such event. This chart is usually drawn in columnar format with inputs shown on the left side, the outputs on the right side and the responsible departments/functions along the top. Processes within each column are represented by appropriate symbols which are connected to each other by lines and arrows.

A system flowchart depicting, sales order processing is illustrated in Figures 2. It may, however, be added that while the preparation of a system flowchart in a columnar format is preferable from the standpoint of clarity, the requirement is not mandatory. In simpler system situations, a non-columnar flowchart may also suffice.

Computer run flowcharts—This type of flowcharts are intended to depict the logical relationship of computer routines alongwith inputs, master files, transfer files and outputs.

The computer run chart is later on replaced by a programmer produced run chart showing the actual program.

A computer run flowchart depicting payroll processing routines is illustrated in Figures 3.

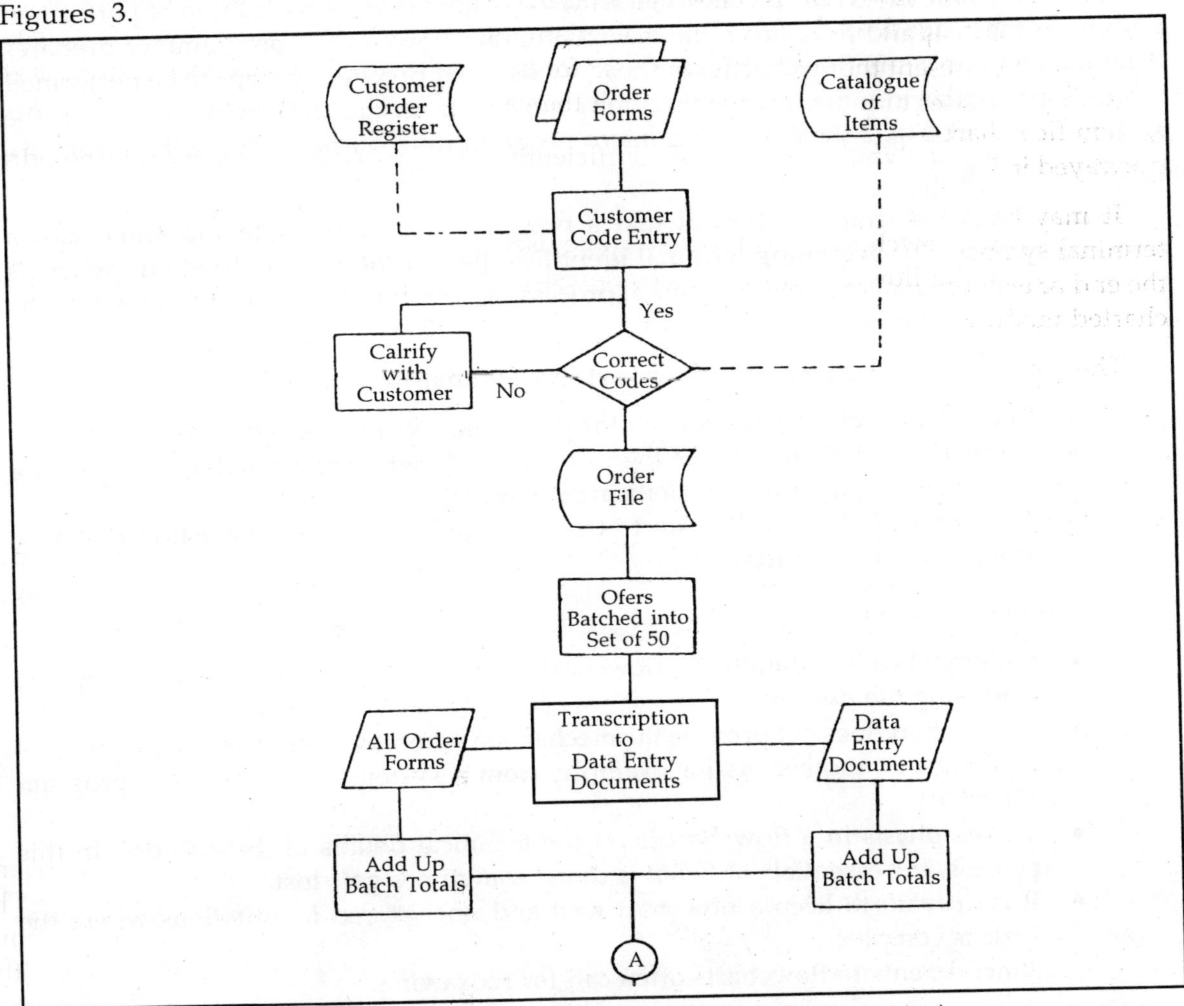

Fig. 1. Clerical Procedure Flowchart (Sales Order Processing)

Program flowcharts—Also, referred to as a *logic diagram*, a program flowchart evolves from a system flowchart. It illustrates, a detail, the various steps (operations, algorithms, etc.) to be performed within the computer for transforming the input into output.

The program flowchart serves as the basis for discussions and communication between the system analysis and the programmers, besides helping the programmers in:

- organising their programming effort
- avoiding certain types of errors

- maintaining (updating, correcting, etc.) an existing program at a later date when the original programmer is not available for consultation.

A program flowchart is usually constructed at two levels: *macro* and *micro*. The macro, a or main program, flowchart is concerned with the major tasks (or *modules*) to be performed within the main application. From the macro program flowchart, a programmer prepares detailed micro program flowchart(s) to show the detailed processing steps to be performed within a particular module. Proceeding, for example, from the step 'built invoice' in the system flowchart, Fig. 2 the macro and micro program flowcharts, evolving therefrom are portrayed in Fig. 4.

It may be noted from the figures that a program flowchart starts and ends with a terminal symbol. The beginning terminal identifies the routine to be carried out, whereas the end or exit terminal connotes the end of processing or return to the routine to which the charted module belongs.

The advantages associated with flowcharts are summarised below:

- Their construction does not call for particular technical knowledge.
- It is easier to understand the logic of a problem when presented in the form of a flowchart on paper than visualising it mentally.
- They provide the mechanism to trace forward from start, the action resulting from a set of conditions.

Their limitations are:

- Different levels of details in a flowchart carry the danger of getting mixed up and confusing the design.
- A flowchart does not provide the mechanism whereby to progress from one level of design to another, as for example, from a systems flowchart to a program flowchart.
- The emphasis in a flowchart is on the technical details of 'how to do'. In this process, the essentials of 'what is done' sometimes gets lost.
- It is difficult to keep a flowchart neat and uncluttered in situations where the logic is complex.
  Amendments to flowcharts often call for redrawing.
- A flowchart does not always provide an easy means to backtrack to the set of conditions that gave rise to the action.

The systems flowcharts and program flowcharts, when produced, constitute an important component of documentation for an application. However, there are also alternatives to flowcharts, a discussion of which follows.

Data Flow Diagrams (DFDs)

Also known as *bubble charts* the *data flow diagrams* may be viewed as a simple method of representing inputs, processes and outputs within an information system. They can be

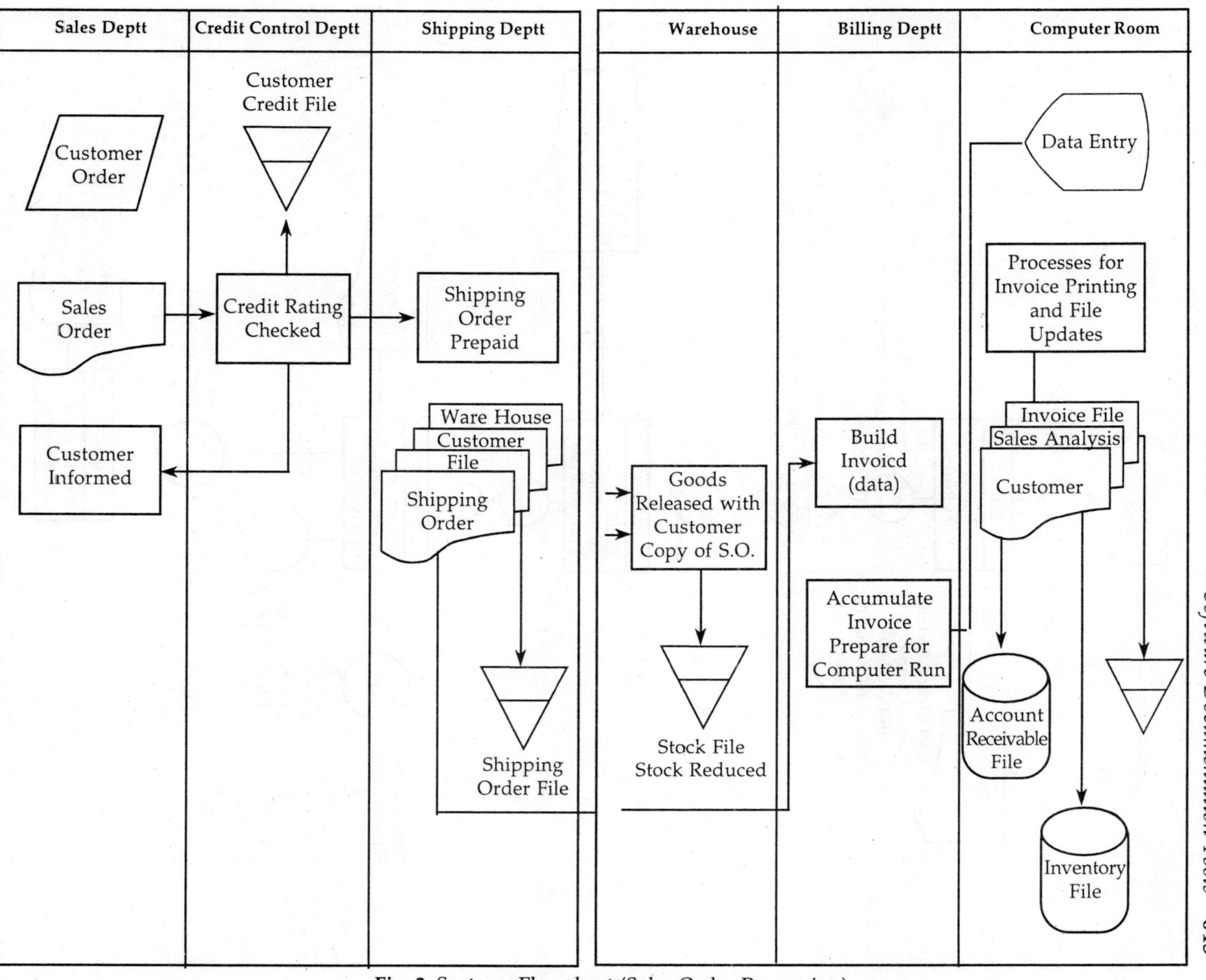

Fig. 2. Systems Flowchart (Sales Order Processing)

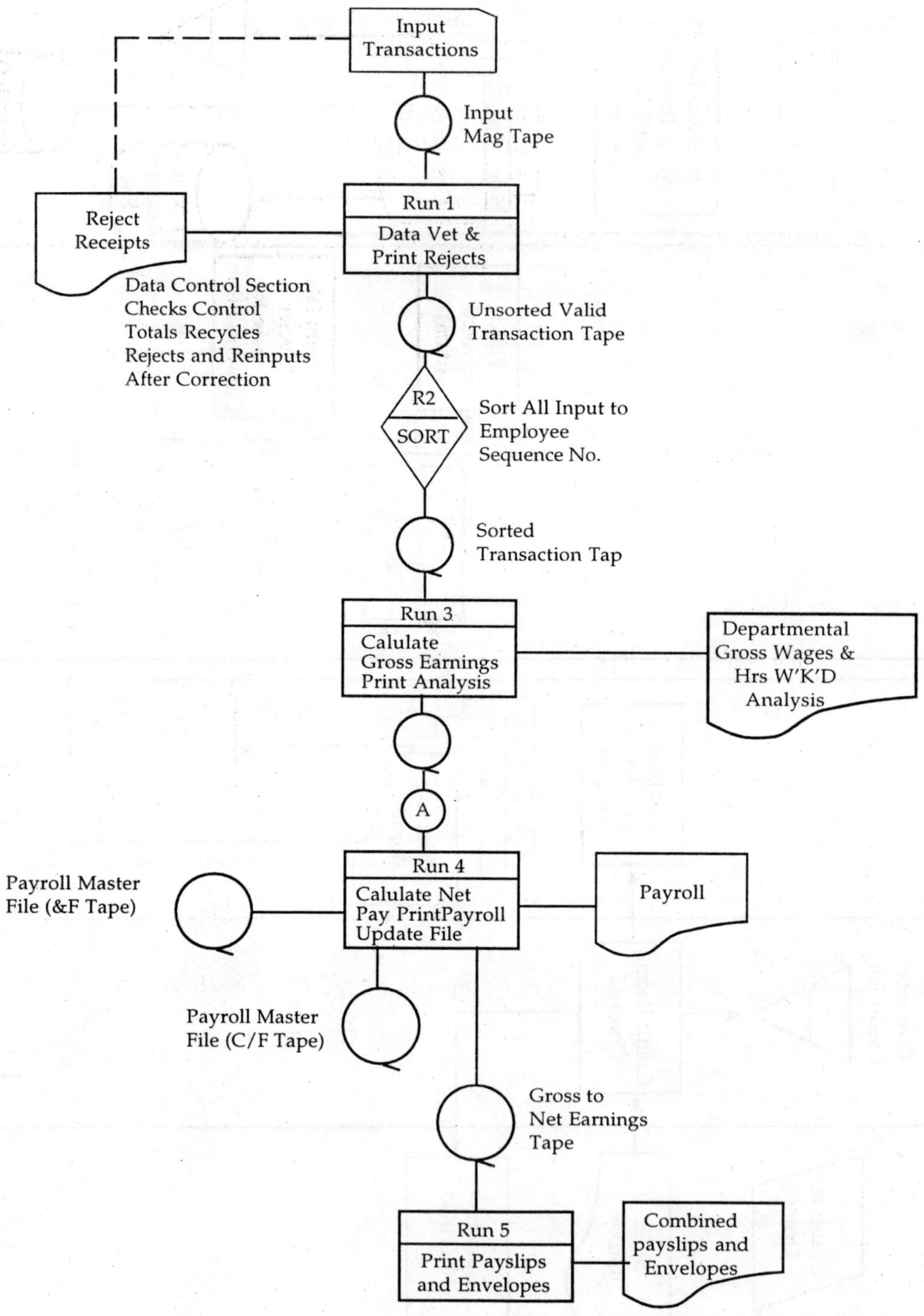

Fig. 3. Computer Run Chart (Payroll Processing)

suitably adapted for use at the data-gathering stage of system analysis for depicting procedures as are being currently carried out as well as at the program design stage for showing the main flow of data through the program and the transformations (or, changes in information) that take place as a result of carrying out a process or a decision. The point of transformation (or, node) is represented by means of a circle (referred to as bubble).

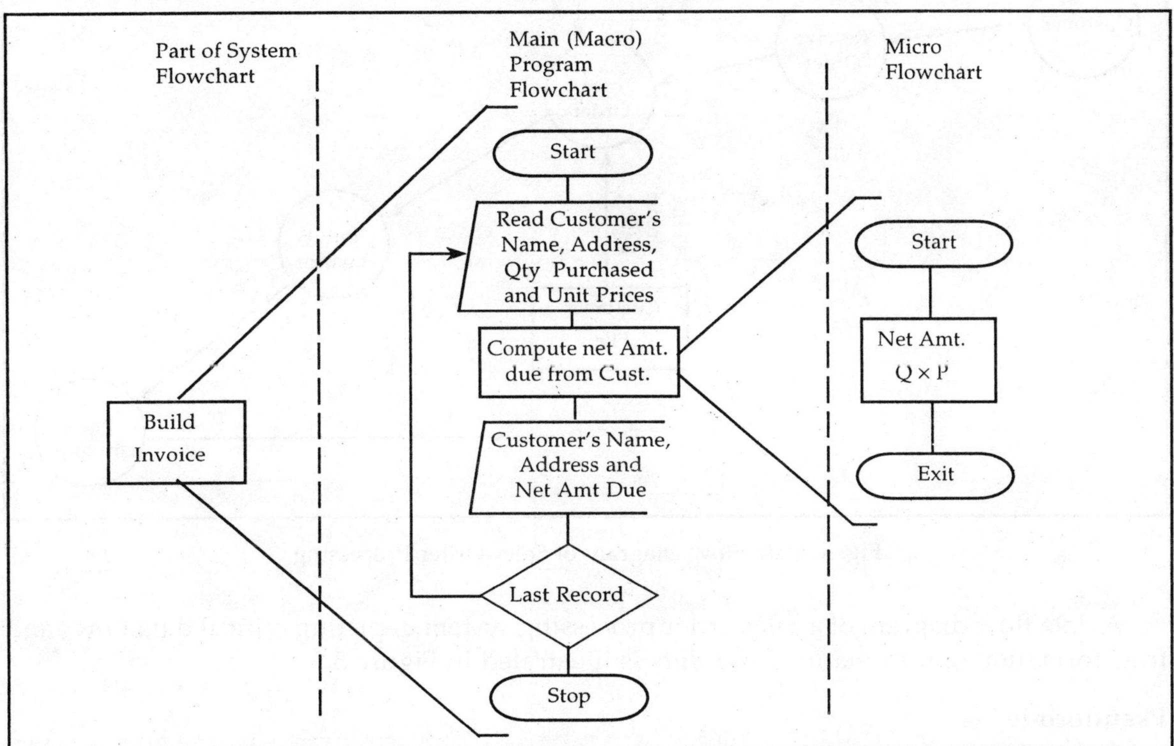

Fig. 4. Macro and Micro Program Flowcharts (evolving from Systems Flowchart)

The techniques employs only a few symbols and their location is somewhat informal. The commonly used symbols, which yet remain to be standardised, are as follows:

Symbol		**What is represents**
	:	Transformation
	:	Data flow
	:	Data storage

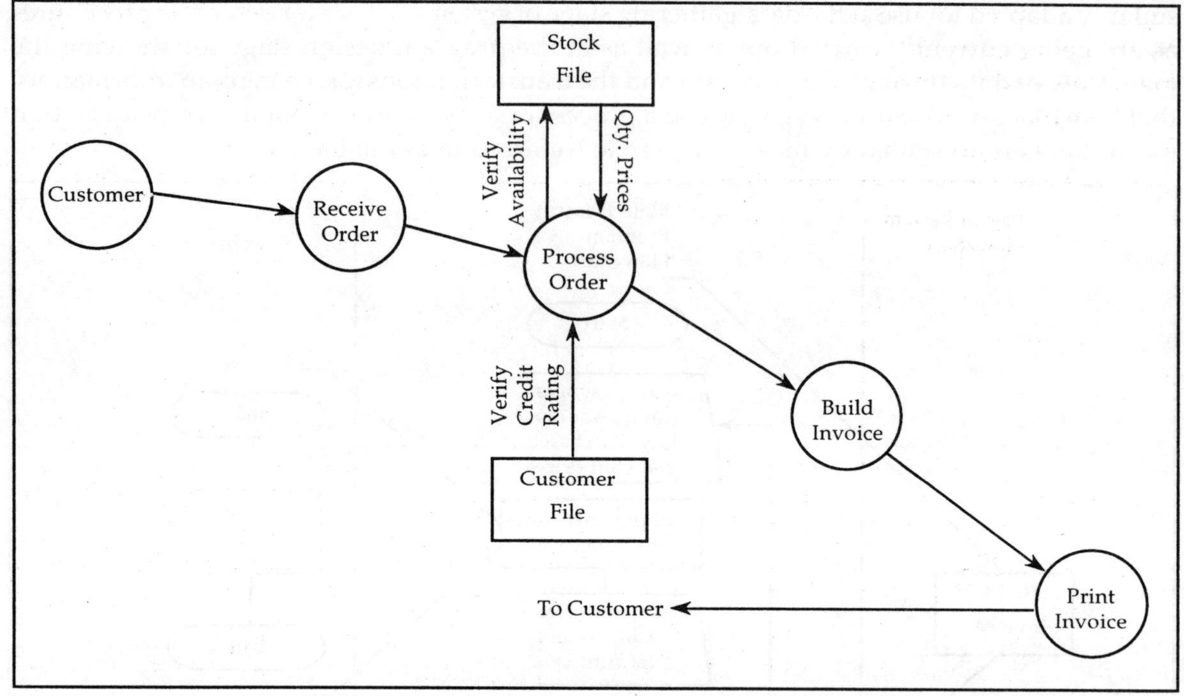

Fig. 5. Data Flow Diagram of Sales Order Processing

A data flow diagram of a sales order processing system depicting critical data flows and transformation of information on orders is illustrated in Figure 5.

Pseudocode

Pseudocode is yet another programming aid. It is a non-graphic way of depicting procedures or data processes that are performed in some scheduled order.

Pseudo means 'counterfeit' and *code* means instructions written in a programming language. The term pseudocode, therefore, connotes actual computer instructions written in a natural language like English but according to certain rules. Programmers using *structured approach* prefer pseudocodes in the preparation of a detailed plan for a program.

Although it might sound an oversimplication, in reality, the entire data processing activity is based on a limited number of actions that can be taken on data. There are : INPUT, OUTPUT, ASSIGN, RETRIEVE, DERIVE and DISCARD.

ASSIGN, here, means identification of a value as belonging to a particular data item. It is accomplished by associating a data item value with a data item name, (as is done by a statement like LET A = 5 in BASIC Programming language).

DERIVE means creating a new data-item value by applying a mathematical (e.g. add, subtract, etc.) or textual function to one or more existing data-item values.

The rest of the terms are self-explanatory.

The first step in developing pseudocode is to connect the required actions in a logical sequence. Any two of the actions can be connected to each other in the following three ways:

- Sequential
- Selective
- Repetitive

These are described below, (followed by a corresponding flowchart representation for greater clarify).

Sequential connectioN—It is simply means carrying out one process to be followed by another. Supposing, it is required to find the total value of a quantity of items at a price. The connections required in pseudocodes will be of the sequential type and will be written as follows.

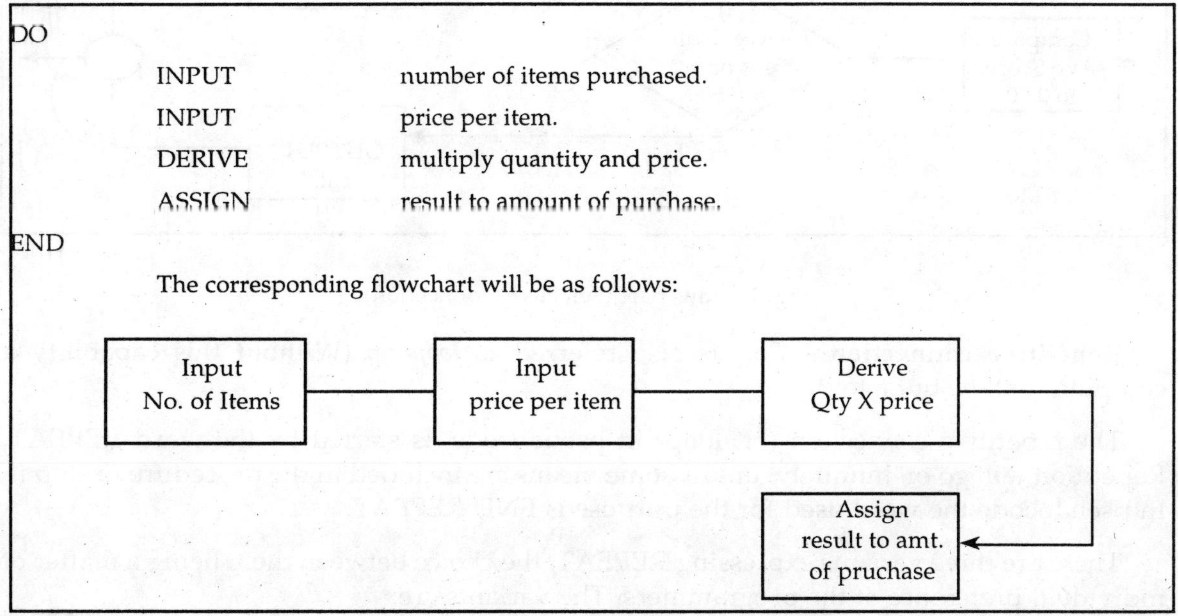

Fig. 6. Flowchart (Sequential Connection)

Selective connection—Selective means choosing among alternatives. In other words, at a particular point in the procedure, a decision has to be made (as logic operation has to be carried out), depending on certain conditions (decision point).

In pseudocode it starts with the word IF, followed by the condition and concludes with the word ENDIF.

The following simplified case will clarify. Supposing, an examiner has to compare the marks obtained by a student with the 'pass' criteria (that is, the examiner has to make a selection). If the total marks are equal to or greater than 50% the student is determined to be 'pass'. if not, 'fail'. The pseudocode depicting this logic will be:

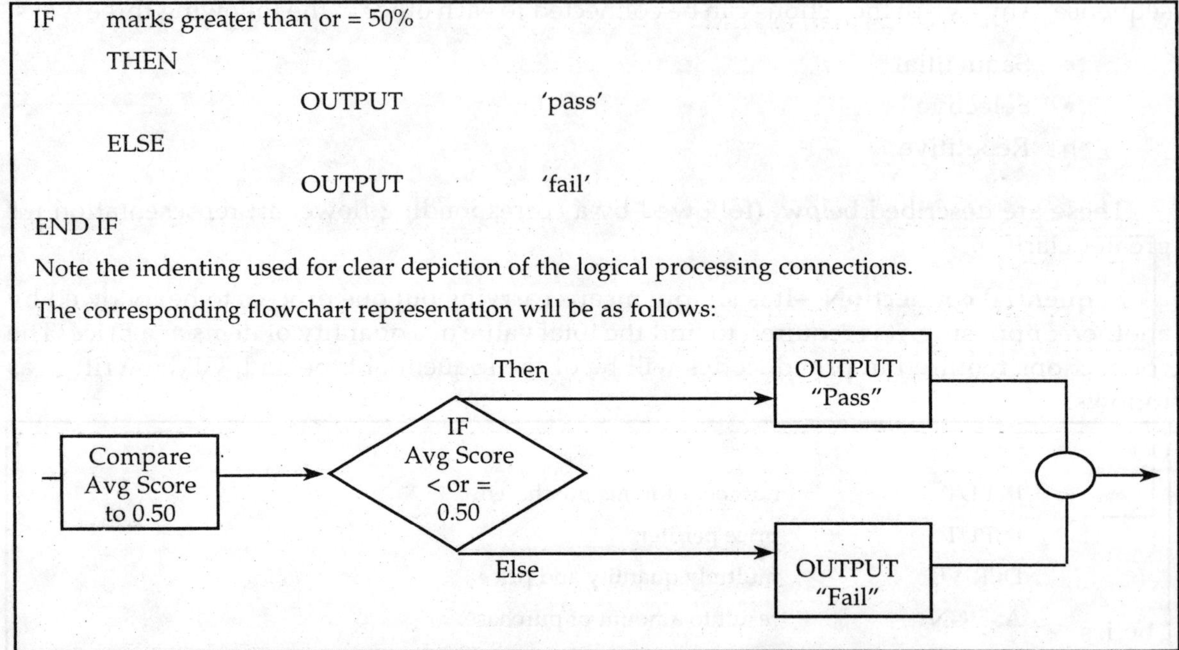

```
IF      marks greater than or = 50%
        THEN
                    OUTPUT          'pass'
        ELSE
                    OUTPUT          'fail'
END IF
```

Note the indenting used for clear depiction of the logical processing connections.

The corresponding flowchart representation will be as follows:

Fig. 7. Flowchart (Selective Connection)

Repetitive connections—This is also referred to *looping*. (Without this capability a computer will be but a toy).

The repetitive connection (or, loop) in pseudocode, is started by the word REPEAT. Repetition will go on infinitely, unless some means are included in the procedure to stop it. In pseudocode the word used for the purpose is END REPEAT.

There are three variants expressing REPEAT, the choice between them being a matter of individual preference of the programmers. The variants are:

REPEAT FOR

REPEAT WHILE

REPEAT UNTIL

The following practical business situation will clarify the procedure. Suppose, it is required to add up the cash sales made during the day from cash vouchers. Starting from zero cumulative total, each amount is added to the cumulative total, until there are no more cash vouchers to add. The pseudocode expression for the activity will be:

ASSIGN cum.total = 0

REPEAT until no more each voucher.

INPUT cash voucher amount

DRIVE cum total + cash voucher amount.

ASSIGN results to cum. total

END REPEAT.

The corresponding flowchart will be:

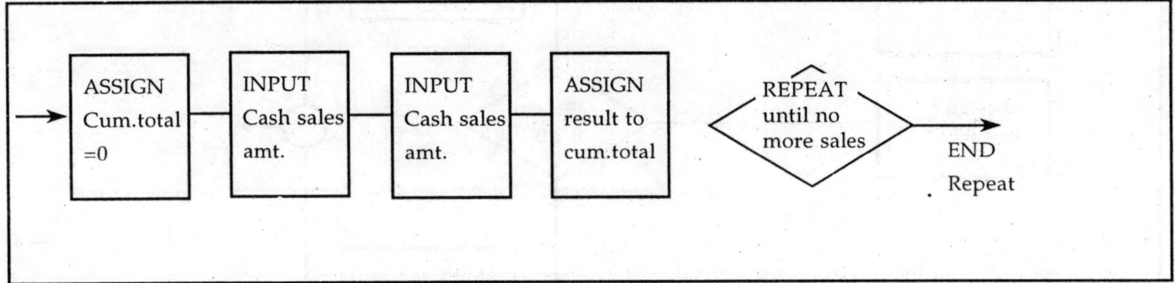

Fig. 8. Flowchart (Repetitive Connection)

A somewhat more complex problem will clarify further. Supposing a new cheque is to be issued after ascertaining that sufficient cash balance exists with the bank to cover the payment. The pseudocode to solve this problem will be as follows:

```
Do Sequentally
        Retrieve                    cash balance (C)
        Input                       amount of cheque (A)
        Derive                      C - A
        Assign                      result to B
        IF B < 0
                Then
                                    Output 'don't write cheque'
                Else                'You may write cheque.'
        End
End Sequence
```

The flowchart for this problem will be as follows:

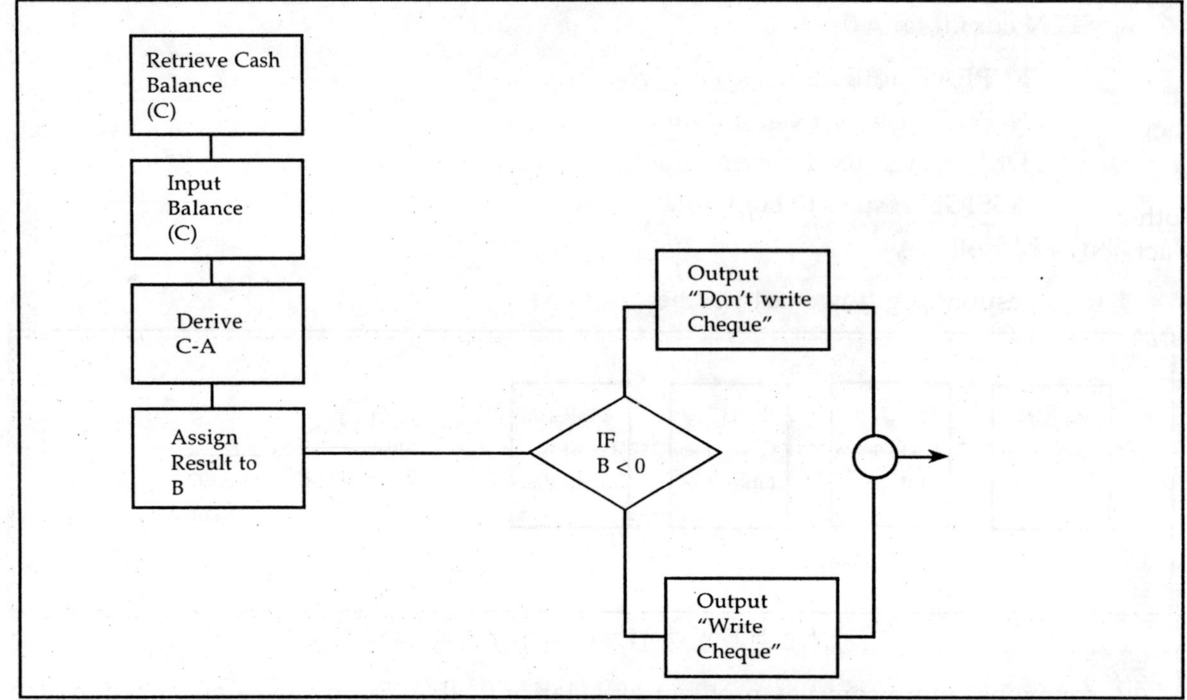

Fig. 9. Flow chart (Complex Connections)

The following advantages are associated with pseudocode:

- Its narative form closely resembles that of spoken language; hence it is easy to learn.
- The format parallels that of many high-level programming languages like Cobol, Basic, Fortran, etc. The program planners thus get a simple and logical description of processing steps which are easy to translate into an actual program.
- Lines of pseudocode text read from top to botom providing a simple path for eye to follow.

Decision Tables

Many data processing procedures involve a multitude of conditions, which necessitate branching to numerous alternative processing pathways when specified conditions are discovered in data after testing (i.e. after carrying out a logic operation). Explaining these multiple conditions, either by means of narrative description or by means of flowchart can often be confusing.

Used either in conjunction with, or in lieu of flowcharts, a *decision table* helps in precisely specifying the branching requirements and in ensuring that all the conditions and actions have been catered for and that the cause and effect relationship is clearly visible.

A decision table may be visualised as a cluster of selective connections. It lists each condition to be taken into consideration, (IF) and the action to be taken if that condition is true (THEN). When more than one conditions are true simultaneously, a more than one action may be required.

The basic format of a decision table consists of two rectangles placed one above the other. The upper rectangle is meant for containing 'condition statements' and the lower for 'action statements'.

The upper rectangle is further sub-divided vertically into the two parts termed *condition stubs* and *condition entries* (also called *rates*). Figure 10 illustrates.

	Table Heading	Decision Rules				
		1	2	3	4	5
Condition	If					
	And stub			entries		
	And					
Action	Then					
	And stub			entries		
	And					

Fig. 10. Basic Format of a Decision Table

The contents of the condition stub, when filled up, correspond to the conditions contained in the decision symbols of the flowchart, while the condition entries correspond to the paths as lead out from the decision symbols. In short, the upper rectangle lists all the conditions and all the questions to be tested in reaching a decision.

The lower rectangle, like the upper one, is also sub-divided into two parts *action stabs* and *action entries*. They are meant to describe the action to be taken in a given set of circumstances. The contents of this rectangle correspond to the non-decision symbols in a flowchart.

The complete decision table, in this way, lists out each condition to be taken into consideration (IF), and the action to be taken if the condition is true (THEN).

The contents of the decision table can be filled up in one of the two ways, respectively called *limited entry* and *extended entry*.

In the limited entry method, the statement of each condition or action is completely contained in (or limited to) appropriate stub and the entry portion merely indicates if a particular rule satisfied the condition or requires the action stated. Conventionally, two symbols are used to fill in the 'condition entry' portion of a decision table. These are:

Y (Yes) if the condition is satisfied.

N (No) if the condition is not satisfied.

In contrast, in the 'action entry' part of the decision table, an X symbol is recorded in signify the required action. If no action is required, the column is left blank.

In the extended entry approach, the statements made in the sub portion are incomplete. In this case, both the stub and entry sections of any particular row in the table must be taken into account together, for deciding whether a condition or action is relevant to the given rule. The advantage of this approach is its brevity. It is also easily possible to convert extended entry format to limited entry format.

These two approaches will become clear if we consider the following typical situations in a bank and attempt construction of limited entry and extended entry decision tables therefrom. the parameters are:

If it is a business account and the minimum balance is less than Rs. 10,000 then the monthly service charges will be Rs. 0.50 per cheque; otherwise there will be no service charge.

In case it is a personal account and the minimum balance is less than Rs. 1000, the monthly service charges will be Rs. 1.00 per cheque.

If the minimum balance is more than Rs. 1000 there will be no monthly service charge.

The limited entry and extended entry decision tables based on these parameters, have been illustrated in the tables, Fig. 11 and Fig 12 below:

Monthly Service Change		Decision Rule Nos.			
		1	2	3	4
A	Business Account	Y	N	N	Y
B	Personal Account	N	Y	Y	N
C	Minimum balance less than Rs. 1000/-	N	Y	N	N
D	Minimum Balance greater than Rs. 10,000/-	Y	N	N	N
E	No mnthly service change	X		X	
F	Change Rs. 0.50 per cheque		X		
G	Change Rs. 1.00 per cheque			X	

Fig. 11. Limited Entry Decision Table

	Monthly Service Charges	Decision Rule Nos.			
		1	2	3	4
A	Business Account	Y	Y		
B	Personal Account			Y	Y
C	Minimum balance	less than Rs. 1000	Rs. 10000	less than Rs. 10000	Rs. 1000
D	No monthly service charge		X		X
E	Charge per cheque	Rs. 0.50		Rs. 1/-	

Fig. 12 Extended Entry Decision Table

Guidelines for Construction of Decision Tables—An important aspect to remember is that there are, theoretically , 2^n rules for n separate conditions. This follows from the number of combinations of the two conditions Y(Yes) and N(No). So, if there are four conditions the result would be 2^4 or 16 rules. Some of the rules are repetitive and it is possible to combine them. Against this background, the further steps are:

- List all conditions and actions.
- Combine redundant rules to simplify the decision table.
- Follow each rule and mark the appropriate 'action' to be taken by using X symbols.

Decision Tables at Two (or More) Levels—In certain situations, where there are many conditions, and the decision table is likely to become large and too complex to follow, the technique is to construct a set of two or more decision tables. The situation below illustrates.

A garment manufacturer allows discounts to customers on the following basis:

Order Quantity	*Normal Discount (%)*
1 - 99	5
100 - 199	7
200 - 499	9
500 and over	10

These discounts apply if the customers' account balance is below Rs. 5000 and does not include any item older than three months. If the account is outside both limits, the above discounts, are reduced by 2%. If only one condition is violated, the discounts are reduced by

1%. If the customer has been of five years standing and conforms to both of the above credit checks, then he is allowed an additional 1% discount.

The decision table in this case can be prepared at two levels. (Accordingly, processing can also be divided into two parts).

	Decision Rules Nos.			
	1	2	3	4
Order Quantity 1 - 99	Y	N	N	N
Order Quantity 100 - 199	N	Y	N	N
Order Quantity 200 - 499	N	N	• Y	N
Give 5% discount	X			
Give 7% discount		X		
Give 9% discount			X	
Give 10% discount				X

Fig. 13(a) Decision Table (Level 1, of two Levels)

Evaluation of Decision Tables—An important advantage of decision tables is that by using specially developed translators called 'interpreters' it is possible to translate decision tables directly into COBOL, and other languages. For this purpose each line of the decision table can be read into the computer and the latter translates it into COBOL statements, bypassing the coding functions for that part of the system.

Other advantages of decision tables are:

- They provide a framework as well as an accurate statement of decision logic for computer processing.
- They facilitate modular programming and improve communication between programmers and system analysts.
- They document applications involving complex variables more clearly than flowcharts.

Their main limitations are:

- They are not well suited to show the flow of processing where there are only a few decisions.
- Flowcharts are better able to express the total sequence of events needed to solve a problem.
- Programmers are, generally, more attuned to flowcharts then to decision tables.

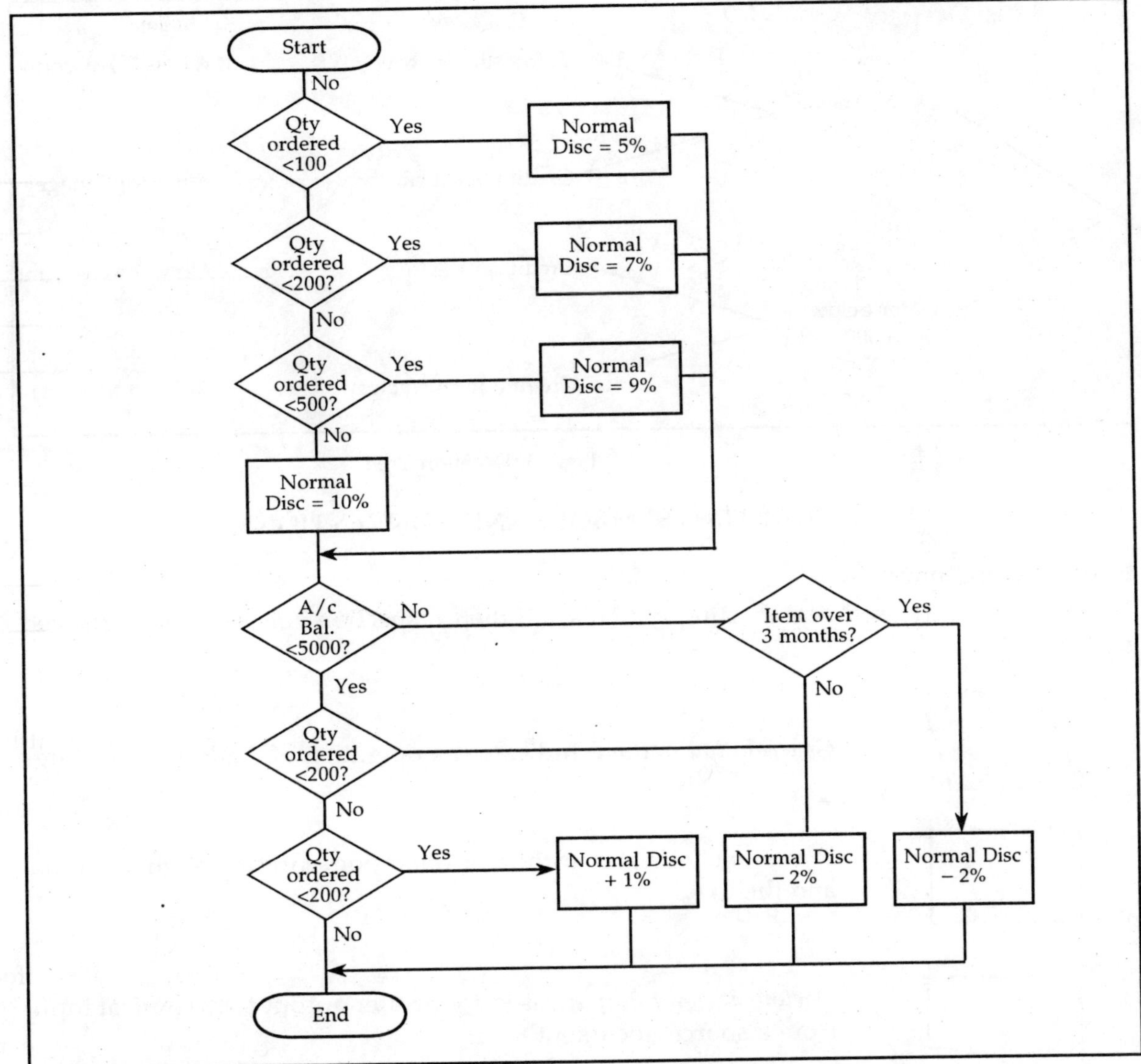

Fig. 14. Decision Table (Fig. 13) Flowcharted.

Decision Trees

The logic in the decision tables can also be expressed in the form of Decision Trees. Supposing the company has the following policy:

If order above Rs. 1000/- and the customer is creditworthy, allow a discount of 5%.

If the order below Rs. 1000/- allow discount only at 3%. Refer all other cases to manager.

The decision tree, in this case, can be constructed in the following manner:

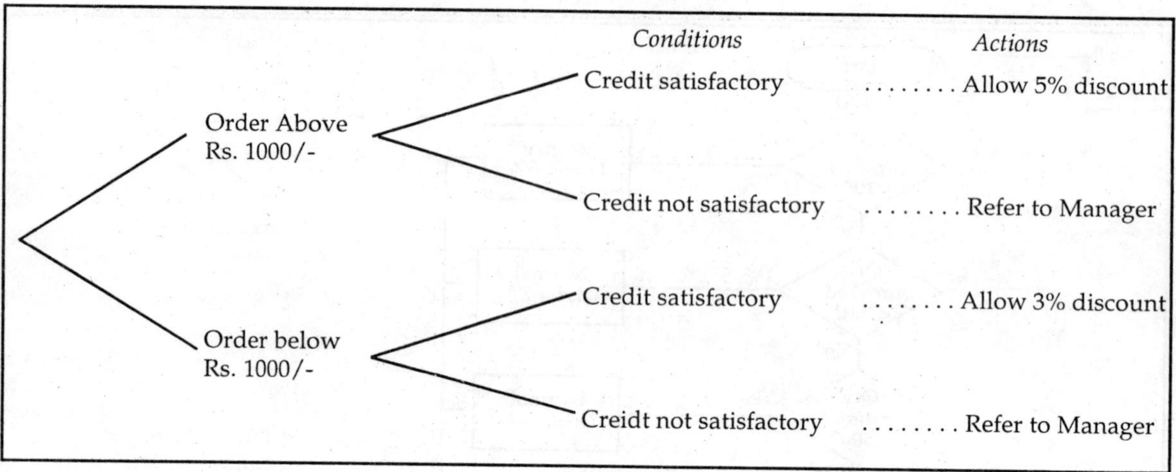

Fig. 15. Decision Tree

FLOWCHARTING SYMBOLS AND CONVENTIONS

Flowcharting Symbols

The commonly used flowcharting symbols and their respective functions are portrayed below:

General input-output. Indicates an operation of reading or writing.

Processing. Indicates arithmetic operation, editing, moving of data, and the like.

Document Input-output. Used for printer output or for optical input from a source document.

Decision. Indicates a decision point. A test is performed and the program flow continues on each outgoing path, conditional on the test.

Pre-defined process. Certain kinds of operations are repented in programs, which can be prepared once and then integrated into other programs. This symbol, depicts such pre-defined processes.

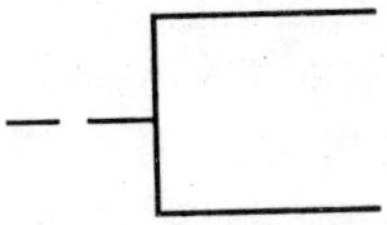

Program comment. Annotation, is given inside the box to clarify some point in the flowchart.

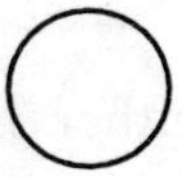

On-page connector. Indicates references to another point in the flowchart on the same page.

Off-age connector. Indicates reference to another point on another page.

Terminal. Indicates the beginning or end of a procedure.

Magnetic lape. Indicates that input-output is from magnetic tape.

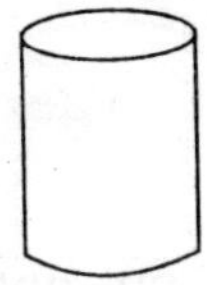

Magnetic disk. Indicates that input-output is from magnetic disk.

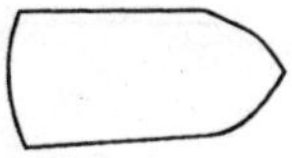

Video Display Unit

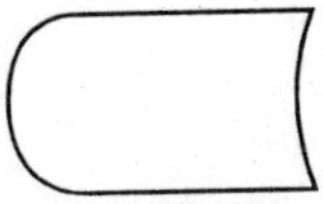

On-line storage

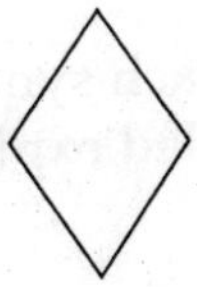

Sort

Flowcharting Conventions

The following guidelines enhance effectiveness in the design and documentation of a computer based system:

Flow The general direction of the flow is as follows:

- For horizontal flow : left to right

- For vertical flow to bottom.

Arrow—These are used to indicate the direction of the flow. If the flow is in either direction, two lines with opposite pointing arrowheads are used.

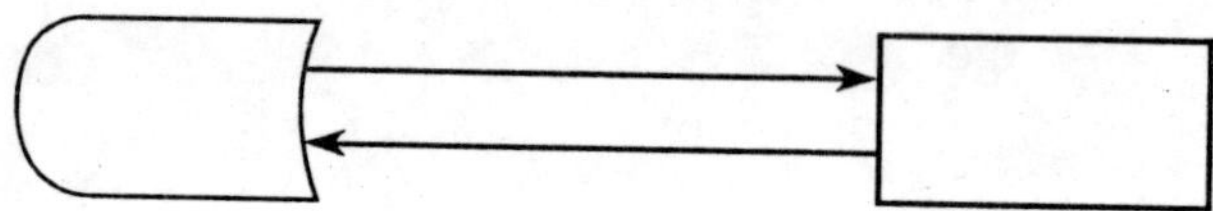

Crossing of Flowlines—This is to be avoided, as far as possible. A bridge symbol, as depicted below is used where crossing cannot be avoided.

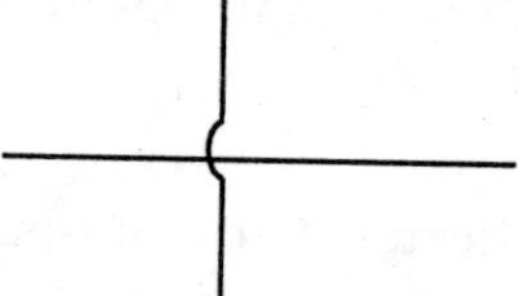

Joining of Flowlines—Two more flowlines may join outgoing flowline, but not at the same point. The convention is depicted below:

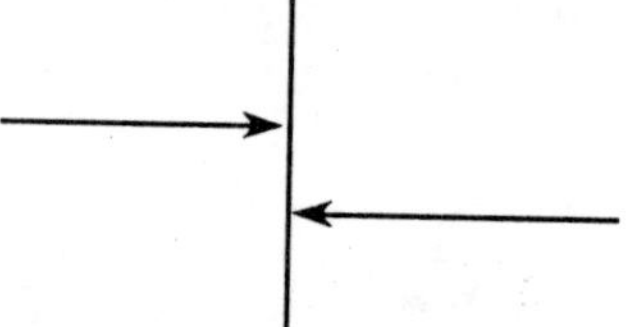

Annotation—A brief annotation (clarifying statement) is given inside each symbol (or, block) in order to describe what is to be done at that stage. Additional detailed explanation is given using an annotation flag, as illustrated below:

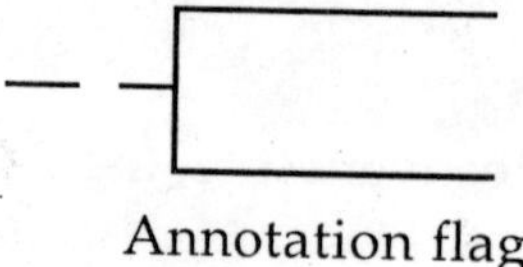

Annotation flag

An annotation flag can be drawn on either side of a symbol.

In annotation, when there is a need to specify a particular physical medium, like disk or magnetic tape, this is done by inserting the name of the medium in a stripe within the lower part of the symbol, as shown below:

Symbol Identification—Symbols, other than connector and terminal symbols are conventionally numbered as, 10, 20, 30, etc, as a means of reference. The scheme of numbering is helpful in situations where a step might have been forgotten in the first instance.

The missing step can be inserted by alloting a number in between, say 15 (between 10 and 20) without disturbing the sequence of other numbers. The number may be placed above and to the left of the symbol, as shown below:

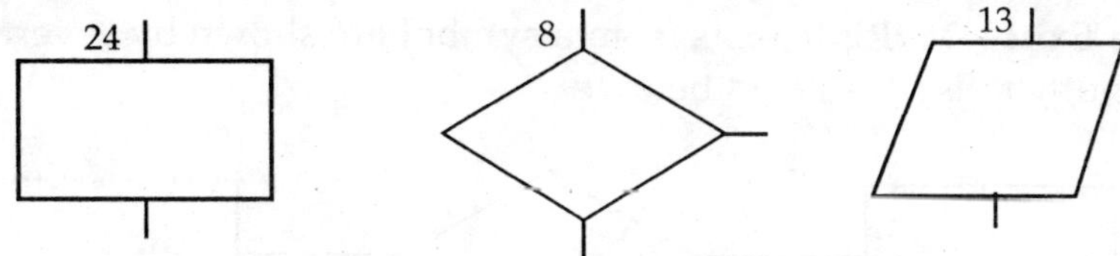

Connectors—These are used to show continuity either between the symbols on the same sheet or between symbols on different sheets of the same procedure. Connectors may be 'out-connectors' or 'in-connectors'. A common identifier, such as all alphabet or mnemonic label is placed within the out-connector and the associated in-connector, as illustrated below.

Terminator—This symbol is portrayed below:

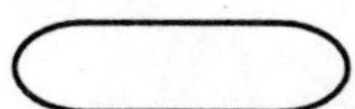

It is used to represent the beginning (START) and the end (STOP) of a program. It is also, additionally, used to show program interruption point when information may enter or exit. Thus, in order to detect certain errors in input data, a programmer may provide a special program branch which may end in a terminator labelled HALT.

Cross referencing and Detailed Representation—Reference to another chart or document, or to the location of detailed representations, within the flowchart, is placed in the upper part of the symbol, as illustrated below:

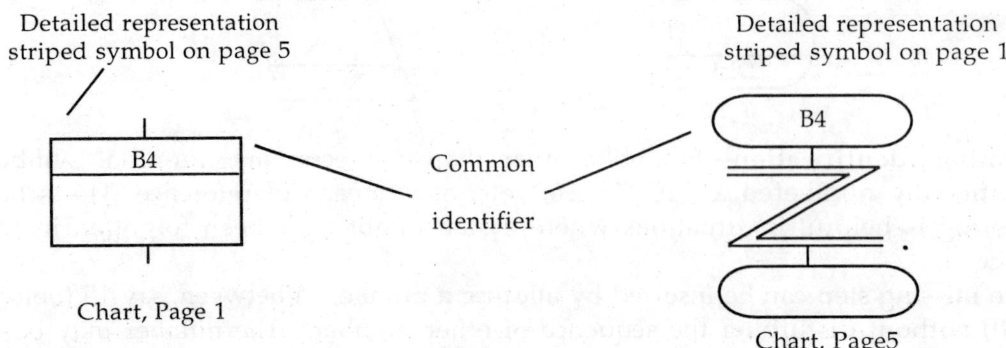

Multiple Exits—Multiple exits from a symbol are shown by several flowlines from one symbol to another, as illustrated below:

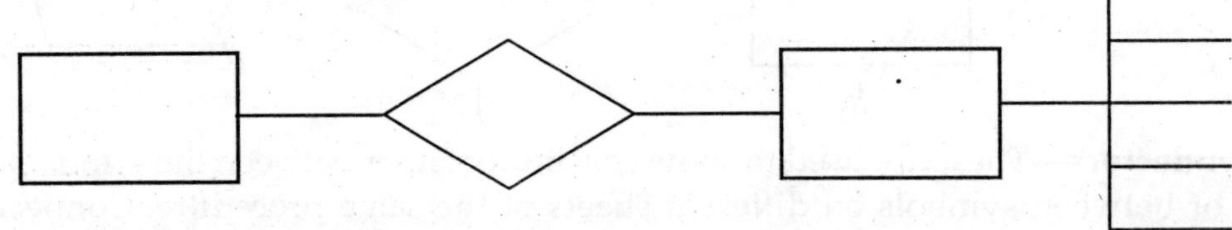

Flowlines with Repetitive Symbols—Flowlines enter or exit from any point on the repetitive (overlay) symbols, as illustrated below:

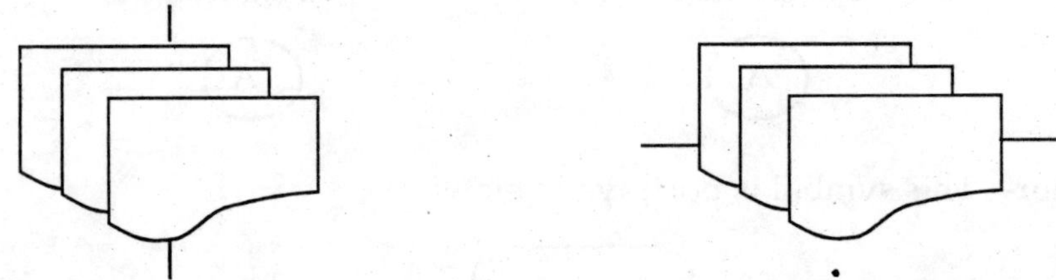

Sub-Structures or a Flowchart

A flowchart basically consists of three sub-structures. These sub-structures are known as:

- sequence
- if-then-else, and
- do-until

All of them can be distinguished in the flowchart (Figure 16), and are depicted below for further amplification.

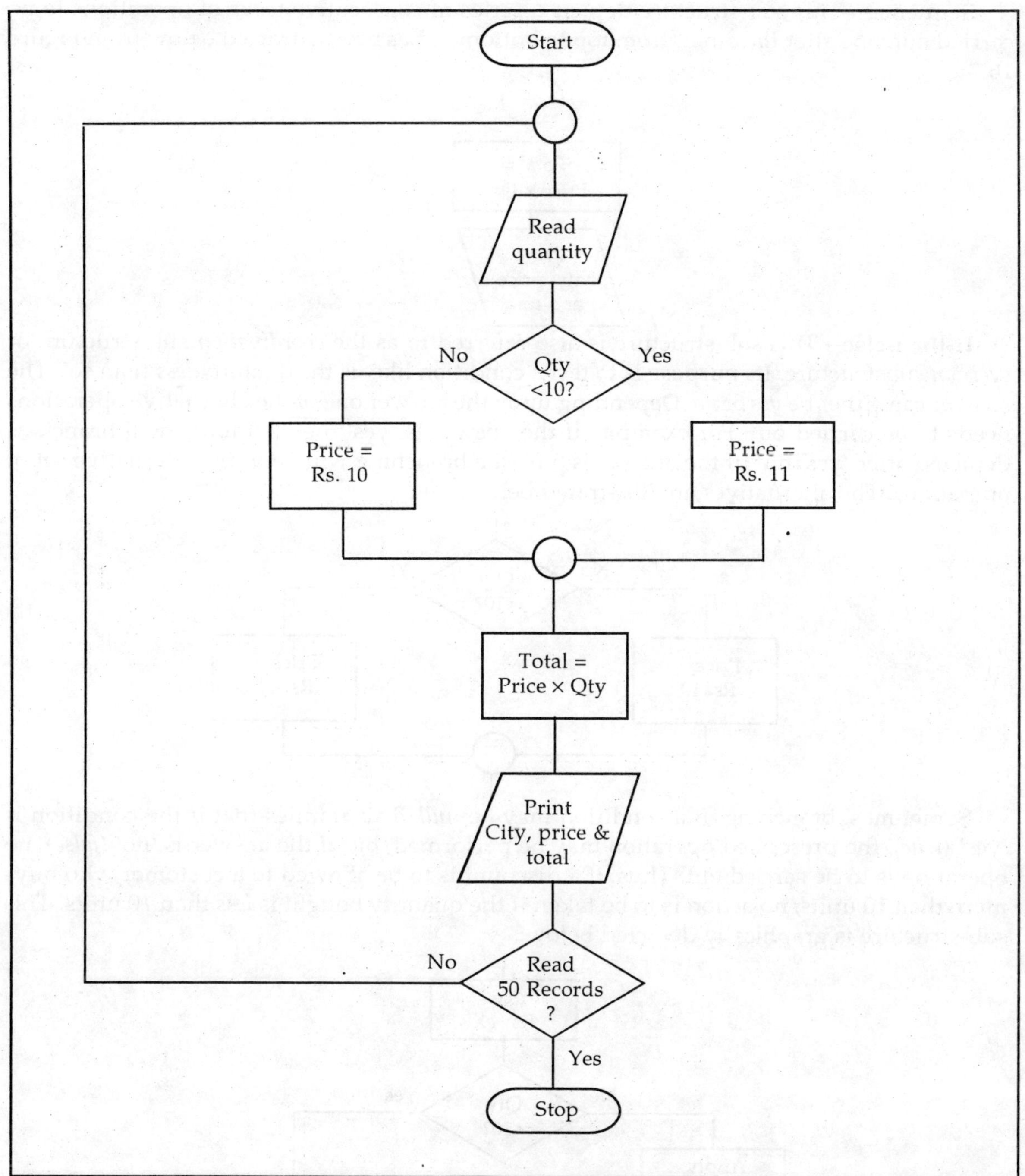

Fig. 16. A Typical Flowchart

Sequence—This sub-structure depicts a series of consecutive tasks of operations to be carried out, one after the other, from top to bottom. It has been extracted below from Figure 16.

Total =
Price × Qty

Print
qty, price
and total

If-then-else—This sub-structure is also referred to as the *coordination* sub-structure or *decision* substructure. Its purpose is to test a condition like 'is the quantity *less* than so'. The answer can either be *yes* or *no*. Depending upon the answer one of the alternative operations needs to be carried out. For example, if the answer is 'yes' the operations will branch as depicted after 'yes' but if the answer is 'no', the branching will be to the alternative set of operations. The alternatives are illustrated below:

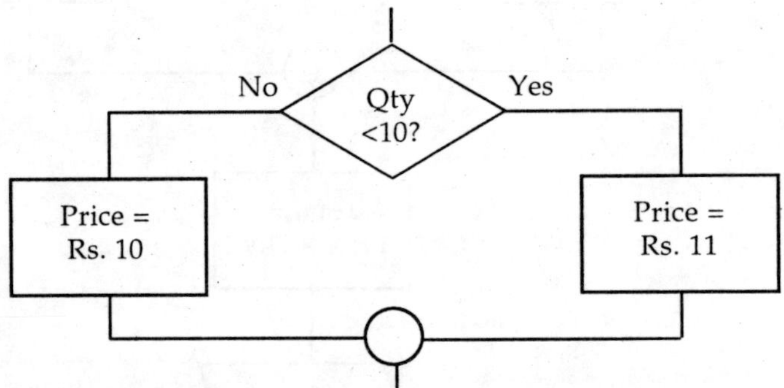

Sometimes, branching in a condition may be *null*. This implies that if the condition is 'yes' (*true*), the prescribed operation may be performed, but if the answer is 'no' (*false*), no operation is to be carried out. Thus, if a discount is to be allowed to a customer who buys more than 10 units, no action is to be taken if the quantity bought is *less* than 10 units. This sub-structure is graphically depicted below:

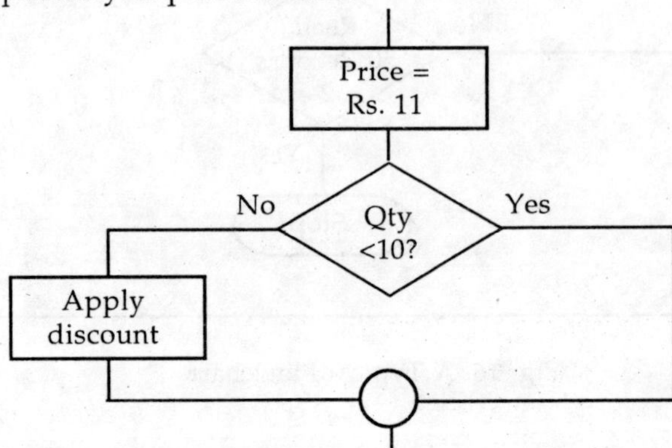

Do-until—This is also referred to the *loop* sub-structure. Its purpose is to specify repeated execution of a program step.

A necessary condition, however, is that the loop must terminate: otherwise execution of operation will continue indefintely. A condition may, therefore, be laid down which will bring about termination, when required. An example of such a condition can be that the loop will terminate after reading 50 records. This sub-structure is graphically depicted below.

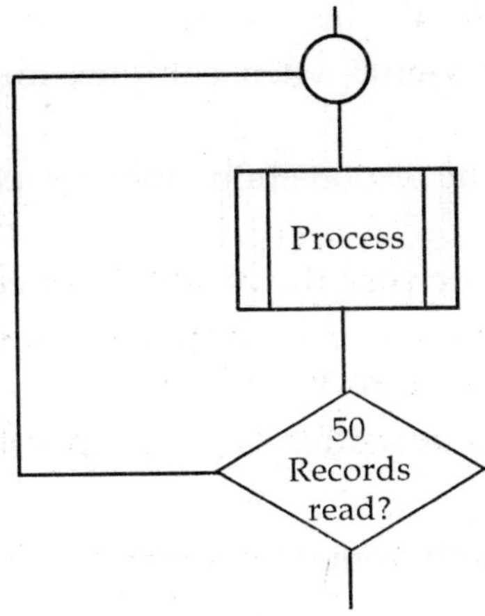

A variant of do-until loop is the *do-while* loop. In such a loop, a test is carried out that if a condition holds good the task may be carried out repeatedly and the operations may stop when the test reveals that the condition no longer holds good.

A graphic representation of the do-while loop follows:

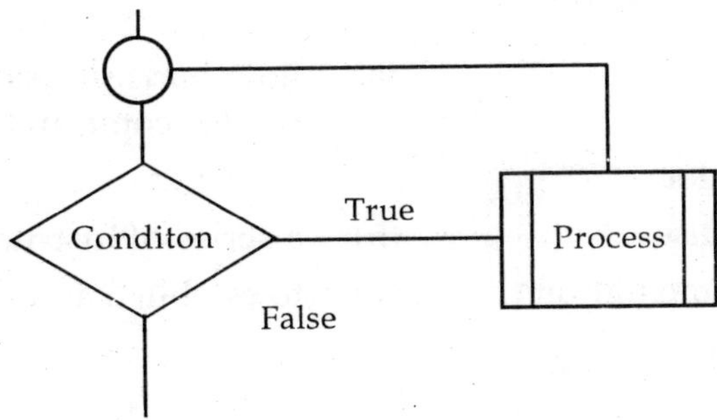

Self-Test

1. Which of the following do not constitute software documentation tools?
   (a) Flowcharts.
   (b) Psedocode.

(c) Microcode.
(d) Decision Tables.
(e) Grid Charts.
(f) Standards Manual.

2. True or false?
   (a) Decision tables were invented to cope with the complex logical relationship which were caused by the introduction of computer hardware.
   (b) Decision tables are useful when complex logical relationships must be analysed.
   (c) Decision tables put the responsibility for specifying the logic parameters on the user.
   (d) Decision tables can increase the reliability of computer data processing.
   (e) A flowchart provides information on relationships of inputs, system and files, which are not obvious from a narrative.
   (f) A narrative provides definition of each input which is difficult to show in a flowchart.

3. The symbols most commonly found on a process chart are:
   A
   B
   C
   D

4. Match the following:

(i) Loop	(a) flowcharts, decision tables, computer programs, etc. for computerised activity.
(ii) Counter	
(iii) Initialise	(b) a series of instructions used repeatedly.
(iv) Documentation	(c) to establish an initial value for a counter.

5. Match the following:

(i) Pseudocode	(a) Concentrates only on important aspects of dataflow with the aid of specially developed symbols, eliminates unnecessary technical details.
(ii) Data Flow Diagram	(b) Consists of phrases, expressing actual computer instructions in ordinary natural language.
(iii) Systems Flowchart	(c) An alternative method of expressing the logic as contained in the decision tables.

(iv)	Decision Tree	(d)	Conceptualises the flow of documents around the computer and the processing performed on them by the computer.
(v)	Extended Entry Decision Table	(c)	Serves as the basis of communication between systems analysts and programmers, besides detailing steps for transforming input into output.
(vi)	Program Flowchart	(f)	In which statements of each condition or action are completely contained in the appropriate stub.
(vii)	Limited Entry Decision Table	(g)	In which stub portions are incomplete and both stub and entry sections of a row in the table must be taken into account for deciding whether a condition or action is relevant to the given rule.

6. Select the respective advantage of (a) Decision Tables and (b) Flowcharts, from the following:
   (a) Provides an accurate statement of decision logic for processing.
   (b) Their construction does not call for any particular technical knowledge.
   (c) Provide the mechanism to trace forward from start, the action resulting from a set of conditions.
   (d) Amendments are not easy to make.
   (e) Emphasis is on technical details of 'how-to-do', whereby essentials of what is done' is sometimes lost.

7. Match the following:

(i)	DOWHILE	(a)	The program structure which involves a series of instructions executed in the order in which they are presented.
(ii)	IF THEN-ELSE	(b)	The program structure which results in the repetitive execution of a segment of program.
(iii)	SEQUENTIAL	(c)	A program structure in which the program takes one path or another, depending on whether or not the condition is met.

21

Logico-Mathematical Models

INTRODUCTION

Many information needs of an organisation can be met by establishing a common data base and from it, providing timely reports or online responses to the users, via remote terminals such as CRTs. An information system is also comprised of a number of information subsystems such as traditional accounting, inventory control, process control and production scheduling, shipping and transportation, sales analysis, and so on. The total information system is management oriented; thus, in addition to being a data processing center, it also uses logico-mathematical models to aid management in its planning, controlling, and decision-making functions. In addition to developing reports and systems for historical record keeping and to satisfy business and governmental requirements, it is also the responsibility of the information systems analyst to select, test, and implement these models to provide alternative, predictive, optimising, and performance information. A systems analyst, therefore, needs a working knowledge of the various logico-mathematical models. In this appendix several models that over the years have proven to be valuable in converting raw data elements into meaningful information are presented.

TRADITIONAL ACCOUNTING MODELS

The traditional accounting function, in addition to handling routine data processing activities, also provides a great deal of information to both internal and external constituents. Much of the information provided by this function is historical, and is stated in terms of money. Traditional accounting, however, also provides information that is performance oriented. In the following subsections most of the traditional accounting models are presented.[1]

Accounting reports derived from models aid management (as well as others) in:

1. Planning, because reporting information on past periods helps the user to make predictions about future events.
2. Controlling, because budgets and standards are set, and performances are measured against these budgets and standards.

3. Decision making, because the reporting of possible outcomes based on alternative inputs allows the decision maker to select the best alternatives.

The accounting function also acts as an overall control device for external constituents such as stockholders. It provides performance measurement via position statements, earnings statements, and funds statements, which together help to indicate how management is doing. It also helps asset control (e.g. cash, securities, receivables, and so on) by promoting efficiency and internal control, which reduces loss through error or fraud. Moreover, it limits needless expenditures by establishing a decentralised system of budgets.

Bookkeeping Model

The bookkeeping model is an equation which sets up a procedure for classifying, recording, and reporting financial transactions of an organisation. It can be states as follows:

Assets (A_t) = Liabilities (L_t) + Contributed Capital (CC_t) + Retained Earnings (RE_t)

Each category represents some financial amount at some point in time. All transactions are classified and recorded in such a way that the total assets equal the sum of the liabilities, contributed capital, and retained earnings.

Retained earnings, at some point in time (usually stated at the end of an accounting period), is the algebraic sum of the retained earnings of the previous period, RE_{T-1}, the earnings for the period E_t, and the dividends declared during the period, D_t. This equation is stated as:

$$RE_t = RE_{t-1} + E_t - D_t$$

Earnings are determined by matching the inputs for the period with the outputs for the period. In business organisations the inputs are measured in terms of revenue, (R), and the outputs are measured in terms of expenses (EXP) required to generate this revenue. Income tax (TAX), is not recognised as an expense, per se, but as a social cost of doing business. The equation for earnings is stated as:

$$E_t = R_t - EXP_t - TAX_t$$

Accounts

Accounts are set up which represent each category in the above equations. These accounts are merely a place to receive transactional data, and to show increases or decreases where, at certain periods, the current amount balance of an item is available. All accounts can be algebraically summed, in accordance with the procedures dictated by the equations, to provide financial statements whenever needed.

These accounts take a variety of forms, depending on whether they are recorded on paper for manual data processing methods or magnetic disk, etc., for computer processing. The basic procedures in classifying, recording, and reporting are the same whatever data processing method is used.

The essential features of an account can be shown in the form of a classical T-account, as follows:

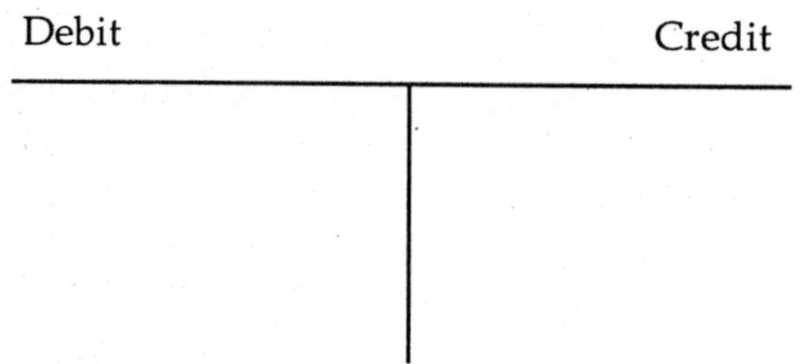

The rules of recording are as follows:

1. *Debits* increase assets, and decrease liabilities, contributed capital, and retained earnings.
2. *Credits* decrease assets, and increase liabilities, contributed capital, and retained earnings.

Retained earnings represent the "meter" for earnings (i.e., revenue increases retained earnings, therefore a credit increases a revenue account). Conversely an expense decreases retained earnings, so a debit increases an expense account.

Accounting data can also be structured in the form of an *m* and *n* matrix with the following general notation:

$$A = \begin{vmatrix} a_{11} & a_{12} & \cdots & a_{1n} \\ a_{21} & a_{22} & \cdots & a_{2n} \\ \cdot & \cdot & & \cdot \\ \cdot & \cdot & & \cdot \\ \cdot & \cdot & & \cdot \\ a_{m1} & a_{m2} & \cdots & a_{mn} \end{vmatrix}$$

Such a matrix is usually represented by the following abbreviation

$$A = (a_{ij}) \qquad i = 1,2........m$$
$$j = 1,2,.......n$$

where i = rows and j = columns.

An accounting matrix, using 16 common accounts, is shown in Figure 1. Notices that the increases and decreases in the accounts work the same as previously explained and that a current balance can be determined at any time. For example, look at Sales (column 10), a revenue account. It obviously has a credit balance (unless there were sales returns, which would be another account) and that balance is $90,000 (row 19). But how were the sales made, cash or credit? Looking at the Cash and Accounts Receivable accounts (rows 1 and 2)

Debits	Credits	01	02	03	04	05	06	07	08	09	10	11	12	13	14	15	16	17	18	19
		Cash	AR	INV	PR	PE	AD	AP	CS	RE	S	CO GS	Wage	Dep	Rent	Oth	Div	Beg DR	Σ DR	End DR
01	Cash		10000						400000		30000								440000	266000
02	Accounts receivable										60000								60000	50000
03	Inventory							150000											150000	150000
04	Prepaid rent	12000																	12000	12000
05	Plant and equipment	75000						25000											100000	100000
06	Accumulated depreciation																			
07	Accounts payable	65000																	65000	0
08	Capital stock																			
09	Retained earnings																			
10	Sales																			
11	Cost of good sold																			
12	Wages expense	22000																	22000	22000
13	Depreciation expense																			
14	Rent expense																			
15	Other expense							8000											8000	8000
16	Dividends																			
17	Beginning credit balance																			
18	Σ Credit totals this period	174000	10000					183000	400000		90000									
19	Ending credit balances	0	0					118000	400000		90000									

Fig. 1. An accounting matrix.

under the Sales account, one can readily determine that $30,000 of the sales were for cash and $80,000 were for credit.

Cost-Volume-Profit Model

Cost react on the basis of activity. We can categorise costs into three basic behavior patterns, which are:

1. *Variable cost behavior*. These costs react in direct proportion to changes in activity.
2. *Fixed cost behavior*. These costs remain the same within a specified range of activity.
3. *Semivariable cost behavior*. These costs vary with the level of activity, but not in a strict proportional way. For example, two shifts might be required to produce X units. However, to produce $X + 1$ units would require another entire shift.

In knowing cost behavior, we can simulate those profits which might be obtained with changes in volume (activity). This simulated activity can be illustrated in a cost volume-profit (CVP) graph, as shown in Figure 2. In this graph, for simplicity, we delineate only two categories of cost—variable and fixed.

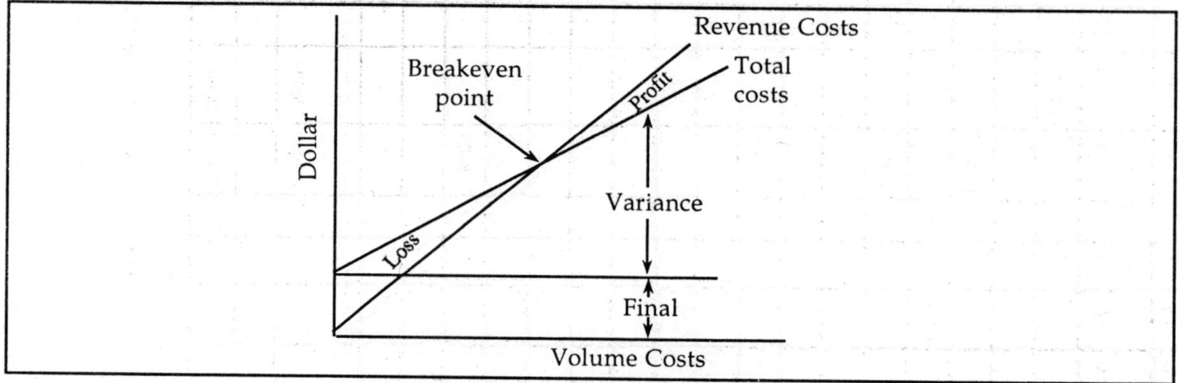

Fig. 2. The cost-volume-profit relationship

Figure 2 shows the relationship between cost and profit at various volume levels. The measure of volume is the number of units produced and sold. At lower volumes, a loss is expected; at higher volumes, a profit is expected; somewhere in between a break even point exists where total cost equals revenue.

The cost-volume-profit relationship provides a useful way for simulating the profit factors of any organisation. The factors which increase profit are:

1. Increased selling price per unit.
2. Decreased variable cost per unit.
3. Increased volume.
4. For a multiproduct company, a change in its product mix.

A typical question from management may be: What would the profit picture look like if we decreased selling price by 5 per cent, variable cost remained constant, decreased nonvariable cost by 8 per cent, and increased volume of sales by 20 per cent? A variety of questions such as this, proposed by management, could generate information which could effectively enhance planning and decision making.

Budget and Performance Analysis Models

A budget is a plan of action, expressed in quantitative terms, which covers some specific time period. the key concept of a budget is to structure it in terms that equate to the responsibility of those who are charged with its execution. In this way the budget is used not only as a planning device but also as a control device. Budgets are of three types[2]:

1. An operating budget, showing planned operations for the forthcoming period.
2. A cash budget showing the anticipated sources and uses of cash.
3. A capital budget showing planned changes in a variety of fixed assets.

The budgeting process involves a planning-control-planning life cycle, which is described as follows:

1. Planning which entails selecting objectives and means for their obtainment.
2. Controlling encompasses two activities:
   (a) Translate objectives into units of output and determine specific inputs to
   (b) Comparison of actual operations with budgeted operations.
3. Planning at this stage uses performance reports for evaluating past operations for planning future operations.

Budgets can also be viewed as being prepared for different levels in an organisation.

Typically, budgets may relate to four levels: (1) entire organisation (master budget), (2) division, (3) department, and (4) subunit. For example, a typical performance report at one level is structured as follows:

	Budgeted	*Actual*	*Variance**
Material	XX	XX	XU
Labor	XX	XX	XF
Other	XX	XX	XU

* U: Unfavorable, F: Favorable.

Budget is a macro concept whereas standards are a micro-concept. For example, the standard cost per labor hour may be $5. The budget for 20,000 hours would show a total labor cost of $100,000. The standard itself is a predetermined estimate of what performance should be under stated conditions. In preparing performance information based on standards, we can use three models:

Quantity Variance	=	(Actual Quantity - Standard Quantity) X Standard Cost Per Unit
Cost Variance	=	(Actual Cost - Standard Cost) X Actual Quantity
Total Variance		Quantity Variance + Cost Variance

Payoff Graph Analysis Model

The payoff graph is another tool that can be used effectively by the analyst to enhance the information received by management. Payoff analysis is a simple, straightforward technique which can be used by analysts to compare costs and savings of alternative systems. For example, examine the set of figures given in the table below.

These figures represent the costs of both systems and the resulting savings (or dis-savings) when compared to each other. Figure 3 depicts a pay off analysis graph that, in a meaningful manner, makes this comparison.

The present system's costs are represented by the cross-hatched areas. Savings are calculated by subtracting the proposed system's costs from the present system's costs. The savings are:

YEAR 1:	450,000 - 700,000	=	-250,000
YEAR 2:	500,000 - 510,000	=	-10,000
YEAR 3:	570,000 - 480,000	=	90,000
YEAR 4:	720,000 - 410,000	=	310,000
YEAR 5:	810,000 - 410,000	=	400,000

The plotted points in the graph indicate the accumulated net annual savings. These points are calculated as follows:

Point 1:	0	+	(-250,000)	=	-250,000
Point 2:	(-250,000)	+	(-10,000)	=	-260,000
Point 3:	(-260,000)	+	90,000	=	-170,000
Point 4:	(-170,000)	+	310,000	=	140,000
Point 5:	140,000	+	400,000	=	540,000

Although this is a useful model in making gross estimates, it ignores the time value of money and a desired rate of return on investments. For these considerations we now turn to the model presented in the next section.

	Year 1	Year 2	Year 3	Year 4	Year 5
Costs:					
Semi-automatic					
(present system)	$450,000	$500,000	$570,000	$720,000	$810,000
Automatic					
(proposed system)	$700,000	$510,000	$480,000	$410,000	$410,000
Savings:	($250,000)	($ 10,000)	$ 90,000	$310,000	$400,000

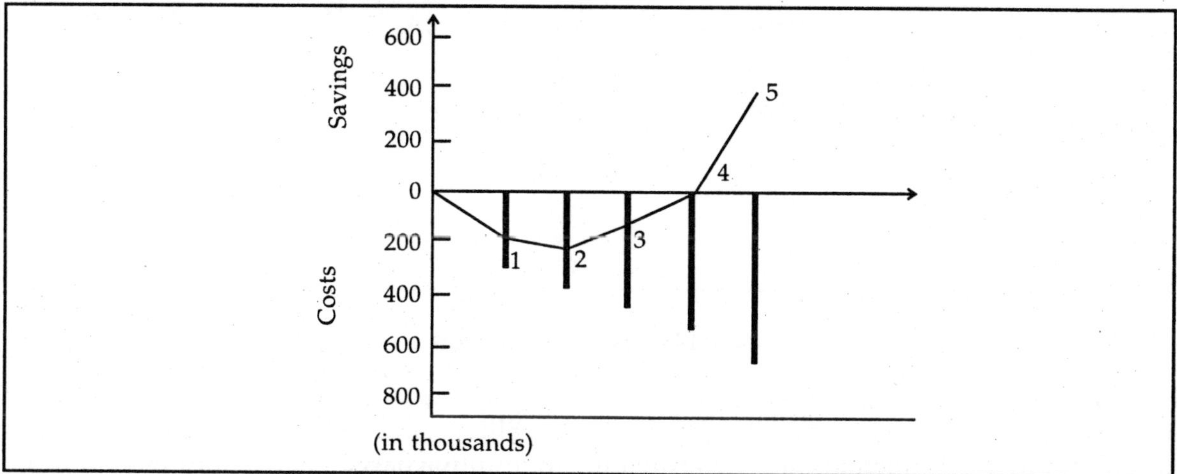

Fig. 3. Payoff analysis graph comparing the proposed system to the present system.

Net Present Value Model

The net present value model can be used to help management make decisions about investment proposals if such a proposal can be reduced to monetary amounts. Stated simply, neglecting nonmonetary considerations, an investment proposal is accepted if the present value of its earnings or cost savings equals or exceeds the amount of the investment required at some desired rate of return.

For example, suppose that management is thinking of purchasing a computer system for $200,000. The useful life of the computer is five years. The cost savings for the first year is $30,000, for the next three years $100,000, and for the last year $80,000. The minimum desired rate of return is 30%. Neglecting other quantitative or qualitative considerations, should management purchase the computer?

In the example below, the net present value of $ –5716 means the investment has not earned what it should at a minimum desired rate of return of 30%. Therefore, the investment is undesirable. If the present value were positive or zero, the investment would be desirable because its return either exceeds or meets the desired minimum.

			Present Value of $1 Discounted at 30%		Present Value
Annual Cost Savings:					
	$36,000	X	.769	$	27,684
	100,000	X	.592		59,200
	100,000	X	.455		45,500
	100,000	X	.350		35,000
	80,000	X	.269		26,900
Present Value of Future Cost Savings				$	194,284
Initial Investment			1,000		- 200,000
Net Present Value				$	- 5,716

Cost Savings Streams

0	1	2	3	4	5
$ 200,000	$30,000	$100,000	$100,000	$100,000	$80,000

ADDITIONAL MODELS

In additional to some of the basic, traditional accounting models presented above other models also help management in planning, controlling, and decision making. In many organisation, these functions are performed on an intuitive basis. That is, minimal effort is made to define and measure variables affecting the organisation. Logico-mathematical methods help to systematise and quantify certain variables in a manner where management can make more knowledgeable decisions. In this section we discuss some of these models.[3]

Probability Concepts

The following concepts of probability and random variables represent the basic knowledge that a systems analyst must have in formulating successful models.

Probability of an Event. The probability that an event E will occur is the ratio between number, n, of cases in which E occurs and the total number, N, of the elementary cases, all equally likely,

$$P(E)=\frac{n}{N}$$

where the assumption of equally likely outcomes describes such processes as tossing coins, rolling a die, and so on.

Random Variable. A random variable, X, assumes the values

$$X_1, X_2 ....X_n$$

with each of these values having a probability of

$$P(X_1), P(X_2) ....P(X_n)$$

where

$$\sum_{i=1}^{n} P(X) = 1$$

and the expected value of X is

$$E(X) = X_1P(X_1) + X_2P(X_2) + ... + X_nP(X_n)$$

For example "what will sales revenue be for the next quarter?" is a typical question an analyst might ask. The estimator states a range of possibilities together with an estimate of the probability each will occur. The sum of the possibilities (X_1, X_2, ...X_n) multiplied by the applicable probability ($P(X_1$, $P(X_2$.....$P(X_n)$ equals the expected value ($E(X)$). The expected value of sales for the next quarter is computed as follows:

Sales (X_1)	*Probability* $P(X)$	*Amount* $X_1P(X)$
$100,000	.1	$ 10,000
120,000	.4	48,000
180,000	.3	48,000
200,000	.2	40,000
	Expected value	$146,000

Compound Probability. This is the probability that both A and B will occur and is written: $P(A, B)$. Compound events are shown in a tree diagram model below.

The probability of a compound event is determined by multiplying branch probabilities. The probability of compound event A_1C_2:

$$P(A_1C_2) = P(A_1) \text{ X } P(C_2) = (.3) \text{ X } (.2) = .06$$

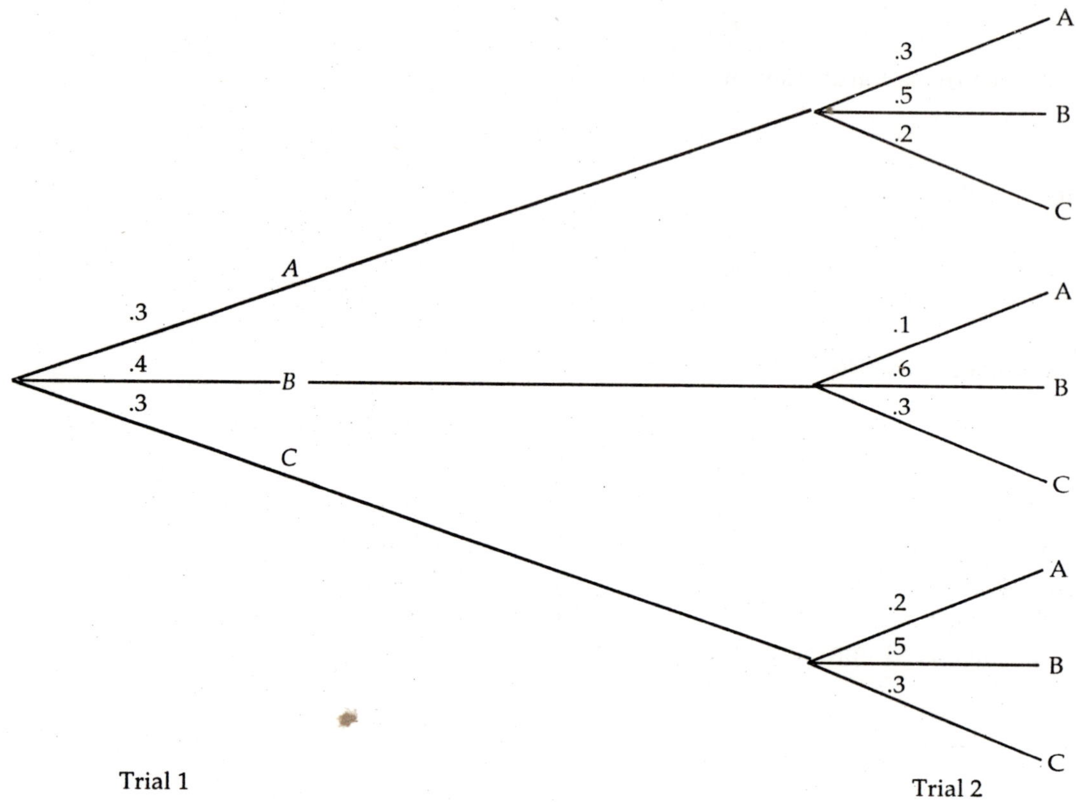

Conditional Probability. The probability that an event A will occur, if it is knows that event *B* has occurred is written *P(A/B)*. For our tree diagram, $P(A_2/B_1) = .1$.

Total Probability. This is the probability of mutually exclusive (nonoverlapping) events occurring. In our example the probability of A_1 or C_1 occurring, written as $P(A_1 + C_1)$ is .6.

Cumulative Probability. This is the process of accumulating the values of *P(X)* which results in the cumulative probability function,

$$P\ (X)\ P(X \leq X) = \sum_{x_1 \leq x} P(X_1)$$

Customer Demand X	*Probability of X*
3	.1
4	.2
5	.3
6	.2
7	.2
	1.0

P (number of units sold ≤ 5) = P (number of units sold = 5) + P (number of units sold = 4) + P (number of units sold = 3) = .3 + .2 + .1 = .6

Statistical Concepts

Statistical concepts represent additional methods of manipulating data to provide information. Some of these basic concepts are indicated here.

Histogram. This is a table showing the number of individual observations falling within each interval or class; this number is called the frequency. Before constructing a histogram, the following must be defined:

1. The limits of the group studied.
2. The data or characteristics measured for each individual.
3. The conditions under which the measurements were made.

Mean. Given a population consisting of N individuals, if f_1 is the frequency of the variate X_I then the mean, $\overline{X}$ is given by the formula:

$$\overline{X} = \frac{1}{N}\sum_{i=1}^{k} f_1\, x_1$$

where k is the number of classes and

$$N = \sum_{i=1}^{k} f_1$$

Mean of the Means. If m measurements are taken in populations of the same nature.

$$X = \frac{n_1\overline{x}_1 + n_2\overline{x}_2 + \ldots + n_m\overline{x}_m}{N}$$

Mode. The mode is the value of χi for which fi is greatest (i.e., the most frequently occurring value).

Median. The median is the value of χi (or lying between two consecutive fi) for which

$$\text{cum f} = \frac{1}{2}N$$

Two Measures of Dispersion. The standard deviation, or mean square deviation:

$$\sigma x = \sqrt{\frac{1}{N}\sum_{i=1}^{k} f_1(x_1 - \overline{x})^2}$$

σ = standard deviation
x = observations
$\overline{x}$ = mean

Random Sample. A sample is considered to be random of it consists of observations that are independently drawn from an identically distributed population.

Network Model

PERT[4] (Program Evaluation and Review Technique) is an example of a network model used for planning and controlling projects with well-defined activities and events. PERT is based on a network composed of activities that take time to accomplish. Between the activities are instantaneous events, which designate the completion of each activity. Probably a better interpretation indicates that events represent a start or finish of the activities.

The activities are placed on network and are represented by arrow. Generally, the arrows or activities flow from left to right. Four rules to follow when placing an activity on the network are:

1. A determination must be made to see if any activities logically precede the activity that is under consideration.
2. A determination must be made to see if any activities are logically concurrent with the activity under consideration.
3. A determination must be made to spot activities which are logically subsequent to the activity under consideration.
4. Events must be clearly defined relative to their beginning and end.

Expected Time

The activity time should be estimated by someone knowledgeable about particular processes. The three time estimates furnished are:

1. *Most likely time.* How long do you expect it would take to complete this particular activity?
2. *Optimistic time.* What is the minimum possible time in which this particular task or activity can be completed?
3. *Pessimistic time.* What is the longest time this particular activity or task has ever taken?

The goal in getting three subjective estimates is to use them to calculate a single weighted average or mean time and variance. This average or mean time is called the expected time of the activity. Briefly, the three time estimates are related to the expected time and standard deviation by the following formulas:

$$t_e = \frac{O + 4M + P}{6}$$

$$\sigma t_e = (P - O)/6$$

where O = optimistic time estimate

M = most likely time estimate

P = pessimistic time estimate

t_e = expected time (weighted average)

σ_{te} = standard deviation of t_e

The above formulas are based on the assumption that the time estimate approximate a beta distribution.

Critical events on the network are those which have zero slack time. Slack time equals the latest event time (T_L)) less the earliest event time (T_E). The latest event time is the latest time that an event can occur without disrupting the project. Earliest event time is the earliest time that an event can occur. A heavy line connecting the critical events represents the critical path for a network. An increase in time along this path will extend the completion date by the same amount. A decrease in time along this path will shorten the time to completion by the same amount or change the critical path.

The network for a batch-project of okra/tomatoes/corn is shown in Figure 4. The activities and time estimates are listed in Table A.1.

Frequently, estimates are required concerning the probability of completing an activity on the critical path by a certain data. Based on the assumption that possible completion times for an activity are approximately normally distributed. PERT has the capability to completing an activity is determined by the number of standard normal units between the completion deadline and the earliest time the activity can be completed. The formula is as follows.

$$Z = \frac{T_D - T_E}{\sqrt{\Sigma\sigma_{t_e}^2}}$$

where Z= number of standard normal units between T_D and T_E

T_D = completion deadline

T_E = earliest completion time

$\sqrt{\Sigma\sigma_{t_e}^2}$ = the square root of the sum of the variances of the pertinent activities on the critical path.

Once Z has been calculated, reference is then made to a standard normal table. The probability that time to completion will exceed the deadline date is equal to the area under the normal curve to the right of the Z value.

For example, we may ask the question, "Can activity 3,7 (cutting okra) be completed by day 13?" The variances associated with the pertinent critical path activities are as follows:

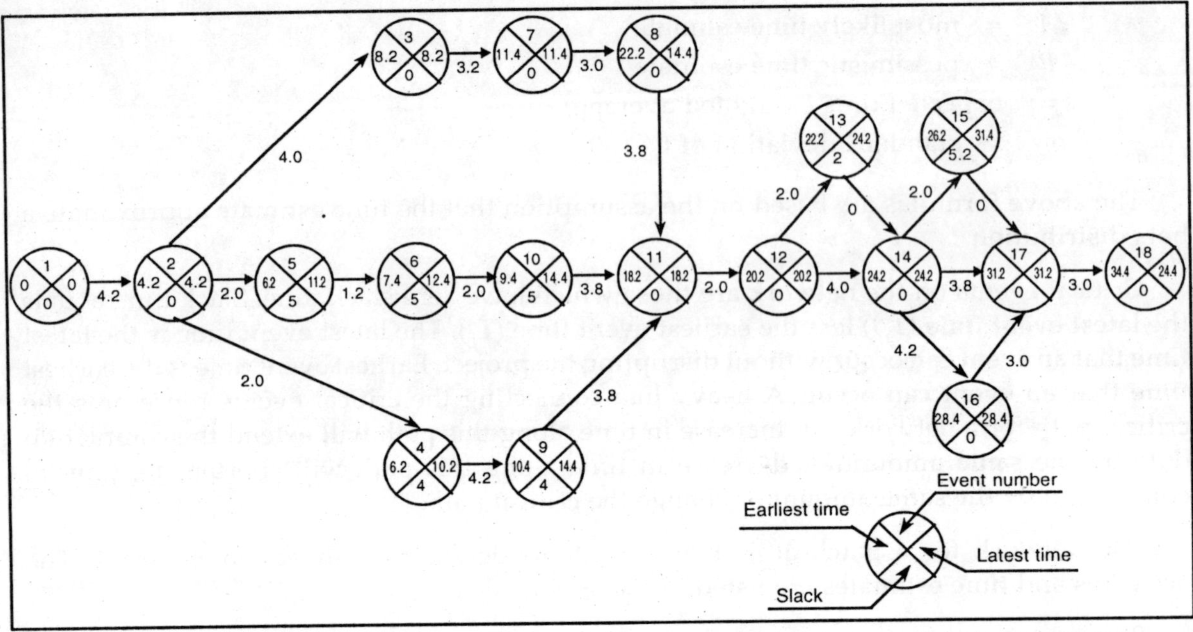

Fig. 4. Network showing earliest and latest time and slack. The heavy line represents the critical path.

Activity	σ_{te}	σ^2_{te}
1,2	.83	.69
2,3	.67	.44
3,7	.50	.25
	Total	1.38

Substituting into our formula for Z,

$$Z = \frac{13 - 11.4}{\sqrt{1.38}}$$

$$= 1.36$$

The area under the normal curve to the right of 1.36 is .0869. Therefore, we can say that the probability of completing activity 3,7 later than day 13 is less than 8.69 per cent. Stated another way, the probability that activity 3,7 will be finished by day 13 is 91.31 per cent.

Decision Model

The elements of a simple decision model consist of actions, outcomes, probabilities of outcomes, and utilities. Let us define the following:

A= set of alternative resource commitments, or actions ((a ε A)

O= set of future states or outcomes (o ε O).

p(o) = set of probabilities that describe the outcome occurrence.

U(o, a)= utility of an outcome occurring given the selection of an action. If an expected utility approach is taken, then the alternative with the highest expected utility would be selected.

$E(U)/a^*$ $MAX\Sigma\ (U\ (o,a).p(o))$

$a\ \varepsilon\ A\ o\ \varepsilon\ O$

TABLE 1

Activities and Time Estimates for the Okra/Tomatoes/Corn Project

		Time in Days		
Activity	*Descriptions*	*Optimistic*	*Most Likely*	*Pessimistic*
1,2	Unloading/testing raw produce	2	4	7
2,4	Washing okra	2	4	6
2,4	Washing/stemming tomatoes	1	2	3
2,5	Loading can racks	1	2	3
3,7	Cutting okra	2	3	5
4,9	Blanching tomatoes	3	4	6
5,6	Mixing device changeover	1	1	2
6,10	Preparation of corn for mixing	1	2	3
7,8	Preparation of okra for mixing	2	3	4
8,11	Loading of okra	2	4	5
9,11	Loading of tomatoes	2	4	5
10,11	Loading of corn	2	4	5
11,12	Canning process	1	2	3
12,13	Quality control-testing	1	2	3
12,14	Pressure cooker process	2	4	6
13,14	Dummy	0	0	0
14,15	Quality control-testing	1	2	3
14,16	Cool bath process	3	4	6
14,17	Warehouse preparation	2	4	5
15,17	Dummy	0	0	0
16,17	Stacking in warehouse	2	3	4
17,18	Cleanup and retooling	2	3	4

Then the expected dollar utility for the alternative resource commitments is as follows:

$$
\begin{aligned}
E(U/a_1) &= U(o_1, a_1) \cdot p(o_1) + U(o_2, a_1) > p(o_2) \\
&= \$2 \cdot .8 + (\$-4) \cdot .2 \\
&= \$1.60 - .80 \\
&= \$.80
\end{aligned}
$$

$$
\begin{aligned}
E(U/a_2) &= U(o_1, a_2) \cdot p(o_1) + U(o_2, a_2) \cdot p(o_2) \\
&= \$0 \cdot .8 + \$1 \cdot .2 \\
&= \$ .20
\end{aligned}
$$

Maximising over alternatives leads us to choose action a_1, accept the shipment.

Many different types of questions can be answered within this decision framework. One of the most interesting is, "What would be the most you would pay for correct information about the contents of shipment?" Let us answer this question by again referring to our example.

Suppose your "perfect" information source was a trained German Shephered dog, who by sniffing the crate could tell with certainty whether or not the grapes were substandard. Your expected utility function would now be,

$$
\begin{aligned}
E(U) &= U(o_1, a_1).\ p(o_1) + U(o_2 a_2).\ p(o_2) \\
&= \$2 \cdot .8 + \$1 \cdot .2 \\
&= \$1.60 + .20 \\
&= \$1.80
\end{aligned}
$$

Notice that the probabilities of the outcomes have not changed. What has changed is that you are no longer making incorrect decisions. You should be willing to pay up to $1.00 ($1.80 – .80) per crate sniffed for this canine's services.

Contribution-by-Value Analysis Model

A very simple, but quite effective, logical model that can be used in almost any kind of performance analysis is termed contribution-by-value analysis (also called ABC analysis). This analysis is based on Pareto's Law, which states that on most situations a relatively small percentage of certain objects contributes a relatively high percentage of output.[5] For instance, it can be shown that in most areas approximately 15-30 per cent of the population contributes 70-90 per cent of the tax revenue. Or, for example, that 20 per cent of the employees in an office do 80 per cent of the work. Many systems analysts find that when inventory items are plotted on a cumulative percentage graph, in order of descending value. Pareto's relationship usually exists. Relative to such a phenomenon, one frequently hears a rule of thumb quoted as: 20 per cent of the items in inventory account for 80 per cent of the sales. Such an analysis is quite effective in that it reveals very clearly the performance of any situation analysed. For inventory analysis, the contribution-by-value analysis can be applied to sales by customer, by salesperson, by product item, by territory, by warehouse, and so on.

An example of contribution-by-value analysis relative to sales by warehouses is discussed and illustrated in Figure 5.

Warehouse Number	*Warehouse Count*	*Number of Warehouse Percentage of Total*	*Annual Sales*	*Cumulative Sales*	*Cumulative Percentage of total Contribution*
1	1	2.00	4,331,927.34	4,331,927.34	56.00
2	2	4.00	1,331,521.32	5,663,448.66	73.20
41	3	6.00	271,765.00	5,935,213.66	76.70
3	4	8.00	189,880.05	6,125,093.71	79.10
50	5	10.00	157,450.05	6,282,543.76	81.20
94	6	12.00	145,175.00	6,427,718.76	83.10
45	7	14.00	123,044.65	6,550,762.41	84.60
14	8	16.00	98,355.30	6,649,117.71	85.90
48	9	18.00	94,579.75	6,743,697.46	87.10
43	10	20.00	86,769.56	6,830,467.02	88.30
42	11	22.00	75,180.12	6,905,647.14	89.20
25	12	24.00	68,287.65	6,973,934.79	90.10
67	13	26.00	66,245.20	7,040,179.99	91.00
26	14	28.00	60,040.40	7,100,220.39	91.80
64	15	30.00	58,352.45	7,158,572.84	92.50
38	16	32.00	42,587.50	7,201,160.34	93.10
39	17	34.00	36,915.80	7,238,076.14	93.50
15	18	36.00	35,601.80	7,273,677.94	94.00
29	19	38.00	32,322.60	7,306,000.54	94.40
36	20	40.00	29,919.65	7,355,920.19	94.80
4	21	42.00	29,322.25	7,365,242.44	95.20
24	22	44.00	29,184.10	7,394,426.54	95.60
19	23	46.00	28,548.05	7,422,974.59	95.90
57	24	48.00	27,129.90	7,450,104.49	96.30

Fig. 5 cont...

95	25	50.00	24,260.13	7,474,364.62	96.60
62	26	52.00	23,379.75	7,497,744.37	96.90
47	27	54.00	23,088.10	7,520,832.47	97.20
16	28	56.00	22,110.39	7,542,942.86	97.50
17	29	58.00	19,293.90	7,562,236.76	97.70
66	30	60.00	18,705.50	7,580,942.26	98.00
71	31	62.00	17,925.20	7,598,867.46	98.20
46	32	64.00	15,764.25	7,614,631.71	98.40
58	33	66.00	14,306.00	7,628,937.71	98.60
18	34	68.00	13,304.20	7,642,241.91	98.80
35	35	70.00	12,741.70	7,654,983.61	98.90
28	36	72.00	11,347.80	7,666,331.41	99.10
65	37	74.00	10,164.25	7,676,495.66	99.20
34	38	76.00	10,087.15	7,686,582.81	99.30
61	39	78.00	9,422.20	7,696,005.01	99.50
27	40	80.00	6,463.10	7,702,468.11	99.50
91	41	82.00	6,196.60	7,708.664.61	99.60
54	42	84.00	5,592.55	7,714,257.16	99.70
55	43	86.00	4,507.80	7,718,764.96	99.70
5	44	88.00	4,049.70	7,722,814.66	99.80
70	45	90.00	3,356.00	7,726,170.96	99.80
37	46	92.00	3,262.10	7,729,433.06	99.90
60	47	94.00	2,402.35	7,731,835.41	99.90
49	48	96.00	1,694.50	7,733,529.91	99.90
23	49	98.00	558.35	7,734,088.25	99.90
68	50	100.00	252.50	7,734,340.76	100.00

Fig. 5. Contribution-by-warehouse sales report.

To prepare the analysis, the following steps are taken.

1. Dollar annual sales are calculated for each warehouse by multiplying sales price times quantity sold for each product and computing a grand total for all products in each warehouse.
2. All warehouses are arranged by dollar annual sales in descending sequence.
3. A list is printed from these ranked ware houses. Included in this report is such information as warehouse number, warehouse count, percentage of total, annual

sales of each warehouse, cumulative sales, and percentage of total contribution. The relevant points of this report are:

(a) The top 10 per cent of the warehouse account for 81.20 per cent of the dollar sales. In other words, a mere 5 out of 50 warehouses account for over four-fifths of the sales of the entire business or close to $6.28 million annually.

(b) The upper 20 per cent of the warehouses account for 88.30 per cent of the sales. An additional 10 per cent increase in the number of warehouses increased sales by 5.20 per cent.

(c) The upper 50 per cent of the warehouses account for 96.60 per cent of the sales.

(d) The upper 74 per cent of the warehouses account for 99-20 per cent of the sales. Conversely, the lower 26 per cent of the warehouses account for only .80 per cent of the sales.

The information from the report is plotted to assist management in visualising the relationships between number of warehouses and their relative contribution to sales volume. A plot of the results of this analysis, with the percentage of cumulative annual sales on the vertical axis, and the percentage of warehouses on the horizontal axis, appears in Figure 6.

The contribution-by-value analysis shows that the company is operating several warehouses which are probably not necessary for efficient and streamlined operations. As surprising as the above relationships are on first exposure, however, they will probably be found in many organisations. It should also be noted that the discernment of such relationships provides management with valuable information even though the contribution-by-value analysis model is, itself, simplistic.

Forecast Models

Good forecasts are vital to the success of every organisation. The sales forecast, for example, is a basic source of information for production, inventory, procurement, and employment plans. Even though inherent errors exist in any forecasting model, an organisation that bases its operations on intuitive decision making is ignoring the possibilities for a more efficient operation.

The Lease-Squares Model

As an extrapolative forecast model, the least-squares technique uses historical data exclusively. When a model of this type is used, two basic assumptions must be made that the recent level of activity will continue and that the recent rate of change will remain about the same. The least-squares line approximating the set of points (X_1, Y_1), (X_2, Y_2),.....(X_n, Y_n) has the equation

$$Y = a_o + a_1 X$$

where the constants a_o and a_1 can be found from the formulas

$$a_0 = \frac{(\Sigma X^2)(\Sigma Y) - (\Sigma XY)(\Sigma X)}{N\Sigma X^2 - (\Sigma X)^2}$$

$$a_1 = \frac{N\Sigma Y - (\Sigma Y)(\Sigma X)}{N\Sigma X^2 - (\Sigma X)^2}$$

Here, X is the independent variable and Y is the dependent variable. The least-squares line passes through the point ($\overline{XY}$) called the centroid or center of gravity of the data.

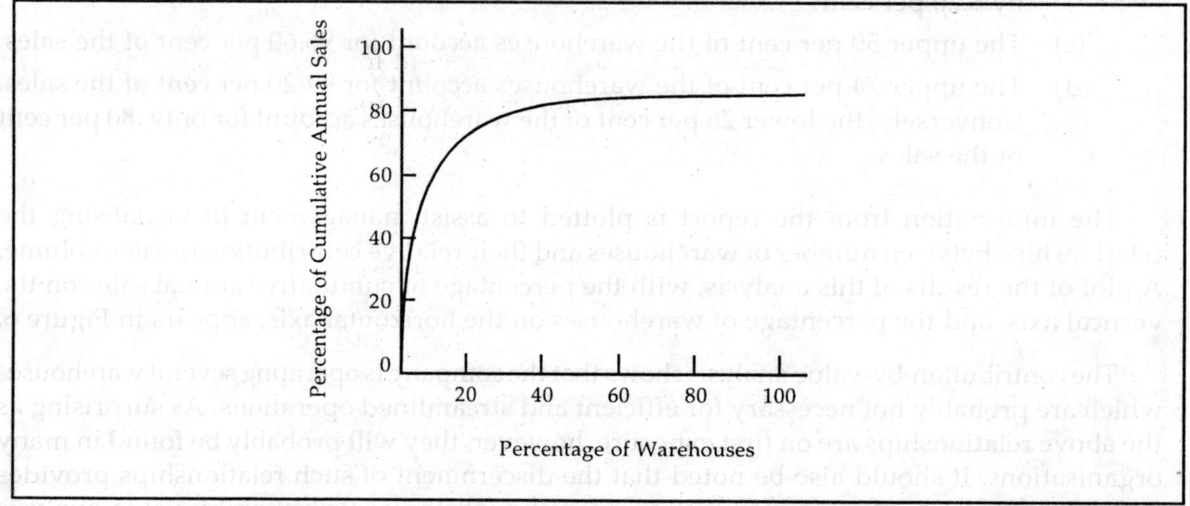

Fig. 6. Graphic representation of the conribution-by-warehouse sales report.

Suppose the value of X represents time, such as months, and the value of Y represents quantities of products sold each month. The value of Y can be extrapolated according to some value of X. In other words, if the independent variable X is time, then the data show the values of Y at various times in the future.

Since Y is estimated from X, $\hat{Y}$ represents the value of $\hat{Y}$ for given values of X as estimated fro m the least-squares regression line of

$$\hat{Y} = a_0 + a_1 X$$

From this, a measure of the scatter about the regression line of X and Y is supplied by the quantity

$$S_{y,x} = \sqrt{\frac{(Y - Y)^2}{N}}$$

which is called the standard error of the estimate of Y on X[6].

The Exponential Smoothing Model

Exponential smoothing is similar to a moving average; however, where applicable, exponential smoothing is normally chosen as a forecasting method for the following two reasons:

1. With the moving average all data in the series are weighted equally. In other words, recent data are given the same weight as older data.
2. Forecasting by the moving average method requires that a great deal of data be maintained.

Exponential smoothing is a form of weighted moving average. All that is needed to use the exponential smoothing model is a smoothing constant, the current forecast, and a new observation.

The computational procedure of exponential smoothing is shown by the following formula:

$$\text{New Average} = \text{Old Average} + \alpha\,(\text{New Demand - Old Average})$$

where α designate a smoothing constant between 0 and 1.

The new average represents the forecast of demand for the subsequent forecast interval. The old average is the new average of the preceding forecast interval, and the new demand is the actual demand for the present period. Said another way, the forecast is part old forecast and part forecast accurate, then the new average would equal the old average.

By controlling the weight of the most recent data, α simultaneously determines the average age of the data included in the estimate of the average. The value chosen for the smoothing constant can be such that the estimate is very stable, or reacts very quickly. For example, $\alpha = 0.5$ would give a greater weight to the new data than $\alpha = 0.1$. Regardless of the value of α8 the weighting of data follows what is called an exponential curve; therefore, the name exponential smoothing.

One of the crucial questions that arise when one uses exponential smoothing is the size of the smoothing constant that should be used. Conceptually, the answer is simple. Enough weight should be given to provide system stability, but it should be small enough so that real (not random) changes in the level of demand will be recognised.

Inventory Control Model

The problem of planning, scheduling, and controlling production in the face of uncertain market conditions, and of maintaining reasonable levels of inventories, is almost universal. In many organisations with a wide product line, the inventory clerks as well as management may not know with reasonable accuracy what the levels are, and an investigation into the inventory will often indicate a wide variation between the actual conditions, and what is thought to be the inventory. When an inventory item is overstocked, the error may not become evident for a long time, if at all. When an item is underlocked and a stockout occurs, customer goodwill is reduced. Any organisation with inventory management system that accomplishes two things: (1) it makes certain that items are available when they are needed, and (2) it prevents an increase of inventory beyond proper limits. Inventory management assures that an adequate supply of inventory is maintained and requires an optimum balance between shortage and overstock. Too many shortages decrease the customer service level. Conversely, an overstock of items ties up working capital that can be used more profitably elsewhere.

Replenishment, Lead Time, and Safety Stock

The first of two approaches to replenishing inventory is shown in Figure 7 and is termed a periodic system wherein an order is placed on a specific date. The disadvantage of this method is that stockouts are risked. The second approach, illustrated in Figure 8, is termed reorder point system in that an order is placed when the inventory level of an item reaches a predetermined level L_{RE}.

The time *T* in the periodic method is always the same, whereas *T* in the reorder point method is unequal. Of the two methods, the second one is used more often. It consists of placing a constant order quantity when the inventory level reaches the reorder level. The reorder level is computed as follows:

Reorder Level =
Lead Time x Forecast of Demand
- Safety Stock

The lead time t_1 to t_2 is that time interval between placement of an order and receipt of that order. In Figure 8, it was assumed that lead time was zero. Such an assumption is normally not realistic. Lead time would probably be similar to that shown in Figure 9. The safety stock allows for a margin of error in estimating lead time or demand.

The Problem of How Much to Order

The best known model of how much to order is the classic EOQ (economic order quantity) model. This model reveals to the inventory clerk how much to buy (or order) when a reorder point is reached.

The order quantity chosen will incur certain costs. Two different set of cost factors are considered. If a greater or lesser quantity is ordered, then some costs will increase, while others decrease. Among those costs that increase are interest, obsolescence, risk, and storage, while the set of decreasing costs included such items as freight and procurement costs. These costs can be lumped into the categories of cost to carry and cost to purchase inventory. The goal is to balance the opposing costs, and thus, obtain a minimum total cost. For an illustration of annual costs versus number of orders, see Figure 10. Two facts are illustrated.

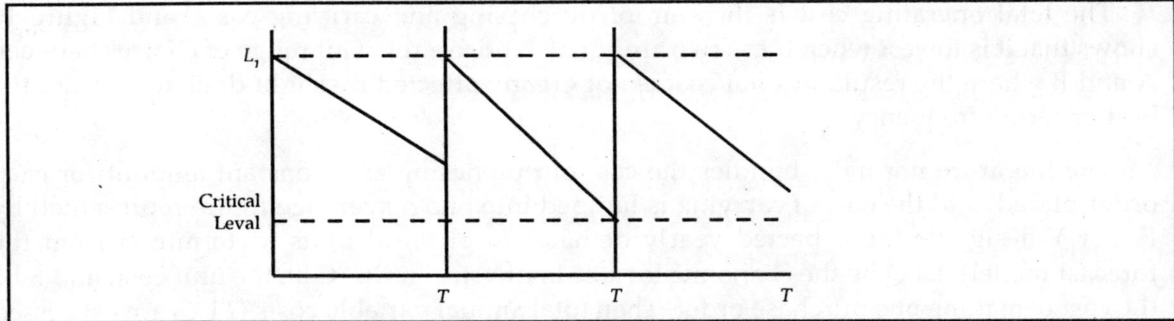

Fig. 7. Periodic replenishment system.

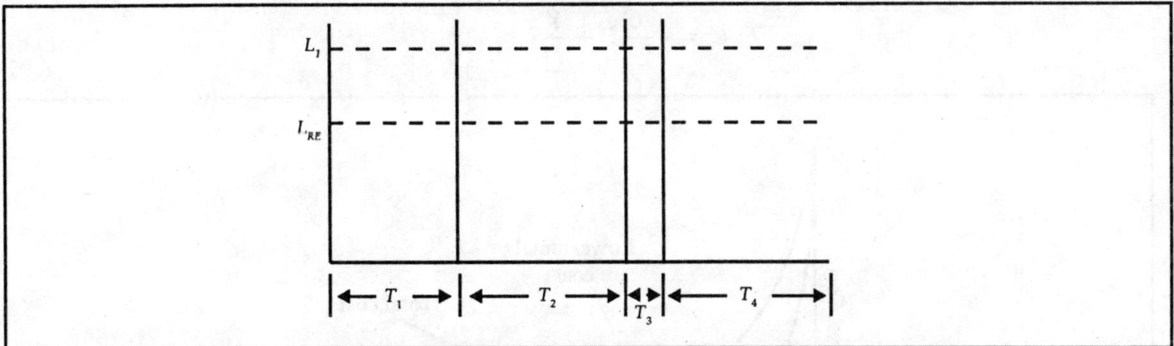

Fig. 8. Reorder point replenishment system.

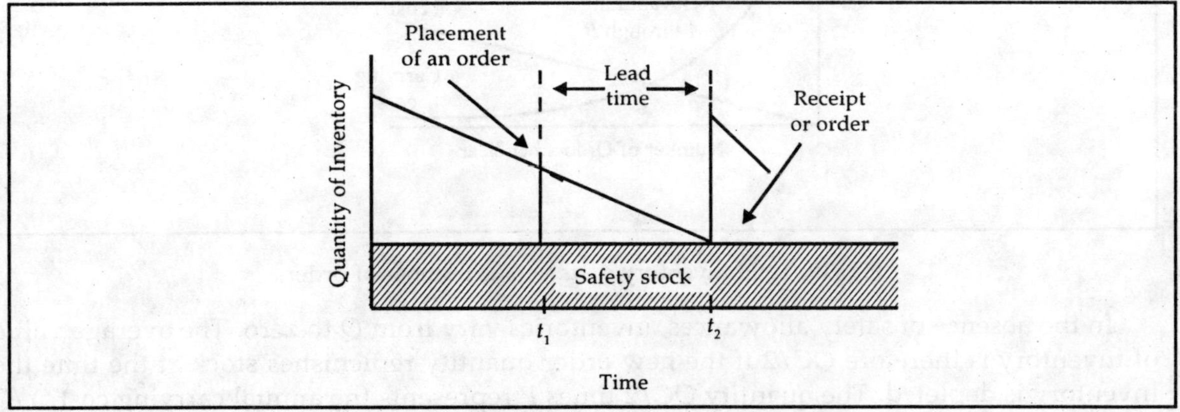

Fig. 9. Illustration of lead time and safety stock.

1. As orders are placed more frequently, carrying costs decrease because the cycle stock (cycle stock is one-half the order quantify) is less.
2. As orders are placed more frequently, purchasing costs increase.

The total operating cost is the sum of purchasing and carrying costs, and Figure 10 shows that it is lowest when these two are equal. Notice a relevant range of choices between A and B where the resultant total cost is not greatly affected by slight deviations from the best ordering frequency.

The literature normally handles the cost of purchasing as a constant amount for each order placed, and the cost of carrying is lumped into one percentage figure represented by *P*. Let *Y* designate the expected yearly demand in physical units (determined from the forecast model), let *Q* be the economic lot size in physical units, *C* be the unit cost, and *S* be the cost of making one purchase order. Then total annual variable costs (*TVC*) are expressed as follows[7]:

$$TVC = \frac{QC}{2}P + \frac{Y}{Q}S$$

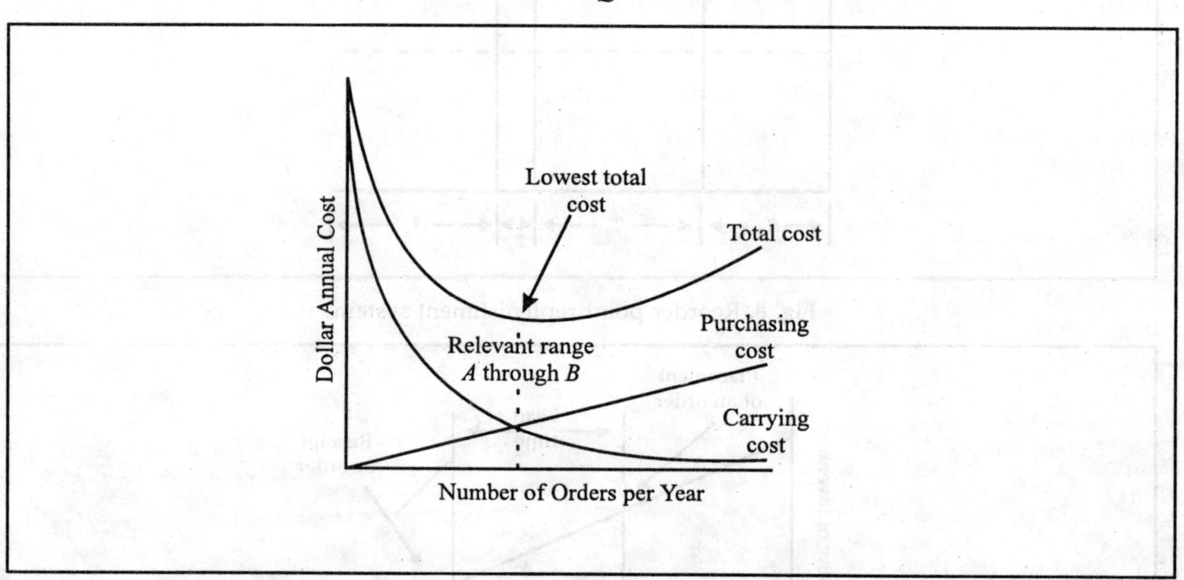

Fig. 10. Total inventory costs versus number of orders.

In the absence of safety allowances, inventories vary from *Q* to zero. The average value of inventory is therefore *QC*/2 if the new order quantity replenishes stock at the time the inventory is depleted. The quantity *QC*/2 times *P* represents the annual carrying cost. *Y*/*Q* represents the number of times a year that orders are placed. Therefore, (*Y*/*Q*)/*S* represents the total annual purchasing costs.

To determine the amount of *Q* which minimizes total cost, the above equation is differentiated with respect to *Q* and set equal to zero. The following equation is obtained

$$\frac{PC}{2} - \frac{YS}{Q^2} = O$$

which, when solved or Q, equals:

$$Q = \sqrt{\frac{2YS}{PC}}$$

This formula states that Q, the economic order quantity, varies directly with the square root of the forecasted demand and the square root of the purchasing costs and varies inversely with the square root of the cost of carrying.

Material Yield Analysis Model

In a number of industries, particularly of the process type, material yield plays a significant role in effecting cost reduction and production improvement. Material yield standards are generally set for various types of raw material. In most cases the yield standards are based on laboratory tests or company records. A substantial cost reduction is achieved through the improvement of the yield of good products based on proper procurement and production efforts. A variance analysis program pointing out and evaluating causes of low yield aids management in minimizing shrinkage and waste in purchasing and production. If, for example, the procurement, personnel purchase defective raw material, then an excess of shrinkage will occur during preparation of this material for processing. Consequently, a yield analysis and reporting system should be installed to determine the degree of shrinkage or waste.

Standards for material usage during the production phase are of paramount importance to top management. The plant manager and top management personnel need to have feedback which will enable them to detect and measure losses of raw produce during the production process. Not only to the reports of material yield disseminate information to responsible persons, but they ensure a significant degree of control of the processing function.

The basic question is whether the standard amount of raw material is used to obtain a given output of the finished product. The difficulty here is that computation of variances is delayed until the production process is completed. At the Yummy Company, however, production is set up so that a number of subbatches comprise an overall batch.

An example of yield information reporting is shown in Figure 11.

The yield analysis report of Figure 11 does not tell why the yield of this particular batch of pimiento is Unfavorable. It does, however, give feedback to the plant manager, the manager of procurement, the president, and other responsible persons that particular phases in the processing function may be faulty. A retracing of the overall process must be set into motion to isolate the cause of the unfavorable variances and take necessary corrective action.

Material Yield Report - Sliced Pimiento				
Product Number	Description	Weight of Input (Raw Product)	Standard Yield Sales	
002	KP SL PIM GL 24/4	32,000#	510	
			Variance from	
Standard Output	Actual Yield Rates*	Actual Output	Percent	Standard Weight
16,360#	.419	13,400#	9.1% UF	2,980 # UF

$$\text{*Actual Yield Rate} = \frac{\text{Weight of Actual Output}}{\text{Weight of Input (Raw Produce)}}$$

$$= \frac{13,400}{32,000}$$

$$= .419$$

Fig. 11. Yield analysis report.

Quality Control Analysis and Reporting

Every organisation, large or small, faces the problem of attaining and maintaining satisfactory quality of their example. First, the quality attributes must be identical. Next accurate standard measurements must be set. Finally, the allowable departures from such standard measurements must be determined. Moreover, satisfactory quantity must be obtained at a reasonable and competitive cost level.

Product quality variation assess out of the variables which constitute a great grocess. The following are basic:

1. The raw materials which enter process themselves vary in form and composition.
2. The production process itself series and resulting output must be below satisfactory quality.

The obvious objectives, therefore are to reduce the amount of the defective raw materials going into production and to dominate defective finished products. These objectives are never fully possible, but a reduction in the number of defectives in the total operation must be sought.

Statistical sampling and concern tables can be used effectively to implementing quality control in organisations. A simple table for this purpose is shown in Figure 12.

Sequence of Samples Which Show Sample Size and Acceptance and Reject Numbers				
Sample	*Sample Size*	*Combined Sample Size*	*Acceptance Number (Cumulative)*	*Rejection Number (Cumulative)*
First	25	25	0	5
Second	25	50	3	8
Third	25	75	6	11
Fourth	25	100	9	14
Fifth	25	125	12	17
Sixth	25	150	15	20
Seventh	25	175	18	23
Eighth	25	200	21	26
Ninth	25	225	24	29
Tenth	25	250	27	32

Fig. 12. A table of acceptance and rejection numbers.

The table indicates that if 5 or more defectives are in the first sample of 25 from some population (batch or lot), the that population being tested is rejected. If more than 0 and less than 5 defectives are found, then another sample of 25 is taken. If in this next sample the cumulative total of defectives is 3 or less, then the population is accepted. If the number of defectives is greater than 3 but less than 8, then another sample is taken. If the cumulative total of defectives at the second sample is 8 or more, then the population is rejected, and so on.

Basic Queuing Models

Many types of problems are described by the build-up of queues of some input to a service facility. The queues result from stochastic or probabilistic phenomena. In all cases inputs arrive at a facility for processing, and the time of arrival of individual inputs at the service facility is random as is the time of processing. The randomness of one or more parameters in a queue system is responsible for the uncertainties associated with it. In all organisations the queuing phenomena is ever present. In production, machines are idle or overburdened. Patients wait for hours in hospitals. Trucks wait in long lines at loading docks. At times inventories are excessive; at other times, too many stock-outs occur. And so if goes. Management must strike a balance between costs of idleness and costs of overburdened service facilities. Consequently, management must know something about the activity and length of a queue, the demand on the service activity, the capacity of the service facility to handle the random demand, and the time spent waiting in the queue plus the time in the service facility.

Four basic structures of queuing situations describe the general conditions of a service facility. The simplest situation is where arriving units from a single queue are to be serviced by a single service facility: for example, a car in a car wash. This structure is called a single-channel, single-phase condition. A simple assembly line has a number of service facilities in series or tandem and represents the single-channel, multiple-phase condition. If the number of service facilities is increased (two or more car washes) but still draws on one queue, then this is represented by a multiple-channel, single-phase condition. Finally, the last structure is a multiple-channel, multiple-phase condition which might be illustrated by two or more parallel production lines.[8] These structures are illustrated in Figure 13.

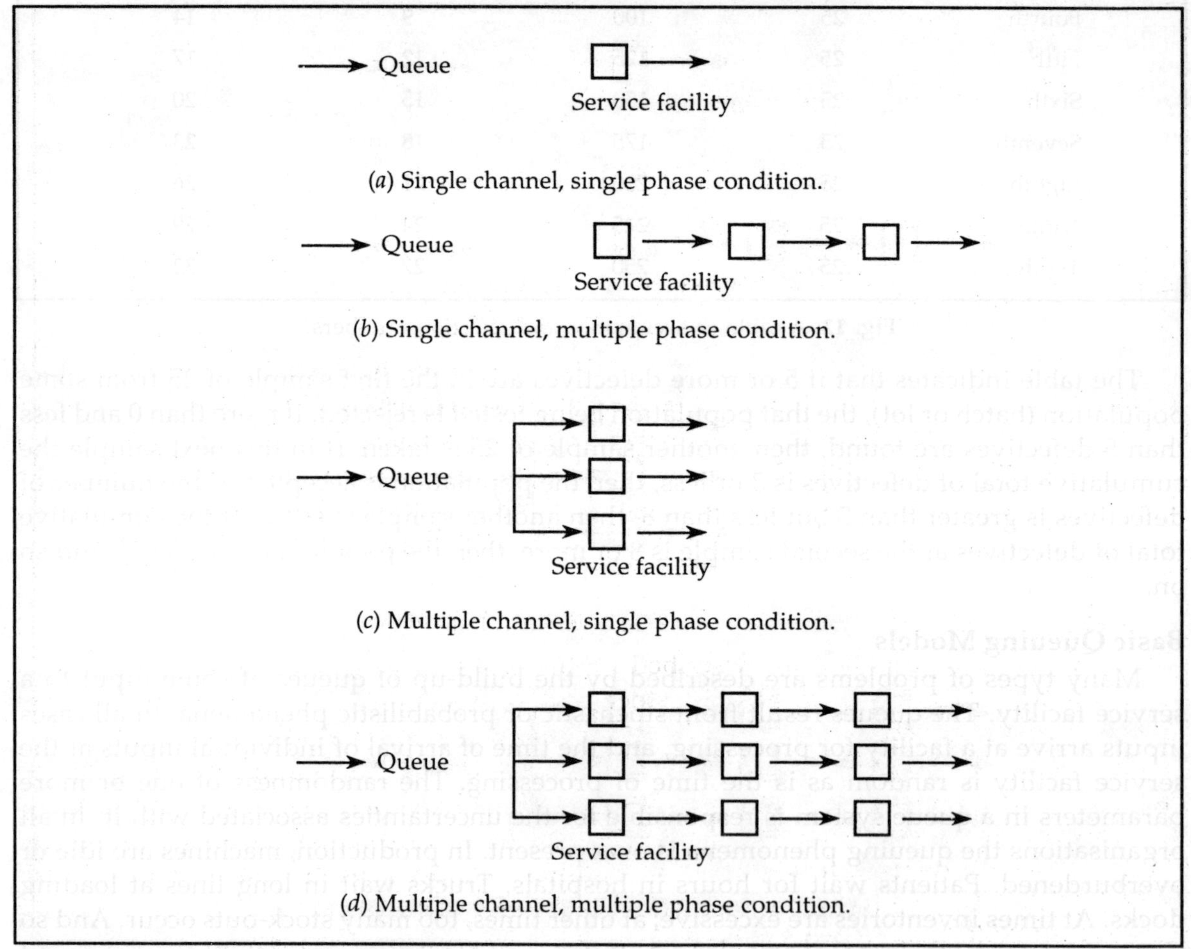

Fig. 13. Four basic structures of queuing conditions.

Simulation Models

In a probabilistic model some dimensions are knows while the value of others is based on phenomena of a stochastic nature. The randomness of one or more parameters in a system is responsible for the uncertainties that exist. Random machine breakdowns, customer demand, labor strikes, and competitor price changes, all occur.

Simulation models help to organise disjointed data and activities, and to illustrate interrelationships previously unknown. The perception of combinational aspects of a complex problem and their effect on a system can, in many instances, be handled only by a model. For example, the problem of smog control is amenable to simulation techniques. A complete understanding of the problem involves the interrelationship of climate, the molecular behaviour of gases, the chemistry of engine exhaust, the number of vehicles, the geographic layout of the city (including the location of the homes, work places, and highway arteries), the availability of alternate means of transportation, the speed of traffic and the timing of traffic lights, the incomes of the population, the chemistry and biology of the lungs and blood stream, and problems of microbes and virus growth under chemical, light and temperature conditions produced by smog-among other problems.[9]

The above smog control problem can be attached through the use of simulation. Decision makers can see more clearly the aspects of the problem and how they interrelate. By so doing, the information produced by the model can aid the decision maker in choosing among a number of alternative courses of action.

Linear Programming Model

The purpose of linear programming is to provide a method of optimising the allocation of scarce resources to competing demands.

Following is a list of kinds of problems which have been solved by liner programming methods. These are the kinds of problems that systems analysts encounter in most organisations; however, this list is not exhaustive and indicates only a few examples.

1. Allocation of energy sources in electrical power generation.
2. Determining optimal mix of food products for beef cattle production.
3. Adapting production to variable and seasonal sales.
4. Allocation of limited raw materials and production facilities to the production of a multiple product line.
5. Optimum multiple plant and warehouse location.

The viewpoint that the analyst should take is to concentrate on the definition of the problem and formulation of the model and leave the technical intricacies and solution of the model to the technical staff of the information system. The technical staff would include, among others, mathematicians, operations research specialists, and application programmers.

Two major assumptions are required in using linear programming techniques: linearity and certainty. Linearity means all the relationships involve variables of the first degree and can be illustrated graphically by straight lines. Certainty requires that the value of all variables must be knows and that all variables are non-negative.[10]

An example of the general form which a linear programming problem may take on. follows:

$$\begin{array}{llllllll} \text{maximise} & p_1x_1 & + & p_2x_2 & + \dots + & p_nx_n & & \\ \text{subject to} & a_{11}x_1 & + & a_{12}x_2 & + \dots + & a_{1n}x_n & \leq & b_1 \\ & a_{21}x_1 & + & a_{22}x_2 & + \dots + & a_{2n}x_n & \leq & b_2 \\ & \vdots & & \vdots & & \vdots & & \vdots \\ & a_{n1}x_1 & + & a_{n2}x_2 & + \dots + & a_{nn}x_n & \leq & b_n \end{array}$$

The pi's in the objective function may refer to profit contributions of the given products $x_1, x_2, \dots x_n$. On the other hand, the a_{ij}'s may refer to the required amounts of manufacturing material for the given products, which are in limited supply according to $b_1, b_2, \dots b_n$. The linear programming problem would then be to maximise the profit contribution subject to the given limitations on manufacturing material.

Let us consider a simple graphical example of a linear programming problem, as follows:

$$\begin{array}{lrcrcl} \text{maximise} & 3x_1 & + & 2x_2 & & \\ \text{subject to} & 2x_1 & + & 3x_2 & \leq & 10 \\ & 3x_1 & + & x_2 & \leq & 6 \\ & x_1 & & & \geq & 0 \\ & & & x_2 & \geq & 0 \end{array}$$

Consider the x_1x_2 coordinate system. Any point (x_1, x_2) can be plotted in this system. For example see Figure 14. All points lying on or to the right of the x_2 axis satisfy the constraint that $x_1 \geq 0$. Similarly, all points lying on or above the x_1 axis satisfy the constraint $x_2 \geq 0$). Therefore a feasible solution to the problem must be contained in the first section (quadrant) of the coordinate system. Now let us consider the other two constraints. If we allow equality to hold, then we would have equations for straightlines and any point on these lines would satisfy the equations. Refer to Figure 15. Observe also, that any point (x_1, x_2) in the first quadrant, which lies on or below one of the given lines, satisfies that inequality. For example, the point (1,2) substituted into the equation $2x_1 + 3x_2 = 10$ yields the value 7, which is less than 10. Therefore, the points satisfying all the constraints lie in the region bounded by $2x_1 + 3x_2 = 10$, $3x_1 + x_2 = 6$ and the x_1 and x_2 axes (the shaded areas).

We must now find the point in the region that maximises the objective function, $3x_1 + 2x_2$. Allowing this function to take on different values produces straight lines which are parallel. We must then find the line that gives the objective function its greatest value and at the same times has at least one point in the constrained region. Let us give $3x_1 + 2x_2$ the value 6 and plot this line in the x_1x_2 coordinate system. See Figure 16. This line has many points within the constrained region, but it should be obvious parallel lines exist above this

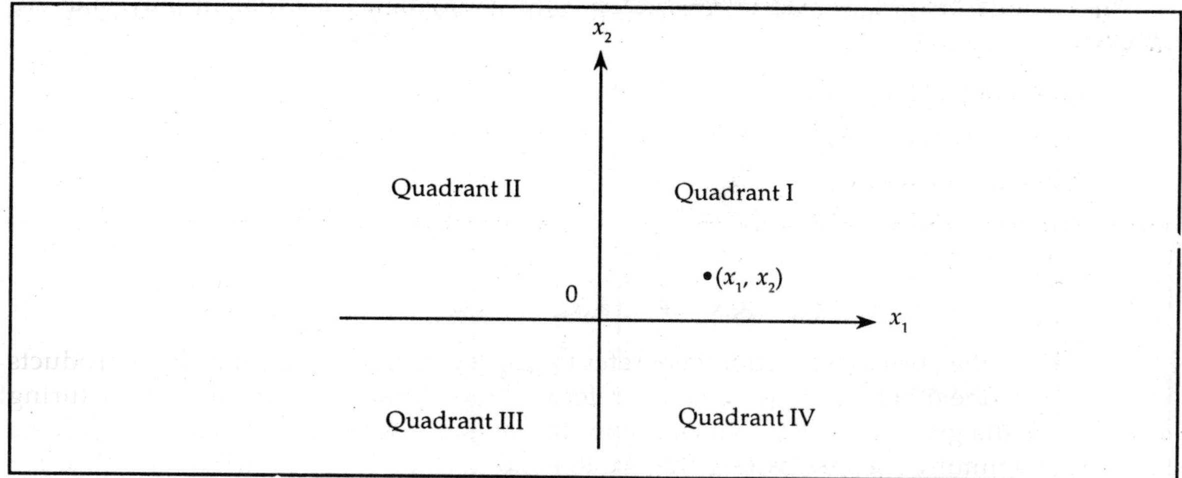

Fig. 14. The x_1, x_2 coordinate system.

line that give the objective function a greater value and still have at least one point within the constrained region. In fact, the line that gives the objective function its greatest value and still contains at least one point within the given region, passes through the point of intersection of the two lines $2x_1 + 3x_2 = 10$, and $3x_1 + x_2 = 6$. Solving these two equations simultaneously, we find $x_1 = 8/7$ and $x_2 = 18/7$. It is these two values that, when substituted into the objective function, give it its maximum value of $= 60/7$

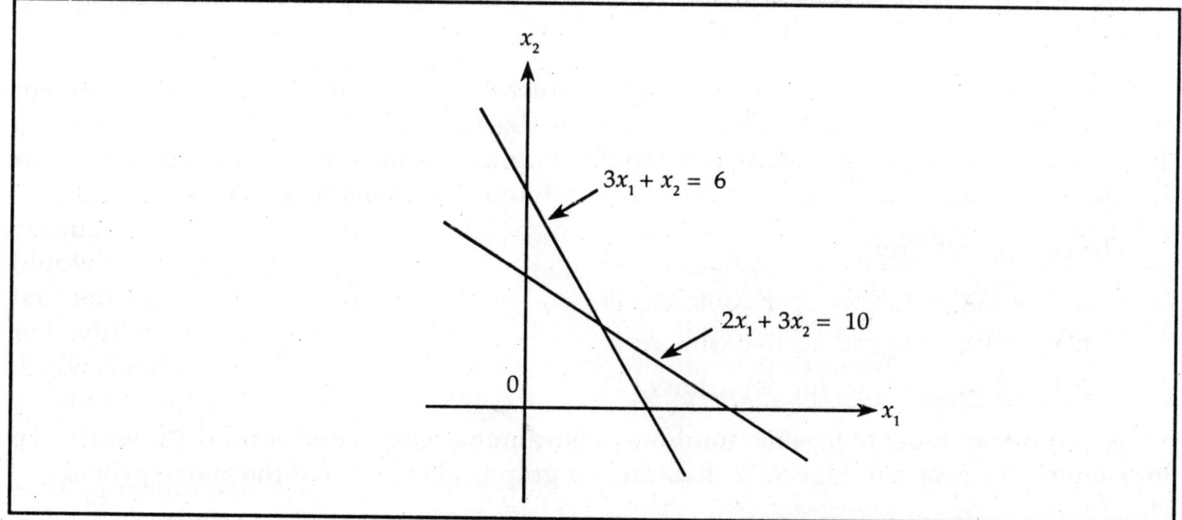

Fig. 15. Graphical example of constraints in a linear programming problem.

For a "real world" application of the linear programming model, assume a company manufactures two products. P_1 and P_2, which are processed by three departments. The products can be processed on any order. Pertinent data are shown in the table above.

The number of minutes each department will be available for operation during the month are as follows:

12,600 minutes for D_1
14,400 minutes for D_2
13,000 minutes for D_3

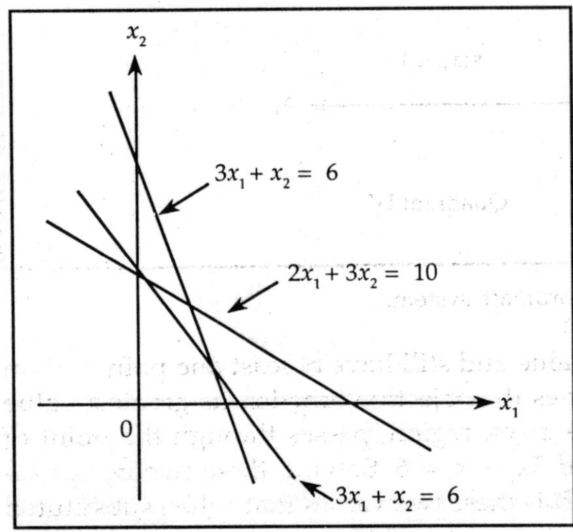

Fig. 16. Graphical exaple of the objective function taking on one of many values.

Fig. 17. Graphical solution.

The question to answer is, how much of Product P_1 and Product P_2 should be produced to maximise the total contribution margin? The objective function, therefore is $Z = 8X_1 + 10X_2$, where X_1 is the number of units of product P_1, and X_2 is the number of units of P_2. Then: $Z = 8X_1 + 10X_2$ the function to be maximised with the conditions $X_1 \geq 0$, $X_2 \geq 0$.

The constraints are:

$20X_1 + 15X_2 \leq 12{,}600$ for department D_1
$12X_1 + 20X_2 \leq 14{,}400$ for department D_2
$26X_1 + 13X_2 \leq 13{,}000$ for department D_3

An infinite number of feasible solutions exist; among them is one or more for which Z is maximum. The graph in Figure 17 illustrated a graphical solution of the above problem.

The area enclosed by abode includes all feasible solutions to the production problem. The maximum solution can be found by computing the values at each corner of the polygon. These computations are made in the table on next page.

	D_1	D_2	D_3	*Contribution Margin*[a]
P_1	20 min.	12 min.	26 min.	8.00
P_2	15 min.	20 min.	13 min.	10.00

a. Contribution Margin = Sales Price - Variable Cost.

The maximum Z is represented by a straight line for a particular value of Z equal to $7600. Since the coefficients $8 and $10 are invariant, this line will remain parallel to itself when the value of Z is changed. The maximum will always correspond to one of the extreme points of the constrained region that is furthest from the point of origin. Therefore, the further this line moves from the origin, the greater the value of Z, and vice versa.

Probably the most important single development in the solution of linear programming problems took place in the late 1940s when George Dantzig devised the Simplex Method. Consider for a moment the graphical example of a linear programming problem treated above. Note that a line drawn between any two points in the constrained area lies entirely within that area. This fact holds for any linear programming problem in which a feasible solution exists and this constrained region is said to be convex (bulges outward from the origin). Also note that an optimal point for the objective function will be at one of the corners of the convex region. The Simplex Method gives us a procedure for moving step by step from a given corner (extreme point) to an optimal corner (extreme point).[11]

	Corner	*Product* P_1	*Product* P_2	*(Objective Function) Total Contribution Margin*
a	0.0	0	0	Z = $8.00(0) + $10.00(0) = $0.00
b	500,0	500	0	Z = $8.00(120) + $10.00(0) = $4000.00
c	250,510	250	510	Z = $8.00(250) + $10.00(510) = $7000.00
d	150,640	150	640	Z = $8.00(150) + $10.00(640) = $7600.00[a]
e	0,720	0	720	Z = $8.00(0) + $10.00(720) = $7200.00

a. Optimum solution.

BIBLIOGRAPHY

Anthony and Reece, *Management Accounting*, Fifth Edition, Homewood IL,: Richard D. Irwin, Inc., 1975.

Archibald and Villria, *Netword-Based Management Systems (PERT/CPM)*, New York: John Wiley & Sons, Inc., 1967.

Bierman, Bonini, and Hausman, *Quantitative Analysis for Business Decisions*, Fourth Edition, Homewood, IL.: Richard D. Irwin, Inc., 1973.

Brown, *Smoothing, Forecasting, and Production of Discrete Time Series*, Englewood Cliffs, NJ,: Prentice-Hall, Inc., 1963.

Buffa, *Operations Management*, Third Edition, New York: John Wiley & Sons, Inc., 1972.

Burch, "Computer Application of Contribution Analysis," *Journal of Systems Management*, August 1970.

Demski, *Information Analysis*, Reading,MA.: Addison-Wesley Publishing Co., 1972.

Dutton and Starbuck, *Computer Simulation of Human Behavior*, New York.: John Wiley & Sons, Inc., 1971.

Evarts, *Information to PERT*, Boston: Allyn and Bacon, Inc., 1964.

Gass, *Linear Programming*, Second Edition, New York: McGraw-Hill Book Co., 1964.

Hadley, *Linear Algebra*, Reading MA.: Addison-Wesley Publishing Co., 1961.

Hillier and Lieberman, *Introduction to Operations Research*, second edition, San Francisco: Holden-Day, 1974.

Horngren, *Cost Accounting: A Managerial Emphasis*, Fifth Edition, Englewood Cliffs, NJ.: Prentice-Hall, Inc., 1982.

Kuhn, *The Study of Society: A Unified Approach*, Homewood, IL.: Richard D. Irwin, Inc., and The Dorsey Press, 1963.

Maisel and Gnugnoli, *Simulation of Discrete Stochastic Systems*, Chicago: Science Research Associates, Inc., 1972.

Martin, *Computer Modeling and Simulation*, New York: John Wiley & Sons, Inc., 1968.

Raiffa, *Decision Analysis*, Reading, MA.: Addison-Wesley Publishing Co., 1968.

Richmond, *Statistical Analysis*, New York: The Ronald Press Company, 1964.

Slaybaugh, "Pareto's Law and Modern Management," *Management Services*, March-April 1967.

Starr and Miller, *Inventory Control: Theory and Practice*, Englewood Cliffs, NJ.: Prentice-Hall, Inc., 1962.

Wagner, *Principles of Operations Research*, Second Edition, Engle-wood Cliffs, NJ.: Prentice-Hall, Inc., 1975.

Whitin, *The Theory of Inventory Management*, Princeton, NJ.: Princeton University Press, 1957.

REFERENCES

1. For a tutorial treatment of these methods, we refer you to Robert N. Anthony and James S. Reece, *Management Accounting*, Fifth Edition, Homewood, III.: Richard D. Irwin. Inc., 1975, and Charles T. Horngren, *Cost Accounting: A Managerial Emphasis* Fifth Edition,. Englewood Cliffs, N.J: Prentice-Hall, Inc., 1982.
2. Anthony and Reece, *op. cit.*, p. 721
3. For an in-depth treatment of a variety of models, refer to H. Bierman, C.P. Bonini, and W.H. Hausman, *Quantitative Analysis for Business Decisions*, Fourth Edition, Homewood, III.: Richard D. Irwin, Inc. 1973, and Howard Raiffa, *Decision Analysis*, Reading, Ma.: Addison-Wesley, 1968.
4. For full treatment of PERT, refer to Russel D. Archibald and Richard L. Villoria, *Network-Based Management Systems (PERT-CPM)* New York: John Wiley and Sons, Inc., 1967. Harry F. Evarts, *Introduction to PERT*, Boston: Allyn and Bacon, Inc., 1964.
5. C. Jay Slaybaugh. "Pareto's Law and Modern Management," *Management Services*, March-April, 1967.
6. The above discussion of least-squares method represents a summarisation of several comprehensive textbooks. For example, see Samuel B. Richmond, *Statistical Analysis*, New York: The Ronald Press Company, 1964, Chapters 2, 7, 18, and 19.
7. For example, see Thomson M. Within, *The Theory of Inventory Management* Princeton, N.J.: Princeton University Press, 1957, pp.32-34. Martin K. Starr and David W. Miller, *Inventory Control: Theory and Practice*, Englewood Cliffs, N.J.: Prentice-Hall, Inc., 1962.
8. Elwood S. Buffa, *Operations Management*, Third Edition, New York: John Wiley and Sons, Inc., 1972, p. 465.
9. Alfred Kuhn, *The Study of Society: A Unified Approach* Homewood III: Richard D. Irwin, Inc., and The Dorsey Press, 1963, p. 4.
10. For detailed analyses of liner programming models, refer to S.I. Gass, *Linear Programming*, Second Edition, New York McGraw-Hill Book Company, 1964;G. Hadley, *Liner Algebra*, Reading, Mass.: Addison-Wesley Publishing Company, 1961; F.S. Hillier and G.J. Lieberman, *Introduction to Operations Research* Second Edition, San Francisco, Holden-Day, 1974; and H.M. Wagner, *Principles of Operations Research;* Second Edition, Englewood Cliffs, NJ: Prentice-Hall, Inc, Inc., 1975.

22

The Computer and Related Technology

INTRODUCTION

The computer and related technology can be divided into three major sections, which are: (1) the central processor, (2) devices peripheral to the central processor, and (3) data communication devices which connect peripheral devices to the central processor.

THE CENTRAL PROCESSOR

The heart of any computer configuration is the central processing unit, or CPU. First, we will analyse the central processor and then present a few technique which help to increase its processing power.

Overview of the Central Processor

The central processor is really the "computer" in a computer configuration and all computer configurations perform the following five basic functions:

Input. The data to be operated upon and the instructions are made available to the central processing unit via input media.

Control. Control is required beside a computer system to: (1) tell the input media what data to enter into primary storage and when to enter the data. (2) tell the primary storage section where to place these data;(3) tell the arithmetic logic section what operations to perform, where the data are to be found and where to place the results; (4) tell what file devices to access and what data to access; and (5) tell what output media on which to write the final results.

Output. This function refers to the results of the data processed within the central processor. This final result is written on various output media.

A schematic of a computer system, emphasizing the central processor, is illustrated in Figure 1. All digital computers, regardless of size, speed, and details of operation, follow this same basic logical structure.

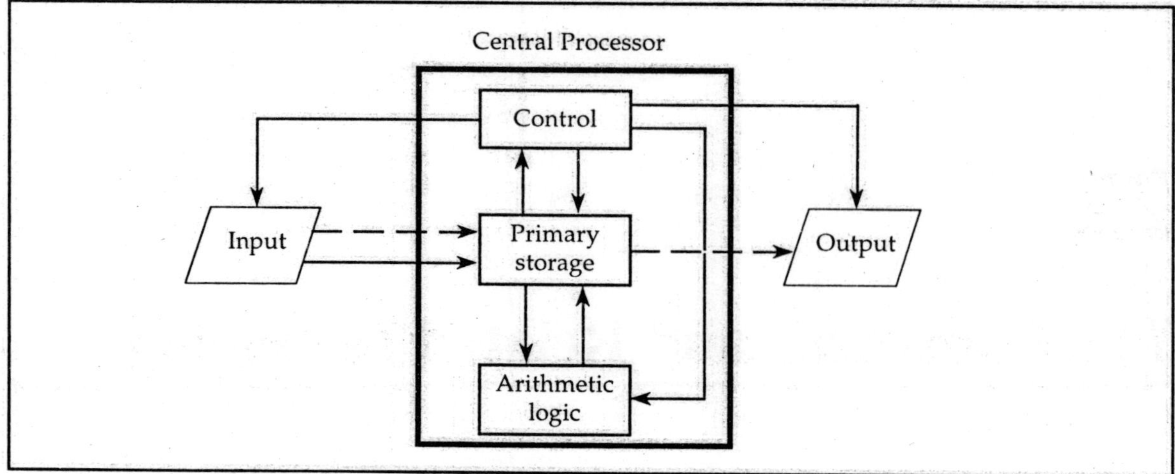

Fig. 1. General diagram of a central processor. Broken line indicates data flow: solid line indicates instruction flow; and heavy line indicates control flow.

Size of the Central Processor

When manufacturers state the size of their processor, they are referring to the size of the primary storage. Size of a processor's primary storage helps to determine the maximum size of programs and the amount of data available for processing at any one time. each primary storage location has a unique address, analogous to a mailbox in a post office. The address identifies the location of the data for both storing and accessing operations. Although all data are represented as binary digits or bits, the smallest addressable location in main storage differs from one computer to another. Depending on the design of the computer, each addressable location is a character or the beginning of a computer word. These storage locations may be designated as follows:

1. Byte-addressable Combination

The basic storage unit of some computers is called a byte. The byte is made up of eight bits and in additional parity bit. Although the byte itself is a fixed binary composition, it can be strung together in different ways to provide structures of varying length. The byte-addressable system is flexible in the sense that each byte is addressable and can represent two numbers or one character. This means that a computer with 64K memory (where K, or kilo, means thousands) has approximately 64,000 bytes of addressable main storage.

2. Character-Addressable

In a character addressable system, it may require a six-bit set (not including control bits) to encode a character. If the number 47 is in storage, the 4 will take up one storage location having an address; the 7 is in another contiguous storage location with a separate address. An eight-bit byte would provide greater storage than a six-bit character because two decimal digits may be packed in a byte.

3. *Word-Addressable*

A computer word consists of an ordered set of bits, which may be of fixed or variable length, depending on the particular computer. Commonly, computers which are designated as word-addressable, have fixed word sizes of 24, 30, 32, 36, 48, 54 and 64 bits.

Speed of the Processor

Other aspects to consider when evaluating primary storage are: access and cycle time. These aspects are discussed here.[1].

1. *Access Time*

Access time refers to the time it takes for the control section to locate instructions and data for processing. It represents the time interval between initiating a transfer of data to or from storage and the instant when this transfer is completed. This time interval varies from one computer to another. In most primary storage devices, access time is measured in microseconds (one-millionth of a second); however, in some large-scale computers access time is measured in nanoseconds (one-billionth of a second).

2. *Cycle Time*

A computer performs its operations on a cycle basis. The computer operates on pulses per length of time like a clock. At any one time, the computer is either in the instruction cycle or the execution cycle. An instruction is obtained from a main memory location and transferred to the arithmetic-logic unit. Here it is decoded according to its operation code, specifying what is to be done, and its operand, specifying the address of the data to be operated upon. The computer then moves into the execution cycle. Here the decoded instruction is executed using the data specified by the instruction. When the execution cycle is complete, the computer automatically goes back into the instruction cycle, and the process begins again.

The amount of data accessed in one cycle depends on the computer design, and is expressed in bytes, characters, or words. For example, Model X may have a slower basic access time then Model Y, but Model X may access four bytes at a time whereas Model Y accesses two bytes. Therefore, two factors combine which result in effective access time: the amount of data accessed during each cycle and the time required to perform each cycle.

Size of storage used is normally based on cost, and cost of storage in turn is based on speed (i.e., as access speed increases, the cost per bit stored also increases). This speed mismatch and cost variation between various storage media have caused a number of processor configuration innovations manifested in different storage hierarchy systems. For example, a hierarchy of storage might consist of very high-speed (nanosecond) semiconductor storage; medium-speed (microsecond) core storage; and large, slow-speed (millisecond) magnetic disk or drum. The hierarchy of storage concept can be illustrated by the virtual storage and buffer storage techniques which are discussed in the following sections.

Virtual Storage Technique

The basic idea behind virtual storage is the dynamic linking of primary storage of the processor to auxiliary storage so that each user (several may be using the system concurrently) appears to have very large primary storage, usually measured in megabytes, at his or her disposal. Parts of a program or data associated with the user's program, may be broken up and scattered both in primary storage and on magnetic disk or drum, thus giving the "virtual" effect of much larger primary storage to the programmer.[2] This technique is illustrated in Figure 2.

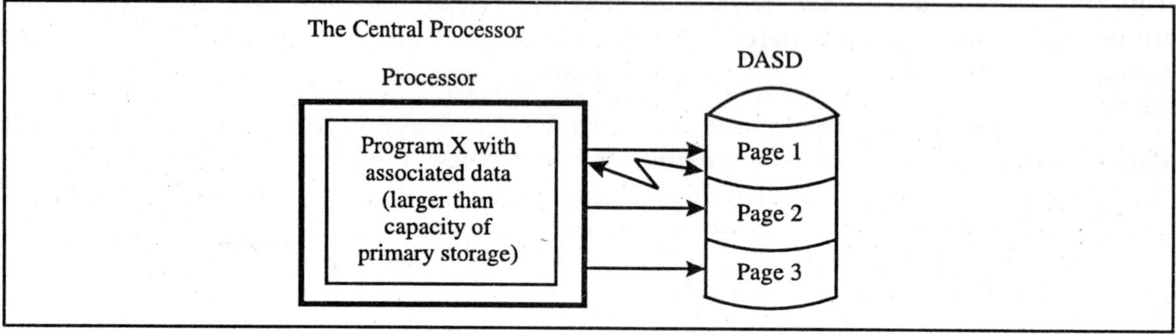

Fig. 2. Illustration of the virtual storage concept.

Normally only the instructions and data necessary for immediate processing will be located in primary storage, in the form of "pages" which are transferred between primary storage and slower auxiliary (DASD) storage automatically.[3] With this approach, jobs are loaded into partitions or regions of auxiliary storage. During processing, small blocks or pages of instructions and data are transferred between auxiliary storage and processor storage according to the momentary needs of each job.[4]

Buffer Storage Technique

This technique, also called cache memory, uses a limited-capacity but very fast semi-conductor storage combined with less expensive, slower, large-capacity core storage to give the overall effect of a faster primary storage. This technique requires careful look-ahead procedures to get the correct data into semiconductor storage when it is required. [5] The buffer storage technique is illustrated in Figure 3.

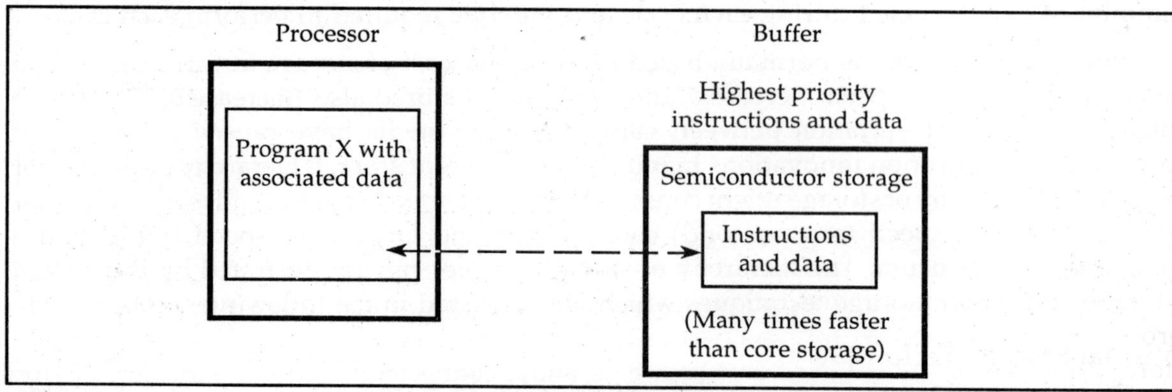

Fig. 3. Illustration of the buffer storage concept

It is the function of the buffer to fetch frequently used instructions and data to be used by the arithmetic-logic part of the central processor. In most-cases, these instructions and data will be available at the buffer rate, rather than at the slower primary storage rate. This technique is based on the theory that adjacent bytes in primary storage will usually be used at the same time. If the required data are in the buffer, they are transferred to the arithmetic-logic unit at buffer-speed. If the required data are not in the buffer then they are obtained from primary storage. On the subject of buffering, studies revealed that the required data are in the buffer 90 per cent of the time. As with the virtual storage technique, the buffer storage technique provides increased performance without adding new responsibilities to the programmer (i.e., the operations of buffer storage is "transparent" to the programmer).

Multiprocessors

It should be recognised by the reader that a computer configuration, in many applications, operates with more than one processor unit (multiprocessing). While one can configure a total computer system in endless ways, for one typical illustration of a multiprocessing system, refer to Figure 4.

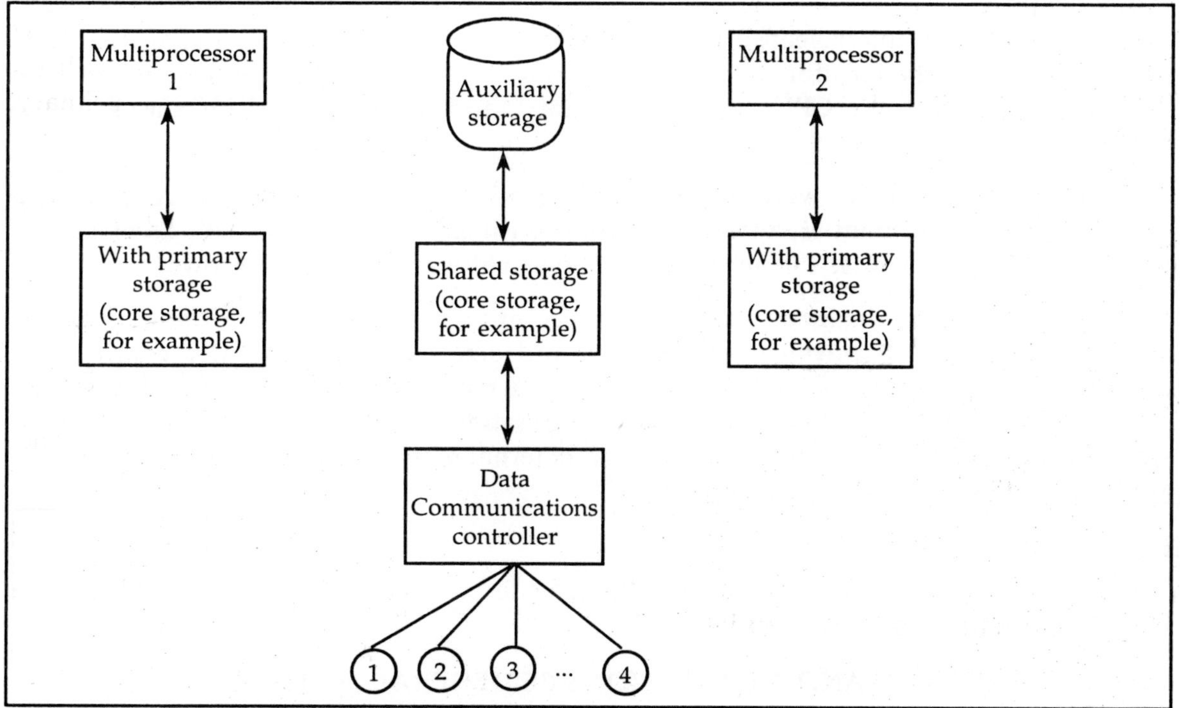

Fig. 4. Illustration of a multiprocessor configuration.

The system above, for an example, could be used as a fall soft backup system where each processor is equipped with its own dedicated core memory, shares common partitioned storage that is used to access the data base files, and is connected to various peripherals. The partitioned core storage configuration allows either processor to operate the entire system in the event the other processor fails.

Minicomputers

Minicomputers are distinguished from large computers on the basis of cost, processor speed, memory size, and software. Today, a typical minicomputer falls within a $15,000 to $75,000 price range. Over three-quarters of all minis support business applications, while about one-half are designed for use in scientific applications.[6]

Features such as virtual memory and small, high-speed cache memory are becoming increasingly popular in minis. The most common size of main memory is from 128K to 512K bytes. Most minicomputers have 16-bit word sizes. The norm of cycle times for a minicomputer is 700 nanoseconds.

Minicomputers typically support up to four languages, with BASIC being the most popular, followed by FORTRAN, COBOL, and RPG.

Microcomputers

The advances in microelectronics that made possible the minicomputer in the early 1970s, have led to the creation of the microcomputer. A system of large-scale integration (LSI) chips contains the CPU, internal memory, and input/output interfaces of the microcomputer.

While microcomputers were originally designed for hobbyists, they have become a viable alternative to manual systems for small businesses. This trend will accelerate as hardware prices fall and as the amount of business software for micros grows.

Though the line of distinction between minicomputers and microcomputers is blurred on the dimensions of physical appearance and size, we can generally characterise microcomputers as having 4K to 64K bytes of internal memory, data entry via keyboard, and a video screen for output. Beyond a basic configuration, a small business microcomputer system may have additional internal memory, external memory in the form of cassettes or minifloppy disks, and a low-speed printer.

Types of Storage

We will conclude this section by presenting a summary classification of storage media. This classification is presented in Figure 5.

DEVICES AND APPLICATIONS PERIPHERAL TO THE CPU

In Figure 6 we present a general schematic of devices peripheral to the computer. In this section we will discuss from a systems application viewpoint five basic areas; (1) aspects of auxiliary storage media, specially magnetic tape, magnetic, disk, mass storage, and microfilm; (2) terminal devices; and (3) data entry techniques.

Analysis of Auxiliary Storage Devices

Primary storage is expensive and can only be used economically to hold programs and data that the computer is presently processing. Auxiliary storage devices are used to store other programs and data which are made available to the computer when needed. Popular storage devices which transfer data or instructions rapidly between primary storage and an input/output drive unit are: magnetic tape, magnetic disk, magnetic drum, and mass storage. Computer output microfilm (COM) can also be considered s auxiliary storage. We will treat, in this section, four of these devices, namely: (1) magnetic tape, (2) magnetic disk, (3) mass storage, and (4) COM.

Magnetic Tape

Magnetic tape is a very popular medium for storage of voluminous amounts of data. It is a sequential medium and is used widely in batch processing environment.

Name of Storage Media	*Primary Storage*	*Online Auxiliary Storage*	*Offline Auxiliary Storage*
Bubble	X		
LSI	X		
Semiconductor	X		
Magnetic core	X	X	
Thin films	X		
Holographic	X	X	
Plated wire	X		
Magnetic drum	X	X	
Magnetic disks	X	X	X
Mass storage		X	
Magnetic tape			X
Punched paper tape			X
Punched cards			X

Fig. 5. Type of storage media.

Physical Characteristics of Magnetic Tape

Data are recorded on seven, eight, nine or ten-channel tape in the form of magnetised sports. Tape widths are normally ½ inch, although some tapes are ¾ and 1, and 3 inches in width. Some new tapes are being marketed which record data in a fashion similar to videotape, (i.e., data are recorded across the tape rather than along it). This technique allows bits to be much smaller and closer together. Some manufacturers claim that packing density is 40 times greater than on regular tape. Usually, reels hold 2400 to 3600 feet of magnetic tape; however, shorter tapes are sometimes used. Further discussion will be based on nine-channel tape.

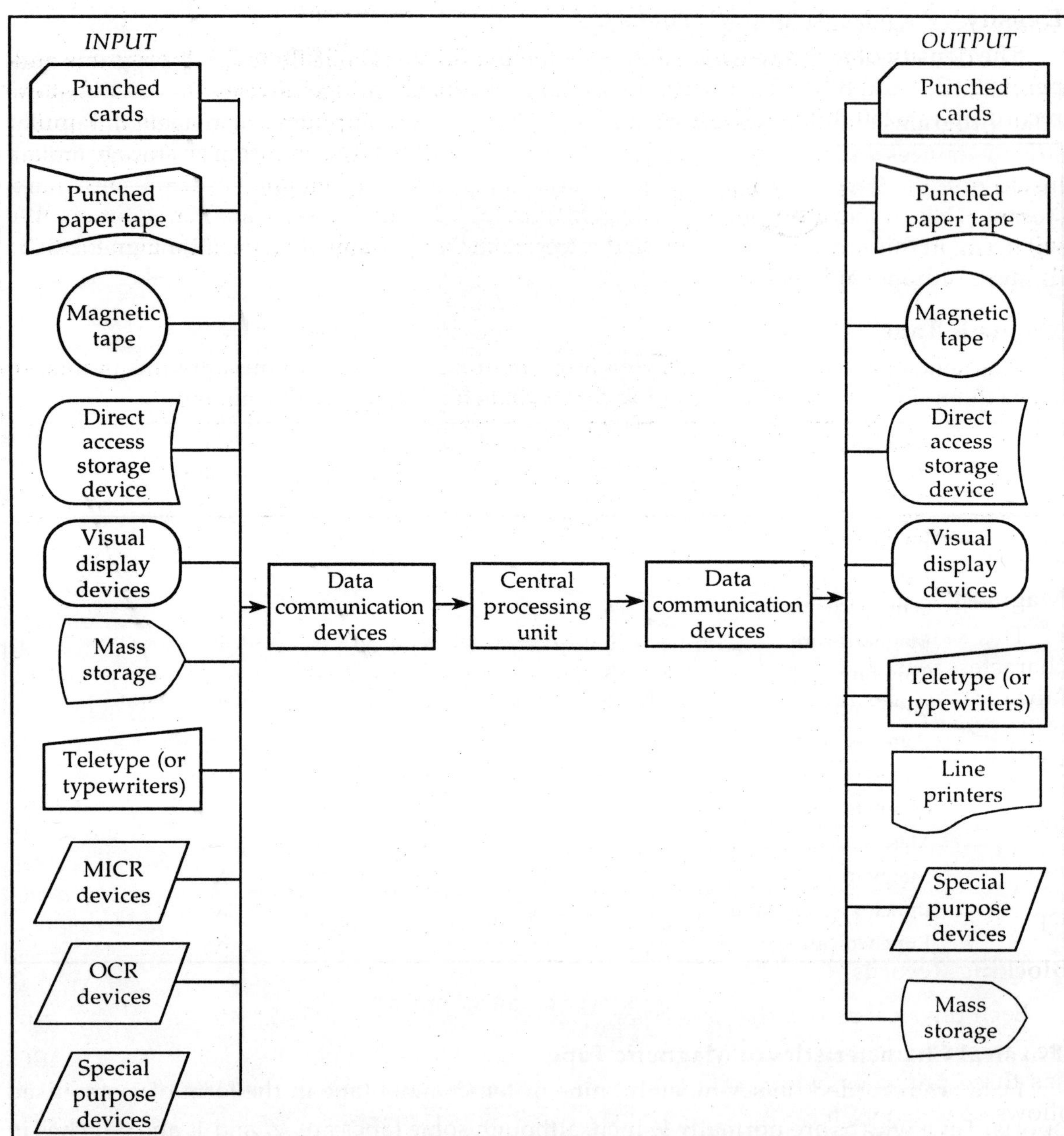

Fig. 6. The computer and its peripherals.

Coding Scheme

The recording of data on magnetic tape is similar in concept to a tape recorder. Magnetic tape for data processing, however, records numbers, and alphabetic and special characters. These data are recorded on tape in channels as shown in Figure 7.

Density

The density of magnetic tape is represented by the number of characters or bits recorded per inch (CPI and BPI). The most common tape density is 1600 BPI. Higher density tapes can record up to 6250 BPI.

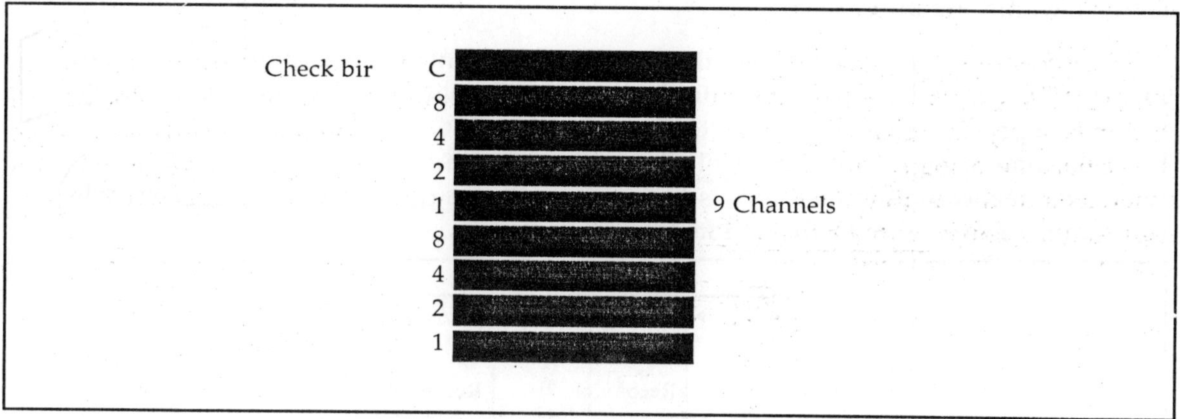

Fig. 7. Magnetic tape using EBCDIC.

Magnetic Tape Transfer Rate

The transfer rate is determined by the speed of a tape drive unit and the density of characters recorded per inch. The tape drive unit functions in much the same way as a home tape recorder (i.e. the tape is wound from one reel to another, passing through a read/write unit where it can be read repeatedly without destroying the data stored). New data can be written over old data, when desired, and the tape can be rewound and backspaced. If the speed of a tape unit is 112.5 inches per second and the characters per inch are 800 then the data transfer rate is 90,000 characters per second (CPS). The common speeds of tape units are: 18.75, 22.5, 36.0, 37.5, 75.0, 112.5, 125.0, and 200.0 inches per second. Some manufacturers use vacuum systems rather than capstan systems. These vacuum systems literally such the tape from one reel to another at speeds of 1000 inches per second.

Blocking Records

Each physical record that is written on a tape is separated by a blank (½ inch, ¾ inch, etc., according to the particular tape system) referred to as an interblock gap (IBG). The IBG has three purposes, which are: (1) it separates a record or block discussed below, (2) it allows space enough for the tape unit to reach its operating speed (i.e., one-half of the IBG is ued for starting speed), and (3) it allows space enough for the tape unit to decelerate after a read or write operation. The tape must be moving at its designated speed before it can be read from or written one. Therefore the IBC gives enough space to get the tape moving at full speed. By the same token, when the end of the record (or block) is reached, in reading or writing, the tape cannot be stopped immediately; therefore, space must also be provided to allow the tape to stop.

The IBG contains no data. For example, if a recording density is 1600 BPI this means that a ½-inch IBG could hold 800 characters of data. Or looking at it another way, approximately the data found in 20-80 column cards could be stored in two ½-inch IBGs. The records in a tape with each record separated by an IBG are shown in Figure 8. The records contain 800 characters and are un-blocked.

Tape economy is realised by combining the records into a block of records by a blocking factor of *N*, where *N* equals the number of records within each block. The block itself becomes a physical group of characters separated by IBGs and the data records within the block become a logical record. A block is therefore said to be a tape-recording concept, whereas a record within the block is logical record, or a data processing concept. Figure 9 represents records with a blocking factor of 5.

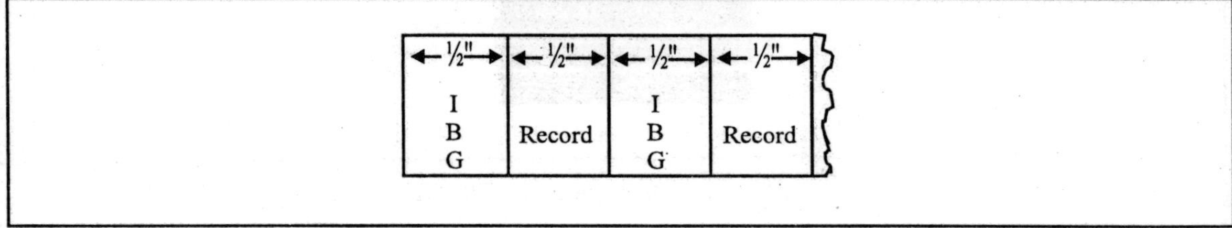

Fig. 8. Unblocked records.

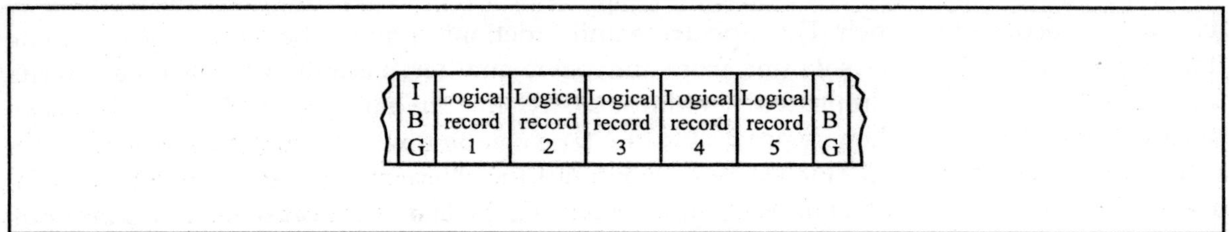

Fig. 9. Records with a blocking factor of 5.

The concept of transfer rate is a little misleading because, as a tape units reads blocks of logical records, it stops each time it comes to an IBG. Consequently, when blocks are being read or written, a certain amount of time is spent at each IBG. The total amount of time required to read or write a given number of blocks is equal to the sum of the time spent reading or writing the data plus the time spent starting and stopping at the IBGs. To realise the effect that start/stop time has on reading and writing speeds, consider the following example:

Tape density	= 1600 BPI
Tape unit speed	= 75.0 inches per second
Therefore, stated transfer rate	= 120,000 CPS
Number of blocks on tape	= 8000

Blocking factor	= 10 where each record contains 30 characters; therefore, each block contains 300 characters or a total of 2,400,000 characters.
Number of IBGs	= 8000
Size of IBG	$= \frac{3}{4}$ inch
Time to pass over IBG	= .010 sec.
Therefore,	
Total start/stop time	= 8000 X .010
	= 80 sec.
Total time for reading data	≐ 2,400,000
	÷ 120,000
	= 20 sec.
Therefore,	
Total time to read all records	= 80 ÷ 20
	= 100 sec.
Effective transfer rate	= 1,200,000 ÷ 100
	= 12,000 CPS

Consequently, it takes 80 sec. to start and stop and tape, and only 20 sec. to read the data. A waste of tape space and, accordingly, processing time results. To reduce this waste more records should be placed in a block. If the blocking factor is 40, then the number of IBGs would be reduced to 2000 instead of 8000. The total time to read the records is 20 sec. for reading data plus 20 sec. (2000 X .010), or 40 sec. When an installation has thousands of tape reels, reducing wasted space becomes quite significant. The reduction in wasted space results in:

1. *Less cost for tape.* Typical costs for tape reels are between$10 and $100. If a system has 1000 tapes with a cost of $80,000 and the space can be reduced 50 per cent then a cost savings of $40,000 can be effected.
2. *Saves time.* Reduction of wait-time of the processing unit resulting either from tapes being moved from the tape units and/or space in tape itself. Obviously, an increased blocking factor increases I/O speeds.
3. *Saves storage.* In order systems that have not had proper data management, and increasing number of applications, combined with increasingly stringent requirements for data retention, have resulted in a squeeze on available storage space. In some instances this squeeze has caused an expenditure for a new wing of the tape library. The principle of large blocking factors can be applied to many

older systems on two levels: (1) The software system should be investigated to ascertain if the largest possible blocking factor is being used by every program. This would be particularly applicable in those installations that have upgraded their central processor storage capacity. (2) The reblocking of archival files should be done to contain the highest blocking factor that the hardware can handle. It is often found that multiple-reel tape files can be reduced to a single reel. The recompilation of source programs to increase blocking factors, the necessary de-blocking factors, the necessary deblocking and file extraction run, and the reblocking of tapes are methods that use computer time, but the time lost on this fairly infrequent procedure would be more than balanced by the overall cost savings. Incidentally, physical space occupied by tapes can be reduced by writing short files on small reels, which are then stored on special racks to maximise the space savings.

Advantages/Disadvantages of Magnetic Tape

The advantages of magnetic tape are as follows:

1. It has a much faster transfer rate than punched cards.
2. Tapes play an important role and remain unchallenged for backup storage and for low-cost, high-capacity applications requiring only sequential access.
3. It requires less storage space than other media such as cards.
4. It is erasable and can be used over and over again for many different applications.
5. Tape manufacturers offer a wide range of specifications to meet particular applications.
6. Relatively speaking, tapes are inexpensive where one cent can buy enough tape capacity to store tens of thousands of characters.
7. In card systems, one or more records can be lost from a file. A tape file is continuous, which means that no record of the file can be lost.

The disadvantages of magnetic tape are:

1. Since tape is a sequential medium, the access of a particular record is made only after all records preceding it have been read. It is, therefore, not applicable for jobs which require rapid, direct access to specific records.
2. Since the tape is also continuous in design, a clerk cannot physically remove, insert, or change a record without reading from the original and rewriting it with the change to another tape.
3. The magnetised spots are unreadable by humans. A printed listing of the tape is required to read or verify tape data.
4. The temperature, humidity, and dust content of the tape environment must be tightly controlled. Particles of dust on a tape can cause improper processing. Temperature and humidity conditions that fall outside of prescribed ranges can cause peculiar and mysterious results from processing.

Magnetic Disk

Magnetic disks have nor become the medium of choice to serve as auxiliary storage. The price per character or byte stored continues to decrease, and the direct access capability of disks gives the systems analyst far more options and flexibility in designing systems (e.g., capability of online inquiry of large files) than does magnetic tape.

Physical Characteristics of Magnetic Disk

A magnetic disk is made up of a stack of rotating metal platters on which records are stored. Direct access to any record can be made without having to read through a sequence of other, irrelevant records. This direct access capability allows random entry of transaction data and random inquiry into the file from a user. The different disk models range from 5 to 100 disks measuring from 1.5 to 3 feet in diameter. The IBM 3330 Disk Storage Facility is used to illustrate the physical characteristics of magnetic disk. A schematic or it is shown in Figure 10.

The illustration portrays a disk unit in which 10 of the 12 surfaces are used for recording data. Each surface is divided into 404 tracks, which are analogous to flattened, circular sections of magnetic tape. Each track has a capacity of 13,030 bytes. The read/write mechanism positions the read/write heads over a separate track which forms a vertical cylinder. Since each surface consists of 404 tracks, we can see that the disk unit is composed of 404 concentric cylinders. In Figure 10, the read/write heads are positioned over the tracks which make up cylinder 013.

Addressing

In Figure 11 we have four 3100-byte records stored o n cylinder 013, track 02. These records, although not shown, are coded in EBCDIC. Each record on the track is numbered sequentially. Therefore, each data record is preceded by a small address record.

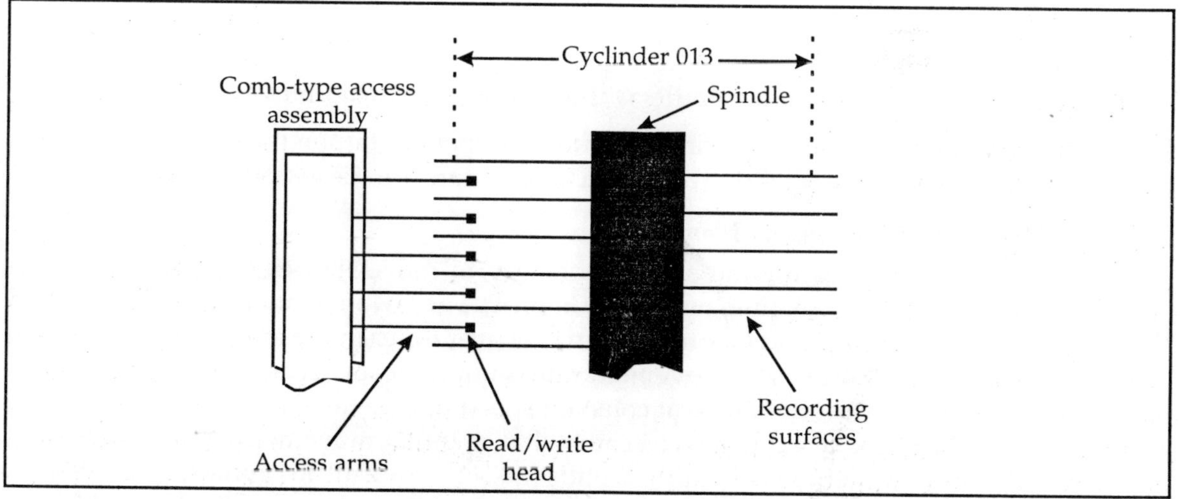

Fig. 10. Side view of a disk pack.

With these addresses, it is possible to access directly any desired record stored on the disk. Note that records are separated by gaps, similar to an IBG in magnetic tape. Since the addresses and gaps require a portion of the track, it is impossible to store a full 13,030 bytes of data on a track when more than one record per track is stored. As the number of records per track increases, the number of gaps and addresses increases, causing the data per track to decrease. For example, if the record size is 500 bytes, then the track capacity would be 20 records, for a total track capacity of 10,000 bytes of data.

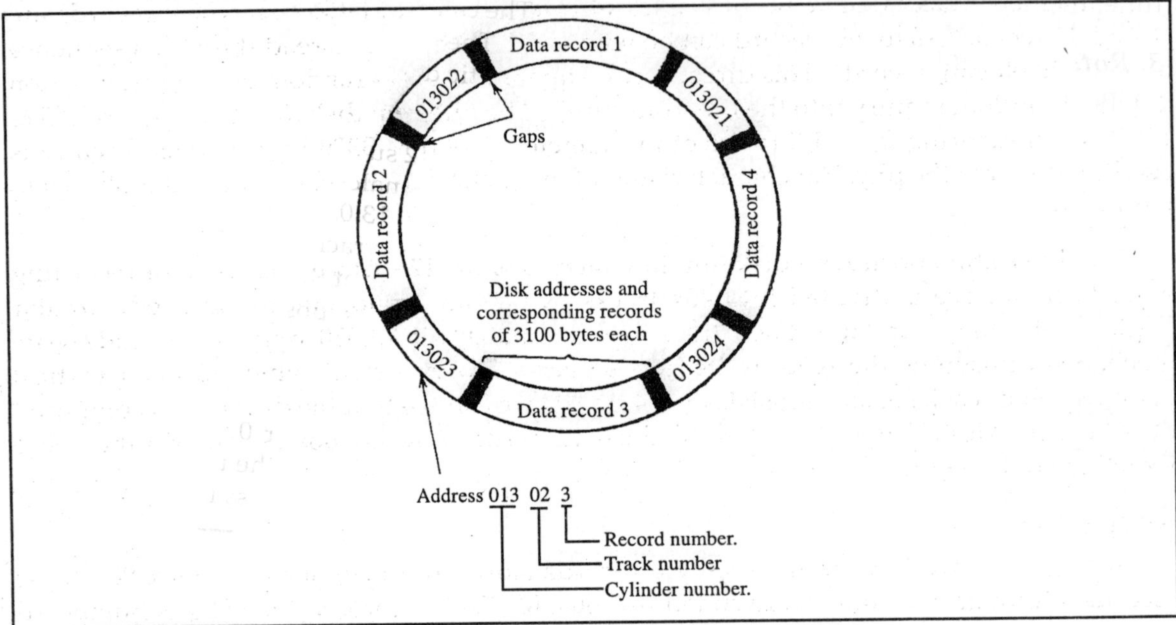

Fig. 11. Four 3100-byte records stored on disk showing an address for each record.

Magnetic Disk Transfer Rate

The disk pack clockwise on a spindle as the access mechanism moves in and out.

The speed with which data are read or written is dependent upon these two factors plus read/write head selection and data transfer. These factors are discussed below:

1. *Access Mechanism Movement Time*

This is the time it takes for the access assembly to move the read/write heads to a specified cylinder (called seek time or access time). The access movement time is based on the number of cylinders the read/write heads travel over to reach the one specified, and the speed of the mechanism itself. The movement rate is not uniform because the mechanism is electromechanical and does not move at constant speed (notice the movement of the player arm of a record; the naked eye can detect a somewhat irregular movement). For a movement of one cylinder, minimum time is 10 milliseconds (msec); across all 404 cylinders, maximum is 55 msec. The average movement speed to over the entire pack is 30 msec. If the read/write heads are already at their proper position during access, they do have to be moved, therefore, the access movement time is zero. On some disk systems the read/write heads are fixed in position over each track (e.g. the IBM 2305 Fixed Head Storage Facility). This eliminates the seek time consideration.

2. *Read/Write Head Selection*

After the access mechanism has been properly positioned on the specified cylinder, the head that is to read or write is switched on. This switching is electronic and the amount of time, therefore, is negligible in all cases.

3. *Rotational Delay*

Before data are read or written the proper location on the track must rotate to the read/write heads. The time spent in rotating to a proper alignment of the read/write heads with the specified location is called *rotational delay*. For the IBM 3330 Disk Storage Facility, a full rotation requires 16.7 msec. If, after positioning the access mechanism over the desired track, the desired record has just passed, then the rotational delay is 16.7 msec. If on the other hand, the desired record has just reached the red/write head, then the rotational delay is zero. For timing calculations, on average rotational delay of 8.4 msec. is used.

4. *Data Transfer*

After the Disk pack has been rotated to its proper location, the record can be read or written. The time required to transfer the record between the disk pack and the main storage is the transfer rate and is a function of rotation speed, the density at which the data are recorded, and the length of the record transferred. The transfer rate of a 3330 unit is 806K bytes per second.

In timing a read or write operation, the actual direct accessing consists, therefore of access mechanism movement time, rotational delay (using average time), and data transfer rate. The total time for a complete processing job requires, in addition, the consideration of additional factors such as program processing time, access method processing time, and control program time.

For example, again using the IBM 3330 as the storage medium, Figure 12 presents an approximate timing summary to read a thousand 5000-byte records randomly distributed over an entire disk pack.

Per record	
Average access time	30.0 msec.
Average rotational delay	8.4 msec
Data transfer time	6.2 msec.
Total	44.6 msec.
1000 records — 44.6 sec.	

Fig. 12. A timing summary.

Floppy Disks

Floppy (flexible) disks were introduced by IBM in 1972 as a low-cst, random access storage medium for minicomputers. Floppy disks are punched out of a polyester film that is coated with iron oxide compound. The flat, 8-inch circular magnetic diskette rotates freely within a jacket that is intended to prevent both data loss and the diskette from being damaged.

The jacket has access and index holes to accommodate the read/write head (which actually touches the disk) and the data timing transducers of the disk drive. Each diskette contains 77 tracks, and has a storage capacity of 512K bytes (double-sides diskettes or "floppies" single density). Track-to-track access time is 3 msec; average access time over all tracks is approximately 90 msec.

Advantages/Disadvantages of Magnetic Disk

The advantages are as follows:

1. Besides having a direct access capability, a disk file may be organised sequentially and processed like a magnetic tape.
2. All transactions can be processed as they occur, thereby keeping the system current.
3. Multiple files can be stored on a single disk pack.
4. Multiple and interrelated files may be stored in a way which permits a transaction to be processed against all pertinent files simultaneously.

The disadvantages are as follows:

1. Magnetic disk is still more expensive than magnetic tape. Falling prices and improved recording densities, however have given real economies to users of magnetic disks (and tapes, too, as far as costs are concerned).
2. For many applications, sequential tape processing is as acceptable and selective as disk.
3. In accounting work, a clearly dissemble audit trail is needed. In updating a file on a magnetic disk, the record is read, updated, and written back to the same location, thus destroying the original contents, if no provision for error detection and file reconstruction is made, costly errors may go undetected.

Mass Storage

Although magnetic tape is being replaced by disk units as the medium immediately below processor memory, large data files, backup files, and seldom-used files still need to be stored on a low-cost, medium of slow access medium. One such system is control Data Corporation's 38500 Mass Storage System (another is IBM's 3851).

This system is intended for processing large active files within an environment where performance and equipment costs are the key criteria for evaluation. Storage capacity of the system ranges from 16 billion to over a trillion bytes. A maximum of 5, and an average of 2.5 sec., is required to access data.

The Control Data 38500 system is built around magnetic tape cartridges. Each enclosed cartridge contains a 150-inch-long, 2.7 inch-wide magnetic tape, capable of storing up to 8 million bytes of data. Within a single-file unit, 2052 tape cartridges are clustered in beehive fashion. To retrieve data, an X-Y selector is positioned at the addressable location, the cartridge is picked by the selector; and the cartridge is then moved to a tape transport. At the transport, the cartridge is opened, and the tape is unwound fully and inserted into vacuum columns. It can then be moved past the read/write station at approximately 129 inches per second, effecting a data transfer rate of over 800,000 bytes per second.

Computer Output Microfilm (COM)

COM provides another medium for storing large amounts of data. This approach is shown in Figure 13. Data output from the central processor is read into a microfilm recorder which is connected to a film developer. The final microfilm output is in two basic forms: (1) microfiche and (2) roll film. Either one can be viewed directly through special readers.

Advantages of COM are:

1. Although COM is generally considered as a replacement for data on paper, in many situations it can be considered as a replacement for magnetic tape.
2. COM is quite applicable for archival files (five or more years), whereas magnetic tape is not made for long-term storage of data. Tape deteriorates over a long period of nonuse and, in addition, the recorded magnetic signals must be insulated from possible damage caused by environmental conditions such as radiation, heat, humidity, and random signals from electrical fixtures.
3. COM significantly reduces the need for storage space because it reduces the paper explosion.
4. Information is available directly from storage in human readable form with the aid of a microfilm reader.
5. It is relatively inexpensive.
6. COM, as a replacement for distributed reports, reduces significantly mailing costs.

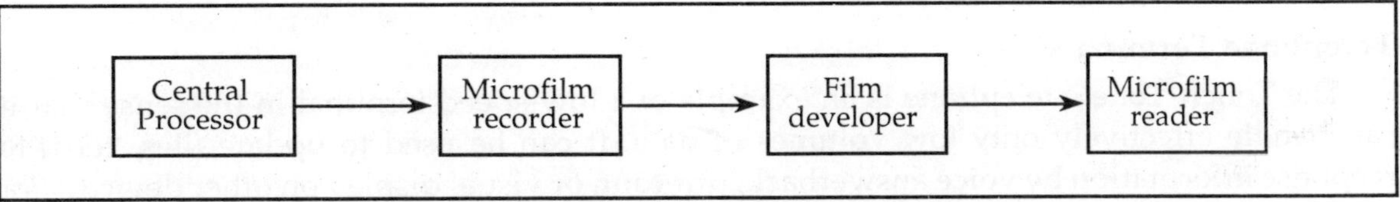

Fig. 13. An illustration of the processes involved in producing C.M.

The major disadvantages of COM are:

1. It is not economical where records within a file require updating continuously.
2. A COM reader is necessary.
3. A COM file cannot be read by a computer.

Summary Characteristics of Auxiliary Storage Devices

We have discussed in detail the four popular auxiliary storage devices— magnetic tape, disk, mass storage, and COM. In seeking the best mix of devices, the high-speed devices such as magnetic drum, magnetic disk, and mass storage are generally the best for quick processing of large quantities of data. In archival files where minimum access speed and high data storage capacity are important, microfilm may be the best choice. Applications that require voluminous amounts of data processed on a periodic basis, requiring little, if any, inquiry capability, are handled best by magnetic tape.

At the slower and lower cost end of the spectrum are punched cards and punched paper tape. It is quite difficult to make a sensible comparison between these two media and other media listed above, because of the great difference in cost, transfer rate, storage capacity, and son on. The decision as to which of the two to select, however, often depends on how the data are to be organised. Paper tape is preferable when files are organised sequentially and there is no need for insertions, modifications, or deletions. On the other hand, punched cards are preferable when the unit-record concept is to be used (i.e., the punched card serves as a record where each card is designed to contain data about a certain transaction).

Terminal Devices

Terminals actually represent devices which are used to get the data into the system and the information from the system. They are fundamental to an online system. Terminal hardware will vary with the needs of the different users throughout the organisation. Terminals vary from simple teletypewriters to card readers, high-speed printers, CRTs, magnetic tape units, and son on. The distance of the terminal from the central processor has no effect on its function. Move a magnetic tape unit to a plant 500 miles from the central processor, add a communication data control unit, connect it to a communication channel, and it becomes a remote job entry (RJE) terminal. Hook up a CRT to the data base and one has an interrogative terminal, and so on.

In this section, we will devote our discussion primarily to two types of terminals: (1) telephones terminals and (2) intelligent terminals.

Telephone Terminals

The Touch-Tone® telephone is an example of a low-speed terminal in the sense that it can handle effectively only low volumes of data. It can be used to update files, retrieve response information by voice answerback, printout, or visual display on other devices. For example, it can be used to provide credit status on credit card customers. Clerks type in to the central processor an access code, the customer's account number, and the amount of the purchase. By voice answer back, heard only by the clerk, the transaction is either approved or the clerk is instructed to call the credit department for further instructions. A similar system to this could be used as an order entry system in conjunction with reporting inventory availability to incoming calls from customers and/or salespersons.

Intelligent Terminals

An intelligent terminal incorporates a processing capability usually in the form of a microcomputer. This microcomputer has the capability to perform operations on the data it handles in addition to transmitting it to a central processor.

Applications of Intelligent Terminals

Intelligent terminals are used to (1) extend the power of the central computer and (2) accept data at its origin and perform some level of processing. Many of the intelligent terminals include microcomputers which can be used for different purposes based on how they are configured and programmed. For instance, by using one set of peripherals and programs a remote job entry (RJE) system is developed, and by using a different set of peripherals and programs a data entry system, such as a remote key-to-disk system, is created.

With the advent of lower costs and greater availability of computers and data communication systems, the use of RJE systems have become cost/effective for small users who cannot economically justify their own data processing systems. Also, this RJE technique is applicable to the distribution information systems structure.

Also, intelligent terminals provide a form of backup for the central computer. With nonintelligent terminals connected to the main processor, if this processor were to fail, the terminals would be disabled and for all practicable purposes, the entire system would be disabled, and for all practicable purposes, the entire system would be down. Transactions could not be entered and processed. At most, transactions might be captured on paper tape or magnetic tape for later transmission to the computer. With an intelligent terminal, it is feasible for the terminal to accept transactions and perform some of the processing if the main computer were down or the data communications system were disrupted. This capability is one of the main reasons why banks and retail stores select intelligent terminals. Sales transactions in a store, or savings transactions in a financial institution, can still be recorded at the terminal for processing and later transmission if necessary, even though the central computer is down.

Another reason for using an intelligent terminal is that it can relieve the central processor of some of the processing workload. This situation helps to reduce an overload on the central processor, allowing the system to get along with a smaller central processor than would otherwise be the case.

Data Entry Techniques

More than half the cost of using computers in many organisations is incurred in the capture and conversion of data. Probably no other aspect of computer processing offers more potential for cost savings than does this one area. The preparation of data for computer processing is truly the big bottle-neck in the entire system and, as a result, it substantially decreases throughout.

In this section on data entry techniques we will direct our attention to five main areas: (1) keyboard-to-storage, (2) point of sale (POS), (3) optical character recognition (OCR), (4) magnetic ink character recognition (MICR), and (5) voice recognition (VR).

Keyboard-to-Storage

The keyboard-to-storage technique consists of several keystations (CRT) connected to a minicomputer or programmed controller which collects the data input, verifies it, provides various other functions, and writes to on tape or disk for processing. Some of the functions that this kind of data entry system performs are:

1. Keyed-in data are input to an edit program to filter out errors.
2. CRT input terminals provide sight verification for the operator, if an error is made, backspacing and deletion allows the operator to correct the error quickly.
3. Operators can work at higher keying rates than is possible with keypunches.
4. Productivity statistics for monitoring and checking operators' efficiency are supplemented by means of a program in the system.
5. Check digits and batch totals are prepared automatically.
6. Certain reasonableness checks and relevancy checks are made.
7. True modular input of data is allowed because blocks of data are merged together into proper sequence for further processing.

The typical keyboard-to-storage system is referred to as key-to-tape or key-to-disk. It consists of a low-cost minicomputer; direct access intermediate storage; and magnetic disk, tape, floppy disk, or cassette for final output. Most manufacturers of these systems offer 8 to 64 keystations per system. Studies indicate that at the present cost levels, disregarding any other benefits, a system has to replace from 10 to 14 keypunches before a key-to-tape system is cost/effective. With falling prices, in the near future, the same basic system may be cost-effective at a five or six keypunch level. A key-to-tape system is shown in Figure 14.

An online data entry system works basically the same way except the data flows directly into the central processor. For an example, refer to Figure 15.

Advantages/Disadvantages of Keyboard-to-Storage Systems

The advantages are as follows:

1. Editing, formatting, combining input data, and dumping data are automatic functions.

2. Supervisors are provided various operational statistics on such things as operator's performance work in progress work completed.
3. Productivity is increased because the operations of card feeding, duplication skipping, and stacking are eliminate.

The disadvantages of keyboard to store of systems are:

1. Buffered keypunch/verifies perform many of the functions that the key is storage systems perform.
2. Practically everyone understands the ubiquitous punched card.

Point of Sale (POS)

Point of sale systems provide a method to which vital data are captured at the point of transaction in department stores, supermarkets, and large discount stores. The same technique is applicable to other user categories where it is important to capture data at the time of an event or transaction.

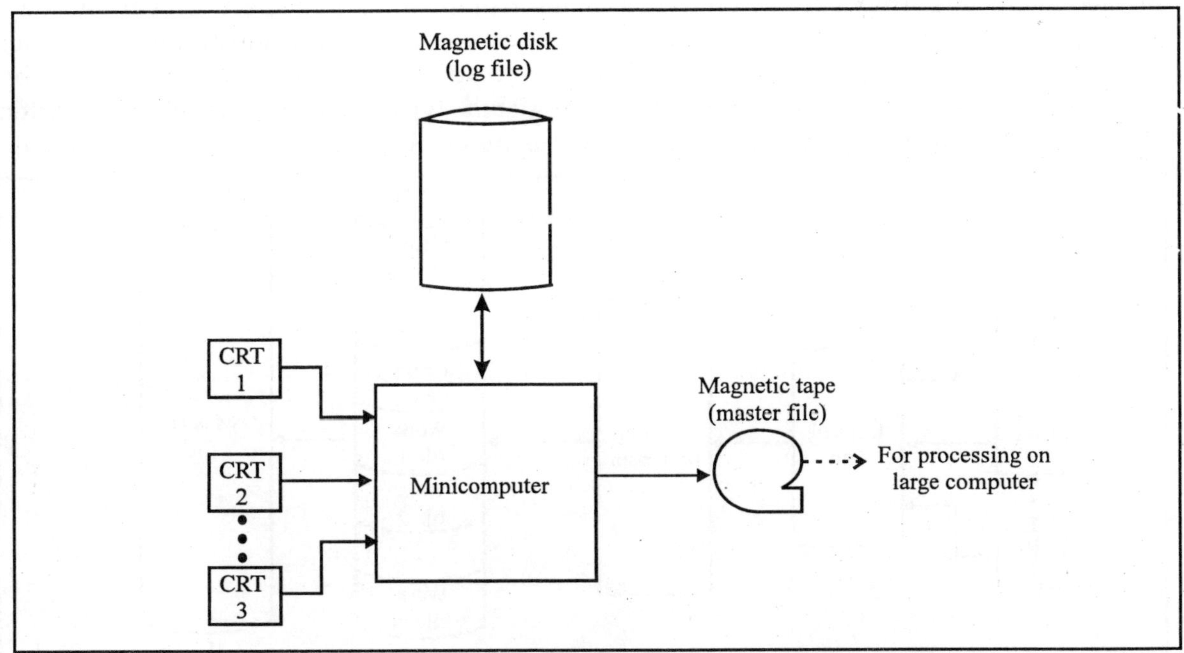

Fig. 14. Illustration of keyboard-to-tape system.

This technique uses either hand-held "wand" readers or stationary sensors, which capture data from merchandise tags or tickets containing optical or magnetic characters. All readers are linked either to a control processor or an intelligent terminal. The main advantages of POS are as follows:

1. Provides large-scale data collection and online capabilities.

2. The method of reading optically or magnetically encoded characters on tickets and product items speeds up the sales transactions to the mutual benefit of the buyer and seller.
3. Input errors are eliminated.

The disadvantages of POS systems are:

1. Currently, many of the systems are too expensive.
2. Requires major revisions to the system in a number of areas (e.g., retagging and recording).

Optical character Recognition (OCR)

The purpose of OCR is to decrease the input bottleneck by reducing the number of keying operations and errors in transcription. Ideally, OCR equipment will read any document and transmit the data to a computer, thus eliminating any intermediate data preparation tasks. Most OCR devices being used in organisations are designed to read marks or machine-printed characters. They operate on the basis of sensing a mark in a specific location in the document. Applications for this device are test scoring, surveys, questionnaires, order entry, inventory control, and payroll. Characters readers read characters generated by computer printers, accounting machines, cash registers, type-writers, and precisely written handprinted characters. A general flow of data using OCR devices is shown in Figure 16.

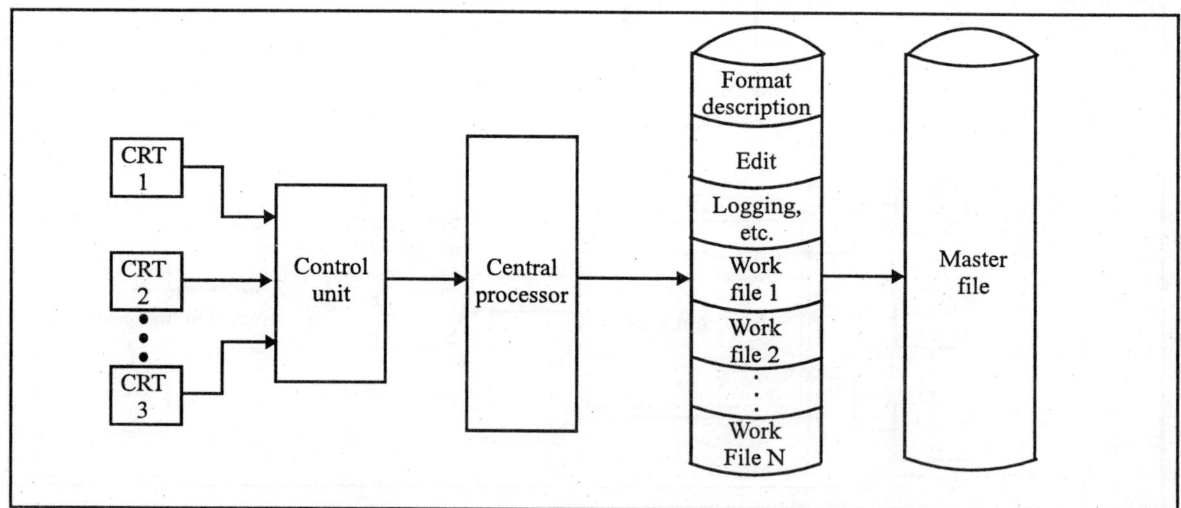

Fig. 15. Illustration of an online entry system.

The advantages of OCR are as follows:

1. Since data conversion is handled photographically, data errors are decreased.
2. Increases throughout.

The disadvantages are as follows:

1. Standardisation problems on type fonts and document inputs.
2. Reject rate is sensitive to the condition of the document (i.e., smudges, creased documents, dirt, and poor quality paper).
3. Low-cost OCR devices have limited throughout and a single-font reading capability. Devices with the capability to read several fonts are expensive.
4. The installation of OCR equipment usually requires complete forms redesign.

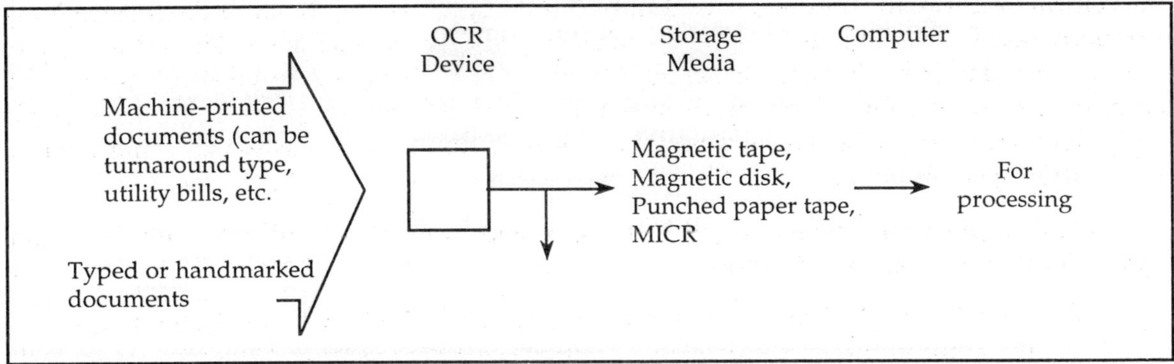

Fig. 16. Illusatration of an OCR application.

Magnetic Ink Character Recognition (MICR)

Magnetic ink character recognition (MICR) is used primarily by financial institutions for sorting and routing financial documents. The MICR characters are preprinted on documents and are composed of the ten decimal digits and four special characters.

Voice Recognition (VR)

On the floor of a commodities exchange, a transaction is completed between two brokers. The reporter speaks into a wireless microphone, "July silver four-four-four" A visual confirmation is given and he says, "Go." Using voice recognition (VR),[7] the data have been captured for further computer processing.

Where a limited amount of data in the form of words and alphanumeric characters are involved, a number of users are finding voice data entry to be cost/effective. By by-passing the writing or keying operations traditionally used to encode data, time may be saved and the cost associated with error correcting minimised. Moreover, VR can serve an important control function, recognising only those commands of authorised personnel.

Operationally, VR systems consists of a microphone or telephone receiver to accept voice input a spectrum analyser to filter the audio signal, and an analog-to-digital converter to change the signal to digital code. The digital code is then matched using a minicomputer to specific code patterns stored on disk or cassette.

Most VR systems have a number of characteristics in common. Normally, VR systems are discrete or isolated. This means that the speaker must pause for a fraction of a second between each sound. Second, each user of the system must train it through repeated utterances to recognise his or her particular enunciation of sounds. Finally, basic voice recognition systems have a limited memory capacity (vocabulary) of 20 to 40 words.

Data Communications

Data communications systems transmit data between peripherals and the central processor and thus, allow people and equipment to be geographically dispersed rather than being at one central location. In computer-based information systems, nearly all of the information produced must be disseminated to a variety of users, some many miles away. This transmission load is increasing each year, making the interdependency of computers and data communications systems even more apparent. Data communications control systems, equipment, and services have, cumulatively, become possibly the fastest growing area of information systems activity.

Typical applications which require design, selection, and implementation of data communication systems are s follows:

1. *Timesharing*. This application allows a number of remote users to gain access to the computational services of a central computer system. Data flow is in both directions (i.e. the terminal is both sending and receiving).
2. *Computer job load sharing*. This application permits the interconnection of two or more computers.
3. *Remote job entry (RJE)*. This application entails the linkage of a central large computer with two or more small computers in separate locations, each of which is equipped with high-speed printers, card read-punches, and magnetic disk and tape. The purpose of RJE is to transmit voluminous amounts of data to a central processor for further processing.
4. *Interrogation*. This application requires the implementation of an online inquiry system using such terminal devices as CRTs and teletypewriters to gain access to the data base. Also, similar to RJE, the user may update records within certain integrated files.

The three major areas of data communications systems are:

1. *Communication channels:* These channels provide a path for electrical transmission between two or more points. These channels are also called circuits, lines, or links.
2. *Modems*. The terms modem is a contraction of modulator-demodulator. These devices modulate and demodulate signals transmitted over communication channels.
3. *Line management*. Line management encompasses the procedures and equipment

necessary to connect several terminals to the same line. Multiplexers, concentrators, and programmable communications processors are devices that enable many different terminals to share a single communications line.

Communication Channels

Communication channels are comprised of one or more of the following :telegraph lines, telephone lines, radio links, coaxial cable, microwave, satellite, laser beam, and helical waveguides. Depending on the terminal equipment and the application required, the channels can be arranged for operation in one or more of the three basic transmission modes:

1. *Simplex*. Transmission is made in one direction only.
2. *Half duplex*. Transmission can be in both directions, but not at the same time.
3. *Full duplex*. Transmission can be made in both directions at the same time.

Data Transmission

Data are transmitted over a wire line (or microwave system) by an electrical signal. It is comprised of three elements: (1) amplitude-strength of the signal, (2) phase-duration of the signal, and (3) frequency-number of times a wave form is repeated during a specified more interval. These elements are illustrated in Figure 17.

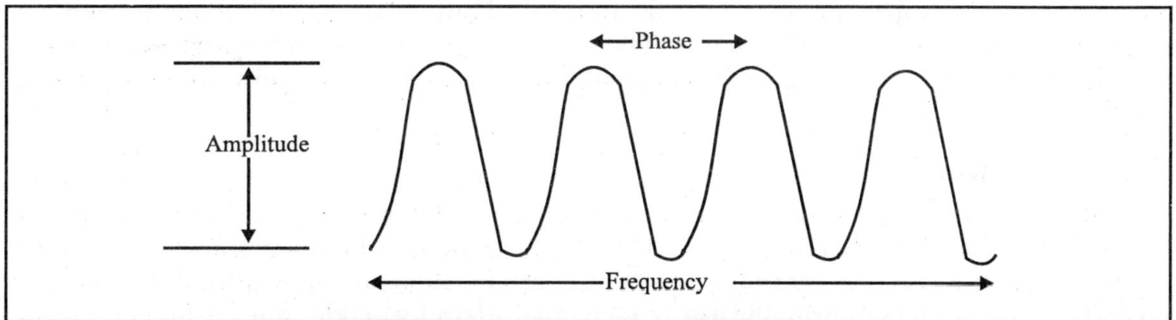

Fig. 17. Schematic of a wave form.

When the binary numbering system is used to represent characters, a pulse for a defined time interval represents a 1-bit and no pulse is used to represent a 0-bit, and no pulse is used to represent a 0-bit. The pulse or no pulse is based on the amplitude, phase and frequency of the signal, which is termed the "state".

Data transmission is either asynchronous or synchronous. Asynchronous transmission, such as in telegraph communication, is the slower of the two. Signal elements are transmitted to indicate the start and stop of each character. Three common asynchronous codes are:

1. *Baudot*. This is a five-level code with 32 possible combinations. With the use of a shift code (shift from a code for numbers to a code for a alphabetics and special

characters), it is possible to code of good combinations. The term, baud, is used for measurement.

2. *Binary Coded Decimal*. The method is similar to the Baudot method It is, however, a six-level code.
3. *American Standard Code for Information Interchange*. This code, termed ASCII uses seven or eight-character bits.

Synchronous transmission is normally used where the transmission rate exceeds 2000 bits per second. The synchronous data transmission requires the receiving terminal to be synchronised bit-for-bit with the sending terminal. This elimination the need for start and top bits, thereby improving the efficiency of data transmission. This system requires, however, a clocking mechanism at both the sending and receiving ends.

Grade of Channels

The above discussion considered the directional flow of data and types of transmission and codes used. Another very important consideration is the grade of the channel. Channels are graded on speed of transmission and this attribute is directly proportional to handwidth. For example, telegraph lines are narrowband, telephone lines are voicehand, and coaxial cable or microwave are broadband. The bandwidth of a channel is measured by a unit called a Hertz (Hz), which means cycles per second. It has been shown that the bandwidth of a channel should be approximately twice the number of bits to be transmitted per second. For example, if one is to transmit data at 1200 bits per second (bps), then a channel with a bandwidth of 2400 Hz is required. Channels may be classified as low-speed, medium-speed, and high-speed.

Low-Speed Channels

This grade was originally developed for use with teletypewriters (TTYs). It transmits data in the range of 55, 75, 110, 150, and 300 bits per second. Data can be transmitted via the teletypewriter online, or paper tape can be prepared offline and transmitted during slack periods. These systems normally use five-channel. (Baudot) code, but, at higher speeds, they also have available the eight-channel ASCII Code.

Medium-Speed Channels

This grade is voiceband and is provided by the Bell System and the independent telephone companies. They are used for voice and data communications, interchangeably. Their typical transmission rate is 300 to 9600 bits per second. There are three types of services available: (1) private line, (2) the dial-up network, and (3) WATS.

1. *Private Lines*. The major difference in this system and a dia-up system is that the channel remains connected for the duration of the lease, the routing can be chosen, and the line can be electrically conditioned so that the transmission rate can be increased up to 9600 bits per second. Private lines are leased on a monthly

basis with unlimited usage and the rate is a function of airline miles from point to point.

Conditioning refers to the process by which the quality of a specific, privately leased line is maintained at a certain standard permissible error rate. Such conditioning adjusts the frequency and phase response characteristics of the channel to meet more exact tolerance specifications.

2. *Dial-up or public switched network.* The dial-up or switched network is currently the most commonly used method of transmitting data. The channel is available as long as the connection is made, and payment varies according to mileage, time of day or night, and duration of connect time. The rate approximates the rate for a normal voice telephone call. The average speed of transmission is generally from 2000 to 2400 bits per second.

   Since each dial-up connection may involve a unique combination of channels, the telephone company does not guarantee the characteristics of dial-up channels. Consequently, to achieve high transmission rates on a dial-up network, the required conditioning must be performed within the modem. Such a modem rapidly determines the channel characteristics and compensates for them at the start of the connection and then continuously adapts to any changes during connect time.

3. *Wide area telephone service (WATS).* WATS is a pricing arrangement for users of large volume data (and voice) transmission over long distances. WATS offers two billing plans: (1) a full period service, and (2) a measured time service. Under full period service, subscriber has unlimited use of the channel at a fixed monthly rate in the geographical area for which he or she subscribes. Under measured time service, the basic monthly rate covers the first ten hours of use per month for calls to Data-Phones (or telephones) within the subscribed service area. An additional charge per hour of actual use is levied beyond the first ten hours; however, the tariff which governs this service is extremely complicated and a full explanation is beyond the scope of this text.

High-Speed Channels

Where data are to be transmitted at high speeds and very high volumes, then a broadband service should be used. Both the Bell System and Western Union offer leased broadband services. These broadband lines comprise of group of channels of voice grade. Each channel, when properly arranged, can carry voice, computer data, or facsimile signals. Two classes of services are offered.

1. *Type 5700 line.* Has a base capacity of 60 voice-grade channels and a maximum equivalent bandwidth of 240 kHz (kilo-hertz).
2. *Type 5800 line.* Has a capacity of 240 voice-grade channels and a maximum equivalent bandwidth of 1000 kHz.

This service is quite flexible because it can be used as a single broadband channel for fast and voluminous data transmission or as several individual lower-speed channels. In certain cases a user group with similar needs may share a line, whereas on an individual basis, they could not afford such a service. A flat monthly rate is charged for this service, regardless ot the volume of data transmitted. This rate is based on the number of channels, total capacity, and distance between transmission points.

Some companies have found it more economical and efficient to develop and use their own private-line microwave systems. The first, National Bank of Boston, for example, has a microwave link between its head office and its operations center four miles away. The microwave link consists of a 1.544-megabit system that is capable of handling data transmission between the two points at speeds up to 19,200 bits per second.

Massachusetts General Hospital has a microwave link between it and Logan Airport in Boston. Doctors at the hospital, through audiovisual contact with patients at the airport, direct tests performed by technicians at the airport medical facility. This system is being extended to nursing homes throughout the Boston area so that expert medical care can be brought to patients who are unable to come to the hospital for treatment.

Arthur C. Clarks, an author of several books on space, believes that satelites will have at least the same impact on people as have telephones. Most major telecommunications companies (e.g. AT&T, GTE) have launched or will launch their own satellites. Western Bancorp for instance, uses satelite links to connect three remote data centers to its corporate data center in Los Angeles. The system supports a bankwide teller-transaction processing system consisting of 5000 terminals in 700 banking offices covering 11 western states.

Fiber optics are AT&Ts terrestrial answer to satellite communications. Optical fibers are embedded in cables and carry communications by bending and bouncing light waves through tiny strands of glass. Fiber optics the size of a human hair offer 1000 times the carrying capacity of today's copper wire pair. The benefits associated with fiber optics as a transmission medium include high handwidth, little noise interference because they are nonelectrical, high security since they cannot be tapped, and suitability for digital transmission because light pulses lend themselves well to binary coding.

A data transmission medium of the 1980s and 1990s is infrared. Infrared is an optical transmission system that uses the infrared spectrum of light-emitting diodes. Like microwave, it is a "line-of-sight" system that is most useful for building-to-building data communications up to 1 kilometer apart. A system called Lite-Link operates at a speed of 500 Kilobits per second.[8]

Modems

Modems, also knows as data sets, are used to handle the data steam from a peripheral device to the central processor, or vice versa, though the common carrier network. The modem can operate in simplex, half duplex, or full duplex mode.

Telephone channels were developed for analog voice transmission. In communication applications involving digital data,, the modulator portion of a modem converts digital pulses, representing binary 1's and 0's generated by the computer or peripheral equipment, into an analog, wavelike signal acceptable for transmission over analog channels. the demodulator reverses this process, converting the analog signal back into a pulse train acceptable to the peripheral or computer at the other end. This is illustrated in Figure 18. If a modem was not used to convert/reconvert data signals, and the computer or peripheral was directly connected to the telephone channel, the signal would be degraded and he data would be made unintelligible by the electrical characteristics of the channel.

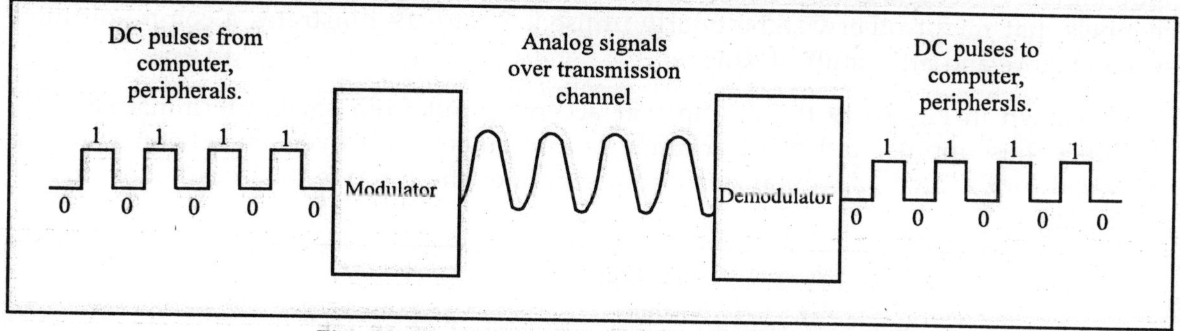

Fig. 18. Illustration of modulation-demodulation

Line Management

Often a single terminal connected to a dedicated line is not active enough of the time to keep the line busy. A common solution to this problem is to connect several terminals to the same line. Because the terminals are "dropped off" the communications line, the configuration is called a multidrop. A multidrop configuration, while decreasing line costs, can produce a garbled message if two or more terminals use the line simultaneously. To overcome this potential problem a polling or contention method of line management is used.

With polling, the central computer asks each terminal if it has something to transmit. If it does, then it is directed to send its message. After transmission of a terminal's message is complete, the computer asks the next terminal if it has something to transmit. This polling continues in turn until all the terminals on the line have the opportunity to transmit. Then the computer polls the first terminal and the entire polling process is repeated. While polling allows the line to be busier, it can waste processor time if terminals do not have messages to send. An alternative method that overcomes this disadvantage is called contention.

With contention, each terminal listens to the communications line before transmitting its message. If the line is free it sends its message. If the line is busy the terminal wishing to send a message waits awhile before listening again. A serious disadvantage of the contention method of line management is that terminals may experience long delays in sending messages because the communications line is too busy or messages are too long.

Multiplexers, concentrators, and programmable communications processors are devices that permit connection of more peripherals to the central computer using fewer channels.

Multiplexer

Where a number of terminals are in one of more areas outside the toll-free zone of the central processor, the common carrier and structure makes it economically attractive to operate a group of such terminals through one voice-grade channel, instead of connecting them separately to the central processor via a number of narrowband channels. In most situations of this type multiplexing will reduce the cost of the communication network by allowing one voiceband grade channel to substitute for many subvoice (slow-speed, telegraph) channels that might otherwise be poorly utilised. Figure 19 illustrates a communication system before and after multiplexing.

As shown in Figure 19 the multiplexer accepts input from several terminal sources, combines these inputs, and hen transmits the combined input over one channel. At the other end (not shown), a similar unit again separates the discrete data inputs for further processing.

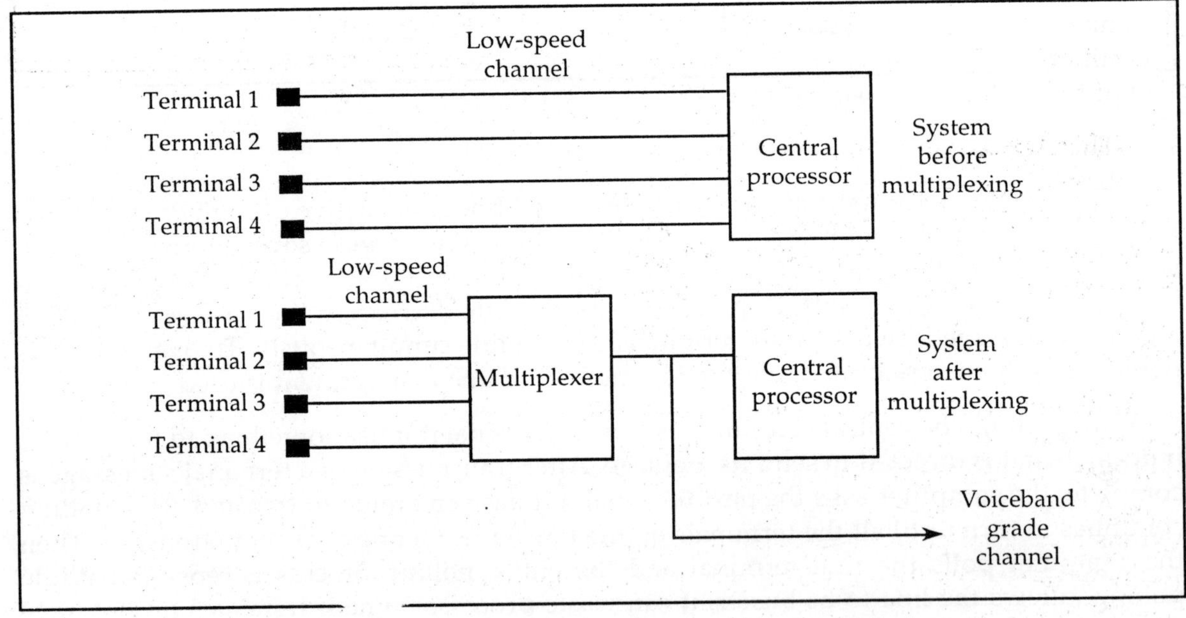

Fig. 19. Communication system before and after multiplexing.

Two basic techniques are used to multiplex data: (1) frequency division multiplexing (FDM), and (2) time division multiplexing (TDM). In FDM the digital pulse signal from each terminal is converted by a modem into an analog signal having a frequency unique to the individual terminal. Each separate signal is allocated its own portion of the frequency of the available band. All the signals are electrically combined and then transmitted over the line. The receiving end of a FDM device demultiplexes the individual signals by using a set of filters, each designed to "hear" a particular tone. The tone is then demodulated by a modem back into a digital pulse signal.

The TDM approach uses transmitting capability according to available time elements. Digital inputs from each terminal are continuously sampled, one by one, for a fixed time period. The sampling time per input corresponds to the time expended to designate a bit (bit-interleaved TDM) or a byte/character (byte-interleaved TDM) by the terminal signal. The bit or byte signal so sampled is time compressed and placed into a time slot in the TDM output signal.

FDM is possibly better where the system has a number of low-speed terminals, geographically dispersed with less than 16 channels. If the transmission rate is 2400 bits per second or more, or a great many channels are used, then the system should use TDM.

Concentrator

A concentrator differs from a multiplexer in that a concentrator accommodates *X* number of terminals but allows only a portion of them to transmit their data over available lines. That is, 12 terminals may compete for only six channels. All terminals must contend for the channels and those which do not make connection are busied out. With a multiplexer, all terminals can be accommodated because the basic assumption is that all terminals are used all of the time.

The concentrator works as a normal switching device that polls one terminal at a time. Whenever a channel is idle, the first terminal ready to send or receive gets control of one of the channels and retains it for the duration of its transaction. If several transactions occur simultaneously. then each terminal must wait its turn on a first in, first out basis.

The cost savings in using a multiplexer are based on combining a data while the cost savings using a concentrator are based on the amount of data traffic in the system. In effect, the use of a concentrator is based on the assumption that all of the terminals will not contend for the available facilities at the same time.

Programmable Communications Processors

As long as the total number of peripherals, local and remote, and the amount of data transmitted are maintained at a certain level, the computer control program (in residence) can execute the interrupts, move the data into and out of storage, and perform the necessary housekeeping without significant throughout penalty. If the number of terminals and volume of data increase to a point beyond that level, however, then computer throughout is reduced significantly. At this point it may be more economical to move these functions out of the computer mainframe and into a communications processor.[9]. These processors perform some, if not all, of the following functions:

1. Housekeeping — the handling of message queues and priorities, processing of addresses, data requests, message blocks, file management, and updating the executive on peripheral activity.

2. Error checking and retransmission requests to prevent incomplete messages from reaching the host processor.
3. Code translation into the "native" code of the host CPU.
4. Preprocessing and editing.
5. Communications analysis processing — error analysis, the gathering of traffic statistics, and so forth.
6. Establishing and acknowledging the required channel connections including automatic dialing, if this is a feature of the system.
7. Verifying successful completion of the message, or detecting line breaks, and either calling for or executing remedial action.
8. Disconnecting after a completed message, to permit polling to resume.
9. Assembling the serial bit steam into a bit-parallel buffered message.
10. Routing messages to and from required memory locations and notifying the software as required.

The major factor in moving these functions from the central processor (host computer) to a communications processor is economic. With a large number of terminals or communications lines, as much as half the processing time of the host computer (even a large one) can be spent in input/output processing and line control. A separate, specialised computer can perform the same functions with fewer steps and simpler software, reducing direct processor time costs, programming costs, and debugging time. The lease or purchase price of the communications processor is often one or two orders of magnitude lower than that of the main computer; if it can assume work which formerly occupied half the main computer's time, it can obviously be economically justified. In Figure 20, a typical configuration is illustrated. [10]

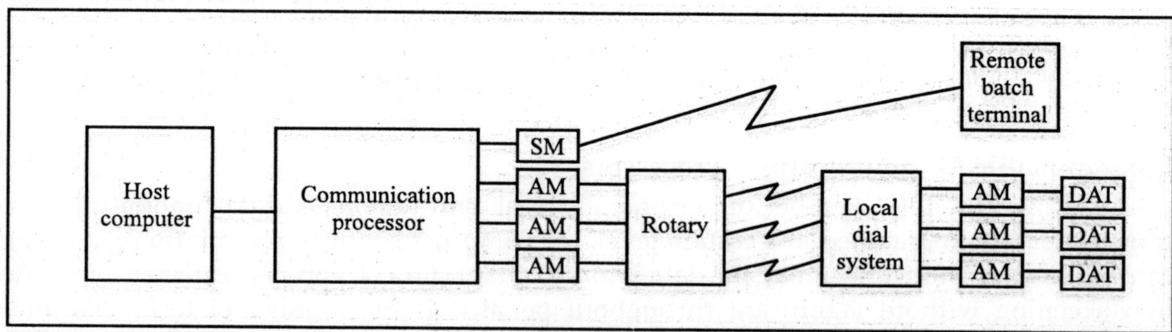

Fig. 20. Computer system with multiple communications ports served by a communications processor. SM: synchronous modem: AM: asynchronous modem; DAT: dial-up terminal.

The increased use of programmable communications processors can be directly attributed to the current proliferation of low cost flexible minicomputers and microcomputers, and also to the developments in integrated circuit technology that have enabled digital computers to be manufactured of greatly reduced costs.

BIBLIOGRAPHY

"All about Minicomputers," *Datapro 70* Delran, NJ.: Datapro Research Corporation, December 1976.

"Control Data 38500 Mass Storage System, *Datapro 70,* Delran, NJ.: Datapro Research Corporation, September 1975.

Davis, *Computer Data Processing,* New York: McGraw-Hill Book Co., 1969.

Havind, "A User's Guide to System Evolution," *Computer Decisions,* June 1971.

Howard, "Telecommunications: 1970-1990," *Computerworld Extra,* March 18, 1981.

"Key to Enhanced Application Development," *Data Processor,* September 1972.

Martin, *Telecommunications and the Computer,* Second Edition, Englewood Cliffs, NJ.: Prentice-Hall, Inc., 1976.

Microcomputer Review, Lexington, MA.: GML Corporation, 1981.

Sardinas, *Computing Today,* Englewood Cliffs, NJ.: Prentice-Hall, Inc., 1981.

"Smart Users Deemphasize' Host, "*Computerworld,* Supplement, July 27, 1972.

Synnott and Gruber, *Information Resource Management,* New York: John Wiley & Sons, Inc., 1981.

Yasaju, "Voice Recognition Comes of Age," *Datamation,* August 1976.

REFERENCES

1. Gordon H. Davis, *Computer Data Processing,* New York: McGraw-Hill Book Company, 1969, p. 150, Used with permission of the McGraw-Hill Book Company.
2. Robert Haavind, "A User's Guide to System Evolution," *Computer Decisions,* June 1971, pp. 26-30. Used with permission.
3. *Ibid.*
4. "Key to Enhanced Application Development." *Data Processor,* September 1972, pp. 2-9 Used with permission.
5. Heavind, *op.cit.,* p. 26.
6. *Microcomputer Review,* Lexington, Mass.: GML Corporation, 1981.
7. Edward K. Yasaki, "Voice Recognition Comes of Age," *Datamation,* August 1976, pp. 65-68.
8. Summarised from Willian R. Synnott and Willian R. Gruber, *Information Resource Management,* New York: John Wiley & Sons, Inc., 1981, pp. 237-420
9. "Smart Users Deemphasize Host'", *Computerworld,* Supplement, July 27, 1972 p. 10. Used with permission. Copyright by *Computerworld,* Newton, Massachusetts 02160.
10. R. L. Aronson, "Data Links and Networks Devices and Techniques," *Control Engineering,* February 1970, pp.105-116. Used with permission.

23

The File System

The UNIX system has a very large number of files. If they are not organised in a systematic manner, it becomes impossible to locate them. It should be possible to group a set of files created by a user, and house them conveniently so that they don't get mixed up with files of other users, or even files used by the system. It should also be possible for two or more users to use the same filename without conflict, and access other files not belonging to them, without infringing on security. All this requires an elaborate storage system with separate "compartments", so that one can *place* himself in any of these compartments, or transfer files from one compartment to another. It also requires an adequate security arrangement so that outsiders are not able to tamper with a file's contents.

An immediate by-product of Ken Thompson's space game, the file system in UNIX is one of its simple and conceptually clean features. The underlying simplicity provides a flexible method of organising information. The system has proved to be so useful that it has been widely adopted by other systems, including MSDOS. In this chapter you will learn how to create directories (the compartments), move around within the system, and perform some basic file related functions. You will also learn about some of the attributes of files, and how to change them.

THE FILE

A UNIX file is a storehouse of information—it is "simply a sequence of characters. UNIX places no restriction on the structure of a file, and you don't need to assume a predefined structure to work with it. A file contains exactly those bytes that you put into it, whether it represents a source program, other text or executable code. A file neither contains its size nor its attributes. It doesn't even contain the end-of-file mark. All file attributes are kept in a separate location in the disk specially earmarked for this purpose. When a file is called up by a command or program, it is this area that is looked up first before the contents are accessed.

The founders' vision of a file is all encompassing; it includes directories and devices too in it's definition. These devices are also considered as files in their own right. The most notable feature of the UNIX file system is that UNIX makes very little distinction between the various types of files. Thus, the printer or tape drive is treated as a file in much the same way as a disk file. The shell is also a file, and so is the kernel. Most commands (which are also files themselves) work with all types of files, and you don't need to indicate specifically the type of file that you are using. With limited exceptions, UNIX doesn't offer separate commands to access these special files.

Although everything is treated as a file by UNIX, it is necessary to divide these files into three categories—ordinary files, directory files and device files. This is because the significance of a file's attributes depends on its type. Thus, read permission for an ordinary file means something quite different from that for a directory or a device. Moreover, you can't directly put something into a directory file, and a device file is not really a stream of characters. While the vast majority of commands work with all types of files, some don't. For a proper understanding of the file system you must understand the significance of these files.

Ordinary File

This is the traditional definition of a file. It consists of a stream of data resident on some permanent magnetic media. You can put anything you want into this type of file. This includes all data, source programs, object and executable code, all UNIX programs, as well as any files created by the user. Commands like **pwd, Is,** etc. are treated as ordinary files. This file is also referred to as as an *ordinary file or a regular file.*

All text files also belong to this type. Any text file in UNIX contains a sequence of lines, with each line terminated by the *LF (linefeed;* character (ASCII octal value 012). This character is also known as the *newline* character, the same character used to terminate a command. This is in sharp contrast to the files used in MSDOS, which use the *CR-LF (carriage return-line feed)* combination to represent the newline character. When you edit a file, the *LF* character is created by hitting the <*Enter*> key.

2. Directory File

A directory can be defined as a storehouse where other programs and sub-directories reside. A directory contains no data, but keeps an account of all the files and sub-directories that it contains. The UNIX file system is organised with a number of such directories and sub-directories, and you can also create them as and when you need. You often need to do that to group a set of files, pertaining to a specific application, in a șeparate directory. This allows two files (or more) in separate directories to have the same filename.

A directory file contains two *fields*—the name of a file and a *pointer* to a separate disk area which contains the file's attributes. If a directory houses, say, ten files, then there will be ten such entries in the directory file. You don't need to concern yourself with further details at this stage because the structure of a directory file has been adequately.

(Sec. 14.8). However, it is worthwhile remembering that, though you can create or remove a directory at will, you can't directly write into it. The system (or specifically the kernel) has the exclusive right to write into such a file. When a file is created or removed, the directory file is automatically updated by the kernel with the relevant information about the file.

3. Device File

The definition of a file has been broadened by UNIX to consider even physical devices as files. This definition includes printers, tapes, floppy drives, hard disks and terminals. Although this may appear confusing initially, it is really an advantage; you don't need any special command or function to use such a file. The device file is special in the sense that any output directed to it will be reflected onto the respective I/O (input/output) device associated with the filename. Thus, when you issue a command to print a file, you are really directing the file's output to the file associated with the printer. When you back up files onto tape, you are "symbolically" using the file associated with the tape drive. The kernel takes care of this by mapping special filenames to their respective devices.

THE STRUCTURE OF THE FILE SYSTEM

Now that you understand the three types of files, you" shouldn't feel baffled by subsequent use of the word in the text. The term *file* will often be used in this text to refer to any of these types, though it will mostly be used to mean an ordinary file. The real meaning of the term should be evident from its context.

All files in UNIX are "related" to one another. The file system in UNIX is a collection of all these related files (ordinary, directory and device files) organised in a hierarchical (an inverted tree) structure. This system has been adopted by MSDOS, and is visually represented in Fig. 1.

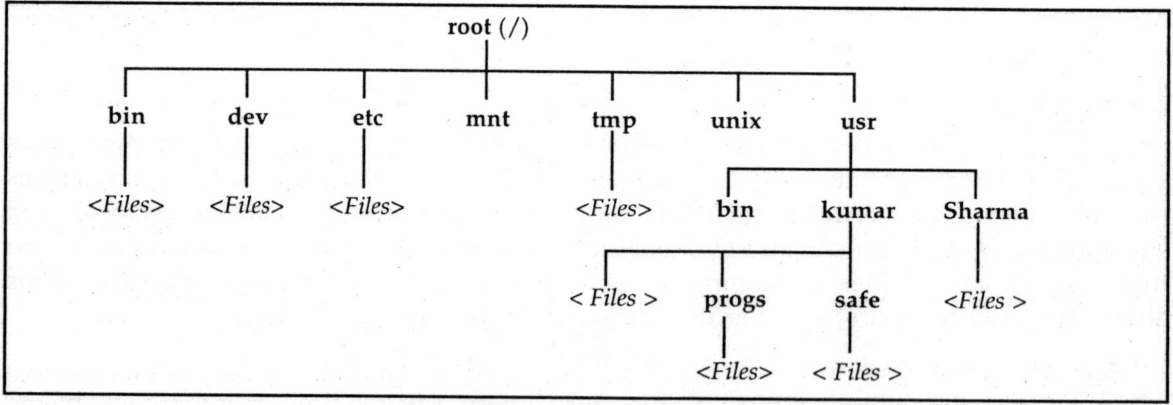

Fig. 1. The UNIX file System

The implicit feature in every UNIX file system is that there is a supremo, which serves as the reference point for all files. Like MSDOS, this top is called *root,* but is represented by a /(frontslash). *root* is actually a directory file, and it has a number of sub-directories (or "branches") under it. These sub-directories, in turn, have more sub-directories and other files ("leaves") under them. For instance, **bin** and **usr** are two directories directly under *root*, while a second **bin** and **Kumar** are sub-directories under **usr.** Note that it is possible for two directories to have the same name. Every file, apart from *root*, must have a *parent*, and it should be possible to trace the ultimate parentage of a file to *root*. Thus, the **usr** directory is the parent of **kumar,** while *root is* the parent of **usr,** and the *grandparent* of **kumar.** If a file can't be traced to its ultimate ancestor, then it is not part of the file system.

Once the relationship between various files is established in this manner, UNIX provides a. simple mechanism of accessing a file. The login directory **kumar** can also be specified as **/usr/kumar.** It is called a *pathname* for the directory file **kumar** Every pathname consists of a sequence of directory names, separated by /'s. If the first character of a pathname is a /, then it indicates that the file's location must be determined with respect to *root*. Such pathnames are called *absolute pathnames.* When you have more than one / in a pathname, for each such /, you have to descend one level in the file system. For instance, **/usr/kumar** is an absolute pathname, implying that **usr** is to be found directly under the *root* directory, and **kumar** under the **usr** directory. In other words, **kumar** is two levels below root, with **usr** as its parent.

When you specify a file by using /'s to demarcate the various levels, you have a mechanism of identifying a file uniquely. The tree-like structure enables you to create as many directories as you wish so that one directory doesn't need to contain too many files. This permits you to use two files with the same name, but in different directories, so that they will have different pathnames. Thus, the file **/usr/kumar/progs/wstovi.c** is different from the file **/usr/kumar/safe/wstovi.c:** While the last name in any pathname can indicate either an ordinary, directory or device file, intermediate names must indicate directory files only. It is obvious that while a branch or a leaf can emanate from another branch, it can't emanate from a leaf. In other words, you can have all the three types of files only under a directory file.

Most UNIX commands use files. Whether you should use ' the command **cat /usr/ kumar/ progs/wstovi.c** or simply **cat wstovi.c** to display the contents of the file **wstovi.c** depends on where you are. You could be placed in the directory **/usr/sharma,** in which case you must use the absolute pathname. However, if you are located in the directory **/usr/ kumar,** then you needn't use an absolute pathname as an *argument* (the meanings of *commands, arguments* and *options are* to be found in Sec. 1) to a command if the file resides in the same directory. The directory where you are placed or located is known as the *current* directory, and is dealt with in Sec. 3.

The directories shown directly under *root* are normally found in every UNIX system (before Release 4), in addition to others. A brief mention needs to be made here about the significance of some of the directories of the file system tree. The directories **/bin, /dev, /etc** and **/lib** are system directories, and you shouldn't try to tamper with their contents (normally you can't even do that). The other directories like **/tmp** and **/usr** are meant for the users.

The commonly used UNIX commands like **who, we, cat**, etc are stored in the **/bin** and **/usr/bin** directories, and made available to every user. You don't need to copy these files into your directory to use them. /**dev** contains the device files of all hardware devices, /**etc** contains those utilities mostly used by the system administrator./**tmp** is used by some UNIX utilities (especially **vi**), as well as by a user to store temporary files. Finally, the /**usr** directory (apart from /**usr/bin**) contains all the files created by a user, including his login directory.

You will learn about the internals of the file system, where the presentation will include some of the complexities and the mechanism by which the kernel handles files. In this chapter, you can safely insulate yourself from knowledge of these internals.

1. Release 4 Changes

Release 4 has modified the structure of the file system. There are more directories now, while some have been dispensed with. Some directories now have different ancestors, **/bin** no longer exists; all the commonly used commands are now stored in **/usr/bin.** Users now belong to the **/home** directory instead of /**usr**. However, since most users are familiar with the structure adopted in Release 3.2 and earlier, it has been assumed throughout the text.

CHECKING YOUR CURRENT DIRECTORY—THE PWD COMMAND

It is a remarkable feature of the UNIX system that both a file, as well as a human user, occupy a certain slot in the file system. When you log in to the system, UNIX automatically places you in a directory called the *home* directory. In most cases, this directory is also your *login* directory, and the name of this home directory is usually the login name. Unless you change your directory, this will be called your *current* directory as well. It is created by the system when a user account is opened. If you log in using the login name **kumar,** you will land up in a directory having the pathname /**usr**/**kumar** (unless you have chosen to be placed in a sub-directory under this directory).

You can always find out the directory where you are currently placed, by using the **pwd** (present working directory) command :

$ pwd

/usr/kumar

$_

The **pwd** command resembles the **CD** command of MSDOS when used without an argument. Note that it displays the absolute pathname of the directory in which the user is placed. It is a general feature of the UNIX system that all users have the /**usr** directory as their parent **(/home** in Release 4).

When a pathname doesn't begin with a /, it means that the search has to start from the current directory. Thus, if **pwd** tells you that your current directory is **/usr/kumar,** you can refer to a sub-directory **progs,** either as **/usr/kumar/progs,** or simply as **progs.** How you should specify a filename depends solely on where you are currently placed. The rules are the same as in MSDOS

CHANGING DIRECTORIES—THE CD COMMAND

You can move around in the tile system by using the **ed** (change directory) command. When used with an argument, it resembles its MSDOS counterpart. It changes the current directory to the directory specified as the argument. You can use it to switch to the directory **progs**:

```
$ pwd
/usr/kumar
$ cd progs
$ pwd
/usr/kumar/progs
$_
```

Though **pwd** displays the absolute pathname, c**d** doesn't need to use one. The command **cd progs** here means that you should change your sub-directory to **progs** (under the current directory). Using an absolute pathname causes no harm either; use **cd /usr/kumar/progs** for the same effect.

When you need to switch to the **/bin** directory where most of the commonly used UNIX commands are kept, then you should use the absolute pathname :

```
$ pwd
/usr/kumar/progs
$ cd /bin
$ pwd
/bin
$_
```

cd can also be used without any arguments:

```
$ pwd
/usr/kumar/progs
$ cd
$ pwd
/usr/kumar
$_
```

Attention, MSDOS users ! This command invoked without an argument doesn't indicate the current directory. It simply switches to the home directory, i.e. the directory where the user originally logged in. Therefore, if you wander around in the file system, you can force an immediate return to your home directory by simply using **cd**:

$ cd /usr/sharma

$ pwd

/usr/sharma

$ **cd**

$ **pwd**

/usr/kumar

$_

The home directory is assigned by the system administrator by making a special entry in the file **/etc/passwd**. This is an extremely important file maintained by the system which keeps track of all the users. When you change your password, this file is updated with the password encryption. Have a look at the file in your system ; it could puzzle you. This file is treated in detail in subsection 15.3.1.

The **cd** command can sometimes fail if you don't have proper permissions to access the directory. This doesn't normally happen unless you deliberately tamper with the permissions of the directory. The technique of doing that is described in subsection 14.8.1.

1. The Iogname Command

As a user, you will often require to **"cd"** to the directory of another user without meaning to cause any damage. Inadvertently, you may even try to create or remove files in that directory, presuming that it is your own login director). Though **cd** (without arguments), followed by **pwd** tells you your home directory, you may want to avoid repeated movements just to check your home directory. The **logname** command tells you the name of your login directory, irrespective of where you are. So, if you move to **/usr/sharma,** the command tells you that your login directory is still **kumar :**

$ cd /usr/sharma

$ logname

kumar

$_

The command doesn't need any arguments, and unlike **pwd,** simply specifies the login directory without the absolute pathname. This name is also stored in a *shell variable* named **LOGNAME,** (Shell variables are taken up in Sec.12.)

LISTING OUT DIRECTORY CONTENTS—THE IS COMMAND

The Is command was used to obtain a list of all files in the current directory, i.e. **/usr/kumar.** Run it once again to have a look at the files now :

```
$ls
chap 0l
chap02
dept.lst
desig.lst
empl.lst
emp2.1st
genie.sh
helpdir
prggen.sh
progs
spcgen.sh ,
user. 1st
$_
```

What you see here is a list of filenames arranged in ASCII *collating* sequence, with one filename in each line. The command is often invoked to check whether a particular file is available. However, when you have several files, it is better to use **an** *option* (i.e. a letter preceded by a - sign and following the command) with Is so that the filenames are displayed in multiple columns. The -**x** option produces a multicolumnar output :

```
$ Is -x
chap 0l      chap 02      dept.ls      desig.lst    empl.lst     emp2.1st
genie.sh     helpdir      prggen.sh    progs        spcgen.sh    user.lst
S_
```

A similar output is displayed in XENIX when the **Ic** command is used. The display in either case shows only the filenames, and is so convenient, that many people have customised the command to display in this format by default (i.e. when used without options). It doesn't, however, show the file attributes, nor does it indicate how many of them, if any, are directory or device files. To identify directories and executable files, the **-F** option should be used. Since UNIX permits the use of more than one option with a command (provided it supports multiple options), the -**x** and -**F** options can be clubbed together to produce a multi-columnar output :

$ ls -F -x

chap 01	chap02	dept.lst	desig.lst	empl.lst
emp2.lst	genie.sh*	helpdir/	prggen.sh*	progs/
spcgen.ss*	user.lst			

$ _

Ex 2.1: Find out all the directories directly under the root directory.

Note the use of two symbols that tag some of the filenames. The indicates that the file contains executable code, while the / refers to a directory. You can now identify the two sub-directories in the current directory; **helpdir** and **progs.**

1. The long Listing—the-I Option

An informative listing of files is obtained when **Is** is used with the **-1** (long) option :

S ls-1

total 264

-rw-r-w--	1 kumar	group	19514	May 10 13:45 chap 0l
-rw-r-r--	1 kumar	group	4174	May 10 15:01 chap 02
-rw-rw-rw-	1 kumar	group	84	Feb 12 12:30 dept.lst
-rw-rw-rw-	1 kumar	group	114	Mar 11 17:37 desig.lst
-rw-rw-rw-	1 kumar	group	236	Mar 18 07:57 emp 1.1st
-rw-rw-rw-	1 kumar	group	392	Mar 18 08:57 emp2.1st
-rw-r-r-	1 kumar	group	9156	Mar 12 1989 genie. sh
drwxr-xr-x	2 kumar	group	64	May 9 10:31 helpdir
-rw-r-r--	1 kumar	group	27012	Mar 11 17:30 prggen.sh
drwxr-xr-x	2 kumar	group	320	May 9 09:57 progs
-rw-r-r--	1 kumar	group	62172	Dec 12 12:20 spcgen.sh
-rw-r-r--	1 kumar	group	74	May 9 16:20 user.lst

This list displays seven attributes of every file in the current directory, which will be discussed shortly. The list is preceded by the words **"total 264",** which indicates that a total of 264 blocks are occupied by these files in the disk, each block consisting of 512 bytes.

Is can be used with one or more filenames as well. You can have a shorter list of only those files that you wish to see, by specifying the filenames in the *command line,* i.e. along with the command. Thus, to see the long listing of files **chap0l** and **chap02,** you need to specify these filenames as arguments to the command :

S Is -1 chap0l chap02

-rw-r- -r- -	1 kumar	group	19514	May 10 13:45	chap0l
-rw-r-r--	1 kumar	group	4174	May 10 15:01	chap02

Note that you didn't need to use the absolute pathname of the files this time. When a filename doesn't begin with a /, it indicates that the file is to be found in the current directory. This is true not only for the **Is** command, but in general for every UNIX command using a filename as argument. But you can use the absolute pathnames also for these files. The output is identical, except for the filenames displayed in the last column :

```
S Is -1 /usr/kumar/chap01 /usr/kumar/chap02
-rw-r—r—    1 kumar    group    19514    May 10 13:45 /usr/kumar/chapOl
-rw-r—r—    1 kumar    group     4174    May 10 15:01 /usr/kumar/chap02
$_
```

The **Is** command has already been used in three ways. First, it was used as it is. Later, it was used with different options (**-x**, **-F** and **-1**), and now you have just specified some filenames to it. It is a general feature of most UNIX commands that they can be used in a number of ways.

The output produced by the **Is** command with the **-1** option will be frequently referred to as the *long listing*, or simply *listing*, and it produces a columnar output showing seven attributes of a file. The significance of each of these attributes is presented in the next subsection.

2. Significance of the Listing Output

The first column shows the type and the *permissions* associated with each file. The first character in this column is usually a -, which indicates that the file is an ordinary one. This is, however, not so for the files **helpdir** and **progs** which shows a **d** at the same position, implying that they are directory files. You then see a series of characters which could take the values **r,w,x** and -. In the UNIX system, a file can have three types of permissions - read, write and execute. You will see how to interpret these permissions and also how to change them in Sec. 10.

The second column indicates the number of *links* associated with the file. This is actually the number of filenames maintained by the system of that file. Unlike MSDOS, UNIX lets a file have as many names as you want without replicating its contents. This attribute will be discussed in Sec. 5.

Ex 2.2: find out the files in the /bin and /usr/bin directories that have links..

The third column shows kumar as the *owner* of all the files. When you create a file, you automatically become its owner. In this case, kumar has created all the files ; hence his name. The owner of a file has certain privileges not normally available with others. Generally, as owner of a file you have full authority to tamper with its contents, permissions and even ownership. Similarly, you can create, modify or remove files in a directory if you are the owner of the directory. This restriction can be altered in ways you will see.

The fourth column stands for the *group* to which the owner belongs. When a user account is opened by the system administrator, he simultaneously assigns the user to some group. Normally, a beginner is assigned to a default group. In the XENIX system, this group is simply called **group**. Ownership and group ownership are also elaborated in Sec. 6.

The fifth column shows the size of the file in bytes, i.e. the amount of data it contains. It is only a character count of the file and not a measure of disk space. The space occupied by a file in the disk is usually larger than this figure since files are written to disk in blocks of 1024 bytes (normally). In other words, even though the file **chap0l** contains 19514 bytes, it occupies more space on the disk.

The sixth, seventh and eighth columns indicate the last modification time of the file. A file is said to be modified only if its contents have been changed in any way. But if you change only the permissions or ownership of the file, the modification time remains unchanged. If the file is less than a year old since its last modification date, then the year won't be displayed. The file **genie.sh** suggests that it has been modified more than a year ago.

The last column displays the filenames arranged alphabetically. A filename can consist of up to 14 characters. If you enter more than 14 characters when specifying a filename, only the first 14 characters are effectively interpreted by the system. Files may or may not have extensions, and can consist of practically any ASCII character. There is no restriction on the selection of these characters. But since the UNIX system has a special treatment for some characters like $, ', ?, *, & amongst others, it is recommended that only alphabets, numerals, the period (.) and the underscore (_) character be used in filenames. Control characters should be definitely avoided.

UNIX imposes no restrictions on the extension, if any, that a file should have. In all cases, it is the application which imposes this restriction. Thus, BASIC requires that files should have **.bas** extension, C language files have the .c extension, and so forth. MSDOS users must remember that UNIX is also sensitive to case. Thus, **chap0l, Chap0l** and **CHAP01** are three different filenames, and it is possible for them to coexist in the same directory.

Ex 2.3: List out the files in the /dev directory with the- I option. Does any column strike you as significant ?

3. Other Options in Is

In the last example you specified some ordinary filenames to **Is** to have a selective listing. But the situation will be quite different if you specify the two directory names **helpdlr** und **progs,** instead:

$ Is -1 helpdir progs
helpdir:
total 1148

```
-rw-r—r—      1 kumar     group      581602    Jan 13 1989 uxmanual

progs:
total 8
-rw-rw-rw-    1 kumar     group          44    May 9 09:08 dept.h
-rw-rw-rw-    1 kumar     group         212    May 9 09:08 dept.q
-rw-rw-rw- 1  kumar       group         154    May 9 09:08 emp.h
-rw-rw-rw- 1  kumar       group         742    May 9 09:08 emp.q
S_
```

This time the contents of the directories are listed, consisting of the UNIX manual in the **helpdir** directory and a number of screen files (for a relational database package named UNIFY) in the **progs** directory. However, if you want to force **Is** to list the directory attributes rather than its contents, then you need to use the **-d** (directory) option :

```
$. Is -1 -d helpdlr progs
drwxr-xr-x    2 kumar     group          48    Jan 30 14:21 helpdir
drwxr-xr-x    2 kumar     group          96    Mar 12 14:50 progs

$-
```

Directories are easily identified from the long listing by the first character of the first column, which here shows a **d**. For ordinary files, this place always shows a - (hyphen), and for device files, either a **b** or a **c**. The significance of the attributes of a directory differ a good deal from an ordinary file. For example, the size of a directory is in no way related to the size of the files that exist in the directory. It only shows the space consumed by the directory file itself. Directories will be considered in the revisit to the file system in Sec. 14.8.

So far, you have confined yourself to working with files in the home directory. To obtain the listing of some of the command files stored in /**bin**, you can supply **Is** with a list of absolute pathnames for them. Alternatively, you can switch to the /**bin** directory, and then simply use the filenames :

```
$ cd /bin
$ pwd
/bin
$ Is -1 -F cat date Is sh who wc cd
cd not found
-rwx- -x- -t    1 bin     bin      9525    Apr 13 1987 cat*
-rwx- -x- -x    1 bin     bin     13950    Apr 13 1987 date*
-rwx- -x- -t    6 bin     bin     18609    Apr 13 1987 Is*
-rwx- -x- -t    2 bin     bin     38477    Apr 13 1987 sh*
-rwx- -x- -x    1 bin     bin      7553    Apr 13 1987 wc*
-rwx- -x- -x    1 bin     bin      1838    Apr 13 1987 who*
$
```

You indeed find all of them in this directory, except for the **cd** command. Even though the filenames were not specified in alphabetic sequence, **Is** sorted them before displaying the listing. Note the * that is suffixed to every filename, indicating that they are all executables. If you are wondering where to locate the **cd** command, then you really won't find it anywhere. It is one of a handful of commands which doesn't exist as a separate executable. It is built into the **sh** (representing the shell) command, which is also included in the listing. In The chapters dealing with the shell, you will encounter a family of commands which perform very useful functions without having an independent existence.

You can reverse the order of the presentation by using the **-r** (reverse) option. The files will then be listed, with the names sorted in reverse ASCII collating sequence :

```
$ Is -1 -r chap0l chap02 dept.lst
-rw-rw-rw-     1 kumar     group        84     Feb 12 12:30 dept.lst
-rw-r—r—       1 kumar     group      4174     May 10 15:01 chap02
-rw-r- -r- -   1 kumar     group     19514     May 10 13:45 chap0l
S_
```

Is doesn't normally show all the files in a directory. There are certain hidden files in every directory, especially in the login directory, which normally don't show up in the listing. The -a option (all) lists out all the hidden files along with the other files :

```
S Is -a -x -F
/          ../         exrc         .profile    chap0l
chap02     dept.lst    desig.lst    empl.lst    emp2.lst
genie.sh*  helpdir/    prggen.sh*   progs/      spcgen.sh*
user. 1st
$_
```

Note the four additional files at the top of the list ; ., .., **.exrc** and **.profile,** all beginning with a period. Use of the **-F** option also suggests that the first two files are directories. MSDOS users will be quick to observe the similarity here which they get with the **DIR** command. UNIX adopts a widely used convention— . (a single period) stands for the current directory while .. (a double period) indicates the parent directory. Whenever you create any sub-directory, these "invisible" directories are created automatically by the system. You can't remove them, nor can you write into them. They provide a shorthand notation for referring to the current and parent directories. These two symbols can be used in a pathname quite gainfully, as will be seen in the topic on relative pathnames (Sec. 8).

The third file **(.profile)** contains a set of instructions, which are performed when a user logs in. It is conceptually similar to **AUTOEXEC.BAT** of MSDOS, and you will know more about it in Sees 4.13 and 12.2. The other file **.exrc** contains a sequence of start-up instructions for the **ex** and **vi** editors. This file is taken up again in Sec. 7.11.

While all these files beginning with a . are normally not listed out with Is, you can either use the **-a** option to include them, or ask for them specifically by using their filenames in the command line. Note that this will display only the regular files ; you have to force the listing for the . and .. directories.

Ex 2.4: Find out the file attributes of the. and.. directories.

Whenever any change is made to a file, the time of such modification is stamped on the file by the system. The **-t** option presents the files in the order of their modification time, the last modified being placed first :

```
$ Is -t-1
total 278
-rw-r—r—      1 kumar    group    10411    May 10 15:56 chap02
-rw-r—r—      1 kumar    group    19514    May 10 13:45 chap0l
-rw-r- -r- -  1 kumar    group       74    May 9 16:20 user.lst
drwxr-xr-x    2 kumar    group       64    May 9 10:31 helpdir
drwxr-xr-x    2 kumar    group      320    May 9 09:57 progs
-rw-rw-rw-    1 kumar    group      392    Mar 18 08:57 emp2.1st
-rw-rw-rw-    1 kumar    group      236    Mar 18 07:57 empl.lst
-rw-r—r—      1 kumar    group     9156    Mar 12 1989 genie.sh
-rw-rw-rw-    1 kumar    group      114    Mar 11 17:37 desig.lst
-rw-r-r--     1 kumar    group    27012    Mar 11 17:30 prggen.sh\
-rw-rw-rw--   1 kumar    group       84    Feb 12 12:30 dept.lst
-rw-r-r--     1 kumar    group    62172    Dec 12 13:20 spcgen.sh
$_
```

You can also use the **-r** option with this option, in which case the files will be sorted in reverse order by the modification time rather than the filenames.

The **-R** (recursive) option, an enhancement from Berkeley, lists all files and sub-directories, as well as the files (and sub-directories) in the sub-directory. This is done recursively till there are no sub-directories:

```
S Is -R -1
total 278 3
-rw-r- -r- -  1 kumar    group    19514    May 10 13:45 chap0l
-rw-r- -r- -  1 kumar    group    10716    May 10 16:0 chap02
-rw-rw-rw-    1 kumar    group       84    Feb 12 12:30 dept.lst
-rw-rw-rw-    1 kumar    group      114    Mar 11 17:37 desig.lst
-rw-rw-rw-    1 kumar    group      236    Mar 18 07:57 emp.lstl
-rw-rw-rw-    1 kumar    group      392    Mar 18 08:57 emp.lst2
-rw-r- -r- -  1 kumar    group     9156    Mar 12 1989 genie.sh
drwxr-xr-x    2 kumar    group       64    May 9 10:31 helpdir
```

```
-rw-r—r—      1 kumar   group    27012   Mar 11 17:30 prggen.sh
drwxr-xr-x    2 kumar   group      320   May 9 09:57 progs
-rw-r—r—      1 kumar   group    62172   Dec 12 13:20 spcgen.sh
-rw-r- -r- -  1 kumar   group       74   May 9 16:20 user.lst
./helpdir:
total 1148
-rw-r- -r- -  1 kumar   group   581602   Jan 13 1989 uxmanual
./progs:
total 8
-rw-r—r—      1 kumar   group       44   Mar 12 14:51 dept.h
-rw-r—r—      1 kumar   group       12   Mar 12 14:52 dept.q
-rw-r—r—      1 kumar   group      154   Mar 12 14:52 emp.h
-rw-r—r—      1 kuma    group      742   Mar 12 14:53 emp.q
$_
```

The list shows the files in three sections—the ones under the home directory, and those under the sub-directories **helpdir** and **progs.** You may be somewhat baffled at the sub-directory naming conventions followed; **./helpdir** indicates that **helpdir** is a sub-directory under . (the current directory) and **./progs** represents the sub-directory **progs** under the current directory. Since **/usr/kumar** happens to be the current directory, the pathnames of the directory files get expanded to **/usr/kumar/helpdir** and **/usr/kumar/progs,** respectively.

TABLE 1

Options in Is

Option	*Description*
-x	Displays multicolumnar output (prior to Release 4)
-F	Marks executables with * and directories with /
-r	Sorts files in reverse order (ASCII collating sequence by default)
-1	The long listing showing seven attributes of a file
-d	Forces listing of a directory
-a	Shows all files including ., .. and those beginning with a dot
-t	Sorts files by modification time
-R	Recursive listing of all files in sub-directories
-u	Sorts files by access time (when used with the **-t** option)
-i	Shows i-node number of a file
-c	Sorts by time of change of the i-node
-s	Displays number of blocks used by a file
-1	One file per line (Release 4)

Ex 2.5. Use ls to produce a listing of all files (including the hidden ones) in the system, arranged in reverse sequence of their modification time.

ls has an enormous number of options, but the ones presented so far are adequate for the time being. The important options are summarised in Table 1, some of which have already been presented in this chapter.

4. Release 4 Enhancements

The default output of the **ls** command, in Release 4, is in multiple columns, similar to the output of the **lc** command in XENIX and the **-x** option used with previous releases of UNIX. To list out a single file in each line, Release 4 provides the **-1** (one) option.

DISPLAYING AND CREATING FILES—THE CAT COMMAND

You encountered this command, which is one of the most elementary and yet quite significant from a conceptual point of view. Like the **TYPE** command of MSDOS, **cat** is used to display the contents of a file. To do that for the file **dept-lst,** simply specify the filename as the argument:

```
$ cat dept.lst
01 | accounts | 6213
02 | admin | 5423
03 | marketing  | 6521
04 | personnel | 2365
05 | production | 9876
06 | sales | 1006

$-
```

This is the most common usage of this command, and can be utilised to display a large file also. In that case, you will find the output rolling off the screen too fast for you to read it. If that happens, you can freeze the scrolling by pressing *<Control-s>*, and resume scrolling by using *<Control-q>*.

cat, like several other UNIX commands, also accepts more than one filename as arguments. You can use it to display the first two chapters of this text :

```
$ cat chap01 chap02
```

The contents of the second file are shown immediately after the first file without any message or header information. What **cat** has done here is to concatenate the two files ; hence its name. Displaying a single file is only a special case of concatenation.

cat is normally used for displaying text files only. Executables, when seen with **cat,** will simply display junk. If you have non-printing ASCII characters in your input, then you can use cat with the -v option to display these characters.

cat is also useful for creating a file. Enter the command **cat**, followed by the > (the right chevron) character and the filename (for example **abc**), and press the <*Enter*> key. Enter the three lines of text as shown below, and then press <*Control-d*> :

$ **cat > abc**

A > symbol following the command means that the output goes to the filename following it. cat used in this way represents a rudimentary editor.

<*Control-d*>

$_

When the command line is terminated after hitting the <*Enter*> key, the terminal goes to the *input mode,* and the prompt vanishes. Enter the three lines, each followed by the <*Enter*> key. Finally use the <*Control-d*> character to signify the end of input to the system, **cat** used in this way resembles the **COPY CON** command of MSDOS, except that the *eof* (end-of-file) character in MSDOS is <*Control-z*>, which also gets into the file. UNIX uses the <*Control-d*> character instead, but this character doesn't get into the file. When this character is entered, the system understands that no further text input will be made. The file is written and the prompt returned. To verify this, simply "**cat**" this file :

$ cat abc

A > symbol following the command means that the

output goes to the filename following it. cat used

in this way represents a rudimentary editor.

$ _

You will learn how to change the eof character with the **stty** command, in Sec. 3.15. **cat** is a versatile command—it can display, concatenate, create and append to files.

Ex 2.6: What happens if you use cat chap0l chap0l chap0l ?

MAKING A DIRECTORY—THE MKDIR COMMAND

Just as in MSDOS, directories can be created by using the **mkdir** (make directory) command. The command is followed by the names of the directories to be created. A directory **pis** is created under the current directory by using this name as the argument to the command:

$ mkdir pis

$ _

Unlike MSDOS, however, a number of sub-directories can be created by one **mkdir** command:

$ mkdir pis pis/progs pis/data

$ _

This creates three sub-directories—**pis**, and two sub-directories in the just created sub-directory pis. The order of specifying the arguments is important; you obviously can't create a sub-directory' before creation of its parent directory. For instance, you can't enter

$ mkdir pis/progs pis/data pis

mkdir: can't access pis/.

mkdir: can't access pis/.

$_

The **pis** directory will still be created in spite of the terse message from the system about its failure to create the sub-directories **progs** and **data.**

Sometimes, the system refuses to create a directory :

$ mkdir test

mkdir: can't make directory test

$_

This can happen when the directory **test** already exists, or the user doesn't have adequate authorisation to create a directory. This will be considered in some detail while dealing with file permissions.

Ex 2.7: Try creating a directory in /bin and /tmp. Find out the directory attributes for each and guess why the system behaved in a different manner with them.

REMOVING A DIRECTORY— THE RMDIR COMMAND

The **rmdir** (**rem**ove **dir**ectory) command removes directories. Like **mkdir,** it can delete more than one directory with a single command. For instance, the three directories and the sub-directories that were just created with **mkdir** can be removed by using **rmdir** with a reversed set of arguments :

$ rmdir pis/progs pis/data pis ;

$_

Notice that when you delete sub-directories, as well as their parent directory **(pis,** in this case), the logic to be applied will have to be the reverse of the one used in creating directories with the **mkdir** command. The following sequence is invalid:

$ rmdir pis pis/progs pis/data

rmdir ; pis not empty

$_

This error message leads to two important rules that you should remember while deleting directories. You can't delete a directory unless it is empty. In this case the **pis** directory couldn't be removed because of the existence of the sub-directories **progs** and **data** under it. liven though the system flashed the error message, it silently deleted the two sub-directories **progs** and **data.** You can now delete the **pis** directory using the same command but with a single argument :

$ rmdir pis

$_

The other important rule is that you can't remove a sub-directory unless you are placed in a directory which is hierarchically *above* the one you have chosen to remove. For instance, you can't remove the **pis** directory by executing the command from the **pis** directory itself. Try doing that :

$ **cd pis**

$ **pwd**

/usr/kumar/pis

$ rmdir pis

rmdir: pis non-existent

$_

The **tnkdir** and **rmdir** commands work only in areas owned by the user. Generally, a user is the owner of his home directory, and he can create and remove sub-directories (as well as regular files) in this directory. When he creates files in any directory owned by him, he automatically becomes the owner of the files as well. By default, kumar doesn't have the right to perform these tasks in some other directory of which he is not the owner. (Ownership of files and directories is revealed in the third column of the **Is -1** listing.)

RELATIVE PATHNAMES

Suppose you have just changed your directory to **/usr/kumar/pis.** To switch to your home directory, you can always use the absolute pathname :

$ **pwd**

/usr/kumar/pis

$ cd /usr/kumar

$ pwd

/usr/kumar

$_

Every absolute pathname must trace its origin to *root*, as discussed earlier in this chapter. The first / indicates the *root* directory, while subsequent ones act as delimiters to sub-directories. This method can be inconvenient and tedious, especially when the absolute pathname is quite long, i.e. when you are located a number of "generations" away from *root*. If you have a long chain of sub-directories, then the use of an absolute pathname is an unsatisfactory solution to the problem of moving a single generation up the hierarchy :

```
$ pwd
/usr/kumar/progs/data/text
$ ed /usr/kumar/progs/data
$ pwd
/usr/kumar/progs/data
$_
```

Fortunately UNIX, like MSDOS, also permits use of a *relative pathname*, which locates a filename with respect to the current directory. In the topic on **Is** you discovered two hidden directories-— . and .. —indicating the current and parent directory, respectively. Using .. as an argument to **cd,** you can issue an instruction to move to the parent directory of**/usr/kumar/progs/data/text:**

i.e. the directory **/usr/kumar/progs/data :**

```
$ pwd
/usr/kumar/progs/data/text
$ cd.
. $ pwd
/usr/kumar/progs/data
$_
```

This method is compact and more useful when ascending the hierarchy. The command **cd** .. translates into this- "Change your directory to the parent of the current directory", You can also combine a number of such sets of.., separated, by /'s. However, when a / is used with... it acquires a different meaning; instead of moving down a level, it moves one level up. For instance, to move to /**usr**, you can always use **cd /usr.** Alternatively, you can also use a relative pathname :

```
$ pwd
/usr/kumar/pis
$ cd ../..
$ pwd
/usr
$_
```

The invisible directories . and .. can be used as shorthand notations for commands which use directory names as arguments. As a general rule, any command which uses the current directory as an argument can very well work with a single dot instead of the directory name. Similarly, the parent directory can always be replaced by two dots (..). Whether you should use absolute or relative pathnames depends solely on the comparative number of keystrokes required to describe the filename.

FILE PERMISSIONS—THE CHMOD COMMAND

Issue the **Is -1** command once again to list some files of the current directory :

$ Is -1 chap02 dept.lst dateval.sh

-rw-r- -r- -	1 kumar	group	20500	May 10 19:21 chap02
-rwxr-xr-x	1 kumar	group	890	Jan 29 23:17 dateval.sh
-rw-rw-rw-	1 kumar	group	84	Feb 12 12:30 dept.lst

$_

The first column contains all details of the permissions of a file. Observe that these permissions take the general form

-rwxrwxrwx

UNIX follows a three-tiered file protection system, which determines the access rights that you have for a file. Each tier represents a category, and consists of a string of **rs, ws** and **xs** to represent three types of permission, **r** indicates read permission, i.e. the file can be read by using, say, the **cat** command, **w** indicates write permission, i.e. you can direct some output to it. **x** indicates execute permission, i.e. the file can be executed as a program. If any of these permissions don't apply to a specific category, then a - (hyphen) occupies the respective slot. You can't read, write or execute every file; the authority to do that is entirely determined by the category of user you belong to, and the permissions applicable for that category. For example, if the file **chap0l** doesn't have any permission for any category, then this expression takes the form

----

If you now try to read this file, say with the **cat** command, the system notifies its failure:

$ cat chap0l

cat: can't open chap0l

$_

You can test the write permission by using

$ > chap0l

chap0l: can't create

$_

Any file is executed by simply invoking the filename :

$ chap0l

chap0l: execute permission denied

$_

If you set your permissions in this way, it not only protects the file from others, but from yourself also. Every time you need to access the file, you have to change the permissions. UNIX adopts a well-defined protection mechanism by which you can have different permissions for different categories of users. This is applicable for all three types of files, and it is important that you understand them. Little learning here can be a dangerous thing. If you don't set the permissions of your files correctly, then disaster could be in store for you.

Now, you can clearly see that the permissions are different for the three files. So, what are the default permissions when you create a file ? The question is easily answered by creating an ordinary file, and then observing the permissions. Use a special operator (>) to create an ordinary file named **note :**

$ > note

$ Is -1 note

-rw-r- -r- -   1 kumar   group   0   May 10 20:30 note

$_

The - at the leftmost position indicates an ordinary file. In this topic, the discussion will be confined to these files only. The first set of three permissions (**rw-**) pertains to the *owner* of the file, in this case, kumar, since the file was created by kumar. The owner has both read and write permissions but no executable permission. The second set (**r- -**) indicates only read permission for the *group* which owns the file, in this case, the default **group** to which kumar belongs. The third set (**r- -**) indicates only read permission for those who are neither the owner, nor belong to the group of the owner. This category is referred to as *others*, and, like the group, has only read access to the file.

This is an important security feature provided by UNIX in the sense that it write-protects a file from all except the owner of the file, though by default, all users have read access. By default, a file doesn't have executable permission. So how does one execute such a file ? To do that, the permissions of the file need to be changed. This is done with the **chmod** (change **mode)** command.

The chmod command is used to set the three permissions for all the three categories of users of a file. It can only be used by the owner of the file and uses the following syntax :

chmod *<category> <operation><permission><filename(s)>*

The command takes as its argument an expression, which combines the category, the operation and the type of permission, by making use of suitable abbreviations. The abbreviations used for the three elements of the expression are shown in Table 2:

TABLE 2

Abbreviations used by chmod

Category	*Operation*	*Attribute*
u - user	+ assign permission	r - read permission
g - group	- remove permission	w - write permission
o - others	= assign absolute permission	x - execute permission
a -all		

To assign executable permission to the owner (here referred to as *user)* of the file **note,** other permissions remaining the same, a suitable expression - needs to be framed by using the appropriate characters from each of the three columns. Since the file needs to be executable by the owner, the expression required will be **u+x**:

S. chmod u+x note

$ Is -1 note

```
-rwxr- -r- -    1 kumar    grou     0    May10 20:30 note
$_
```

The command assigns (**+**) executable (**x**) permission for the user (**u**) , other permissions remaining unchanged. You can now execute the file if you are the owner, but the other categories (i.e. group and others) still can't. To enable all of them to execute this file, you should use more than one character for the first column, each indicating the category :

S chrnod ugo+x

note S Is -I note

```
-rwxr-xr-x    1 kumar    group     0    May 10 20:30 note
$ _
```

The string **ugo** combines all the three categories—user, group and others. UNIX also offers a shorthand symbol a (all) to act as a synonym of the string. There is an even shorter form which combines these three categories. When it is not specified, the permission applies to all categories. So the previous sequence can be replaced by either of the following :

$ chmod a+x note

$ chmod +x note

chmod also accepts more than one filename in the command line. When you need to assign the same set of permissions to a group of files, all the filenames can be specified with a single **chrnod** command:

$ chmod u+x note notel note3
$ _

Permissions are removed with the - operator. To remove the read permission from both group and others, use the expression **go-r** :

```
$ Is -1 note
-rwxr- -r- -     1 kumar     group     0     May 10 20:30 note
$ chmod go-r note
$ Is -1 note
-rwx- - - - -    1 kumar     group     0     May 10 20:30 note
S _
```

More than one permission can also be set with the same command. Use multiple expressions with the , (comma) as delimiter. For instance, to restore the original permissions to the file **note,** you have to remove the executable permission from the user and assign read permission to the group and others:

```
$ chmod u-x,go+r note
$ Is -1 note
-rw-r—r—         1 kumar     group     0     May 10 20:30 note
$_
```

Setting write and executable permissions for others entails use of multiple permissions tor the same category. This can be done very easily:

```
$ chmod o+wx note
$ Is -1 note
-rw-r- -rwx      1 kumar     group     0     May 10 20:30 note
$ _
```

Ex 2.8. Create a file test1 and then use chmod to assign all permissions to the owner and remove all permissions from others.

Absolute assignment is also possible with the = operator. Unlike the + or - operators, it assigns only those permissions that are specified along with it, and removes other permissions. Thus, if you want to assign only read permission to all three categories, and remove all other permissions, then you can do it either by

$ chmod u-w,o-wx note

or simply by using the = operator in any of the three following ways :

$ chmod ugo=r note

$ chmod a=r note

$ chmod =r note

Remember that, irrespective of the privileges that are applicable to a file, only the owner of the file, in this case kumar, can change the file protection modes, kumar can't change the permissions of files owned by, say, Sharma. You will see how the super user can always tamper with a file owned by anybody. But for the time being, you can feel secure with the knowledge that the power to change file permissions rests only with the owner of the file, **chmod** is way ahead of **ATTRIB** of MSDOS, which also provides a rudimentary level of security, but not one that is unbreakable.

1. The Octal Notation

There is a short-hand notation available for changing the file permissions, **chmod** also takes a numeric argument that describes both the category as well as the permission. The notation takes the form of an octal representation of the permissions. Thus, read permission is assigned the value 4, write permission the value 2, and executable permission the value 1. When there is more than one permission associated with a particular category, the respective numbers are added. Like the = operator, the assignment is absolute.

To take a simple example, if a file has read and write permissions for the owner, then the octal representation of the permissions will be 4 + 2 = 6. When this exercise is repeated for the other categories, the result will be a three digit number, with each digit indicating the permissions for the category. The sequence followed is user, group and others.

You can use this method to assign read and write permission to all the three categories. Without octal numbers, you should normally be using **chmod ugo+rw note** to achieve the task. But now you can use a different method :

```
$ chmod 666 note
$ Is -1 note
-rw-rw-rw- 1 kumar group 0 May 10 20:30 note
$_
```

The **6** indicates read and write permissions (4 + 2). Thus, to restore the original permissions to the file, you need to remove the write permission (2) from the group and others :

```
$ chmod 644 note
$ Is -1 note
-rw-r- -r- - 1 kumar group 0 May 10 20:30 note
$ _
```

To absolutely assign all permissions to the owner, read and write permissions to the group and only executable permission to the others, you should use either of the two following forms:

```
$ chmod u=rwx,g-rw,o=x note
```

$ **Is -1 note .**

-rwxrw- - -x 1 kumar group 0 May 10 20:30 note

$ **chmod 76l note**

$ **Is -1 note**

-nvxrw- - -x 1 kumar group 0 May 10 20:30 note

$ _

Thus, **chmod** 777 **note** assigns all permissions to all categories, while **chmod 000 note** removes all permissions from all categories.

Ex 2.9: Assign to the file note, read and executable permissions for the owner, write permission fur the group, and executable permission for others.

Ex 2.10: How do the permissions change if you use the command chmod 753 note ?

Although the permissions dealt with here pertained only to ordinary files, you shouldn't assume-that the permissions correctly set for such a file automatically protects it. It is possible that a file can't be read even though it has read permission, and can be removed even when it is write-protected. Read and write access to a file set with **chmod** are also influenced by the permissions of the directory housing them. If the default directory permissions are not altered, then the **chmod** theory still applies. But if they are changed, then unusual things can happen. Though directory permissions are taken up in subsection 14.8.1, it is a good idea to know now what its default permissions are.

$ **Is -1 -d progs**

drwxr-xr-x 2 kumar group 320 May 9 09:57 progs

$ _

If you find unexpected things happening to your files, then check up the directory permissions. If the permissions differ from what you see here, then look up for remedial action.

2. Release 4 Enhancement

It is now possible to apply the **chmod** command recursively to all files and sub-directories in a directory. This is done with the -R (recursive) option, and needs only the directory name as the argument :

$ **chmod -R a+x progs**

$_

This makes all files and sub-directories in the directory executable by all users.

COPYING A FILE—THE CP COMMAND

The **cp** (copy) command copies a file or a group of files. Similar to the **COPY** command of MSDOS, **cp** creates an exact image of the file on the disk with a different name. The syntax requires at least two filenames to be specified in the command line. When both files are ordinary files, then the first is copied to the second. To copy the file **chap0l** to **unit1,** you have to use

$ cp chap0l unit1

$_

If the destination file doesn't exist, it will first be created before copying takes place. If not, it will simply be overwritten. UNIX assumes that a user is aware of the consequences of the actions he takes. It doesn't warn him if a file is to be overwritten. So, be careful when you choose your destination filename. Just check with an **Is** command whether or not the file exists.

If there is only one file to be copied, then the destination can be either an ordinary or a directory file. For example, to copy the file **chap0l** to the directory **progs,** you can use

$ cp chapOl progs/unit1

$_

or simply

$ cp chapOl progs

$_

In the first case, the file **chap0l** is copied to the directory **progs** with the name **unit1.** You can specify' the same filename ; identical filenames in two separate directories don't conflict with each other. In the second case, the explicit specification was avoided, which copied the file **chap0l** to the directory **progs.**

Ex 2.11: Try copying a file from /etc. How do the file attributes change when a file is copied in this way ?

If there are a group of files to be copied, then they can all be specified in the command line ; the syntax requires the destination file to be a directory, and copies the files into the directory. For example, to copy the various chapters of this text to the **progs** directory (provided it exists), you can write

$ cp chapOl chap02 chap03 progs

$_

All files after copying will retain their original names. It is not possible to specify target filenames for each file, and copying takes place only if the **progs** directory exists. Remember that if these files are already resident in **progs,** then they will simply be overwritten (unless used with the -1 option in Release 4).

One important point that should be remembered is that you can't copy a file if it is read protected, and can't create a copy if the destination file or directory is write protected. You can't also copy a file into a directory you don't own. For instance, kumar can't copy the files he owns to a directory which he doesn't own, say **/usr/sharma :**

$ **cp chap0l /usr/sharma**

cp: can't create /usr/sharma/chap0l

$ _

even though Sharma may usually be able to copy these files from kumar's directory !

$ **pwd**

usr/sharma

$ **cp /usr/kumar/chap0l .**

$ **ls -1 chap0l**

-rw-r—r— 1 Sharma group 19514 May 10 23:45 chap0l

$ _

When Sharma copies the file **chap0l** owned by kumar, he then becomes the owner of the copy. He can now manipulate the file permissions with **chmod** Note that the new naming convention for the current directory (.) permits you to enter simply a . as the destination filename. This copies the file **chap0l** in the directory **/usr/kumar** to Sharma's current directory. The destination file obviously retains its original name.

Release 4 Enhancements

This problem of overwriting an existing file by the copying process has been taken care of in Release 4. The **-1** (interactive) option, originally a Berkeley enhancement, used with **cp,** warns the user before overwriting the destination file. If the file **unit1** exists, then you get a different response with the latest release :

$ **cp -1 chap0l unit1**

cp: overwrite unit1 ? y

$_

A **y** at this prompt overwrites the file, while any other response (including n) terminates the process.

It is now possible to copy an entire directory structure using the **-r** (recursive) option. This is an idea borrowed from the **copy** command that is found in some UNIX systems (e.g. XENIX). The following command copies all files and sub-directories in **progs** to **newprogs:**

$ cp -r progs newprogs

$_

Since the process is recursive and copies all the files resident in the sub-directories, **cp** here has to create the sub-directories as well, if it doesn't find them during the copying process.

DELETING FILES—THE RM COMMAND

Files can be deleted with **rm** (remove). Unlike its MSDOS counterpart **DEL,** it can delete more than one file with a single instruction. It normally operates silently and has, therefore, to be used with a great deal of caution. When invoked without options, it deletes the files specified in the command line. The following command deletes the first three chapters of the text:

$ rm chapOl chap02 chap03

$_

rm won't normally remove a directory, but it can remove files from one. You can remove the two chapters from the **progs** directory without having to **"cd"** to it :

$ rm progs/chap0l progs/chap02

$_

You may sometimes require to delete all the files of a directory as part of a cleaning-up operation.

This method of specifying all the filenames explicitly in. the command line is obviously a poor solution. You will see how the UNIX system uses certain special characters which can be used to frame a pattern for matching more than one file. One of the characters that you will be using is the * (asterisk), which is interpreted to include all files in the current directory. This character was also used in an argument to **Is,** in the previous chapter. Using this symbol, you can easily delete all files in this directory :

$ rm *

$ _

MSDOS users, beware ! When you delete files in this fashion, the system won't prompt you with the message **"Are you sure ?"** or **"All files in directory will be deleted",** before removing the files ! The **$** prompt will return silently, suggesting that the work has been done. The * used here is equivalent to V used in MSDOS.

When **rm** is invoked with options, different things start happening. The -i (interactive) option makes the command prompt the user with each filename and a ?, before acting on it:

$ rm -i chap0l chap02 chap03

chap0l: ?*y*

chap02: **?n**

chap03: ?y

$_

If you press a **y** after this message, then the file will be deleted. This process will be repeated till all the files in the list are displayed. A **y** removes the file, any other response leaves the file undeleted.

When used with the **-r** option, **rm** performs a deadly recursive search for all sub-directories and files within these sub-directories, and then deletes all these files (as well as the sub-directories !). **rm** will not normally remove directories, but when used with this option, it will. Therefore when you issue the command

$ **rm -r** *

$ _

you will be deleting all files in the current directory, as well as all files and sub-directories in the sub-directories **helpdir** and **progs,** as well as the sub-directories themselves. If you don't have a backup, then these files will be lost forever. -

rm won't delete any file if it is write protected, but may prompt you with its mode (in octal) before it decides to delete them. The **-f** option overrides this protection also. It will force removal even if the files are write protected. So the deadliest usage of the command will be

$ **rm -r -f** *

$_

Note that you can't normally delete a file which you don't own. The default permissions for any ordinary file is, you will recall, read and write permission for the owner, and read permission only for the group and others. That is why kumar can't delete a file in **/usr/sharma,** unless Sharma has negligently assigned write permission to the group or others. If kumar belongs to the same group as sharma, all he needs is write permission for the group. If not, he needs to have write permission for others. But then, in that case, any user can delete that file! And a file once a file once deleted can't be recovered. UNIX doesn't have its own PCTOOLS or NORTON UTILITIES that MSDOS does.

RENAMING FILES—THE MV COMMAND

The **mv** (**move**) command simply renames a file or a group of files. It is similar to the **REN** command of MSDOS, and the syntax is similar to the **cp** command, **mv** doesn't create a copy of the file ; it merely renames it. No additional space is consumed, only the directory housing the file is updated with the new name. To rename the file **chap01** to **man01,** you should use

$ mv chap01 man01

$ _

If the destination file doesn't exist it will be created. Unlike MS, however, **mv** overwrites the destination file if it exists. So be careful, again.

Like **cp**, a group of files can be *moved*, but only to a directory. The following command

$ mv chapOl chap02 chap03 progs

$_

moves the files **chap0l, chap02 and chap03** to the progs directory. (This feature is not available in MSDOS.)

There is one important distinction, however, with the **cp** command, **mv** can be used to rename a directory, provided that both source and target directories have the same parent. The command

$ mv pis perdir

$_

renames the directory **pis** to **perdir.**

You may be surprised to learn that the **cp** and **mv** commands are actually a single file, operating in two different *modes*. This is possible because UNIX lets a file have two different names, and the operation that is performed depends on the name by which it is invoked. If you see the listing of these files (in the **/bin** directory), then you will observe that they have multiple links.

Ex 2.12: There is one more file which has a link with cp and mv. Locate it in the/bin directory.

Release 4 Enhancements

As in **cp**, Release 4 comes 10 the rescue of the user if he afraid that he may overwrite a file accidentally. If he is too lazy to check up with **Is** whether the target file exists, he can use the **-i** option which prompts him with the same message that he gets while using **cp** with the same option. This option again is a Berkeley enhancement, which has now been included in Release 4.

A single **mv** statement can now be used to move all files and sub-directories recursively to another directory. This requires two directory names to be specified as the two arguments of the command. No separate option is called for, and it is not necessary for these two directories to have the same parent. While moving files and sub-directories, **mv** creates them as and when required during the move process.

REVIEW

This chapter featured files and treated them in a simplistic manner. A file contains just what you put into it, and the UNIX system maintains the attributes of a file in a separate area of the disk, and not in the file itself. It is however, necessary to divide these files into three categories —ordinary, directory and device. While most commands work with all files, the significance of the file attributes depends on the type of file being used. The inverted tree structure brings all these files within a single family or file system. Every file in this family has a pathname, which traces its ultimate ancestry to *root.* Though you can write into an ordinary file, writing into a directory is the sole prerogative of the system.

The **Is** command is used to display the various file attributes, and you can change at least one of them with the **chmod** command. You also observed the hidden directories . and .., which can be used by any command, with the current or parent directory as argument. They are particularly useful in framing relative pathnames. Though UNIX makes little distinction between the various types of files, this wasn't really established in this chapter. You used exclusive commands to handle directories (**pwd, cd, mkdir** and **rmdir),** and equally exclusive ones to handle ordinary files (**cat, cp** and **rm**). Later chapters will gradually unfold this aspect of the UNIX philosophy.

Internally the file system is quite complex, and some of these internals are featured, which takers a second look at it. The owner of a file usually reserves the sole right to tamper with a file's contents or its attributes. Ownership is an important aspect in the UNIX system, extending beyond files and into processes. You will discover that the file attributes for directories and devices differ a great deal from those of ordinary files. You will also see other file permissions having far-reaching implications. Moreover, while there is a single file system tree, it can spread over many physical devices. To baffle you further, one physical device can contain more than one file system, each with its own *root.* The revisit to the file system will examine these aspects in some detail.

Most of this textbook is.concerned with all the wonderful commands that you can find in the UNIX system, Each command is treated as a black box ; you need only to know what it does, and not how it does it. There are a large number of commands in the UNIX repertoire.

24

Programming with the Shell

You have seen the role played by the shell in processing a command line and rebuilding it in a form that the command understands. But the activities of the shell are not restricted to command interpretation alone; they involve much more than that. The shell also has rudimentary programming features which, coupled with the use of UNIX commands and other programs, make it an extremely useful programming language. In this chapter and the next one, you will be exploring these features in some detail.

The scope of shell programming often goes beyond the limits of conventional languages. In addition to the external commands (like **grep**, **sed**, etc.), you can use the entire set of shell's internal commands inside a shell program. These internal commands can be stringed together as a language, with its own variables, conditionals and loops. What makes shell programs powerful is that an external command can be used as a control command for any of the shell's constructs. The language has features borrowed from C, though most of its constructs are compact and simpler to use than those in C. In these two chapters, the shell's built-in commands will be termed as *statements*.

These two chapters also pursue and finally realise the central objective of the book-application development. You will learn how to develop professional grade applications using the programming features of the shell. You will be designing menus, data entry and validation routines, and other useful scripts which take care of the daily chores. However, shell programs run slower than those written in high-level languages, and the shell is often used as an intermediate platform to finally code the program in C. But it speed is not a hurdle (especially with modern hardware), or if you have a shell compiler installed in your system, the shell is certainly a very fascinating language which every serious UNIX user must know.

The discussions in these two chapters are drawn up with reference to the Bourne shell. However, all the features are equally applicable to the C and Korn shells. If you are using the latter, then you should look up Appendix A for an understanding of its exclusive features.

SYSTEM VARIABLES

The use of shell variables, and noted the role played by the shell in evaluating them before the command is executed. While you are free to set up your own variables, there are a number of variables, that are separately set by the system, some during the booting sequence, and some after logging in. These variables are called *system variables*. You need to know the significance of most of them because they determine the environment in which you work. You can even alter their values to your liking. To have a complete list of all these variables you can use the **set** statement (a concise list is displayed here).

```
$ set
HOME=/usr/kumar
IFS=

MAIL=/usr/mail/kumar
PATH=/bin:/usr/bin:
PS1=$
PS2=>
SHELL=/bin/sh
TERM=ansi
$_
```

By convention, such built-in variable names are defined in upper case. If you use variables of your own, then for the purpose of distinguishing them from the ones built in, it is preferable to use lowercase names only. The important thing to remember is that the shell, which expands these variables, is sensitive to case. Thus, the variable **x** is not the same as **X**. The significance of some of the important system variables is presented in the following.

1. The PATH Variable

This sets the search path for any executable command, MSDOS users need no further elaboration as the same variable is used for the same purpose in that system. However, in UNIX, you can find out its value only by echoing a **$**-prefixed variable name:

```
$ echo $ Path
/bin:/usr/bin:
$_
```

This shows a list of directories (in order of precedence) that have to be scanned by the shell while hunting for a command. In this case, the search will begin from **/bin**, through/ **usr/bin**. and finally to the current directory indicated by a . (dot). This sequence makes the commonly used UNIX commands universally available to every user, since, by default, every user has the directories **/bin** and **/usr/bin** included in his **PATH** variable.

You can modify this value to include another directory name in its list. For example, you can store all your shell programs in a separate directory named **progs**, and then modify **PATH** to include this directory in its search path:

```
$ PATH = $ PATH:/usr/kumar/progs
$ echo $PATH
/bin:/usr/bin:.:/usr/kumar/progs
$_
```

The assignment uses the pathname/**usr/kumar/progs** to be appended to the existing value of the variable.

Ex 1: If you have a program named awk in your current directory, how can you execute it?

2. The HOME Variable

When you log in, UNIX normally places you in a directory named after your login name. This directory is called the *home* or *login* directory, and is controlled directly by the variable **HOME**. In the chapter on system administration (subsection 15.3.1) you will see how this variable, in turn, is set by a certain field in the file/**etc/passwd**. You can switch from any directory to your home directory by using the evaluated variable **$HOME** as an argument to the **cd** command:

```
$ pwd
/usr/bin
$ cd $HOME
$ pwd
/usr/kumar
$_
```

The **cd** command used without arguments also resets the current directory to the directory assigned to **HOME**. In other words, simple invocation of the command **cd** will mean **cd $HOME**.

3. The IFS Variable

IFS contains a string of characters which are used as word separators in the command line. The string normally consists of the space, tab and the newline characters. All these characters are invisible, but the blank line following it only suggests that the newline character is part of this string. You can confirm the contents of this variable by taking its octal dump:

```
$ echo      "$IFS" I od-bc
0000000     \t              \n              \n
            040     011     012     012
0000004
$_
```

The space character is represented by the ASCII octal value 040 , while **\t** and **\n** universally represent the tab and newline characters, respectively. You can reset the value of this variable to a #, for instance, and use this character as the word delimiter:

```
$ IFS=#
$ cat#emp.Ist
```

Ex 2: If reassigned in this way, does it mean that the space can't be used as the delimiter any more?

You will sometimes require to change the value of **IFS** while parsing a group of characters on a different delimiter. This will be done in Sec. 16 while using the **set** statement.

4. The MAIN Variable

MAIL determines where any mail addressed to the user is to be stored. In the previous chapter, mention was made of this variable, with the remark that all incoming mail is stored in the directory defined by this variable. This directory is searched by the shell every time a user logs in. If any information is found here, then the shell informs the user of this with the familiar message "**you have mail**".

Ex 3: If kumar defines his MAIL variable as MAIL=/usr/sharma, can be expect to see his mail in sharma's directory?

5. The Variables PSI and PS2

UNIX has two prompts, stored in **PS1** and **PS2**. The primary prompt string **PS1** is the one you normally see ($). You have seen, especially while using the **sed** and **awk** commands, that a multi-line command makes the shell respond with a >. This is the secondary prompt string, indicated by **PS2**. Normally, **PS1** and **PS2** are set to the characters $ and >, respectively.

You can change the primary prompt string to C> if you find the MSDOS environment more reassuring:

```
$ PSI="C>"
C>_
```

To reset this variable to the familiar $, simply make the reassignment at the C> prompt:

```
C> PSI= "$"
$_
```

Ex 4. How could you use the $ within double quotes, and still have it interpreted literally?

While the $ is the most commonly used primary prompt string, the system administrator uses the # as the prompt while working in the *root* directory, or as a super user. You should avoid using this character because that can give the impression to other users that you are the system administrator, which you may not be!

6. The SHELL Variable

SHELL determines the type of shell that a user sees on logging in. Today, there are a host of shells that accompany any UNIX system, and you can select the one you like the most. Besides the Bourne shell, which is the most popular shell in the UNIX world, the C and Korn shells have also carved out a niche for themselves, because of certain inherent advantages. The C shell is known by the program **csh**, and the Korn shell by **ksh**.

If you wish to use either of these as the default shell, then the variable needs to be assigned accordingly. However, this assignment is made by the system after reading a field in the file **/etc/passwd**. If you wish to change the setting permanently, then this file needs to be edited. The system administrator usually sets up your login shell while creating a user account, though he can change it whenever you request him to.

7. The TERM Variable

TERM indicates the terminal type being used. There are some utilities which are terminal dependent and they require to know the type of terminal you are using. One of them is the **vi** editor, which makes use of a control file in a sub-directory under the directory **/usr/lib/terminfo**. If **TERM**, is not set correctly, **vi** won't work, and the display will be faulty. On 80286-based systems running XENIX, ansi (**A**merican **N**ational **S**tandards **I**nstitute) terminals are often used. This textbook was developed on a machine using one.

Now that you understand variables, you can use some of them in shell scripts. It is the facility to integrate these variables with command arguments that makes these variables so useful and easy to work with. The script **sysvar.sh** makes use of some of them:

```
$ cat sysvar.sh
# This script explains the functions of the system variables
echo "Our home directory is $HOME" #Used by the cd command
echo "The two prompt strings are $PSI and $PS2"
echo "And the path for command search is $PATH"
$_
```

All programming languages use a character or word to specify comments in the programs; the shell uses the # character for this purpose. This character is normally the first character in any line, though it can be placed anywhere else. Notice that comments have been made, both at the beginning of a line and after specifying a command. The shell simply ignores any text placed after this character. Make the file executable, and then run the program:

```
$ chmod u + x sysvar. sh
$ sysvar. sh
Our home directory is /usr/kumar
The two prompt strings are $ and >
And the path for command search is /bin:/usr/bin:
$_
```

The variables have been evaluated by the shell, and echoed by the program. But how were the variables defined in the first place? The next section answers this question.

THE SCRIPT EXECUTED DURING LOGIN TIME- THE. profile

Issue the **ls -a** command to locate the **.profile** in your login directory. This, you will recall, is the **AUTOEXEC.BAT** file of UNIX, and mention of this script has been made several times throughout the text. This file is created when a user is added to the system by the system administrator. It is really a shell script, which is executed by the shell when one logs in. These "profiles" can be quite large, depending on users' requirements, but an abridged one should do for the purpose of initial comprehension:

```
$cat .profile
#User $HOME/ .profile - commands executed at login time

HOME=/usr/kumar/progs
PATH =/bin:/usr/bin::/usr/kumar/progs
MAIL =/usr/mail/kumar #mailbox location
IFS =

PSI = $
PS2 =>
echo "Today's date is `date`"
cd
echo "You are now in the $HOME directory"
calendar
news
$_
```

Some of the system variables have been assigned in this script. The later statements show that the file has been edited to taste. The **HOME** variable here is set to the **progs** sub-directory, so that when you use **cd** without arguments, you will switch to this directory. Note that you won't be placed in this directory when you log in; that is determined by **/etc/passwd**. It is quite expedient to store the **calendar** and **news** commands in the file, so that you are reminded of your immediate engagements, and can also look at any messages from the system administrator.

The **.profile** alters the operating environment of a user, which remains in effect throughout the login session. That is why every time you make changes to it, you should log out and log in again (for the time being, at least). The file is routinely executed during login time by the shell in a special manner. It is not easy to execute it in the way you execute a shell script. In the next chapter you will know why that is so. The following output is seen on the terminal when a user logs in with the login name **kumar:**

```
    Todays date is Fri Feb 22 12.30:II EST 1991
    You are now in the /usr/kumar/progs directory
    The payslips have to be printed on Feb 25
  meeting (root) Fri Feb 22 09:02:10 1991
    There is a weekly review meeting with the manager
    in Feb 26, 1991 at 10.30 a.m.
$_
```

You must learn to exploit the features of this startup file, because there are certain things you can do with this file which are difficult or impossible to do otherwise. By manipulating these variables and adding and modifying statements in this file, you can customise your operating environment to suit your requirements.

DATA IN THE SAME FILE - THE HERE DOCUMENT

So far, you have used the < redirection symbol to redirect the standard input to come from a file. While this is the normal and most frequently used method of handling input, there are occasions when the data involved is fairly limited. It will be a better idea if it can be kept in the shell script requiring it. Fortunately, the shell offers a mechanism of doing so; it is the << symbol. This symbol is often referred to as a *here document*, signifying that the data is here rather than in a separate file.

Any command using standard input can also have the input from a here document. This represents the fourth source of standard input. But it is discussed here because it is most useful when placed in a shell script. However, the following example shows that it can be used at the prompt, too:

```
$ grep director << end
> 5678 | sumit chakrobarty    | d.g.m       | marketing   | 19/04/43 | 6000
> 1006 | chanchal singhvi    | director    | sales       | 03/09/38 | 6700
> 2476 | anil aggarwal       | manager     | sales       | 01/05/59 | 5000
> 2345 | j.b saxena          | g.m.        | marketing   | 12/03/45 | 8000
> 9876 | jai sharma          | director    | production  | 12/03/50 | 7000
3564 > | sudhir Agarwal      | executive   | personnel   | 06/07/47 | 7500
> end
1006 | chanchal singhvi      | director    | sales       | 03/09/38 | 6700
9876 | jai sharma            | director    | production  | 12/03/50 | 7000
```

The standard input symbol here is indicated by the here document (<<), followed by the data (six lines of text), and a delimiter (the string **end**). The shell treats every line following the command, and delimited by the string **end**, as input to the command. Judging by the appearance, of the **PS2** prompt, you can say that the accompanying text following the here document symbol is also part of the command line. When this sequence is placed inside a script, execution is faster, because a single file is called up from the file system (the command **grep**).

The here document is also quite useful when used with commands which don't accept a filename as argument. You issued the **mail** command to send messages to any user by utilising redirected standard input in this way:

```
$ mail sharma < letter.msg
```

Some of the commands used in electronic mail (like **mail, write** and **wall**) don't accept filenames as arguments; they always use the standard input as the source of input. However, if the message is short (which any **mail** message is normally expected to be), then you can have the **mail** command, as well as the message to be mailed, in the same script.

```
$ cat updt.sh
flname= 'ls -t emp*.lst | head -l'        #most recently modified file
awk -f empawk5.awk $flname lp             #used by awk
mail sharma << marker
Your program for printing the biodata has been executed on 'date'. Check the print queue
The updated file is known as $flname
marker
$_
```

This script runs an **awk** program and then mails a message taken from a here document, to the user. Because the here document is actually part of the command invoking, it you can use command substitution ('**date**') and variables (**flname**) in the input. The advantage of using this method is that no separate file needs to be opened to take input; it comes from the same file.

With the discussion of the here document, all the possible sources of the standard input and standard output steams have now been covered. Six sets of operators are required to make use of them; -, l, >, >>, < and <<. Later in this chapter, you will be using this special form of redirection to validate input from a user.

Throughout this chapter, you will be devising scripts to search for a single pattern or more from a file. This script will be enhanced progressively to include more features as and when a shell feature is introduced. The first of these scripts is taken up in the next section.

4. MAKING SHELL SCRIPTS INTERACTIVE - THE read STATEMENT

The **read** statement is the shell's internal tool for taking input from the standard input. Functionally, it is similar to the **INPUT** statement of **BASIC**, and the **scanf ()** function in C. But it has one or two interesting features. It can be used with one or more variables to make shell scripts interactive. Input supplied through the standard input during interaction is read into these variables. The script **emp 1.sh** uses the statement to take the search string and the filename from the terminal:

```
$ cat emp 1.sh
# Script: emp 1.sh - Interactive version
# The pattern and filename to be supplied by the user

echo "\nEnter the pattern to searched: \c"
read pname
echo"\nEnter the file to be used: \c"
read flname
echo"\nSearching for $pname from file $flname\n"
grep "$pname" $flname
echo "\nSelected records shown above\n"
$_
```

Shell variables have been used to take input from the user. The echo statement has also been used with the required escape sequences to insert blank lines between textual matter. During runtime, you have better readability when messages are separated with such blank lines. The sequence \c, you will recall, places the cursor at the end of echo's argument, rather than on the next line. Run it, and specify the input accordingly:

```
$ emp 1. sh
Enter the pattern to be searched ; director
Enter the file to be used: emp2. lst
Searching for director from file emp2.lst
9876 | jai sharma        | director    | production    | 12/03/50  | 7000
2365 | barun sengupta    | director    | personnel     | 11/05/47  | 7800
Selected records shown above
$_
```

When the script is run, it pauses at two points. First, a waits for the pattern to be entered. Input the string **director**, and press the <*Enter*> key. The value is assigned to the variable **pname** Next, it asks for the filename; enter the string **emp2. lst,** and also press <*Enter*>. This time the variable flname gets assigned. In line with UNIX tradition, the input values are assigned to variables only after the <*Enter*> key is pressed. After accepting these inputs from the keyboard, the gıep and echo statements are executed.

read can also be used to make the script pause without accepting any input from the user. It can simply wait for <*Enter*> key to be pressed for program execution to continue (somewhat like the **WAIT** command of dBASE). You can also condense the above program to some extent by accepting both the arguments in one line; a single **read** can also be used with two or more variable names. Create a file **emp 2.sh,** and then execute if:

```
$ cat emp2. sh
echo "Press the <Enter> key to continue \c"
read pause
tput clear # to clear the screen
echo "\nEnter the pattern and the filename:\c"
read pname flname
grep "Spname" $flname
$_
```

When the script is executed, it pauses once, clears the screen, and then accepts two arguments in one line. Remember to separate the two inputs by while space:

```
$ emp2. sh
Press the <Enter> key to continue <Enter>

<...Screen clears...>

Enter the pattern and the filename: director emp 1. 1st
1006 | chanchal singhvi  | director    | sales         | 03/09/38  | 6700
6521 | lalit chowdury    | director    | marketing     | 26/09/45  | 8200
$_
```

Ex 5 What is the value of the variable pause after execution of this script?

What happens if the number of arguments supplied is less than the number of variables accepting them? The answer is that, after the assignments are made in the usual manner, any left-over variables will simply remain unassigned. But when the condition is reversed, i.e. the number of arguments exceeds the number of variables, you have an unusual response:

$ emp2. sh

Press the <Enter> key to continue <*Enter*>

<...*Screen clears....*>

Enter the pattern and the filename: **director emp 1. 1st emp 2. 1st**

emp 1.lst:1006	I chanchal singhvi	I director	I sales	I 03/09/38	I 6700
emp 1. lst:6521	I lalit chowdury	I director	I marketing	I 26/09/45	I 8200
emp2. 1st:9876	I jai sharma	I director	I production	I 12/03/50	I 7000
emp2.lst:2365	I barun sengupta	I director	I personnel	I 11/05/47	I 7800

$_

What has actually happened is that the word **director** got assigned to the variable **pname,** and the remaining words **emp 1. lst** and **emp2. lst** were assigned to the leftover variable **flname.** This is the format used by **grep** while scanning multiple files for the string.

Ex 6: How can you make the script take the input from a file instead of the keyboard?

SPECIAL PARAMETERS RELATED TO COMMAND LINE ARGUMENTS

Shell procedures accept arguments in another situation too — when you specify them in the command line itself. The C language also accepts arguments in this way. You do that most of the time when you use UNIX tools (which are written in C) in a non-interactive manner by specifying the arguments in the command line. This non-Interactive method of specifying arguments is quite useful for scripts requiring few inputs. It also forms the basis of developing tools which can be used with redirection and pipelines.

When arguments are specified along with the name of the shell procedure, they are assigned to certain special "variables", or "parameters". The first argument is read by the shell into a special parameter $1, the second argument into $2, and so on. These variables are appropriately called *positional parameters*. You can't technically call them shell variables, because all variables are evaluated with a $ before the variable name. In the case of $1, say, you really don't have a variable 1 which is evaluated with $.

Apart from these positional parameters, there are a few other special parameters used by the shell; some of them pertain to the positional parameters already mentioned. For example, the parameter $* stores the complete set of positional parameters as a single string. The parameter $# is set to the number of arguments specified. This lets you design scripts which check whether the right number of arguments have been entered. The command itself is stored in the parameter $0. The next script illustrates these features:

```
$ cat emp3.sh
echo "Program: $0
The number of arguments specified is $#
The arguments are $*"
grep "$1" $2
echo "\nJob Over"
$_
```

Invoke this script with the pattern **director** and the filename **emp1.lst** as the two arguments

```
$ emp3.sh director emp1. lst
Program: emp3.sh
The number of arguments specified is 2
The arguments are director emp 1.lst
1006    | chanchal singhvi    | director    | sales        | 03/09/38   | 6700
6521    | lalit chowdury      | director    | marketing    | 26/09/45   | 8200

Job Over
$_
```

When arguments are specified in this way, the first word (the command itself) is assigned to the special parameter $0, the second word (the first argument) to $1, and the third word (the second argument) to $2. You can use more positional parameters in this way up to $9 (and using the shift statement, you can go beyond). All the arguments have been collectively displayed with the notation $*, while the number of arguments have been correctly shown as 2, using the symbol $#.

Since the script accepts three arguments, how do you search for a multi-worded pattern, say **barun sengupta** from the **file emp2. lst**? When the string is quoted, the shell understands it to be a single argument:

```
$ | emp3.sh "barun sengupta" emp2.lst
Program: emp3.sh
The number of arguments specified is 2
The arguments are barun sengupta emp2.lst
2365 | barun sengupta    | director    | personnel | 11/05/47 7800

Job Over
$_
```

Here, the entire string **barun sengupta** was assigned to $1, and the filename **emp2.lst** to $2. $# correctly identifies the number of arguments, in spite of quoting.

There is one more parameter related to command line arguments. It is the $@, which bears a resemblance to $*. However, its subtle difference will be brought out after we discuss loops at the end of this chapter (Sec. 15)

OTHER SPECIAL PARAMETERS

This section deals with the other special parameters which the shell understands. These are not related to command line arguments, but more to the command itself. Two of them hold the PID number of the current shell and the last background job, while the third remembers whether the last command was executed successfully.

1. PID of the Current Shell - the $$

How you can refer to the PID number of login shell as $$. When you log in, the shell stores the process-id of itself. This value is seen in the output of the **ps** command. You can always find out its value separately by evaluating the parameter $$.

```
$ echo $$
49
$_
```

Since the PID is numeric, it is often used to form temporary files which are not likely to conflict with any file that may exist in the current directory, for instance the output of a filtering action. The following sequence uses a file named 49 to temporarily hold a **sed** output before being moved out to the original file:

```
$ echo $$
49
$ sed 's/UNIX/& System V/g' text1 > $$
$ mv $$ text1
$-
```

You can also use this parameter to log out of the system by "surely" killing your login shell"

```
$ kill -9 $$
login:
```

2. PID of the Last Background Job — the $1

$! stores the PID number of the last background job, the same number that the shell throws out whenever the & is affixed to a command. Note that, when you run more than one job in the background, this parameter stores the PID number of only the last one. Now, instead of using the ps command to find out the PID number, and then using the **kill** command after it, you can do that in one shot. Thus,

```
$ sort -o emp.lst emp.lst &
345
$ kill $!
$-
```

kills the last background job running on the machine, and owned by the user. This is a shorthand method of killing the job, which can also be done by issuing **kill 345**.

3. Exit Status of a Command

Before the next parameter is taken up, you should know the consequences of a command not executing according to your expectations. You used UNIX commands in every chapter: some commands executed in the way you wanted, and some didn't, For example, the command

```
$ cat abc
cat: can't open abc
$_
```

generates as error message to the standard error, probably on account of the file **abc** not being present or being unreadable. Similarly, **grep** simply returns the $ prompt when the pattern is not found. Every command returns a value after execution. This value is called the *exit status* or *return value* of the command. A command is said to be true if it executes successfully, and false if it fails. The **cat** command shown above didn't succeed, and is thus said to return a false exit status. And if **grep** can find and display the pattern, it is said to return a true exit status.

These return values are of great importance to the programmer because he can devise program logic which branches into different paths, depending on the success or failure of a command. For example, there is no point in continuing with script execution if an important file doesn't exist or can't be read. The shell offers a number of operators and statements which test these values and make use of them.

4. The Exit Status of the Last Command - the $?

The parameter $? stores the exit status of the last command. It has the value 0 if the command succeeds, and a non-zero value if it falls. For example, if **grep** fails to find a pattern, then the return value is 1, and if the file scanned is unreadable in the first place the return value is 2. In any case, return values exceeding 0 are to be interpreted as failure of the command. Try using the **grep** command in different ways:

```
$ grep director emp.lst > /dev/null: echo $?
```

```
0
$ grep manager emp.lst >/dev/null ; echo $?
1
$ grep manager emp3. lst >/dev/null; echo $?
grep: can't open emp3.lst
2
$_
```

grep is one command which returns these values; 1 if the pattern can't be found, and 2 if the file can't be opened. All commands, however, don't behave in a similar manner. For example: neither **sed** nor **awk** returns a non-zero value if a pattern can't be located in its input. This is the reason why it is advantageous to use **grep** rather than **sed** and **awk** in shell scripts if the course of the script is to be determined by the success or otherwise of locating the pattern.

These special parameters will be used over and over again in shell programs, and it is important that you understand their meanings and significance right at this stage. They are reproduced in Table 1.

TABLE 1

Special Parameters Used by Shell

Shell parameter	*Significance*
$0	Name of executed command
$*	Complete set of positional parameters —$ 1, $2, etc.
$#	Number of arguments specified in command line
$@	Same as $* except when enclosed in double quotes
$S	PID number of current shell
$!	PID number of last background job
$?	Exit status of last command

You should note that all assignments to the positional and special parameters are automatically made by the shell. You can't really tamper with their values, except in an indirect fashion. But you can use them to great advantage in several ways.

CONDITIONAL EXECUTION — THE LOGICAL OPERATORS && AND | |

In a previous script, you must have observed that there was no mechanism to prevent the display of the message. **"Selected records shown above"** if the pattern wasn't found. That is because you had not used the information of the exit status of the **grep** command to generate an appropriate message. The shell provides two operators to control execution of a command depending on the success of failure of the previous command. They are && and | |.

The && operator is used by the shell in the same sense as it is used in **awk** and C. It delimits two commands; the second command is executed only when the first succeeds. You can use it with the grep command in this way:

```
$ grep 'director' emp 1.lst && echo "pattern found in file"
1006    | chanchal singhvi    | director    | sales        | 03/09/38   | 6700
6521    | lalit chowdury      | director    | marketing    | 26/09/45   | 8200
pattern found in file
$_
```

You can also conditionally execute more than one command by using a set of parentheses to enclose the command group. In the following example, the **date** and **echo** commands will be executed as a group only when the **grep** command succeeds:$

```
$ grep 'director' emp.lst && (date; echo "pattern found")
```

Ex 7 Write a command sequence to search for a pattern only if the input file exists.

The || operator is execute the command following it only when the previous command fails. If you "grep" a pattern from a file without success, then you can notify the failure:

```
$ grep 'manager' emp2.lst || echo "Pattern not found"
Pattern not found
$_
```

You can also use more than one operator in the same command line. All commands barring the first will be conditionally executed:

```
$ cat emp2.lst >/dev/null &&
> grep 'manager' emp2.lst ||
>echo "pattern not found"
pattern not found
$_
```

The cat command was executed to test whether the file abc existed and was readable. The existence of this file was tested right at the beginning because there was no point in continuing the sequence if the first test failed. Note that, when you terminate each line with a logical operator, you needn't escape the <Enter> key. The shell automatically understands that the line is not complete, and responds with the secondary prompt string (PS2).

SCRIPT TERMINATION - THE exit STATEMENT

The **exit** statement is used to prematurely terminate a program. When this statement is encountered in a script, execution is halted and control is returned to the calling program, in most cases the shell. You have used this statement, you will remember, to terminate the introductory session in the first chapter.

You don't need to place this statement at the end of every shell script, because the shell understands when script execution is complete. The **exit** statement is quite often used with a command when it fails. The script **emp3.sh** can be modified to include this feature:

```
grep "$1" | | exit 2
echo "Pattern found - Job Over"
```

This segment achieves something more in that it takes rudimentary two-way decisions which the previous scripts couldn't. The program is aborted when the **grep** command fails, and a message is printed if it succeeds. Notice that the **exit** statement also takes a argument. This argument is optional, but when you specify one, the script will terminate with a return value as specified with the statement. If no return value is specified, then the value returned will be zero (true). This value is assigned to the parameter $?.

By using the logical operators && and | | in these ways, you have been encroaching on territory which rightfully belong to the shell's conditionals. These operators have their limitations, and are recommended for making simple decisions. When complex decision making is involved, they have to make way for the if statement.

Ex 8. Try using exit as the last statement in your .profile. How can you explain the behaviour of the system ? (Contact the system administrator first.)

THE IF CONDITIONAL

The **if** statement, like its counterpart in other programming languages, takes two-way decisions, depending on the fulfillment of a certain condition. You have already encountered it in **awk**, where you used it to control the flow of an **awk** program. In the shell, the statement uses the following form, much like the one used in other languages:

```
if        <condition is true>
then      <execute commands>
else
          <execute commands>
fi
```

if evaluates a condition which accompanies its command line. If the condition is fulfilled (i.e. returns a true exit status), then the sequence of commands following it is executed. Mark the keywords **then** and **fi** which must necessarily accompany every **if** conditional. The construct also provides for an alternate action using the optional keyword **else**. This is not always required, and the simplest form of the if statement thus condenses to:

```
if <condition is true>
then
<execute commands>
fi
```

The condition to be evaluated is actually the exit status of a program or command placed in the "command line". This program or command has already been referred to as the *control command* in the chapter on **awk** (Sec. 9.14). It is first executed, and if uses its return value to control the program flow. If the command executes successfully, then those statements following the keyword **then** are executed in a sequence. If the command fails, then the commands following the keyword **else** are executed, if there is an **else** segment.

You may not understand the far-reaching consequences of this property right now. But soon you will see how the use of a UNIX command as the condition makes the shell remarkable as a programming language. For a taste of that, enter the following sequence at the prompt to check whether the pattern **director** can be located in the file emp.lst:

```
$ if grep "director" emp.lst
> then echo "Pattern found - Job Over"
> else echo "Pattern not found"
> fi
9876    | jai sharma         | director  | production  | 12/03/50  | 1700
2365    | barun sengupta     | director  | personnel   | 11/05/47  | 7800
1006    | chanchal singhvi   | director  | sales       | 03/09/38  | 6700
6521    | lalit chowdury     | director  | marketing   | 26/09/45  | 8200
Pattern found - Job Over
$_
```

First note that every shell construct can be entered at the prompt itself. The **if** conditional is interpreted by the shell only after the keyword **fi** is entered. The **grep** command is here executed first, its output is displayed on the standard output, and its return value used as input to **if**. You can use if in this way with any executable which returns a value. Amazing power indeed!

1. If's Companion - test

When you utilise if to evaluate expressions, the **test** statement is invariably used as its control command. On most UNIX systems, it is an internal feature of the shell **test** evaluates the condition placed on its right, and returns either a true or false exit status. This return value is used by **if** for taking decisions. For this purpose, **test** uses certain operators to evaluate the condition. You will know the relational operators first, which you see in other languages, but **test** uses a different form. the complete set of operators is shown in Table 2.

TABLE 2

Relational Operators Used by if

Operator	Meaning
-eq	Equal to
-ne	Not equal to
-gt	Greater than
-ge	Greater than or equal to
-lt	Less than
-le	Less than or equal to

These operators always begin with a - (hyphen), followed by a two-character word. There must not be any white space between the - and the word, and the operator must be enclosed on either side by white space. Numeric comparison in the shell is a bit different from other languages in the sense that the test is confined to integer values only. Decimal values re simply truncated.

test doesn't display any output, but simply returns a value, which is assigned to the parameter $?. To verify that, assign some values to three variables, and check whether they are equal or not:

```
$ x = 5
$ y = 7
$ z = 7.2
$ test $x -eq $y ; echo $?
1
$ test $s -lt $y ; echo $?
0
$test $z -gt $y ; echo $?
1
$ test $z -eq $y ; echo $?
0
$_
```

The first two tests are obvious enough. The last two show that 7.2 is not greater than but equal to 7. This is a serious drawback in the Bourne shell, which makes it totally unsuitable for testing conditions with decimal numbers. However, a certain degree of computing capability is now available in the Korn shell.

Having seen how **test** can be utilised as a stand-along feature, you can now use it in the command line of the **if** conditional. The next script uses three arguments to take the pattern, as well as the input and output filenames. But first it checks whether the right number of arguments have been entered:

```
$ cat emp4. sh
if test $# -ne 3   # 3 arguments not entered
then
        echo "You have not keyed in 3 arguments"
        exit 3
else
        if grep         "$1" $2> $3
        then
                echo "Pattern found - Job Over"
        else
                echo "Pattern not found - Job Over"
        fi
fi
$_
```

Here, you have two **if** constructs, each terminated with its **fi**. One **if** is nested within the other. The statement

```
test $# -ne 3
```

tests whether the number of arguments entered is not equal to three. When you run this script with, say, one or even no argument, then this condition evaluates to true, the first message appears, and the script is terminated. The second if construct now tests for the exit status of the **grep** command, and echoes suitable messages, depending on the success or failure of **grep**. Invoke the script without any arguments, and then check its exit status:

```
$ emp4. sh
You have not keyed in 3 arguments
$_
$ echo $?
3
$_
```

The script here exists with a return value as used in the exit statement. Now run the script with the right number of arguments:

```
$ emp4. sh manager emp.lst man.lst
Pattern found - Job Over
$ cat man.lst
1265   | s.n. dasgupta    | manager   | sales   | 12/09/63  | 5600
2476   | anil aggarwal    | manager   | sales   | 01/05/59  | 5000
$_
```

How do you send a message to all users (with /etc/wall) after ensuring that there is at lest one user (apart from the sender) logged in? Since the pipeline **who | wc -1** counts the number of users in the system, you can use the feature of command substitution too:

```
$ if test 'who |  we -l' -gt 1
> then
> /etc/wall < warning
> fi
```

What **test** evaluates here is whether the output of the pipeline sequence is a number greater than 1. When there are at least two users in the system, this condition returns a true value, and the **wall** command is executed. Since pipelines can produce extremely complex sequences, the applicability of the if conditional is limited only by your imagination.

Ex 9: Write a script which accepts a pattern as an argument, and then searches either of two files, depending on which one has the greater number of records.

test is so widely used that fortunately there exists a shorthand method of executing if. A pair of rectangular brackets enclosing the expression can replace the word **test**. Thus, the following two forms are equivalent

```
test $x -eq $y
[$x -eq $y ]
```

The second form is more convenient to remember, and will be used henceforth. Just remember that the pair of brackets should be separated from the enclosed expression on either side by white space.

if also permits multi-way branching. In other words, you can evaluate more conditions if the previous condition fails. For each condition that is evaluated, you can have a set of commands which are executed if evaluation is found to be true. This form uses the **else** keyword, and optionally it also uses the **else** segment in the same sense as the first form. It has the following structure:

```
if <conditional is true>
then
```

```
<execute commands>
elif        <condition is true>
then
<execute commands>
<...>
<...>
else
<execute commands>
fi
```

A single **fi** closes the construct, even through there may be a couple of **elif** statements for testing alternate conditions. The **elif** here is used in identical manner as its counterpart of the *IF-ELSEIF-ENDIF* structure used by CLIPPER (Summer '87and later). It also resembles the *else-if* form used by other languages. You can use this form to improve the previous script **emp4. sh**:

```
$ cat emp4a.sh
if $# -ne 3
then
echo "You have not keyed in 3 arguments" ; exit 3
elif grep "$" $2> $3  2>/dev/null
then
     echo "Pattern not found -Job Over" ;
else
     echo "Pattern not found -Job Over" ; rm $3
fi
$_
```

A minor feature of removing the output file, if **grep** fails, is also added. This serves to curb the building up of unnecessary files in the disk.

All these scripts have a serious shortcoming. They don't indicate why a pattern is not found. This message appears even if file does'nt exist at all, and the redirection of the diagnostic stream with **2>** ensures that **grep's** complaints are not seen on the terminal. A script ideally should check that before starting a search. This is taken up next.

2. file — tests

test can be used to test the various file attributes. For example, you can test whether a file has the necessary read, write or executable permissions. An abridged list of the possible file related tests is shown in Table 3.

TABLE 3

File-related Tests with Test

Test	*Exit Status*
-a <file>	True if <file> exists (Release 4)
-f <file>	True if <file> exists and is a regular file
-f <file>	True if <file> exist and is readable
-w <file>	True if <file> exists and is writable
-X <file>	True if <file> exists and is executable
-d <file>	True if <file> exists and is directory
-s <file>	True if <file> exists and has a size greater than zero

Any of the **test** options can be negated by the ! (bang) operator. Thus [**! -f file**] negates [-**f file**]. You won't find these elaborate testing arrangements in other languages, where file attributes are either not available to a program, or tested by using a good deal of programming. The file testing syntax used by **test** is quite compact, and you can test some attributes of the file **emp.lst** at the prompt:

$ ls -l emp,lst

-rw-rw-rw- 1 kumar group 870 Jun 8 15:52 emp.lst

$ [-f emp. lst]; echo $?

0

$ [-x emp.lst]; echo $?

1

$ [! -w emp.lst] echo "False that file is not writeable"

False that file is not writeable

$_

First you checked whether the file existed; it was true. The second test checked whether the file was executable; it was false. Finally, you checked whether the file was *not* writeable: it was false (indicating that the file was writeable).

Using these features, you can design a script which accepts the name of a file from the standard input, and then performs a number of tests on it:

```
$ cat filetest.sh
    echo "Enter the name of the file: \c"
read flname
if [ ! -f $flname ]
then
    echo "File does not exist"
```

```
elif [ !-r $flname]
then
    echo "File is not readable"
elif [ ! -w $flname]
then
    echo "File is not writeable"
else
    echo "File is both readable and writeable"
fi
$_
```

Test the script with two filenames — one that does'nt exist and one that does:

```
$ filetest. sh
Enter the name of the file: cmp3. lst
File does not exist
$_
$ filetest.sh
    Enter the name of the file:emp.lst
File is both readable and writeable
$_
```

A common mistake made by many, when using **test** for testing file attributes, is to use the shell's wild-cards as a substitute for file names. **test** doesn't accept them at all, and uses only literal strings.

3. test—string Comparisons

The third type of usage of the **test** statement is in testing and comparing strings. There is nothing unusual in these tests which you can't find elsewhere, though **test** uses a different syntax. Table 4 lists the string handling tests.

TABLE 4

String Tests Used by Test

Test	Exit Status
-n *sig*	True if string stg *is not a null string*
-z stg	*True if string* stg *is a null string*
s1 = s2	True if string s1 = s2
s1 ! = s2	True if string s1 is not equal to s2
stg	*True if string* stg *is assigned and not null*

String quality is performed with the = operator, while the C-type operator != checks for inequality. Like the other **test** operators, these also should have white4 space on either side. You can use the string comparison features in the next script (**emp5. sh**) to check whether the user actually enters a string, or simply presses the <Enter> key:

```
$ cat emp5.sh
echo "Enter the string to be searched: \c"
read pname
if [ -z "$pname"]
then
        echo "You have not entered the string"
        exit 1
fi
echo "Enter the file to be used: \c"
read filname
if [! -n "$filname"]
then
        echo "You have not entered the filename"
        exit 2
else
        echo "Search for $pname from $flname?:\c".
        read answer
        if ["$answer" = "Y"]
        then
        grep "$pname" "$filname" echo "Pattern not found"
else
        exit 3
fi
$_
```

The script checks whether the user actually enters something when the script pauses at the first two points; once in accepting the pattern, and then while accepting the filename. Notice the check for null string is made with **[-z "$pname"]**, as well as with **[! -n "$filname"]** since they are really two different ways of saying the some thing. The script aborts if one of the inputs is a null string:

$ emp5. sh
Enter the string to be searched: **director**
Enter the file to be used: <Enter>
You have not entered the filename
$_
$ emp 5. sh
Enter the string to be searched: **director**
Enter the file to be used:**emp 1.lst**
Search for director from emp 1.lst?:**Y**
1006 | chanchal singhvi | director | sales | 03/09/38 | 6700
6521 | lalit chowdhury | director | marketing | 26/09/45 | 8200
$_

test also permits the checking of more than one expression in the same line. Like the dBASE operators .**AND** and .**OR**., it also uses similar operators performing identical functions. The **-a** operator performs the AND function, while **-o** simulates OR. Unlike dBASE, however, the entire compound conditions have to be flanked on either side by one set of the symbols [ ]. You can now simplify the earlier script to illustrate this feature. Remove the first **if** construct, and use this sequence after both strings have been accepted:

```
if [-n "$pname" -a -n "$filname"]
then
        grep "$pname" "$flname" || echo "Pattern not found"
else
        echo "At least one input was a null string"
        exit 1
fi
```

The **test** output is true only if both the variables are non-null strings, i.e. the user enters some non-whitespace characters when the script pauses twice.

Ex 10. Implement the above logic with the -o operator

A word of caution here before terminating this discussion on the **if** conditional, as well as the **test** statement. While using shell variables with **test**, it will be preferable to enclose the variable within a pair of double quotes, as has been consistently done here. A variable without quotes will create problems when a multi-word string is assigned to it. Another point that you should remember is that **test** accepts simple strings only. It doesn't accept the shell's wild-cards or a regular expression used by the sophisticated UNIX filters.

Ex 11: Why can't you use single quotes?

THE case STATEMENT

The **case** statement is the second conditional offered by the shell. It doesn't have its parallel in most languages. dBASE and C use a similar form, though. The statement matches an expression for more than one alternative, and uses a compact construct to permit multi-way branching. It also handles string tests, but in a more efficient manner than **if**. The general syntax of the **case** statement is as follows:

```
case        <expression> in
            <pattern 1>    <execute commands> ;;
            <pattern 2>    <execute commands> ;;
            <pattern 3>    <execute commands> ;;
            <....>
            <....>
esac
```

The keywords here are **in** and **esac**, and the symbols ;; are used as option terminators. The construct also uses the) to delimit the pattern from the action. It matches the **expression** first for **pattern 1,** and if successful, executes the commands associated with it. If it does'nt then it falls through and matches **pattern2** and so on. Each command list is terminated by a pair of colons, and the entire construct is closed with an **esac** (reverse of **case**).

Consider a simple example using this construct. You can devise a script, which accepts values from 1 to 5, and performs some action depending on the number keyed in. The code for this menu is stored in the file **menu.sh**:

```
$ cat menu.sh
cat << END
          MENU
  1.  List of files
  2.  Processes of user
  3.  Today's Date
  4.  Users of system
  5.  Quit to UNIX
END
echo " Enter your option: \c"
read choice
echo
```

```
case "$choice" in
 1)  ls -l ;;
 2)  ps -f ;;
 3)  date ;
 4)  who ;;
 5)  exit ;;
esac
$_
```

The five menu choices are displayed with a here document using the **cat** command. The meanings attached to these choices are obvious enough. The user response from the keyboard is accepted to the variable **choice**. The **case** statement then matches the value of this variable for the strings **1, 2, 3, 4** and **5**, as shown in the five lines below the keyword **case**. It than relates each value to a command that has to be executed. For example, if the user enters a **1**, then the **1s -1** command will be executed. Script termination is achieved by entering the number **5**, or for that matter, any other value not matched in the program logic.

You can list the processes on your terminal by choosing the second option:

```
$ menu.sh
     MENU
  1.  List of files
  2.  Processes of user
  3.  Today's Date
  4.  Users of system
  5.  Quit to UNIX
Enter your option: 2
UID     PID   PPID   C   STIME     TTY   TIME   COMMAND
kumar    30      1   0   09:16:10   01   0.03   -sh
kumar    81     30   0   10:05:40   01   0.06   vi dentryl. sh
kumar    82     81   0   10:06:16   01   0.00   sh -1
kumar    83     82  11   10:06:20   01   0.00   ps -f
$_
```

The same logic can also be implemented using the **if** statement, but **case** certainly is more compact. But **case** can't handle relational and file tests; it can only match strings. However, you can use the shell's features to fetch a string, for example, by command substitution.

Design a calendar service which reminds you of certain things, depending on the day of the week. The day of the week is obtained from the first field of the output of the **date** command. The relevant **case** logic is shown below:

```
case 'date | cut -d" " -f1' in

        Mon) <commands> ;;
        Tue) <commands> ;;
        Wed) <commands> ;;
        <....>
        <....>
esac
```

The preceding example is fairly straightforward; a different option exits for each day of the week.

case can also match more than one pattern with each option. Programmers frequently encounter a logic which prompts the user for a response, for example , **"Do you wish to continue ?(y/n)"**. It is always a good idea to include both upper and lowercase responses in the programming logic. To do that, the **if** statement will have to test for both **y** and **Y** using the compound condition feature.

```
if [ "$choice = "y" -o "$choice" = "Y"
```

It is here that **case** offers a superb and compact pattern matching feature. Like **egrep**, it uses the delimiter to separate the various patterns, so you can use the expression **y/Y** to match both upper and lowercase:

```
echo "Do you wish to continue ? (y/n): \c"
read answer
case "$answer" in
        y l Y) ;;
        n l N) exit ;;
esac
```

A null statement using only the delimiters ;; implies that no action is to be performed if a match is made there, and control flows out of the construct. You can match a number of strings in this way, each string separated from the other by the l. The above sequence, however, doesn't take into account the possible patterns like **Yes, YES** or **yES**, etc., which a user may enter at the prompt. But **case** offers a solution to these problems too.

case becomes even more powerful in its handling of the shell wild-cards for matching patterns. **case** and the **for** loop are the only shell control flow statements that accept the same set of metacharacters as used in matching filenames. The revised **case** construct lets the user answer the preceding question in several ways:

```
case "$answer" in
        [yY] [eE] [sS] ;;
        [nN][oO] exit ;;
        *) echo "Invalid response" ;;
esac
```

If you have understood wild-cards, then interpretation of this sequence should be a fairly simple matter. Since control breaks out of the construct once a match has been performed, the shell metacharacter * is normally used as the last option to any **case** construct. In this case, the * matches any number of characters (or none) not matched by the previous options.

```
????
```

and since the emp-id contains numerals only, the following pattern will be more restrictive:

```
[0-9][0-9][0-9][0-9]
```

Ex 12: Write a script which prompts for a name, and accepts it only if it contains alphabetic characters, spaces or dots.

The **case** conditional is valuable programming tool available with the UNIX system. Since UNIX treats numerals as strings, **case** can also be used to match numbers. Moreover, the wild-card matching feature also makes **case** compact and easy to use. If you have only strings to match, then **case** is the best construct to handle them.

LOOPING - THE while STATEMENT

The pattern scanning scripts developed so far still suffer from serious defects. You have no way of giving the user another chance when he has made a faulty response. And you are able to scan only one pattern at a time. Loops let you perform a set of instructions repeatedly. The shell features three types of loops - **while, until** and **for**. the first two are basically complementary to each other. All of them repeat the instruction set enclosed by certain keywords as often as the control command permits.

The **while** statement should be quite familiar to most programmers. It repeatedly performs a set of instructions till the control command returns a true exit status. The general syntax of this command is as follows:

```
while      <condition is true>
do
           <execute commands>
done
```

The keywords here are **do** and **done**. The set of instructions enclosed by **do** and **done** are to be performed as long as *condition* remains true. Like in the **if** statement, this condition is actually the return value of a UNIX command or program. This means that you can use the **test** statement here also, with its associated expressions, numeric and string comparisons, and file tests.

The following loop displays the **ps -f** output after a regular interval:

```
$ x = 5
$ while [ $x -gt 3]
> do
> ps -f
> sleep 5
> done
```

Any loop is treated as complete only when the words **do** and **done** are entered in the right order. The assignment **x = 5** is made before the **while** construct, and then the condition **[$x -gt 3]** is tested. It is true, and the loop executes. After the first iteration, the condition is again tested, and the instructions are again executed. The result is display every five seconds of the **ps -f** command output with an infinite loop. You can terminate the session by pressing the interrupt key.

This is an indirect and unsatisfactory method of setting up an infinite loop. A dummy command in **while**'s command line which always returns a true exit status, can help set up one. Fortunately there is such a command; even if it didn't exist, you would have had to invent it. The UNIX command **true** does nothing except return a true exit status (0). So you can substitute the **while** construct with one:

```
while true
> do
> ps -f
> sleep 5
> done
```

Similarly, there is a command **false** which returns a non-zero value. And if you are wondering what the commands **true** and **false** actually contain, "**cat**" them to find out:

```
$ cat /bin/true
#true do -nothing, successfully
exit 0
$_
$ cat/bin/false
```

```
#false - do nothing, unsuccessfully
exit 255
$_
```

true and **false**, in fact, are simple shell scripts which do nothing except return an exit status, **true** returns 0, while **false** returns a non-zero value.

There is a short-hand notation for the **true** command. The: (colon) command also does nothing except return a true value. This command can be placed anywhere in a script, where it is mandatory to have a dummy command. You can replace the statement **while true** with

```
while:
```

to set up an infinite loop. You can have the: too inside an **if** construct:

```
        if [-f emp.lst]
        then:
```

or even at the prompt:

```
$:
$ _
```

When you write programs, you repeatedly compile, reedit or execute them, depending on the success of compilation or execution. Automation of this set of activities can be an ideal application for **while**. The script **edcomrun.sh** achieves this automation:

```
$ cat edcomrun. sh
# Script to edit, compile and execute a program

while true
do
        cc $1                   # Compiling a C program
        case $? in
                0)  echo    "Compilation successful"
                    echo    "Executing Program a out"
                    a.out,  exit ;;
                *)  echo    "Compilation unsuccessful"
                    echo    "Press the <Enter> key to edit"
                    read pause

        vi $1;;
done
$_
```

This script accepts the filename as a positional parameter (**$1**). The loop body first compiles the C program. the compilation status (true or false) is stored in the parameter **$?**. The file **a.out** is executed on successful compilation and the script terminated. Unsuccessful compilation generates the message to that effect, and waits for the user to press the <*Enter*> key. The **vi** editor is then invoked to enable editing work. Control then returns to the top of the loop for the next iteration. The compilation process begins and the statements are repeated.

1. Break and Continue

With this knowledge, you should now be able to devise a data entry program for adding an entry to the file **desig.lst**. This is the file which contains the code table for the designations. The script must offer the user a second chance if he defaults in input. It should also validate the code entered with the ones that already exist in the file. The code and description should be appended to this file only after they pass the validation tests.

To do that, you need to use another two keywords -**break** and **continue**. They have their counterparts in **awk** and the C language with the same names. dBASE users can recall the **EXIT** and **LOOP** statements for a close parallel. The **continue** statement suspends execution of all statements following it, and switches control to the top of the loop for the next iteration. The **break** statement, on the other hand, causes control to break out of the loop. They optionally also use arguments, but that will be taken up only in the next chapter.

The script **dentry 1.sh** makes use of all these features:

```
$ cat dentry 1.sh
filname = desig.lst
while echo "Designation code " \c"
do
        read desig
        case "$desig" in
        [0-9][0-9] if grep "^$desig" $flname >/dev/null #if code exits
              then
                        echo "Code exists"
                        continue
              fl;;
                    *)  echo "Invalid code"
                        continue ;;
              esac
while echo "Description        :\c"
do
```

```
            read desc
            case "$desc" in
            *[!\a-zA-Z]*)    echo "Can contain only alphabets and spaces"
                             continue ;;
                       "")   echo "Description not entered"
                             continue ;;
                        *)   echo "$desig l $desc" >> flname
                             break
            esac
        done
        echo "\nWish to continue? (y/n): \c"
        read answer
        case "$answer" in
            [yY]  *)    continue ;;
                  *)    break ;;
        esac
done
echo "Program terminated"
$_
```

The script prompts for two fields—the designation code and the name—and uses two loops, one enclosed by the other. Since an **echo** command always produces a true exit status, the statements issuing the two prompts are used as the control commands of the two loops. The code is accepted into the variable **desig,** and first checked in the **case** conditional for a two-character numeric pattern. the file **desig.lst** is then scanned for a match. The code has to be reentered if it exists in the file or if it doesn't have a two-digit structure. This is ensured by the two **continue** statements that switch control to the top of the loop.

Next, it prompts for the description, and uses the variable **desc** to hold the user response. The expression ***[!\a-zA-Z]*** checks the input for at least one character which is neither a letter of the alphabet nor a space. Since **case** uses the wild-cards that are used in matching filenames, the space character needs to be escaped. Filenames can't have this character, that is why the shell's wild-cards don't match it literally. The next option tests for a null response. The **continue** statement here stops further processing, and starts the next iteration of the inner loop.

The valid, code, along with the description, is then appended to the file, using the pipe as the delimiter between them. The **break** statement in the inner loop makes sure that the loop is not iterated after a record is added. After that, the user is prompted for more entries.

A response beginning with **y** or **Y** starts the next iteration, while any other response causes control to break out of the loop.

The logic becomes convincing after you undèrtake a dialogue with the script:

```
$dentry 1.sh
Designation code          :  01
Code exists
Designation code          :  07
Description               :  security officer
Wish to  continue ? (y/n) :  Y
Designation code          :  8
Invalid code
Designation code          :  08
Description               :  vice president 1
Can contain only alphabets and spaces
Description               :  vice president
Wish to continue ? (y/n): n
Program terminated
$_
```

When you cat the file **desig.lst** you will see the two appended entries:

```
$ cat desig.lst
01 | chairman
02 | d.g.m.
03 | director
04 | executive
05 | g.m.
06 | manager
07 | security officer
08 | vice president
$_
```

This is first of the data entry scripts. You will be developing three more, using less code and more features. This will be done only in the next chapter.

REDIRECTION — A SECOND LOOK

The discussion here applies equally to each of the other loops as well, but since the **while** loop is taken up first, the examples are drawn up with reference to it. You will have noticed that the singular statement for adding a record to the file uses the >> symbol. Redirecting the output of a command with this symbol is good enough, but it makes script execution very slow. This is because, the output file **<desig.lst>** has to be opened every time the **echo** command is called up. Opening and closing a file involve disk I/O, resulting in significant overheads. And when large data files are processed in this way, performance is bound to suffer.

Fortunately, the shell provides a very simple way of avoiding such multiple file openings and closures. All the shell's conditionals (**if** and **case**) and loops (**while, until** and **for**) can be redirected. Though they are internal commands the shell accords them the same status as the external commands, All these constructs are redirected by sing the redirection symbol after the final keyword (i.e. **fi, esac** and **done**). That is why when you use redirection in this way the file is opened only once, at the beginning of the iteration, and is closed finally when the loop iteration ends. This speeds up execution time, but has a very serious consequence. When you redirect a loop in this way, all individual statements inside the loop also get redirected. In other words, the "error" messages (i.e. the **echo** statements) also land up in the same file, instead of being displayed on the terminal.

To solve this problem, you should explicitly redirect the output of all the other **echo** commands to the special file /**dev**/**tty**. This file, representing everybody's terminal, can be used to direct output explicitly to one's own terminal, irrespective of the terminal he is working on. Using this knowledge, you can rephrase the inner **while** loop to look like this:

```
while echo "Description: \c" >/dev/tty
do
        read desc
        case "$desc" in
        *[*\a-zA-Z]*) echo "Can contain only alphabets and space" /dev/tty
                      continue ;;
                 ")   echo "Description not entered" >/dev/tty
                      continue ;;
                 *)   echo "$desig l $desc"
                      break

        esac
done >> $flname
```

This is an acceptable solution, with two steams making their way to two different destinations. However, the problem with this approach is that the output of all the **echo** commands (barring one) go to the terminal, and there is simply no way that you can save such "error" messages in a file.

What if a script contains more than one of these loops, and the output of each one has to go to the same file ? You can't use the redirection feature like this with each of these loops; it will be a better idea to redirect the entire script itself. Thus, instead of effecting the redirection at the **done** keyword, you can redirect the script as a whole:

$ dentry 1.sh > sclist

When you redirect a shell script in this way, you must ensure that statements inside the script, requiring to send the output to the terminal, have been separately redirected with >/**dev/tty**.

The preceding discussion centred round output redirection. However, the same considerations apply to input redirection as well. As a variation of the standard procedure of using the keyboard or positional parameters to specify the patterns, you can try placing them in a file. The parameter file **empid.lst** has a list of four of them:

```
$ cat empid.lst
2233
9876
2476
3564
$_
```

Can you use the following sequence to take the patterns from this file?

```
while true
do
        read string < empid.lst
        grep $string emp.lst
done
```

This opens the file **empid. lst** in every iteration of the loop. Thus, the **read** statement will read the first line of this file every time it is invoked. Moreover, the script holding the sequence will never terminate, because the control command (**true**) always evaluates to true. Redirecting the **done** keyword only partially solves the problem:

```
while true
do
        read string
        grep $string emp.lst
done< empid.lst
```

Here, the loop as a whole takes its input from the file **empid.lst**. The variable **string** is assigned the contents of each line of the file **empid.lst** in turn, and the **grep** command executed with each iteration. While this loop will work, and show the selected lines on the terminal, the problem of the infinite loop still persists.

You may be surprised to learn that the **read** statement itself returns an exit status, and **while** is often used with **read** itself as the control command in this way:

```
$ cat searchpat.sh
while read string
do
        grep $string emp.lst
done < $1
$_
```

When you run the script with the file **empid.lst** as argument. this is what you will get:

```
$searchpat.sh empid.lst
2233 | a.k. shukla      | lg.m.      | lsales      | l12/12/52| 6000
9876 | jai sharma       | director   | production  | 12/03/50 | 7000
2476 | anil aggarwal    | manager    | sales       | 01/05/59 | 5000
3564 | sudhir Agarwal   | executive  | personnel   | 06/07/47 | 7500
$_
```

The characteristic feature of the **read** statement is that it evaluates to false only when it encounters the end of input. Otherwise, the statement always returns a true exit status, even when assigned a null string. While the script works perfectly, the next chapter will reveal its inadequacy for a simple reason; the value of any variable inside the loop will never be available outside it. This can pose a number of problems in application shell programming, but the present solution should suffice for the time being.

The **while** structure is ideal for developing data entry shell scripts with extensive validation features. You have already had a taste of this in this section. Advanced validation features are taken up in the next chapter.

while's COMPLEMENT - THE until STATEMENT

The **until** statement complements the **while** construct in the sense that the loop body here is executed repeatedly as long as the condition remains false. It is simply another way of viewing the whole thing. Either form can be used interchangeably, except for the fact that the expression has to be negated while switching from one form to another. The **while** loop introduced at the beginning of the previous topic can now be rephrased as:

```
$ until false
>do
> ps -f
> sleep 5
> done
```

Here, the previous **while** command line has been replaced by its complementary **until** statement. Thus,

while true

has now become

until false

while the instruction set remains unchanged. Even though the two forms are structurally identical, you should choose the form you like best, and use it throughout. Most users, however, prefer the **while** form to the **until**.

The **until** loop is an ideal tool to develop certain programs which involve great programming effort in other languages. There are situations when a program can be executed only when a certain file has been created. You can use a script which periodically monitors the disk for the existence of the file, and then executes the program once the file has been located. Have a look at the script before you execute it:

```
$ cat monitfile.sh
until [-r empmas]          # until the file empmas can be read
do
        sleep 60
done
updt. sh
mail sharma < mail.msg
$_
$ monitfile.sh &
270
$_
```

This is an interesting and very useful program, and illustrates a few features. The loop sleeps for 1 minute, and then wakes up to check for the existence of the file **empmas.** If the file is readable, the program **updt.sh** is executed, and sharma is mailed a message. The entire script is executed in the background, which is responsible thing to do.

LOOPING WITH for

The **for** loop is different in structure from the ones used in other programming languages. There is no **next** statement there, neither can a step be specified. Unlike **while** and **until**, it doesn't test a condition but uses a list instead. The syntax of this construct it as follows:

```
for variable in list
do
        <execute commands>
done
```

The loop body is identical in structure to the **while** and **until** loops. The additional keywords here are *variable* and **list**. The list consists of a series of character strings, with each string separated from the other by white space. Each item in the list is assigned to the variable in turn, and the loop body is executed. It performs the loop as many times as there are words in the list. A simple example can help you understand things better:

```
$ for x in 1 2 4 5
> do
> echo "The value of x is $x"
>done
The value of x is 1
The value of x is 2
The value of x is 4
The value of x is 5
$_
```

This is how the construct works — the list here consists of four strings **1, 2, 4** and **5**. First the string **1** is assigned to the variable **x**, and the single instruction, i.e. the **echo** statement is executed. In the next iteration, the variable **x** is assigned the value **2**, and the instruction repeated. This process continues till the list is exhausted. You normally use the same variable in the loop body, but there is no compulsion for you to do so.

In the previous example, you used a set of literal strings to form the list for the loop to act on. What else can this list be made up of? It an consist of practically any of the expressions that the shell understands and processes — variables, wild-card expressions, command substitution and positional parameters, **for** is probably the most often used loop in the UNIX system, and it is important that you understand it thoroughly.

1. List from Variables

Variable usage is simple. You can use a series of them in the command line. They are evaluated by the shell before executing the loop:

```
$ for war in $PATH $HOME $MAIL
> do
> echo "$var"
>done
/bin: /usr/bin:
/usr/kumar
/usr/mail/kumar
$_
```

for also treats a multi-word string as separate components of the list. For example, you can assign a three-word string to the variable **chstring**, and then execute a suitable **for** loop:

```
$ chstring = "unit01 unit02 unit03"
$ for var in $chstring
> do
> wc $var
> done
        541     9703     56895    unit01
       1010    10999     64908    unit02
        833     8921     49489    unit03
$_
```

The fact that **wc** didn't print the total at the end indicates that it was executed three times, with a single argument each time. However, you will come across a situation when you need to alter this behaviour. That will be taken up later.

2. List from wild-card Expressions

When the list consists of wild-cards, the shell automatically interprets them as filenames, and reproduces an alphabetically sorted list of filenames (from the current directory, by default) matching the wild-card pattern. Like **case, for** accepts the complete metacharacter set used by the shell for matching filenames. Since the *matches any number of characters, you can use it to compile all C programs:

```
$ for file in *.c
> do
> cc $file
$_
```

This loop compiles all C programs in the current directory with the compiler command **cc**. The above program, however, has the limitation that all C programs will overwrite the same executable file **a.out**. It won't be possible to maintain executables separately for each program in this way. To do that, you have to make use of the shell's feature of concatenating a variable and a string. This is done in either of the two ways:

```
cc -o $file "x" $file
cc -o $file[x] $file
```

Thus, the program **pay.c** will have an executable **pay.cx**

3. List from Positional Parameters

One of the most important uses of **for** lies in its ability to process positional parameters. It accepts the special notation $*, as well as the individual arguments ($1, $2, $3 etc.) as constituents of the list. This implies that the parameters have to be supplied externally as arguments to the script itself. The next script **emp6.sh** scans the file repeatedly for each argument:

```
$ cat emp6. sh
echo "\nThe number of patterns entered is $#"
echo "The patterns are $*"
for pattern in $*
do
        case    "$pattern" in
                ????) grep "^pattern" emp.lst ll
                        echo  "Pattern $pattern not found" ;;
                *)      echo  "Not a four character pattern $pattern" ;;
        esac
done
$_
```

Execute the script by passing four arguments:

```
$ emp6.sh 2345 1265 4379 367

The number of patterns entered is 4
The patterns are 2345 1265 4379 367
2345 | j.b. saxena     | g.m.      | marketing     | 12/03/45 | 8000
1265 | s.n. dasgupta   | manager   | sales         | 12/09/63 | 5600
Pattern 4379 not found
Not a four character pattern 367
$_
```

The four emp-id's supplied as arguments to the script have been stored in $*, which form the list for this construct. This loop is processed, along with the **case** routine, to scan a file for a number of four-character patterns. The first gets stored as $1, the second as $2 and so on. The advantage of using this approach is that you can specify a variable number of arguments to the script; $* accepts them all.

Since **for** is mostly used with **$*** to access command line arguments, a blank list defaults to this parameter. Whenever you have a **for** loop with the list omitted, you can interpret this invisible list as the parameter **$***. Thus, when you see the statement

for *variable*

it actually expands to

for *variable* in $*

4. List from Command Substitution

Finally, you can use command substitution to produce the list. When the list is large, and you don't think it practicable to specify its contents individually, you can store them in a separate file, say **clist**, and then use **'cat clist'** as the argument to **for**. The **for** command line will then look like this:

```
for file in 'cat clist'
```

The advantage of using this feature is that you need change only the contents of the file **clist**, without disturbing the contents of the main program.

Ex 13. Print the man pages for all commands in the /bin directory.

ANOTHER SPECIAL PARAMETER -$@

The previous script scanned the file **emp.lst** with four-character emp-id's. The **for** loop creates problems when you use names instead. Modify the previous script to remove the restriction on four-character patterns, and then use it with three multi-word strings. The script **emp7.sh** is as follows:

```
$cat emp7.sh
[$# -eq 0]&& exit    #Quit fi no patterns entered
echo "\nThe number of patterns entered is $#"
echo "The patterns are $*"
echo "Enter output filename: \c"
read flname
for pattern in $*
do
        grep "$pattern" emp.lst ll echo "Pattern $pattern not found" > /dev/tty
```

```
done > $flname
$_
```

Now run this script with three names, and then have a look at the contents of the output file:

```
$emp7.sh "jai sharma" "v.n.singh" "karuna ganguly"
The number of patterns entered is 3
The patterns are jai sharma v.n. singh karuna ganguly
Enter output filename:dup.lst
Pattern v.n. not found
$_
$ cat dup. lst
9876 | jai sharma        | director | production | 12/03/50 | 7000
9876 | jai sharma        | director | production | 12/03/50 | 7000
1006 | chanchal singhvi  | director | sales      | 03/09/38 | 6700
6213 | karuna ganguly    | g.m.     | accounts   | 05/06/62 | 6300
6213 | karuna ganguly    | g.m.     | accounts   | 05/06/62 | 6300
$_
```

This produces some interesting but deceptive output—while **$#** correctly assesses the number of arguments that have been specified, **$*** can't. **for** treats **jai** as one argument, **sharma** as another, **v.n.** as one argument, and **singh** as another, and so forth. That is why some of the records have been shown twice. Though **v.n** couldn't be found, **singh** was found embedded in **singhvi**.

Enclosing the **$*** parameter in quotes like this

```
for pattern in "$*"
```

can make matters worse:

```
$emp7.sh "jai sharma" "j.b. saxena" "karuna ganguly"
The number of patterns entered is 3
The patterns are jai sharma j.b. saxena karuna ganguly
Enter output filename: dup.lst
Pattern jai sharma j.b. karuna ganguly not found
$_
$ cat dup. lst
$_
```

All the three arguments here are viewed as a single argument by "$*" and consequently by **for**. Note that **$#** still correctly assesses the number of arguments. You haven't been able to perform a search with multi-word strings yet.

The answer to this problem lies in the special parameter **$@**. Like the **join** command, it appears to be the most neglected special parameter of the shell. But then, it comes to your rescue in critical situations. It behaves exactly lie **$*** when used without quotes. But when used with them, it treats each quoted argument as a separate one, which is exactly what is required here. Modify the **for** statement to look like this:

for file in "$@"

and then invoke the script as you have done before:

```
$ emp7.sh "jai sharma" "j.b. saxena" "karuna ganguly"
The number of patterns entered is 3
The patterns are jai sharma j.b. saxena karuna ganguly
Enter output filename: dup.lst
$_

$ cat dup.lst
9876 | jai sharma      | director  | production  | 12/03/50 | 7000
2345 | j.b. saxena     | g.m.      | marketing   | 12/03/45 | 8000
6213 | karuna ganguly  | g.m.      | accounts    | 05/06/62 | 6300
$_
```

This output has important implications. When you employ multi-word strings in the command line of a shell script, then you should use the **"$@"** parameter with the relevant programming construct to iterate for each argument of the script. The use of **"$@"**, rather than **$*** or **"$"** is highly recommended, because **"$@"** can handle single-word arguments in just the same way as **$*** has been handling all along.

THE set AND shift STATEMENTS

Unlike shell variables, the positional parameters as well as the parameters associated with it (**$#, $*** and **$@**) can't be set by making a direct assignment with the = operator. You can't obviously make an assignment with the statement **1=abc** and then evaluate it with **echo $1**; that is simply absurd. However, you can put some values into these positional parameters in an indirect manner. This is done with the **set** statement.

The **set** statement makes it possible to convert is arguments into positional parameters. A simple use of this statement can be

```
$set 9876 2345 6213
$_
```

This assigns the value **9876** to the positional $**1, 2345** to **$2** and **6213** to **$3**. It also sets the other parameters **$#, $*** and **$@**. You can verify this by echoing each parameter in turn:

```
$echo $1
9876
$echo $2
2345
$echo $3
6213
$ echo $#
3
$ echo $*
9876 2345 7213
$ echo $@
9876 2345 6213
$_
```

This feature is especially useful for picking up individual fields from the output of a program. Thus, using command substitution, you can assign values to the shell's positional parameters with the output of the **date** command:

```
$set 'date'
$echo $*
Wed Oct 24 14.02.43 IST 1990
$echo $2 $3 $6
Oct 24 1990
$_
```

and use them individually in a UNIX command:

```
$ echo "The data today is $2 $3, $6"
The date today is Oct 24, 1990
$_
```

A different problem arises while using the **for** loop with positional parameters. Many scripts are designed in a way which uses the first argument to indicate a separate entity, say a filename, while the other arguments represent a series of strings, say different patterns to be selected from a file. This wasn't done in the previous script, because the **for** loop would have interpreted the filename as one of the patterns. To illustrate this point, modify the **for** loop of the previous script so that the input filename is now replaced by the positional parameter **$1**:

```
for pattern in "$@"
do
        grep "$pattern" $1 ll echo "Pattern $pattern not found"
done
```

The script won't work because the loop iteration will start with a wrong argument, viz. **$1**, which is meant to indicate a filename. However, if you can arrange things in such a way that the iteration starts with **$2** instead of **$1**, then you can make the sequence work. In other words, you should be able to shift the parameters to the *left*. That is possible with the shell, which offers the facility of renumbering these parameters with the **shift** statement.

shift transfers the contents of a positional parameter to its immediate lower numbered one. This goes on as many times as the statement is called. When called once, **$2** becomes **$1, $3** becomes **$2**, and so on. Try this on the positional parameters that were filled up with the **date** command:

$echo $*
Wed Oct 24 14:02:43 IST 1990
$ **echo $1 $2 $3**
Wed Oct 24
$shift
$echo $1 $2 $3
Oct 24 14:02:43
$ **shift**
$ **echo $1 $2 $3**
24 14:02:43 EST
$_

The important thing to remember is that the contents of the leftmost parameter, i.e. **$1** are lost every time **shift** is invoked. In this way you access than one positional parameters in a script, which you couldn't have done earlier. So if a script now uses twelve arguments, you can shift thrice and then use the ninth parameter:

$ **echo $#**
12
$ **shift**

```
$ shift
$ shift
$ echo $#
9
$_
```

From Release 3 onwards, **shift** accepts an argument as well. Thus, **shift 3** replaces the three individual statements in the above sequence.

How can you then use this principle to accept both a filename, as well as a set of patterns, as positional parameters to a script? The script **emp8.sh** that:

```
$cat emp8. sh
# Script using the shift feature
case $# in
        0l 1) echo "Insufficient number of arguments"
        *)    flname = $1  # Store $1 as a variable it gets lost
              shift
              for pattern in "$@"
              do
                   grep "$pattern" $flname ll echo "Pattern $pattern not found"
                   esac
$_
```

Since the script now requires at least two arguments, you should verify their presence before you act on the patlerns. The contents of **$1** are stored in the variable **flname** because they will be lost after the *shift* operation otherwise. Now you can use the script with a variable number of arguments (not less than 2):

```
$ emp8 .sh emp1.lst
insufficient number of arguments

$_
$ emp8.sh emp1.lst "j.b. saxena" 10006 9876
2345 | j.b. saxena          | g.m.       | marketing       | 12/03/45 | 8000
1006 | chanchal singhvi     | director   | sales           | 03/09/38 | 6700
Pattern 9876 not found
$_
```

Ex 14: How can you achieve the same, but using the while construct instead of a for loop?

All these scripts still have one major limitation; since the **grep** command operates inside a loop, it is called as many times as the loop is iterated. This can consume time, since it involves scanning the entire file with each pattern. It will be a better idea to convert the patterns into a form which is accepted by **egrep**. The script **emp9.sh** does this conversion:

```
$ cat emp9.sh
# Uses egrep to scan file
flname = $1
shift

egpat=
for pp in "$@"
do
        egpat = $egpat$[pp]" l"
done
egpat = 'echo $egpat l sed 's/ls$//'
egrep "$egpat" $flname l l echo "None of the patterns found"
$_
```

Here "$@" represents the entire set of arguments except the first one. The variable **pp** picks up each positional parameter (barring the first one) from the list. With each iteration, the variable **egpat** is reset by suffixing the value **$pp** and a pipe to its old value. Since **egpat** now contains an extra l at the end of the iteration, it is better removed with **sed**. This script now performs faster because the file is searched only once:

```
$ emp9.sh emp1. 1st "j.b. saxena" 1006 9876
1006 l chanchal singhvi    l director   l sales        l 03/09/38 l 6700
2345 l j.b. saxena         l g.m.       l lmarketing   l 12/03/45 l 8000
$_
```

Ex 15: How can you build the pattern without using a loop?

1. Set Options

set has a host options; it is simply not a practicable idea to discuss even most of them. But there is one option (-x) which can be quite useful in debugging shell scripts. When used inside a script (or even at the $ prompt), it echoes each statement on the terminal, preceded by a + as it is executed. Modify the previous script to place the statement

```
set -x
```

at the beginning, and the statement

```
set +x
```

at the end of the script. A set option preceded by a + turns of the feature turned on by the corresponding option used with a -. This is what you 'll get when you invoke the script in the following manner:

```
$ emp9. sh emp 1.lst 2233 1265 0110
flname = emp1.lst
+shift
egpat =
egpat = 2233
egpat = 2233 | 1265 | 01101 |
+ sed s/$//
+ echo 2233 | 1265 | 0110 |
egpat = 2233 | 1265 | 0110 |
+ egrep 2233 | 1265 | 0110 emp 1.lst
2233 | a. k. shukla      | g.m.      | sales      | 12/12/52 | 6000
1265 | s.n. dasgupta     | manager   | sales      | 12/09/63 | 5600
0110 | v.k. agrawal      | g.m.      | marketing  | 31/12/40 | 9000
+ set +x
$_
```

This is an ideal tool to use if you have trouble finding out whey scripts don't work in the manner expected. Note how the shell prints each statement as it is being executed, the statement being preceded by a +. It evaluates the variables, and also printes them. What is most interesting is the way the shell shows the value of the variable **egpat** with each iteration of the loop. Next it shows how sed removes the last l from the string. It even shows you what the egrep command line finally looks like !

The **-v** option also works in a similar fashion, but the **-x** option is preferable. For the other set options, look up the UNIX documentation.

You may often require to use **set** with command substitution. If the output of the executed command begins with a - **set** will interpret it as one of its own options:

```
$ set 'Is -I unit01'
-rw-r- -r-: bad option(s)
$_
```

The reason why this happens is that set interprets the permissions field as an option of its own. Since the entire permission set begins with a -(for regular files), **set** displays it is a "bad" option.

set can also cause problems when the argument in its command line evaluates to a null string.

Suppose you use

$ set 'grep secretary emp.lst'

and the pattern can't be located in the file, **set** will then operate with no arguments, and will display all the environment variables on the terminal. This can be most disconcerting for the user who suddenly sees the screen filled with a variable list having no connection with the program.

The solution to these problems lies in the use of — (two hyphens) immediately after the statement **set** then understands that the arguments following — are not to be treated as options. The two hyphens also make **set** understand that if the arguments evaluate to a null string, then it should suppress its default behaviour.

The **set** and **shift** features can be used in developing a script which validates the department code, when one is entered through the keyboard. You did a similar thing with an earlier script, but here you will be using it to flash the department name when the code is located. The unusual feature of this script is that uses the here document to maintain the code list in the script file, rather than externally. The script has the name **valcode.sh**

```
$ cal valcode.sh
IFS = "l"                       # Reset field separator to pipe
while echo "\nEnter department code: \c"
do
        read dcode
        set — 'grep "^$dcode" << limit
01  l accounts    l 6213
02  l admin       l 5423
03  l marketing   l 6521
04  l personnel   l 2365
05  l production  l 9876
06  l sales       l 1006
limit'
case $# in
```

```
        3)    echo "Department name      :$2\nEmp-id of head of dept: $3"
              shift 3 ;; # Flush out the positional parameters
        *)    echo "Invalid code" ; continue
              esac
$_
```

The script holds a user-supplied code in the variable **dcode.** It then searches the data in the here document, and assigns the output of the **grep** command to positional parameters. Since a here document is considered to be a part of the command itself, the closing backquote for command substitution has been placed after the word (limit) that marks the end of standard input.

Usually **set** breaks up text on white space, i.e. the characters specified in the IFS variable. Here you need to change this variable to a | so that **set** can interpret the three fields of the selected line as three positional parameters. If the number of these parameters is not equal to three (the second **case** option), it means that the pattern can't be located. But when it locates the pattern, it outputs the department name and the emp-id of the departmental head. Finally, it clears the values from these parameters (**shift** 3) before starting the next iteration.

The script doesn't terminate he normally, but you can use the interrupt key at any time to abort the program. When you execute the script, this is how it behaves:

```
$ valcode.sh
Enter department code     :  99
Invalid code
Enter department code     :  02
Department name           :  admin
Emp-id of head of dept    :  5423
Enter department code     :  04
Department name           :  personnel
Emp-id of head of dept    :  2365
Enter department  code    :  <Control-c>
$_
```

It is often an advantage to hold the input in a file in the script itself, as has been done here. This is also feasible when the code list is small. The response is faster because **grep** doesn't have to open any file to scan a pattern; it finds the input in the command line itself.

INTERRUPTING A PROGRAM—THE trap STATEMENT

The previous script was terminated by pressing the interrupt key, *<Control-c>* in that instance, by default, shell scripts terminate whenever this key is pressed, and control returns to the parent shell, usually the login shell. It is not a good idea to terminate shell is scripts in this way because that can leave a lot of temporary files in the disk.

How you could kill processes using the **kill** command. What **kill** actually does is send some signals, designated by some numbers, to terminate the process abnormally. Recall that you had used an option with this statement, for example **kill -15 345,** to kill the process having PID 345, with the signal numbered 15. Some programs are built to respond to these signals differently, and you will see how.

The **trap** statement is used by shell programmers to specify the course of action to be taken in case a signal is received during execution. The statement is normally placed at the beginning of a shell script to indicate how it should respond to such signals. The syntax of the **trap** statement is fairly simple:

trap <*command list*> <*signal list*>

When the script is sent any of the signals that may be in *signal list* **trap** executes the commands it *command list*. The signal list can contain one or more of the 32 signals that are now available in Release 4, and which you used with the **kill** command.

If you habitually create temporary files named after the PID number of the shell, then it will be a good idea to remove them whenever an interrupt occurs:

trap 'rm $$* ; echo "Program interrupted" ; exit' 1 2 15

This tells the script that, in the event of encountering signals having numbers 1,2 or 15, the script should first remove all files expanded from the expression $$*. It should then flash the **echo** message before exiting to the calling program. When you interrupt a program by pressing the interrupt key of your terminal, it sends the signal number 2. It is thus a good idea to include this number in all advanced scripts.

You may also like to ignore the signal, and continue processing. In that case, you should make the program immune to such signals by using a null command list:

trap '' 1 2 15

It is not mandatory to have a **trap** statement in your shell scripts. However, if you have one, then don't forget to include the **exit** statement at the end of the command list, unless you want the script to ignore the specific signals. The inclusion of this statement changes the default behaviour of a script, so it doesn't exit unless specifically instructed to do so. You can have more than one **trap** statement in the same script, but the last executed **trap** overrides the previous ones.

REVIEW

The shell is a remarkable language which will fascinate a programmer. It has most of the standard features of modern day languages, including variables, conditionals and loops. Besides, the facility to use the exit status of a program to control the program flow is a highlight of the UNIX system. Since programming is a built-in feature of the shell, that again leads to further advantages. This gives it a certain kind of power which is somewhat unique in the programming world.

System variables let you alter the operating environment. The *here document* enables you to keep the data in the same script that holds the command line. The **read** statement is used with one or more variables to make shell scripts interactive. Arguments can also be passed on to a script using the positional parameters ($1, $2). There are parameters related to command line arguments ($# $* and $@) which are available to the user. Other parameters let you know the exit status of the last command ($?), the PID of the current shell ($$), and the last background job ($!)

The principle of the exit status was used with the logical ll and **&&** to perform a limited amount of program branching. The **if** conditional is as powerful construct, and its tests are not confined to evaluating expressions alone. Apart from using relational and string tests, it can also file attributes. The **case** statement offers certain special advantages within a compact construct. It accepts alternate patterns as well as wild-card expressions, and is probably the best way to implement string matching in program logic.

Like C, the shell also uses three types of loops. The **while** and **until** loops are complementary to each other, using a reversed control command. Both can handle the same tests that are used by **if**. The **for** loop uses a list of strings for iteration. This list can be generated by using any of the shell's processing capabilities like variable evaluation, command substitution, positional parameters and wild-card expressions. The **set** statement puts values into positional parameters and the **shift** statement is used to reassign the parameter list, **trap** lets you determine the fate of a script when it receives a signal, by pressing the interrupt key for instance.

The shell is really a string-oriented language; the Bourne shell doesn't have any built-in computational facility. There are commands in the UNIX system which can do that, and when used inside a program, overcome the deficiency to some extent. Besides, the shell also possesses some advanced and yet very useful features. It can identify several streams, not merely the three standard ones, and can also merge one steam with another. It can handle multiple files, simulate handle strings and perform unusual steam manipulation. All these, along with a host of other features, will be presented in the next chapter.

25

Overview and System Features: DB2, Oracle, and Ingres

In Chapter this chapter you will learn about relational database management systems (RDBMS). We will provide enough information for you to understand the concepts and the potential of the relational approach in storing and retrieving data. We will cover the basics of three mainframe RDBMS that are available - DB2, ORACLE and INGRES. There are many others as well as systems that run on personal computers.

1. What is a DBMS?
2. What is a Relational DBMS?
3. RDBMS Components
4. DB2
5. The DB2 Environment
6. DB2 Catalog
7. DB2's Related Products
8. DB21
9. ORACLE
10. ORACLE Products
11. INGRES
12. INGRES Products

1. What is a DBMS?

A database management system (DMBS) is a generic term for computer software that acts as an electronic filing or record-keeping system. See Figure 1.

Modern DMBSs come in many different classifications, and with many different processing capabilities, but in general they try to accomplish three things.

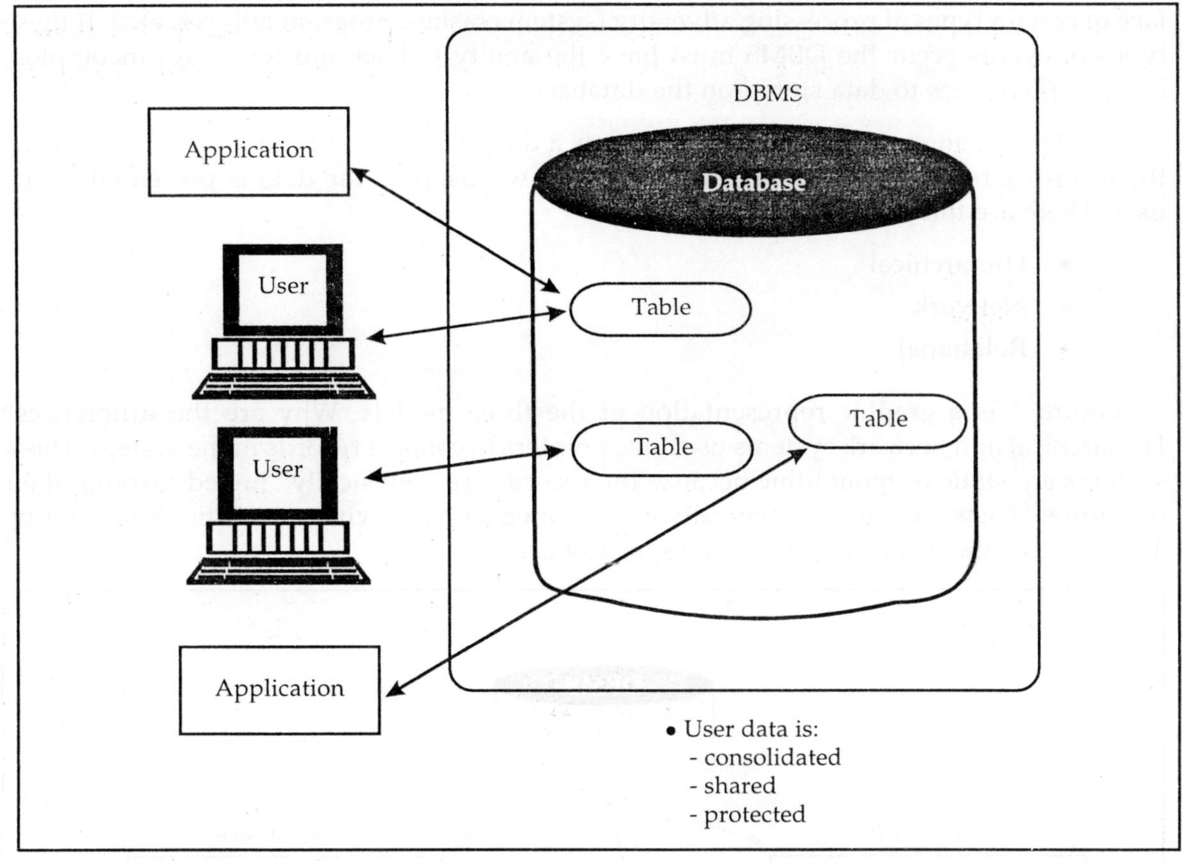

Fig. 1. What is database management system?

1. Data consolidation
2. Data sharing

Data consolidation refers to the combining or unifying of separate data files into a centralised structure, and storing the data in a nonredundant format. A redundant format is a structure that stores the same data items in two or more locations. For instance if within a company an employee address is stored on not only the payroll file, but a department file, project file, employee history file. etc., you have noncentralised structures carrying redundant information. An integrated (nonredundant) system carries the employee address in one location.

Data sharing refers to the ability of the system to allow multiple users concurrent access to individual pieces of data in the database. (You can think of the database as a "pool" of shareable information.)

Data protection refers to the ability of a DBMS to maintain the integrity of its data in the face of certain types of processing adversity (system crashes, program failures, etc.). If these types of events occur the DBMS must have the ability to back out (or undo) incomplete erroneous changes to data stored on the database.

DBMS's organise data in what is known as a data model. You think of a data model as the infrastructure of the data organisation other words, how the data is presented to the user. There are three basic data models:

- Hierarchical
- Network
- Relational

Figure 2 is a graphic representation of the three models. Why are the differences? Hierarchical and network systems use links pointers to connect records in the system. These systems are static or monolithic because the records are "physically" linked through their definition. The structures are typically complicated to work with and difficult to modify. This disadvantage is tempered by the speed of access.

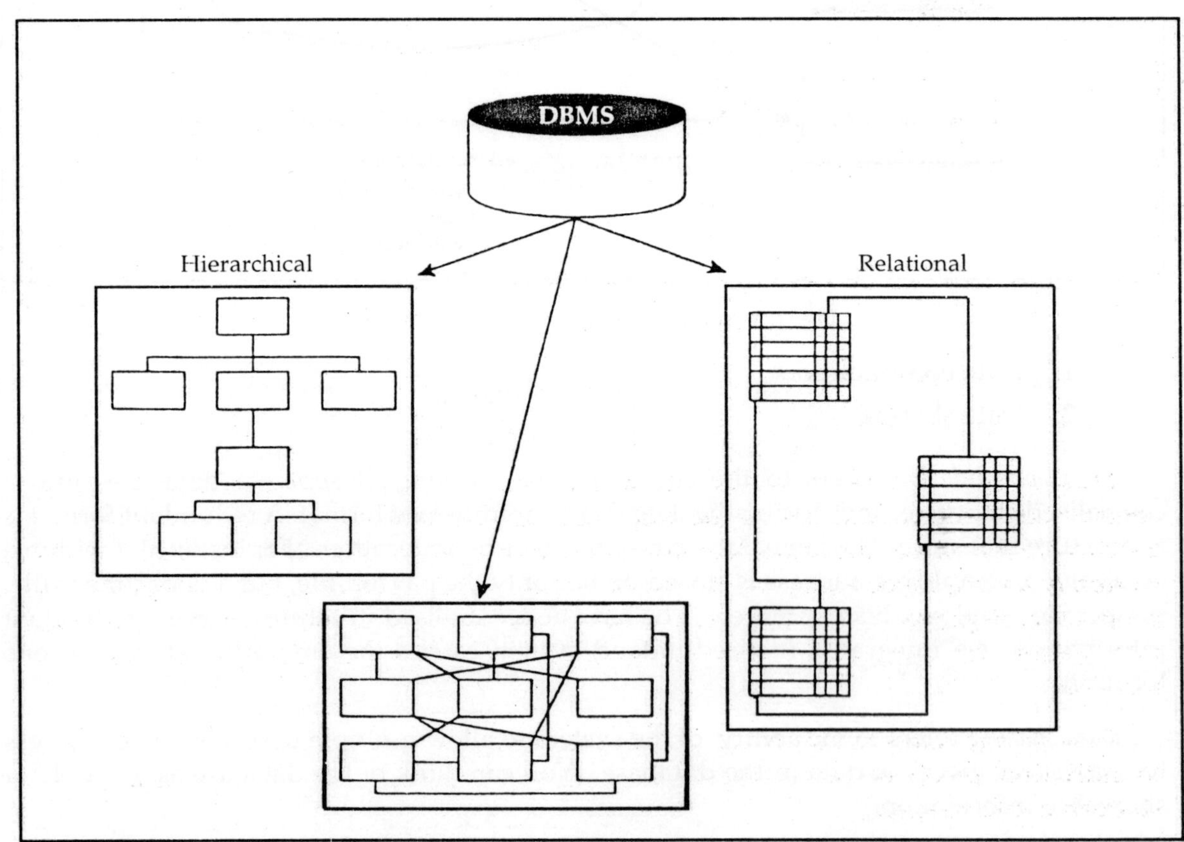

Fig. 2. Data model comparison

Relational systems are not physically linked between records by printers. Associations are based on real field names such as IDs, names, employee numbers, etc. The records in the system are content addressable in that you access them by matching stored data values.

2. What is a Relational DBMS?

Now let's take a look at what a relational database management system is.

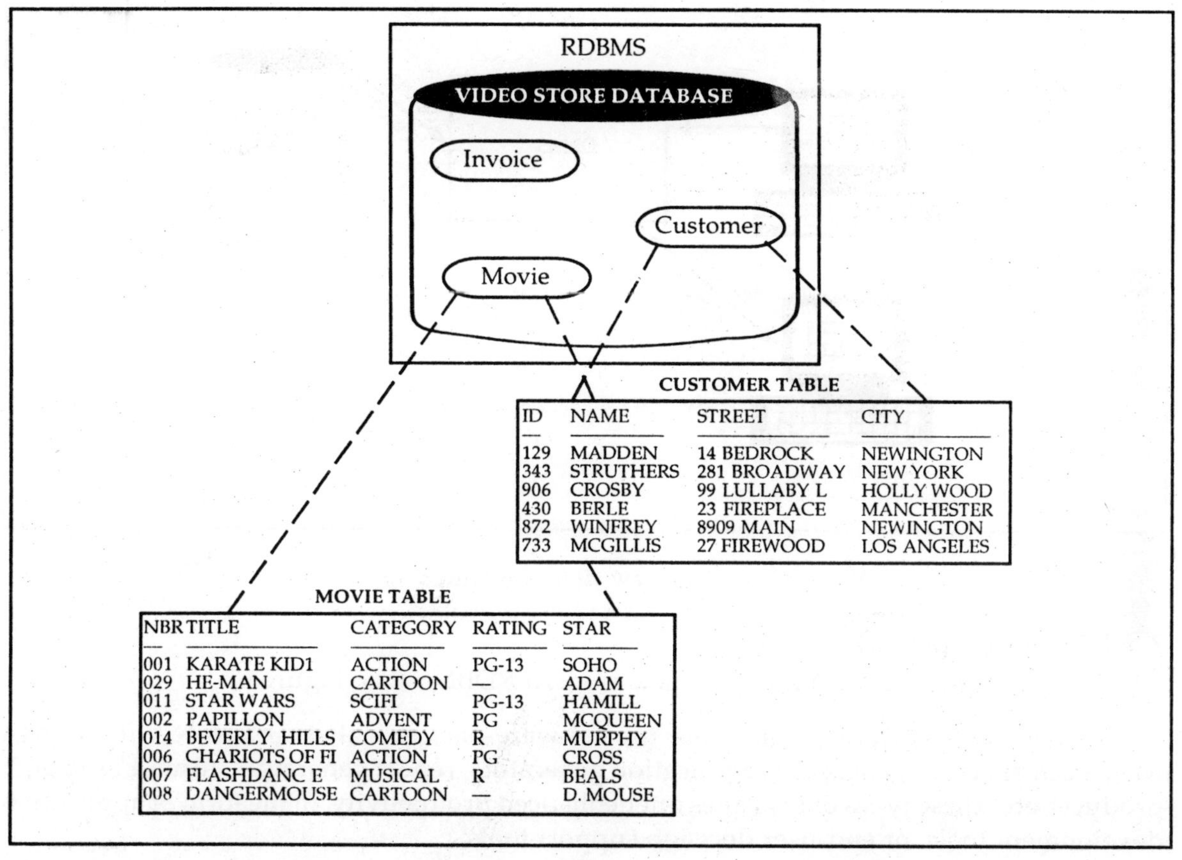

ID	NAME	STREET	CITY
129	MADDEN	14 BEDROCK	NEWINGTON
343	STRUTHERS	281 BROADWAY	NEW YORK
906	CROSBY	99 LULLABY L	HOLLY WOOD
430	BERLE	23 FIREPLACE	MANCHESTER
872	WINFREY	8909 MAIN	NEWINGTON
733	MCGILLIS	27 FIREWOOD	LOS ANGELES

NBR	TITLE	CATEGORY	RATING	STAR
001	KARATE KID1	ACTION	PG-13	SOHO
029	HE-MAN	CARTOON	—	ADAM
011	STAR WARS	SCIFI	PG-13	HAMILL
002	PAPILLON	ADVENT	PG	MCQUEEN
014	BEVERLY HILLS	COMEDY	R	MURPHY
006	CHARIOTS OF FI	ACTION	PG	CROSS
007	FLASHDANC E	MUSICAL	R	BEALS
008	DANGERMOUSE	CARTOON	—	D. MOUSE

Fig. 3.

As of this writing, there are over 200 "relational" DBMS products on the market. Of these about 100 products use SQL on a mainframe, mini, or personal computer. True relational products can be distinguished from non - or pseudo-relational systems. by these three criteria:

1. The data is presented to system users as a collection of tables. These tables are a simple, two-dimensional representation of rows and columns. (See Figure 3.)
2. The system allows users to generate new tables using existing tables. These new, generated tables can be temporary structures (typically when they are the outcome of queries used for reports), or permanent structures. (See Figure 4)

3. Relational systems allow three distinct relational operations on tables: (See Figure 5)
   - SELECT - accessing specific table rows
   - PROJECT - accessing specific table columns
   - JOIN - combining data stored in two or more separate tables

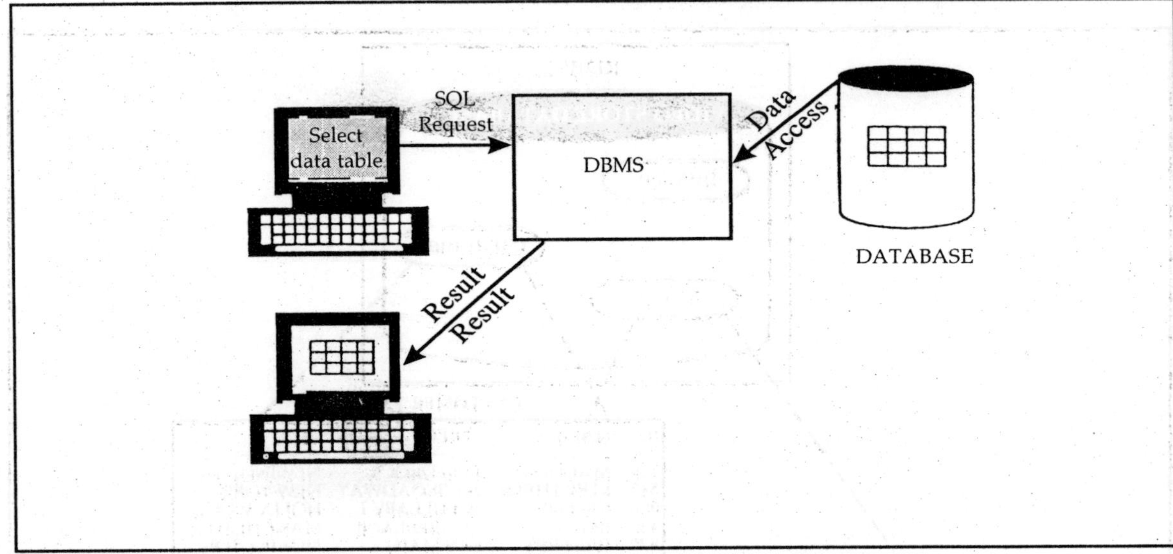

Fig. 4. Generating new tables from existing tables.

3. RDBMS Components

There are three basic components of a modern RDBMS (See Figure 6):

Front-end user interface products are the software packages that interface with system users such as screen generators, application generators, report generators, forms based SQL products, etc. These types of packages offer enhanced productivity in the form of application development tools, or end-user decision support tools.

Back-end data management services supply the engine that powers the system, providing data access, data integrity, and data control mechanisms.

Data access language is the means of communicating system user requests to the data management services. More and more the language of choice is SQL.

Some RDBMS products such as Ingres and Oracle have concentrated on DBMS functionality, providing a veritable cornucopia of front-end products. The strength of the IBM offerings (DB2 and SQL/DS) lies in their sophisticated data control and integrity mechanisms.

Now let's take a quick look at three of the more popular relational DBMS products: DB2 Oracle, and Ingres.

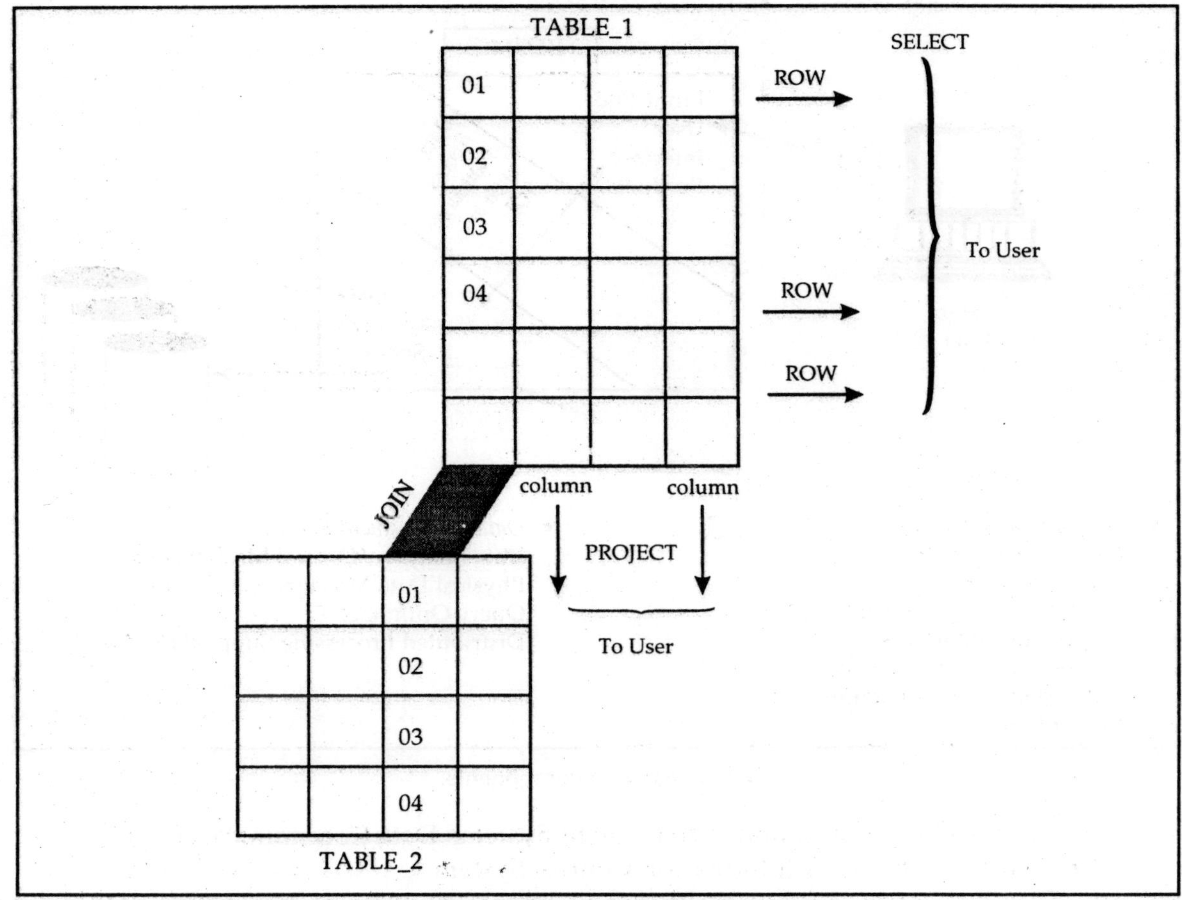

Fig. 5. Relational operations.

4. DB2

DB2 (Database 2) is IBM's relational database management system for large mainframe computers running under the MVS/SP, MVS/XA and MVS/ESA operating systems. The first commercial release of DB2 was in 1983 and DB2 remains the single most talked about database product in a decade. Its strengths lie in its data management capabilities and (as of DB2 version 2.1) its online transaction processing speed — DB2 was benchmarked at over 430 transactions per second in a typical debit/credit application.

5. The DB2 Environment

DB2 runs under the supervision of one of the transaction managers shown in Figure 7. A transaction is any complete unit of business processing: a transaction manager is the software responsible for the successful completion of the unit of work involved in a transaction.

- TSO — Time Sharing Option

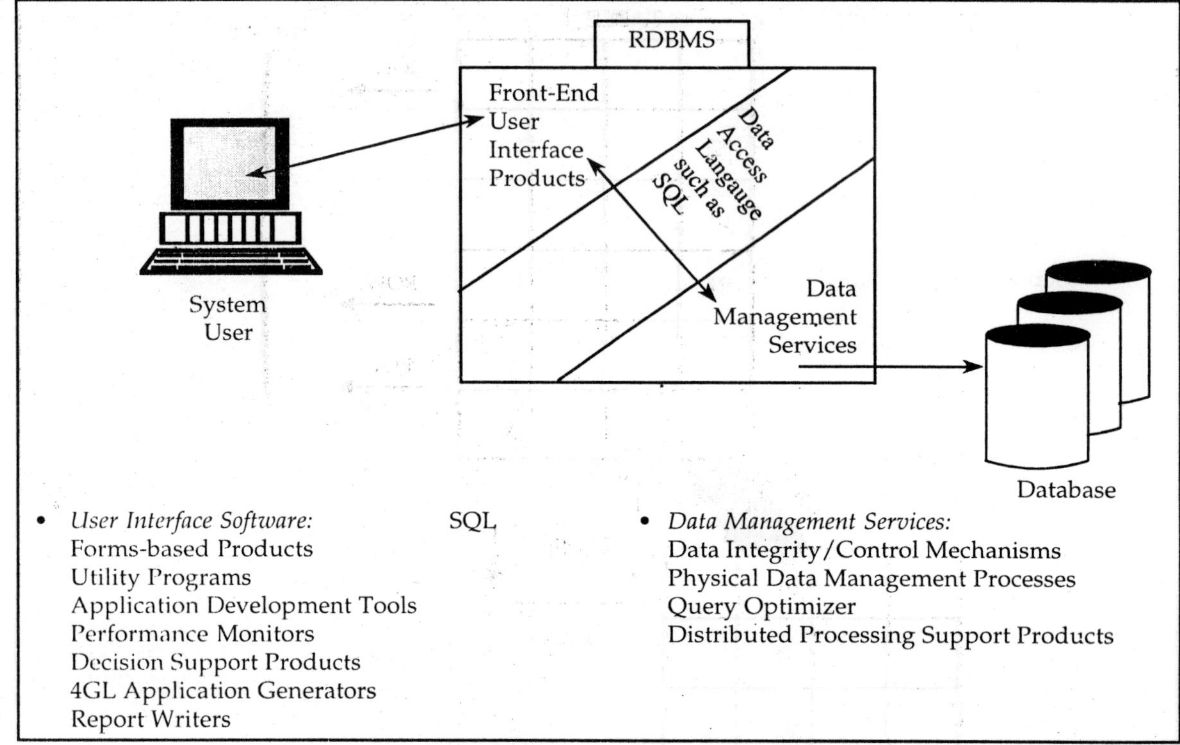

Fig. 6. RDBMS components.

- IMS DC — Information Management Systems Data Communication
- CICS — Customer Information Control System

The transaction manager provides essential services to DB2 including:

Data Communications — the ability to communicate with users at remote terminals.

Data Integrity — the ability to maintain DB2 or other data in an uncompromised and consistent state.

6. DB2 Catalog

DB2 contains basically two different kinds of databases, user databases and a catalog database. The catalog database is used by DB2 to direct and control the operation of the system. On it are stored descriptions of all the data and data objects that DB2 manages.

The catalog itself consists of tables just like a user database. These tables can be queried (but not updated or defined) with SQL statements, just like user tables.

The catalog is used as an active, functioning data dictionary by various parts of the DB2 system for system security, system performance, and SQL query optimisation. (A data dictionary is a structure that maintains information on the content of a database.).

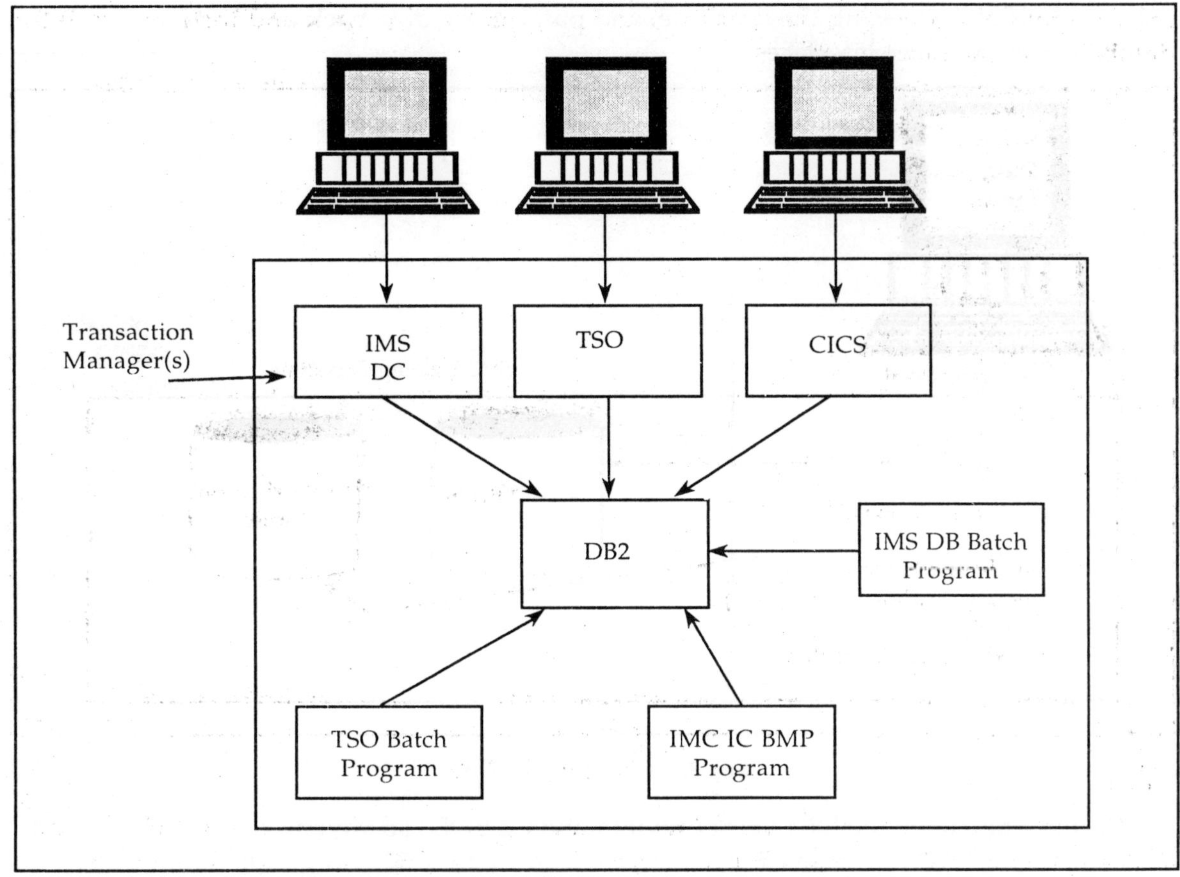

Fig. 7. DB2 environments, DB2 relationships to TSO, CICS, IMS/DC.

*As of this writing, a special type of connection needs to be made from IMS DB programs of DB2.

The DB2 catalog consists of around thirty tables such as:

- SYSTABLES — which contain a row of information on each table in the system;
- SYSCOLUMNS — which contain a row of information for each column in each table in the system;
- SYSINDEXES — which contain a row of information for each index on each table in the system.

Most, if not all, of the popular RDBMS products feature a similar catalog of some sort.

7. DB2's Related Products

As you can see from Figure 9. the system is conceptually layered with the DB2 RDBMS at the kernel. This kernel basically functions as a data manager, accepting or rejecting requests for data, accessing the database, and passing the data back and forth between the database and the other interfaces.

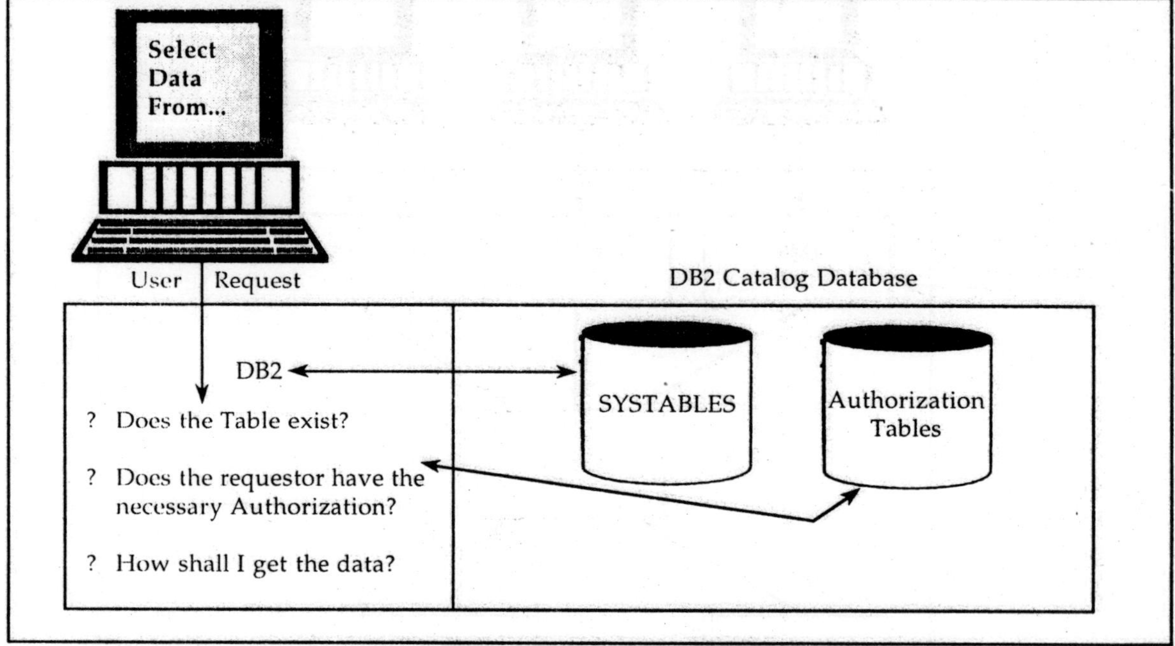

Fig. 8. Catalog use by DB2.

The only language the DB2 kernel understands is SQL., so anyone requesting access to data stored on DB2 databases must communicate with DB2 using SQL statements. The following products are:

- DB21 (DB2 Interactive Interface); A user-friendly interface consisting of a main menu and seven options that allows programmers and database administrators to accomplish work interactively and productively in the DB2 environment.
- QMF (Query Management Facility): A front-end/report-writing program that is meant for the true business end-user. QMF consists of an easy to follow collection of PF-key-driven menus and options. It provides user-friendly access to SQL- and DB2.
- DXT (Data Extract); A data fascimile (data copy) program that allows us to transfer information from other file organisations (like sequential, indexed, and hierarchical file structures) into a format that is ready for loading into DB2 tables.
- DBEDIT: A custom forms front-end program.
- VSAM Transparency: A utility program designed to make DB2 data accessible to application programs that expect to find the data stores as VSAM (virtual sequential method) files.

8. DB21

DB21 is an easy-to-use, menu-driven interface for DB2. It runs under the supervision of TSO. DB21 provides for interactive processing and execution of seven important DB2 facilities (see Figure 9):

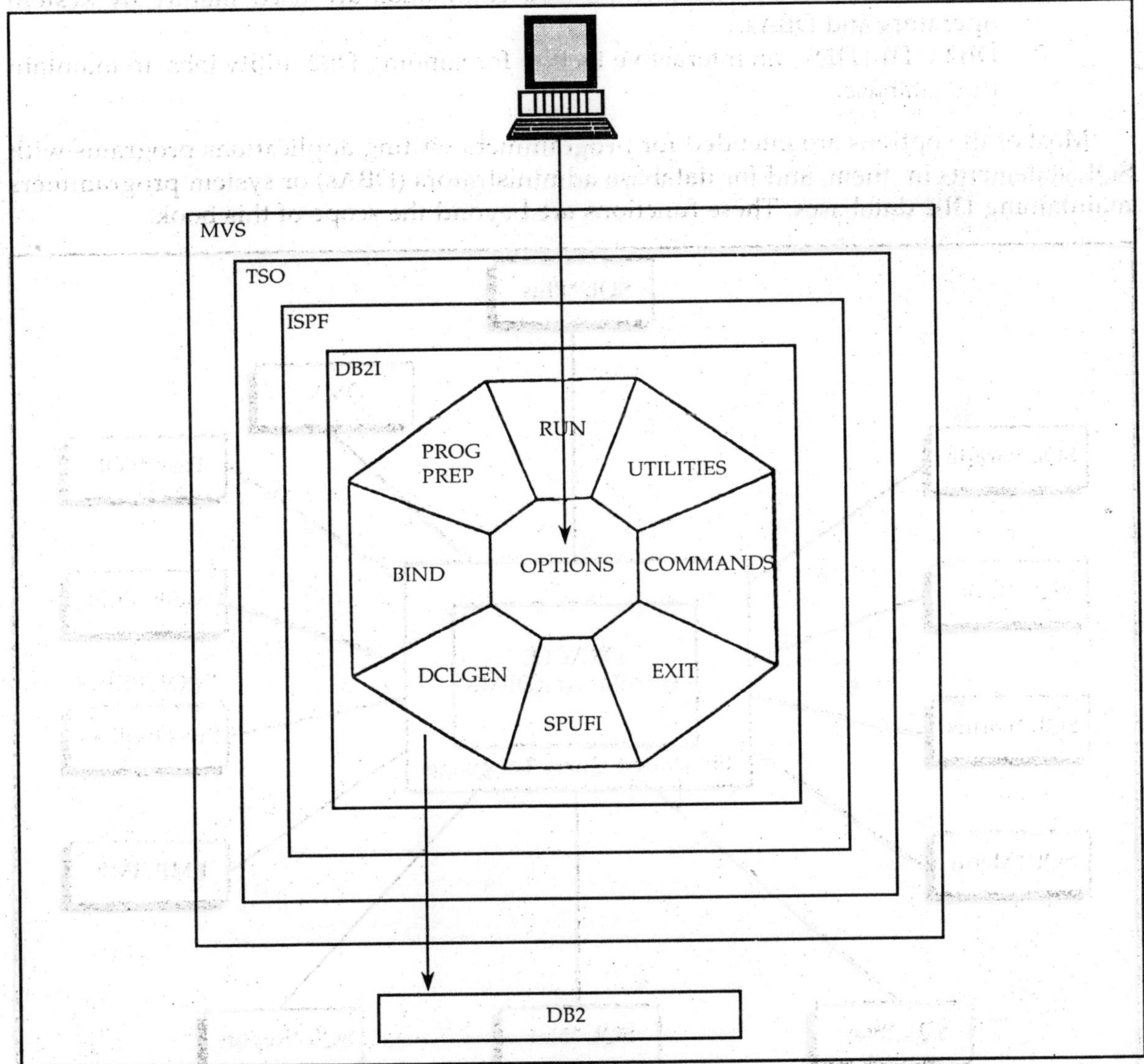

Fig. 9. DB21 environment.

1. SPUFI (SQL processor using File Input) - an interactive SQL statement execution facility
2. DCLGEN (Declarations [Copybook] Generator) - an application program data description generator

3. BIND - an embedded SQL compiler
4. PROGRAM PREPARATION - an application program/SQL precompiler
5. RUN - an application program foreground execution
6. DB2 COMMANDS - an interactive facility for issuing DB2 commands (not to be confused with SQL statements). DB2 commands are used mainly by system operators and DBAs.
7. DB2 UTILITIES - an interactive facility for running DB2 utility jobs to maintain the database.

Most of the options are intended for programmers writing applications programs with SQL statements in them, and for database administrators (DBAs) or system programmers maintaining DB2 databases. These functions are beyond the scope of this book.

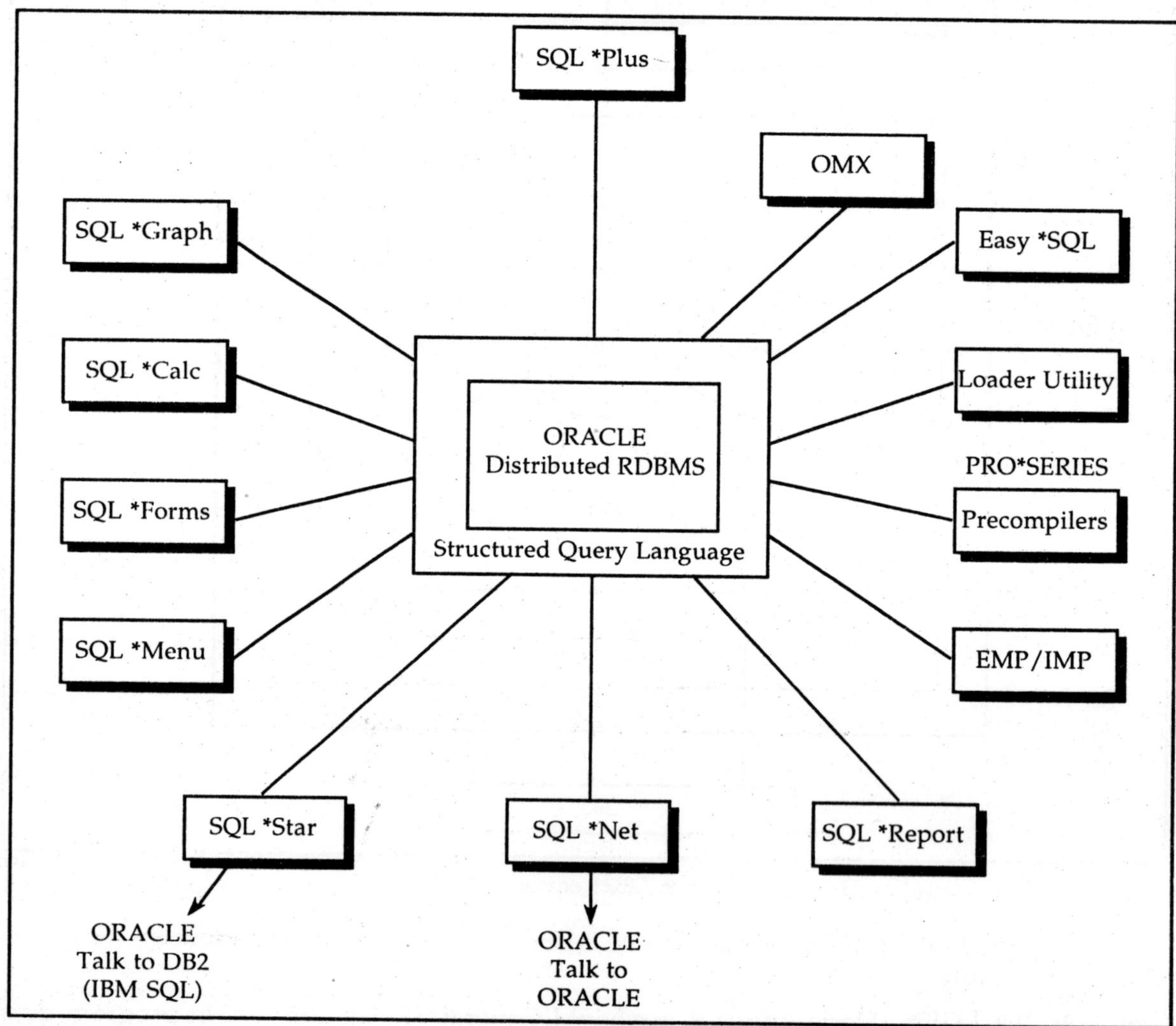

Fig. 10. Oracle Products

9. Oracle

ORACLE is a distributed relational database system created by ORACLE Corporation of Belmont, California, Versions of ORACLE exist for micro. mini. and mainframe systems. ORACLE's first commercial release was in 1977 and as of this writing, the product is at version 5.x. ORACLE's SQL engine is written in C. Language, and because of C's portability (and popularity) ORACLE is available on over sixty different machines and operating systems. The same basic product and add-ons are presented across all these different platforms allowing for what is called vertical integration of a company's DP systems, data, and human resources.

10. Oracle Products

When it comes to front-end user interface products ORACLE's offerings are both varied and powerful (see Figure 10):

SQL*PLUS — The ORACLE version of SQL, which has many powerful operators and functions missing from the IBM SQL dialect.

SQL*FORMS — A forms-based prototype or application development package that allows you to build applications by creating the screens (or forms) that users will access, and building sophisticated controls and integrity features into the panels themselves.

- SQL*CALC — A spreadsheet interface into the ORACLE database, which looks (and behaves) remarkably like Lotus 1-2-3
- SQL*GRAPH — A graphics interface for displaying query results
- SQL*MENU — An ORACLE application front-end development tool
- EASY*SQL — A forms-based product that allows end-users to access table information without SQL statement coding.
- SQL*NET — The ORACLE networking communications software
- SQL*STAR — The ORACLE distributed database software that enables distributing ORACLE and non-ORACLE systems
- SQL*REPORT — The ORACLE forms-based report writer
- QMX — A report/writer query product for end-users that imitates the IBM QMF software.

*PRO*SERIES* — The ORACLE embedded SQL precompilers and third generation language interface products currently available for COBOL. FORTRAN. PASCAL, C. PL/I. BASIC. and ADA.

Oracle gives the potential application developer almost too many product choices. Also. Oracle's version of the SQL language - SQL*PLUS - is in the opinion of this writer, the most functionally complete and powerful SQL on the market. SQL*PLUS has outer-join, hierarchical structuring, output formatting, minus/difference and data/time operators, as well as a formidable selection of row functions such as standard deviation, soundex, and null value replacement.

11. Ingres

INGRES is a distributed relational database system offered by RTI Corporation of Alameda, California. Versions of INGRES also exist for micro, mint, and mainframe systems. however, INGRES is written in the Assembler language of the target system, and is available on fewer machines and operating systems than Oracle.

12. Ingres Products

While the ORACLE products execute from the operating system of the host computer (giving even the PC version of ORACLE a mainframe look and feel), INGRES products are accessed through an integrated wrap around, Lotus 1-2-3 like menu. This approach is very comfortable for business end-users, and in general, the Ingres system offers more of a forms-based data access strategy than either ORACLE or DB2 does.

The application development and decision support tools available in Ingres include (see Figure 11.)

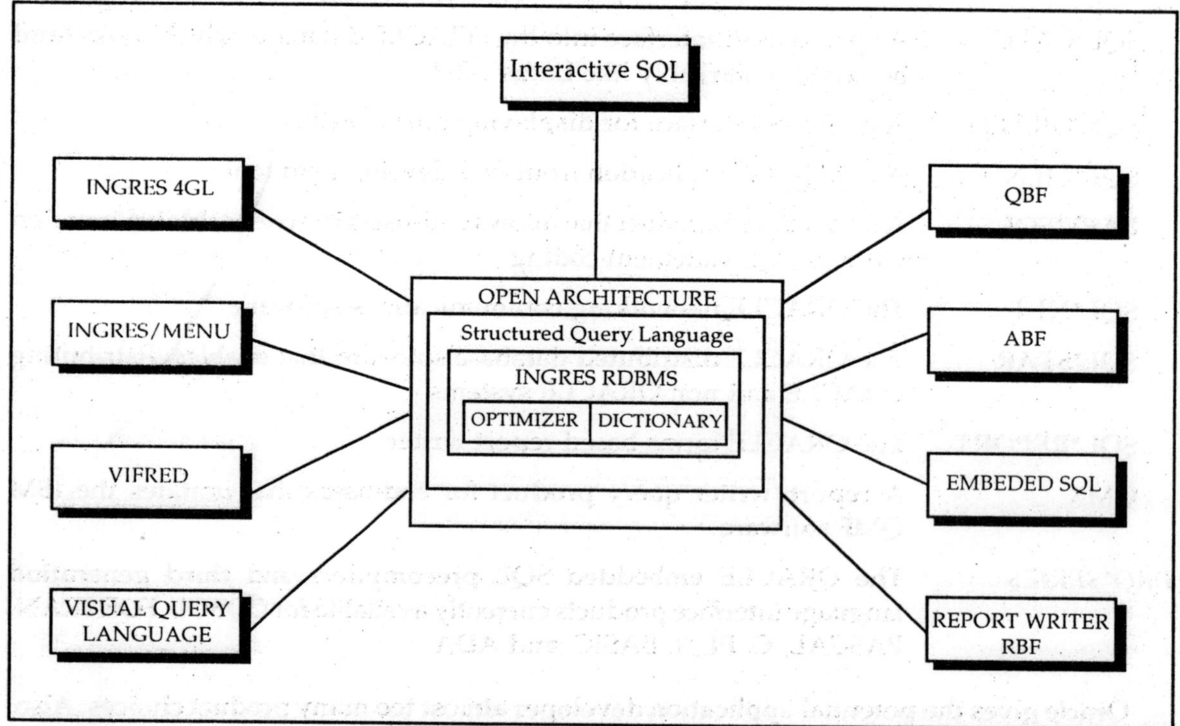

Fig. 11. Ingres product overview.

ISQL	Interactive SQL - similar to SQL*PLUS except that ISQL supports full screen editing capability
INGRES/MENU	A forms-driven interface to all of the INGRES integrated tools and capabilities
INGRES/4GL	A fourth generation language application generator
VIFRED	Visual Forms Editor - A full-screen forms editor for creating custom panels for applications and data access requests
VQL	Visual Query Language - a forms-based tool for data transfer
ABF	Application by Forms - a panel-based application generator
QBF	Query By Forms - a forms-oriented interface to INGRES data, both to some of the above tools and to other access panels
RBF	Report by Forms - The INGRES forms-based report writer

INGRES features some interesting integrity constraints and transaction journaling features not available on other systems s well as an extremely user-friendly front-end to the product in general.

There are minor differences in the SQL syntax as used by DB2. ORACLE and INGRES. In order to use a computer to do the exercises in this book, you will have to modify your answer to fit the system you are using.

26

Data Retrieval Statements

If you have entered the data as shown earlier, you may do the exercises on your computer. If not, write your answers in the space provided. Check your answers with the answer key. Let's proceed.

The SELECT Statement

SELECT retrieves data from tables. It provides a query capability. This means that by executing SELECT statements, information currently in tables will be displayed.

You can think of SELECT as a request to the DBMS for a snapshot image of the table information.

SELECT is the most important SQL statement you will learn. With it you can:

- Display some or all of the COLUMNS fro, tables
- Display some or all of the ROWS from tables
- Display calculated values from tables
- Display statistical information from tables, like averages or sums of column values
- Combine information from two or more tables

SELECT has many options and formats. The basic ones will be covered in this book.

1. Select Statement Format

The format or layout of SELECT statements is as follows:

SELECT <columnname(s)>From<tablename>:

This is interpreted as:

SELECT (what?) One or more column names from a table. If you SELECT more than one column, the column names must be separated from each other with commas **(you may optionally add blanks or spaces for**

readability). Note that there is no comma following the last column name.

FROM (where?) A correctly spelled table name.

SELECT and From are the two mandatory words in a Select query. Other additional words and qualifiers will be covered shortly. In SELECTing data., your main concerns for now will simply be to spell the column and table names correctly. This should not be a problem., because we will be showing them to you on the same page where we ask you to code SELECTs. Again, the structure of the command is:

```
SELECT <columnname(s)> From <tablename>;
```

Example 1: Read the Movie table, and display the title and star columns from all the rows.

```
SELECT TITLE, STAR FROM MOV;
```

Example 2: Read the Invoice table, and get the number, rental data, and return date from all the rows.

```
SELECT NBR, RENT, RETURN FROM INV;
```

Note the use of spaces for readability. We recommend you leave a space between every keyword. For example:

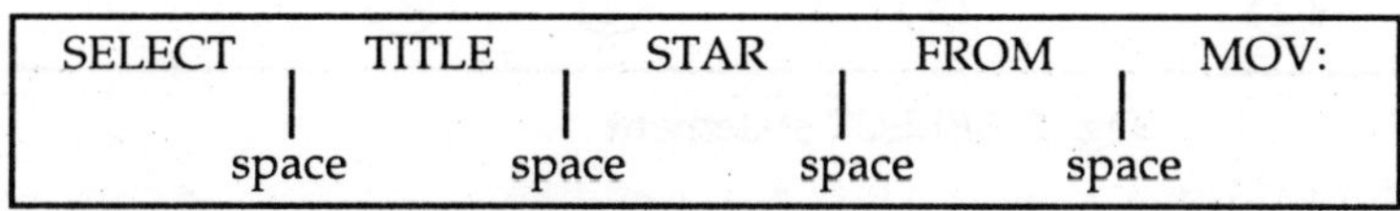

2. Select Statement Results Tables

The output of any successful SELECT statement execution is an unnamed, temporary table knows as a results table. Results tables represent a copy of the data as it exists in the database. These results tables can have zero rows, or up to as many rows as the original table — this depends on your query statement.

Example 1:

```
SELECT TITLE, STAR FROM MOV:
```

Results Table:

The results table will display all titles and stars from the movie table:

TITLE	STAR
Gone with the Wind	Gable
Friday the 13th	Jason
Top Gun	Cruise
Splash	Hanks
101 Dalmations	
Body Heat	Turner
Risky Business	Cruise
Cocoon	Ameche
Crocodile Dundee	Harris
TOOTSIE	HOFFMAN

Coding Select Statements

SQL statements are easy to code (create) when compared to almost any other programming language. There are no rules for column justification (right or left positioning). This means that you don't have to use certain SQL. Words in certain columns as you do when using some other languages.

There are five parts to a SELECT statement, as seen in Figure 1.

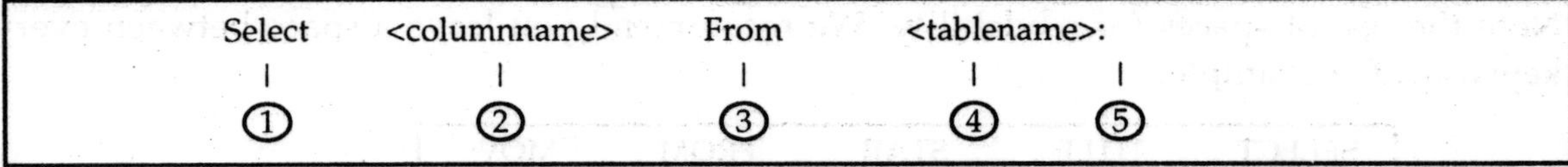

Fig. 1. SELECT statement

1 *Select* is the first word in your query. ***It must be separated by a blank or space from the column names,*** and of course, must be spelled correctly.

2 ***Column names*** must be the next items in your query. They must be separated by a comma, exist in the table you are querying, and of course, must be spelled correctly.

3 ***From*** must be the next word in your query. ***It must be separated by a blank or space from the column names.***

4 ***Tablename*** must be the next item in your query. ***It must follow a blank or space.***

5. ***Semicolon*** lowercase key. The ; tells SQL that the query is complete and may be executed.**

Even though we have not covered some of the details of the statements shown in the following. Look at them carefully. Notice that whether you put the statement on the same line, or break it up onto two lines, the results table is the same. Remember to press **ENTER** after typing each command

Type: SELECT LNAME, FNAME FROM CUST;

RESULTS TABLE

LName	FName
Dangerfield	Rodney
Field	Sally
Nicholson	Jack
Murray	Fred
Madden	John
West	Mae
Woodward	Joanne
Rogers	Roy
Ringwald	Molly
ROGERS	FRED

Type: SELECT LNAME, FNAME FROM CUST;

RESULTS TABLE

LName	FName
Dangerfield	Rodney
Field	Sally
Nicholson	Jack
Murray	Fred
Madden	John
West	Mae
Woodward	Joanne
Rogers	Roy
Ringwald	Molly
ROGERS	FRED

* If you are using SQL on a mainframe using QMF, you do not used a semicolon at the end of the statement.

Layout of Task Specification Sheet

For the remainder of this book, you will be completing exercises to achieve mastery in SQL. The exercises will be presented in the format shown in Figure 2.

1. SQL TOPIC. This represents the SQL concept or statement on which we are currently working.
2. EXERCISE. This represents out business specification written in English.
3. INPUT TABLE. This represents the table that holds the information that will complete our task.
4. SQL STATEMENT STRUCTURE OR FORMAT. This describes the general syntax for your statements. In particular, notice the two variable areas for column and table names;
   - 4a. <columnname> represents the column name(s), which will change from request to request.
   - 4b. <tablename> represents the table name, which will change from request to request.
5. After reading the exercise over two or three times to gain a thorough understanding of the problem to be solved, follow these steps to complete the exercise:
   1. Write your answer in the space provided.
   2. Type in your statements (watch <columnname> and <tablename> spelling) and execute them.
   3. Verify that your answers are correct by both looking at the results table 6 and the input table. For further verification, look at the answer key. 7

SELECTing Single Columns Exercises

Because these are your first SQL statements, we'll go through the procedures step by step.

Exercise 1 asks you to display (SELECT) all of the movie titles using the movie table. This is a very straightforward request, asking you to SELECT the TITLE column From the MOV table. Remember our steps;

Steps Towards Problem Solution

1. Red the exercise carefully.
2. Formulate the solution mentally. Try rephrasing the task using SQL-like syntax (SELECT, FROM. etc.). Check the format box and write your answer in the space provided.
3. Type in your statements and execute them.
4. Verify that your answers are correct by both looking at the results table given and looking up the input table.

1. TOPIC: How to Complete This Book
2. EXERCISE: This is an example.
3. INPUT TABLE:

SQL Statement Structure
Format

4. SELECT <columnname> From <table name>

space space space

5. STEP 1.____________________________________
   Write your answer.
   ____
   ____
   ____

   STEP 2. Enter your answer into the computer.

   If you are using a computer, complete the exercise. Otherwise, check your answer by looking at the answer key.

   STEP 3. Check your results.
6. RESULTS TABLE:

7. If your screen does not look like this, try again or look at the answer key and execute the solution given.

Fig. 2. Exercise format.

The answer you will write down and type is:

Select Title From Mov;

After you press the **ENTER** key, the data on your screen should look like the results table in Exercise 1. If your screen doesn't look like this, check for spelling errors in the <columnname> or <tablename>. Make sure the words are in the correct order as shown in the format box, and that a semicolon(;) appears at the end.

Now do Exercise 1

EXERCISE 1

1. TOPIC: SELECTing Single Columns
2. EXERCISE 1. Display the movie Title(s) from the Mov table.
3. INPUT TABLE:

Mov

NBR	Title	Type	Rating	Star	Qty	Price
1.	Gone with the Wind	Drama		Gable	4	39.95
2.	Friday the 13th	Horror	R	Jason	2	69.95
3.	Top Gun	Drama	PG	Cruise	7	49.95
4.	Splash	Comedy	PG 13	Hanks	3	29.95
5.	101 Dalmations	Comedy	G		3	59.95
6.	Body Heat	Drama	R	Turner	3	19.95
7.	Risky Business	Comedy	R	Cruise	2	44.55
8.	Cocoon	Scifi	PG	Ameche	2	
9.	Crocodile Dundee	Comedy	PG 13	Harris	2	69.95
10.	TOOTSIE	COMEDY	PG	HOFFMAN	1	29.95

Format

4.

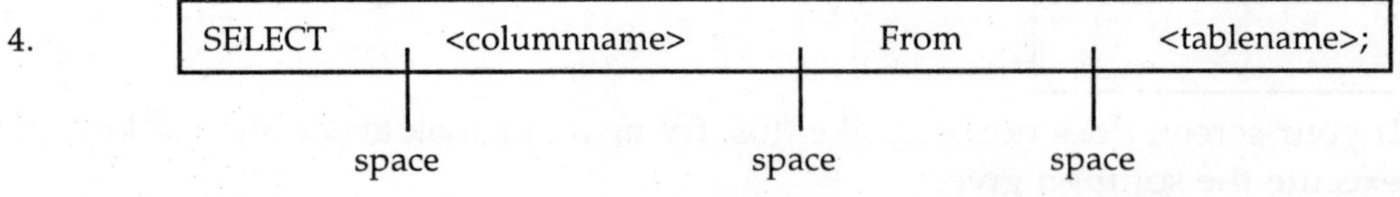

5. STEP 1. ______________________________

Write your answer.

____

____

____

STEP 2. Enter your answer into the computer.

If you are using a computer, complete the exercise. Otherwise, check your answer by looking at the answer key.

STEP 3. Check your results.

6. Results Table:

Title
Gone with the Wind
Friday the 13th
Top Gun
Splash
101 Dalmations
Body Heat
Risky Business
Cocoon
Crocodile Dundee
Tootsie

7. If your screen does not look like this, try again or look at the answer key and execute the solution given there.

Note: We have given you the answer to Exercise 1. From now on, you will write your own answers.

EXERCISE 2

1. TOPIC: SELECTing Single Columns
2. EXERCISE 2. Display the movie Type(s) from the MOV table.
3. INPUT TABLE:

Mov

NBR	Title	Type	Rating	Star	Qty	Price
1.	Gone with the Wind	Drama		Gable	4	39.95
2.	Friday the 13th	Horror	R	Jason	2	69.95
3.	Top Gun	Drama	PG	Cruise	7	49.95
4.	Splash	Comedy	PG 13	Hanks	3	29.95
5.	101 Dalmations	Comedy	G		3	59.95
6.	Body Heat	Drama	R	Turner	3	19.95
7.	Risky Business	Comedy	R	Cruise	2	44.55
8.	Cocoon	Scifi	PG	Ameche	2	
9.	Crocodile Dundee	Comedy	PG13	Harris	2	69.95
10.	Tootsie	Comedy	PG	Hoffman	1	29.95

FORMAT

4. 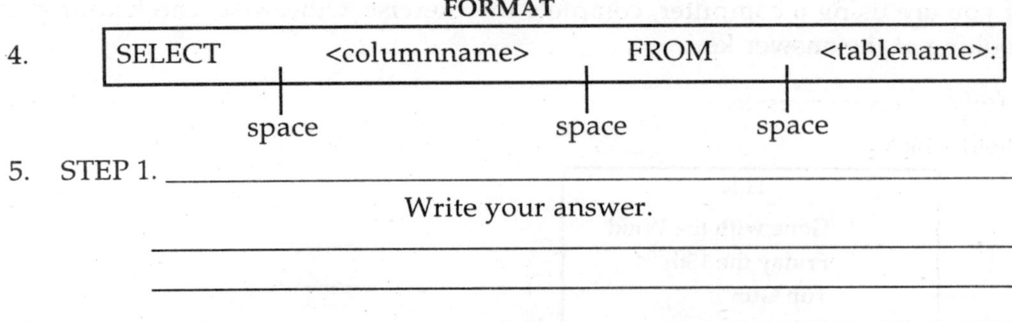

5. STEP 1. ____________________

Write your answer.

____

____

____

STEP 2. Enter your answer into the computer.

If you are using a computer, complete the exercise. Otherwise, check your answer by looking at the answer key.

STEP 3. Check your results.

6. Results Table:

Type
Drama
Horror
Drama
Comedy
Comedy
Drama
Comedy
Scifi
Comedy
Comedy

7. If your screen does not look like this, try again or look at the answer key and execute the solution given there.

EXERCISE 3

1. TOPIC: SELECTing Single Columns
2. EXERCISE 3. Display the CITY column from the CUST table.
3. INPUT TABLE:

CUST

ID	LNAME	FRAME	CITY	ST
01.	Dangerfield	Rodney	Hartford	CT
02.	Field	Sally	Franklin	NY
03.	Nicholson	Jack	Hartford	CA

04.	Murray	Fred	Bozrah	CT
05.	Madden	John	Bratilebord	VT
06.	West	Mae	Park Place	CA
07.	Woodward	Joanne	Gettysburg	PA
08.	Rogers	Roy	Happy Trails	TX
09.	Ringwald	Molly	Pinksville	CA
10.	Rogers	Freed	Park Palace	CA

FORMAT

4. SELECT <columnname> FROM <tablename>:

space space space

5. STEP 1. ______________________________

Write your answer.

____

____

____

STEP 2. Enter your answer into the computer.

If you are using a computer, complete the exercise. Otherwise, check your answer by looking at the answer key.

STEP 3. Check your results.

6. Results Table:

City
Hartford
Franklin
Hartford
Bozrah
Brattleboro
Park Place
Gettysburg
Happy Trails
Pinksville
Park Palace

7. If your screen does not look like this, try again or look at the answer key and execute the solution given there.

Exercise 4 asks you to retrieve the names contained in the Star column, on the movie (MOV) table.

EXERCISE 4

1. TOPIC: SELECTing Single Columns
2. EXERCISE 4. Display all the stars from the MOV table.
3. INPUT TABLE:

MOV

NBR	TITLE	TYPE	RATING	STAR	QTY	PRICE
1.	Cone with the Wind	Drama		Cable	4	39.95
2.	Friday the 13th	Horror	R	Jason	2	69.95
3.	Toy Gun	Drama	PG	Cruise	7	49.95
4.	Splash	Comedy	PG 13	Hanks	3	29.95
5.	101 Dalmations	Comedy	G		3	59.95
6.	Body Heat	Drama	R	Turner	3	19.95
7.	Risky Business	Comedy	R	Cruise	2	44.55
8.	Cocoon	Scifi	PG	Ameche	2	
9.	Crocodile Dundee	Comedy	PG 13	Harris	2	69.95
10.	Tootsie	Comedy	PG	Hoffman	1	29.95

FORMAT

4.

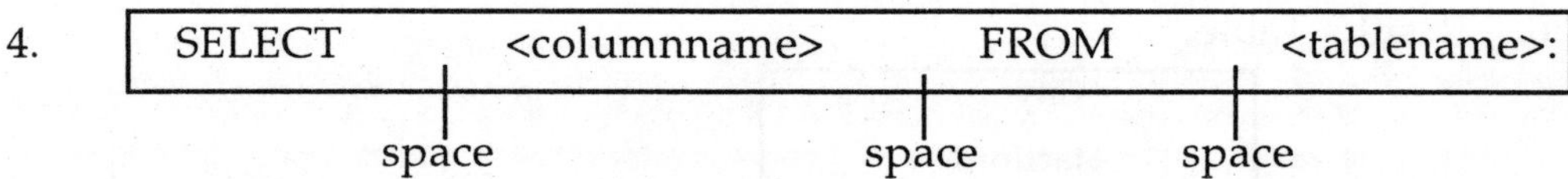

5. STEP 1. Select Title From Mov;

Write your answer.

____

____

____

STEP 2. Enter your answer into the computer.

If you are using a computer, complete the exercise. Otherwise, check your answer by looking at the answer key.

STEP 3. Check your results.

6. Results Table:

Star
Cable
Jason
Cruise
Hanks
Turner
Cruise
Ameche
Harris
Hoffman

7. If your screen does not look like this try again or look at the answer key and execute the solution given there.

Select Distinct - Eliminating Duplicate Rows

In Exercise 4, you may have noticed that CRUISE, was listed twice in our results table. This kind of redundant information is often unnecessary and than clutter up our reports. SQL does not eliminate duplicate rows from the results table unless explicitly requested. The way to accomplish this is with the Distinct modifier.

DISTINCT eliminates duplicate rows from our results table, Its syntax is very straightforward:

```
SELECT DISTINCT <columnname> FROM <tablename>;
```

Just remember that DISTINCT comes after SELECT and before the first column name.

The next three Exercises are easy to accomplish and short, so you might want to run the queries with and without DISTINCT to see its effect more clearly.

EXERCISE 5

1. TOPIC: DISTINCT-Eliminating duplicate rows
2. EXERCISE 5. Display the different stars on the MOV table, and do not duplicate any rows.
3. INPUT TABLE:

MOV

NBR	TITLE	TYPE	RATING	STAR	QTY	PRICE
1.	Gone with the Wind	Drama		Cable	4	39.95
2.	Friday the 13th	Horror	R	Jason	2	69.95
3.	Top Gun	Drama	PG	Cruise	7	49.95

4.	Splash	Comedy	PG 13	Hanks	3	29.95
5.	101 Dalmations	Comedy	PG 13	Hanks	3	29.95
6.	Body Heat	Drama	R	Turner	3	19.95
7.	Risky Business	Comedy	R	Cruise	2	44.55
8.	Cocoon	Scifi	PG	Ameche	2	
9.	Crocodile Dundee	Comedy	PG13	Harris	2	69.95
10.	Tootsie	Comedy	PG	Hoffman	1	29.95

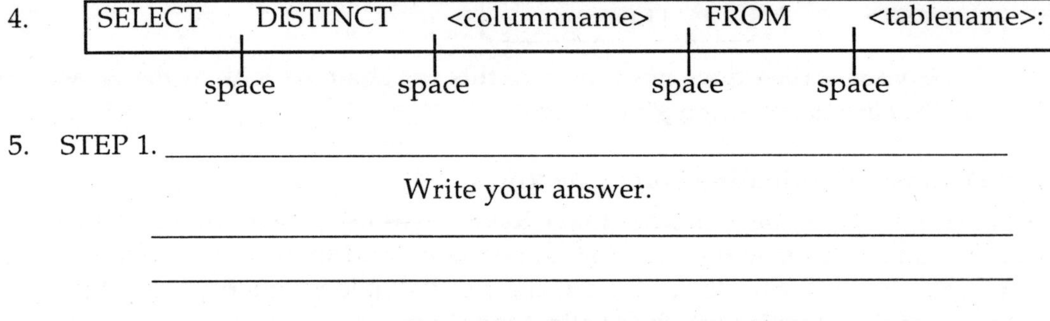

5. STEP 1. ________________________________

Write your answer.

____

____

____

STEP 2. Enter your answer into the computer.

If you are using a computer, complete the exercise. Otherwise, check your answer by looking at the answer key.

STEP 3. Check your results.

6. Results Table:

Star
Ameche
Cruise
Cable
Hanks
Harris
Hoffman
Jason
Turner

7. If your screen does not look like this, try again or look at the answer key and execute the solution given there.

Note that DISTINCT sorted our output here on Star's name. This is purely coincidental. We will learn how to sort our Results Tables in SQL.

EXERCISE 6

1. Topic: Distinct—Eliminating duplicate rows
2. Exercise 6. Display the different movie types on the MOV table. Remove duplicate rows from your output.
3. Input Table:

MOV

NBR	TITLE	TYPE	RATING	STAR	QTY	PRICE
1.	Gone with the Wind	Drama		Cable	4	39.95
2.	Friday the 13th	Horror	R	Jason	2	69.95
3.	Top Gun	Drama	PG	Cruise	7	49.95
4.	Splash	Comedy	PG 13	Hanks	3	29.95
5.	101 Dalmations	Comedy	G		3	59.95
6.	Body Heat	Drama	R	Turner	3	19.95
7.	Risky Business	Comedy	R	Cruise	2	44.55
8.	Cocoon	Scifi	PG	Ameche	2	
9.	Crocodile Dundee	Comedy	PG 13	Harris	2	69.95
10.	Tootsie	Comedy	PG	Hoffman	1	29.95

FORMAT

4. SELECT DISTINCT <columnname> FROM <tablename>:

   space space space space

5. STEP 1. ______________________________

   Write your answer.

   ____

   ____

   ____

   STEP 2. Enter your answer into the computer.

   If your are using a computer, complete the exercise. Otherwise, check your answer by looking at the answer key.

   STEP 3. Check your results.

6. Results Table:

Type
Comedy
Drama
Horror
Scifi

7. If your screen does not look like this, try again or look at the answer key and execute the solution given there.

Note: **Mainframe users may see a results table with these rows displayed a different order.**

EXERCISE 7

1. TOPIC: DISTINCT—Eliminating duplicate rows
2. EXERCISE 7. Find out which movies have been rented by displaying the different movie numbers on the I_M table. Remove duplicate rows from your output.
3. INPUT TABLE:

I_M

I_NBR	M_NBR
1	4
1	5
2	3
3	1
3	10
4	6
4	3
4	5
4	1
5	1
5	7
7	1
7	3
7	5
8	4
8	7
9	9
9	2

10	4
10	4
10	1
10	5
10	4

FORMAT

4. SELECT DISTINCT <columnname> FROM <tablename>:

   space space space space

5. STEP 1. ______________________

   Write your answer.

   ____

   ____

   ____

   STEP 2. Enter your answer into the computer.

   If you are using a computer, complete the exercise. Otherwise, check your answer by looking at the answer key.

   STEP 3. Check your results.

6. Results Table:

M_NBR
1
2
3
4
5
6
7
9
10

7. If your screen does not look like this, try again or look at the answer key and execute the solution given there.

6 SELECTING MULTIPLE COLUMNS FROM A TABLE

SELECTing multiple columns is as easy as retrieving single columns. Just type the column names after your SELECT statement (but before the FROM clause) and separate each column name with a comma. You can optionally add spaces after each comma to make your query more readable.

The columns will be displayed from left to right, in the same order in which they appear after Select.

Note that DISTINCT applies to all of the columns selected in the query, so that if you request more than one column, one results table row must duplicate another results row in every column before it is eliminated by DISTINCT. Exercise 10 will show you this more clearly.

Try these exercises. Refer to the table listings shown to get the correct spelling for the columns requested.

EXERCISE 8

1 TOPIC: SELECTing Multiple Columns

2 EXERCISE 8. Display all the title, quantities, and prices on the MOV table.

3 INPUT TABLE:

MOV

NBR	Title	Type	Rating	Star	Qty	Price
1.	Gone with the Wind	Drama		Cable	4	39.95
2.	Friday the 13th	Horror	R	Jason	2	69.95
3.	Top Gun	Drama	PG	Cruise	7	49.95
4.	Splash	Comedy	PG 13	Hanks	3	29.95
5.	101 Dalmations	Comedy	G		3	59.95
6.	Body Heat	Drama	R	Turner	3	19.95
7.	Risky Business	Comedy	R	Cruise	2	44.55
8.	Cocoon	Scifi	PG	Ameche	2	
9.	Crocodile Dundee	Comedy	PG 13	Harris	2	69.95
10.	Tootsie	Comedy	PG	Hoffman	1	29.95

FORMAT

4.

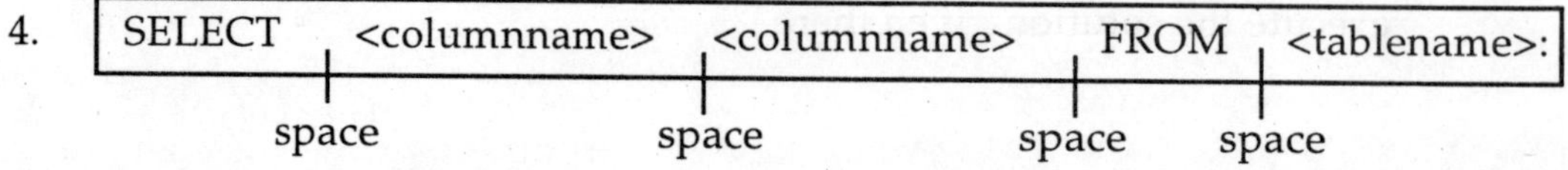

5. STEP 1. ____

Write your answer.

____

____

____

STEP 2. Enter your answer into the computer.

If you are using a computer, complete the exercise. Otherwise, check your answer by looking at the answer key.

STEP 3. Check your results.

6. Results Table:

Title	Qty	Price
Gone with the Wind	4	39.95
Friday the 13th	2	69.95
Top Gun	7	49.95
Splash	3	29.95
101 Dalmations	3	59.95
Body Heat	3	19.95
Risky Business	2	44.55
Cocoon	2	
Crocodile Dundee	2	69.95
Tootsie	1	29.95

7. If your screen does not look like this, try again or look at the answer key and execute the solution given there.

EXERCISE 9

1. TOPIC: SELECTing Multiple Columns
2. EXERCISE 9. Display all the last and first names on the Cust table.
3. INPUT TABLE:

Cust

ID	LNAME	FNAME	CITY	ST
01.	Dangerfield	Rodney	Hariford	CT
02.	Field	Sally	Franklin	NY

03.	Nicholson	Jack	Hariford	CA
04.	Murray	Fred	Bozrah	CT
05.	Madden	John	Brattleboro	VT
06.	West	Mae	Park Place	CA
07.	Woodward	Joanne	Gettysburg	PA
08.	Rogers	Roy	Happy Trails	TX
09.	Ringwald	Molly	Pinksville	CA
10.	Rogers	Fred	Park Place	CA

FORMAT

4. 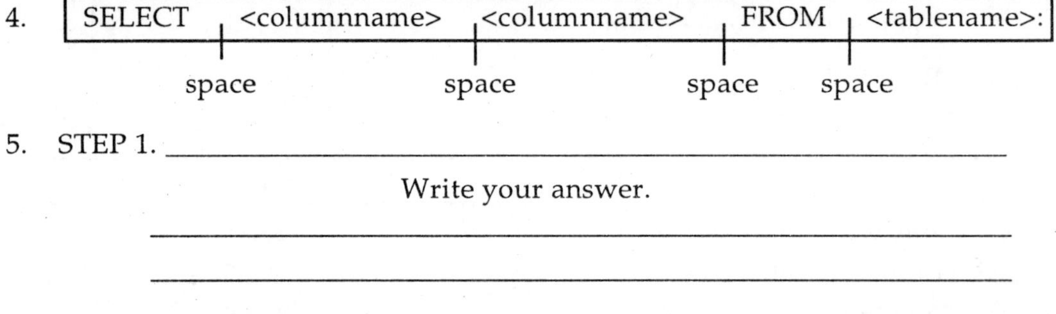

5. STEP 1. ____________________

Write your answer.

____

____

____

STEP 2. Enter your answer into the computer.

If you are using a computer, complete the exercise. Otherwise, check your answer by looking at the answer key.

STEP 3. Check your results.

6 Results Table:

LName	FName
Dangerfield	Rodney
Field	Sally
Nicholson	Jack
Murray	Fred
Madden	John
West	Mae
Woodward	Joanne
Rogers	Roy
Ringwald	Molly
Rogers	Fred

7. If your screen does not look like this, try again or look at the answer key and execute the solution given there.

EXERCISE 10

1. TOPIC: Distinct—Selecting multiple columns
2. EXERCISE 10. Select all of the different combinations of movie types and ratings.
3. INPUT TABLE:

MOV

NBR	Title	Type	Rating	Star	Qty	Price
1.	Gone with the Wind	Drama		Cable	4	39.95
2.	Friday the 13th	Horror	R	Jason	2	69.95
3.	Top Gun	Drama	PG	Cruise	7	49.95
4.	Splash	Comedy	PG 13	Hanks	3	29.95
5.	101 Dalmations	Comedy	G		3	59.95
6.	Body Heat	Drama	R	Turner	3	19.95
7.	Risky Business	Comedy	R	Cruise	2	44.55
8.	Cocoon	Scifi	PG	Ameche	2	
9.	Crocodile Dundee	Comedy	PG 13	Harris	2	69.95
10.	Tootsie	Comedy	PG	Hoffman	1	29.95

FORMAT

4. Select Distinct <columnname> <columnname> From <tablename>:

   space space space space

5. STEP 1. ______________________________

   Write your answer.

   ____

   ____

   ____

   Step 2. Enter your answer into the computer.

   If you are using a computer, complete the exercise, Otherwise, check your answer by looking at the answer key.

   Step 3. Check your results.

6 Results Table:

Type	Rating
Drama	
Horror	R
Drama	PG
Comedy	PG 13
Comedy	G
Drama	R
Comedy	R
Scifi PG	
Comedy	PG

7. If your screen does not look like this, try again or look at the answer key and execute the solution given there.

Note: **DISTINCT eliminated only one movie which duplicated "comedy" and "PG-13".**

7 ELECT* — DISPLAYING ALL COLUMNS FROM A TABLE

Select* is a shorthand method of telling SQL that you want all of the columns in a table displayed. Its format is very simple (see the Format box below). It can save time in your SQL coding efforts.

Select * is convenient, and we will be using it quite a bit throughout the next few lessons to allow you to concentrate on learning new SQL concepts, and to spend less time typing.

EXERCISE 11

1. TOPIC: SELECTing All Columns
2. EXERCISE 11. Display all the rows and columns to the INV table.
3. INPUT TABLE:

INV

NBR	Custid	Tot	Rent	Return
1.	01	9.55	87055	
2.	02	13.55	87030	
3.	02	21.01	87041	87042
4.	01	11.25	87042	87072
5.	03	12.55	87045	87051

6.	02	9.75	87047	87051
7.	04	10.35	86355	
8.	04	12.55	87051	87053
9.	05	10.35	87052	
10.	02	7.55	87030	87060

FORMAT

4. Select* From <tablename>:

5. STEP 1. ____________________

Write your answer.

____

____

____

Step 2. Enter your answer into the computer.

If you are using a computer, complete the exercise. Otherwise, check your answer by looking at the answer key.

Step 3. Check your results.

6. Results Table:

NBR	Custid	Tot	Rent	Return
1.	01	9.55	87055	
2.	02	13.55	87030	
3.	02	21.01	87041	87042
4.	01	11.25	87042	87072
5.	03	12.55	87045	87051
6.	02	9.75	87047	87051
7.	04	10.35	86355	
8.	04	10.35	87051	87053
9.	05	10.35	87052	
10.	02	7.55	87030	87060

7. If your screen does not look like this, try again or look at the answer key and execute the solution given there.

EXERCISE 12

1. TOPIC: SELECTing All Columns
2. EXERCISE 12. Display the contents of the CUST table.
3. INPUT TABLE:

CUST

ID	LName	FName	City	ST
01.	Dangerfield	Rodney	Hartford	CT
02.	Field	Sally	Franklin	NY
03.	Nickolson	Jack	Hartford	CA
04.	Murray	Fred	Dozrah	CT
05.	Madden	John	Bratilebord	VT
06.	West	Mae	Park Place	CA
07.	Woodward	Joanne	Gettysburg	PA
08.	Rogers	Roy	Happy Trails	TX
09.	Ringwald	Molly	Pinksville	CA
10.	Rogers	Fred	Park Place	CA

FORMAT

4. | Select* | From | <tablename>: |
|---|---|---|

5. STEP 1. ______________________

Write your answer.

____

____

____

Step 2. Enter your answer into the computer.

If you are using a computer, complete the exercise. Otherwise, check your answer by rocking at the answer key

Step 3. Check your results.

6. Results Table:

ID	LName	FName	City	ST
01	Dangerfield	Rodney	Hariford	CT
02	Field	Sally	Franklin	NY
03	Nicholson	Jack	Hartford	CA
04	Murray	Fred	Bozrah	CT
05	Madden	John	Braitleboro	VT
06	West	Mae	Park Place	CA
07	Woodward	Joanne	Gettysburg	PA
08	Rogers	Roy	Happy Trails	TX
09	Ringwald	Molly	Pinksville	CA
10	Rogers	Fred	Park Place	CA

7. If your screen does not look like this, try look at the answer key and execute the solution given there.

EXERCISE 13

1. TOPIC: Selecting All Columns
2. EXERCISE 13. Display the entire Mov table.
3. Input Table:

MOV

NBR	Title	Type	Rating	Star	Qty	Price
1.	Gone with the Wind	Drama		Cable	4	39.95
2.	Friday the 13th	Horror	R	Jason	2	69.95
3.	Top Gun	Drama	PG	Cruise	7	49.95
4.	Splash	Comedy	PG 13	Hanks	3	29.95
5.	101 Dalmations	Comedy	G		3	59.95
6.	Body Heat	Drama	R	Turner	3	19.95
7.	Risky Business	Comedy	R	Cruise	2	44.55
8.	Cocoon	Scifi	PG	Ameche	2	
9.	Crocodile Dundee	Comedy	PG 13	Harris	2	69.95
10.	Tootsie	Comedy	PG	Hoffman	1	29.95

FORMAT

4.

```
Select*    From    <tablename>:
```

5. STEP 1. ____

Write your answer.

____

____

____

Step. 2. Enter your answer into the computer.

If you are using a computer, complete the exercise. Otherwise, check your answer by looking at the answer key.

Step 3. Check your results.

6. Results Table:

NBR	Title	Type	Rating	Star	Qty	Price
1.	Gone with the Wind	Drama		Cable	4	39.95
2.	Friday the 13th	Horror	R	Jason	2	69.95
3.	Top Gun	Drama	PG	Cruise	7	49.95
4.	Splash	Comedy	PG 13	Hanks	3	29.95
5.	101 Dalmations	Comedy	G		3	59.95
6.	Body Heat	Drama	R	Turner	3	19.95
7.	Risky Business	Comedy	R	Cruise	2	44.55
8.	Cocoon	Scifi	PG	Ameche	2	
9.	Crocodile Dundee	Comedy	PG 13	Harris	2	69.95
10.	Tootsie	Comedy	PG	Hoffman	1	29.95

7. If your screen does not look like this, try again or look at the answer key and execute the solution given there.

EXERCISE 14

1. TOPIC: Selecting All Columns
2. EXERCISE 14. Display everything on the I_M table.
3. INPUT TABLE:

I_M

I_NBR	M_NBR
1	4
1	5
2	3
3	1
3	10
4	6
4	3
4	5
4	1
5	1
5	7
7	1
7	3
7	5
8	4
8	7
9	9
9	2
10	4
10	4
10	1
10	5
10	4

FORMAT

4. Select * From <tablename>:

5. STEP 1. ______________________________

Write your answer.

____

____

____

Step 2. Enter your answer into the computer.

If you are using a computer, complete the exercise. Otherwise, check your answer by looking at the answer key.

Step 3. Check your results.

6. Results Table:

I_NBR	M_NBR
1	4
1	5
2	3
3	1
3	10
4	6
4	3
4	5
4	1
5	1
5	7
7	1
7	3
7	5
8	4
8	7
9	9
9	2
10	4
10	4
10	1
10	5
10	4

7. If your screen does not look this, try again or at the answer key and execute the solution given there.

8 SUMMARY

So far we have covered three ways to SELECT data:

1. Select <columnname>, <columnname>, <columnname>, etc.
2. Select Distinct <columnname>, etc.
3. Select*, etc.

In the next chapter, you will learn how to tell SQL which particular rows to select.

9 INTERPRETING SQL STATEMENTS

In these examples, try to write out an English translation, or picture the results of executing the SQL statements shown. The fourth example uses the WHERE clause, which we haven't covered yet. What do you think its effect will be on SELECT statement?

1. Select Distinct I_NBR From I_M;
2. Select Distinct Custid. Rent From Inv;
3. Select FName, LName, City From Cust;
4. Select* From Mov Where Type = 'Drama';

1. ______________________________
2. ______________________________
3. ______________________________
4. ______________________________

10 ANSWER KEY

There may be more than one answer to an exercise. However, the one given emphasises the chapter topic.

Exercise	1	Select Title From Mov;
Exercise	2	Select Type From Mov;
Exercise	3	Select City From Cust;
Exercise	4	Select Star From Mov;
Exercise	5	Select Distinct Star From Mov;
Exercise	6	Select Distinct Type From Mov;
Exercise	7	Select Distinct M_NBR From I_M;
Exercise	8	Select Title, QTY, Price From Mov;
Exercise	9	Select LName, FName From Cust;
Exercise	10	Select Distinct Rating, Type From Mov;
Exercise	11	Select * From INV;
Exercise	12	Select * From Cust;
Exercise	13	Select * From Mov;
Exercise	14	Select * From I_M;

Interpreting SQL statements

1. Check to see that no duplicate invoice numbers exist on the I - M Table. ______

----

2. Find out who rented movies - remove duplicates. ______________________

3. Display our customer first and last names and their cities. ______________________

4. Display all of the rows and columns for DRALA movies ______________________

27

Joining Tables

In this chapter you will learn how to:

1. Select data that is contained on more than one table with a select statement.
2. Combine the information from three and four tables on a query.

1. Join — Retrieving Data From Two or More Tables

Suppose we wanted a report listing the customer name (LNAME), in number (NBR), and return data (RETURN), for all the invoices that the report columns are spread across two tables. LNAME is of CUST table, and NBR and RETURN are on the INV table. We need way to merge the columns from these two tables. We do this by join them on a column that carried the same information. In this customer identification number — which is called ID on the CUST and CUSTID on the INV table — provides the link. Although ID CUSTID are different column names, they contain the information.

This technique is called joining tables, because the corresponding columns from two or more different tables are actually "joined together" to from a single row in the results table. The ability to join rows and combine data from two or more tables is one of the most powerful features of relational systems. Review Figure 1.

- It is often necessary to access data stored in two or more tables in the same query.
- For example:
  List the customer name, invoice number, and RENT for all items on the INV table
- Solution:

```
Select LNAME, NBR, RENT
From INV. CUST
Where ID = CUSTID;
```

This SQL, statement combines or merges columns from the CUST and INV table, based on a data value (Column), that is common to both tables — customer ID

- The WHERE condition dictates that the only rows to be SELECTED will be those in which the number for CUSTID matches in both tables

Figure 1. Selecting from more than one table (join).

There are several reasons to join tables. Study these two examples.

1. **Merge columns from two or more tables.** If for instance, as in the example above, we wanted a list of the customer LNAMEs and their corresponding invoice NBRs, we would use the following statement:

```
Select LName, NBR From Cust, INV Where ID = Custid;
```

LName	NBR
DangerField	1
Field	2
Field	3
DangerField	4
Nicholson	5
Field	6
Murray	7
Murray	8
Madden	9
Field	10

2. **Select data from one table, based on another table.** For instance, if we wanted customers who have videos yet to be returned, we following statement:

```
Select LName, ID From Cust, INV Where
ID = Custid and Return is Null;
```

LName	ID
DangerField	01
Field	02
Murray	04
Madden	05

2. Join Graphic

Notice that the customer identification number is tables. It is used as the joining column in the WHERE "link" the tables togeher.

The key to understanding the subtleties of joining WHERE condition that links the tables together. This WHERE is called (appropriately enough) a "join condition. Let's more closely.

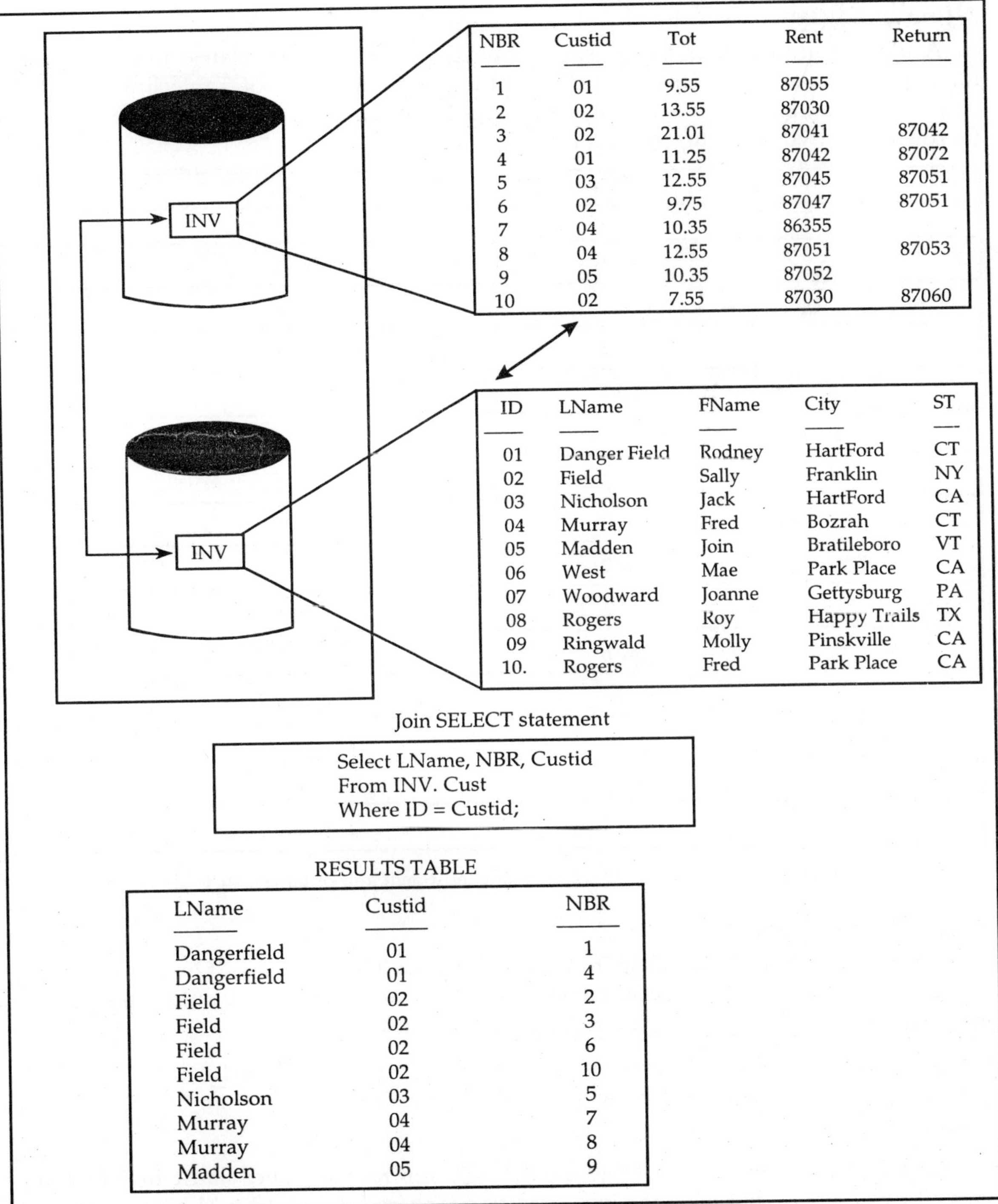

NBR	Custid	Tot	Rent	Return
1	01	9.55	87055	
2	02	13.55	87030	
3	02	21.01	87041	87042
4	01	11.25	87042	87072
5	03	12.55	87045	87051
6	02	9.75	87047	87051
7	04	10.35	86355	
8	04	12.55	87051	87053
9	05	10.35	87052	
10	02	7.55	87030	87060

ID	LName	FName	City	ST
01	Danger Field	Rodney	HartFord	CT
02	Field	Sally	Franklin	NY
03	Nicholson	Jack	HartFord	CA
04	Murray	Fred	Bozrah	CT
05	Madden	Join	Bratileboro	VT
06	West	Mae	Park Place	CA
07	Woodward	Joanne	Gettysburg	PA
08	Rogers	Roy	Happy Trails	TX
09	Ringwald	Molly	Pinskville	CA
10.	Rogers	Fred	Park Place	CA

Join SELECT statement

```
Select LName, NBR, Custid
From INV. Cust
Where ID = Custid;
```

RESULTS TABLE

LName	Custid	NBR
Dangerfield	01	1
Dangerfield	01	4
Field	02	2
Field	02	3
Field	02	6
Field	02	10
Nicholson	03	5
Murray	04	7
Murray	04	8
Madden	05	9

Fig. 2. Join (another view).

3. Join Condition

A join condition refers to the specific portion of a WHERE clause that links tables together in a table join. This WHERE condition contains a set of Table linking column names—one column from each table. This join condition is the condition that SQL uses to tie rows from two tables together in the join process.

Table 1	*Table 2*
row 1	row 1
row 1	row 2
row 1	row 3
row 1	row 4
row 1	row n
row 2	row 1
row 2	row 2
row 2	row 3
row 2	row 4
row 2	row n
row n	row 1
row n	row 2
row n	row 3
row n	row 4
row n	row n

Fig. 3. Cartesian Product Table — unconditional join of table 1 to Table 2.

4. SQL. Join Process

Whenever SQL finds two or more table names in a FROM clause, it builds a "holding" table, which is a temporary results table. This table is stored in the computer's memory and may take a great deal of space, as well as time, to build.

This table is known as a Cartesian Product Table (see Figure 3), and you can picture it as a table that SQL, creates, containing all possible row combinations from the tables you are joining:

Once the Cartesian Product Table is built, SQL applies the Where clause to it, and filters out all rows that do not meet the join condition (Where MOV.NBR = M NBR as shown in Figure 4).

Actually, the entire join process is quite simple to visualise. and is shown in Figure 4.

1. SQL creates a large, temporary table that contains all possible row combinations from the tables you are joining — the Cartesian Product of the two tables.
2. SQL applies the Where clause, like a filter on the table, to sift out rows that do not meet the Where condition. These rows become the results table.As you might imagine, Cartesian Product Tables can be rather large. In spite of the fact that they are only temporary structures, the amount of disk space and internal SQL

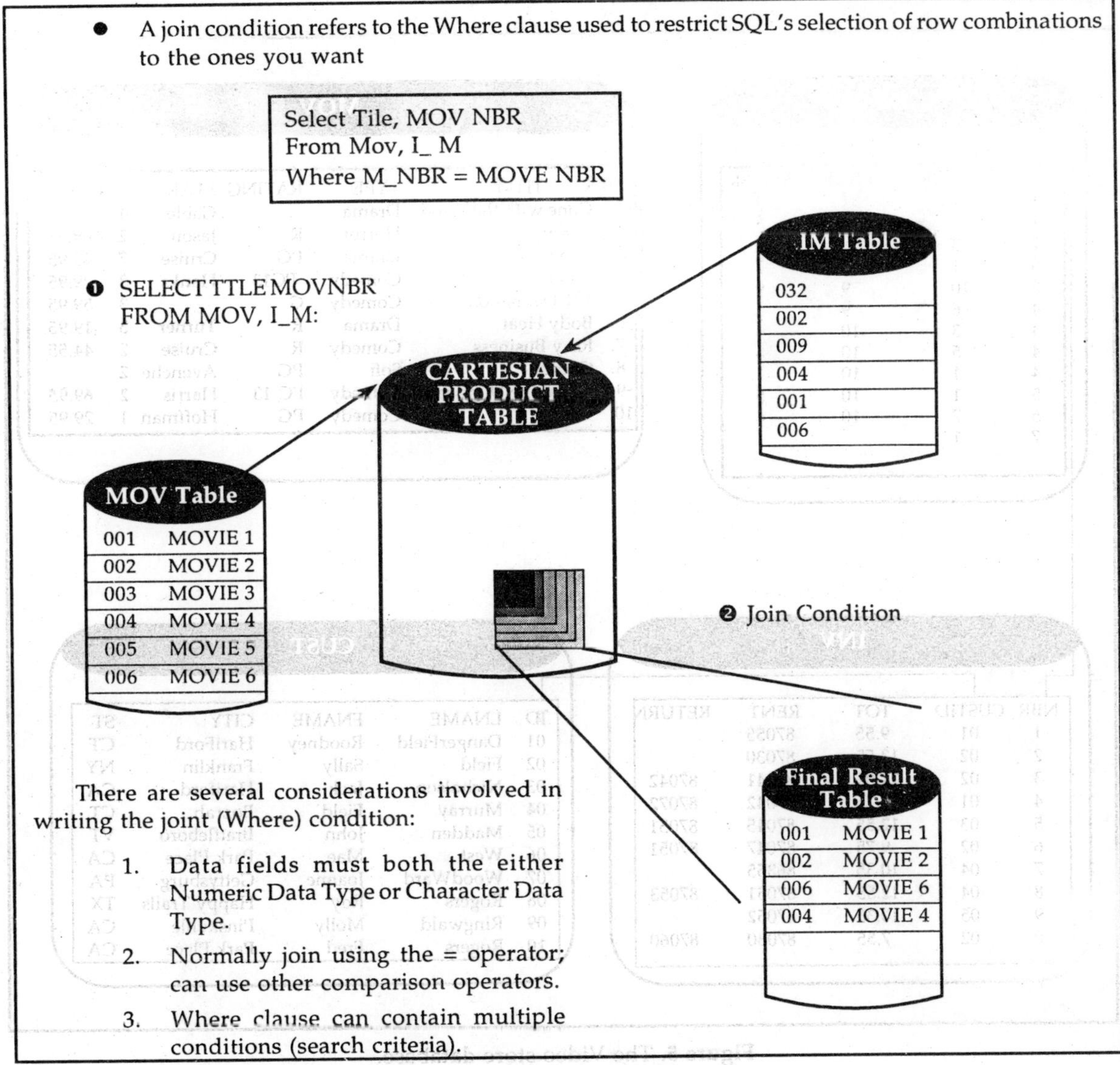

Fig. 4. Join condition.

processing that occurs places exhaustive demands on the system. Joins of large tables (over 100,000 rows) can produce major performance problems.

5. Table-Linking Columns

Figure 5 shows the table-linking columns for our video database. These columns hold the "intertable values" necessary to correctly join two or more tables together. Look at the actual column information in Figure 5 and study the values stored in the fields that are specified as the table-linking columns.

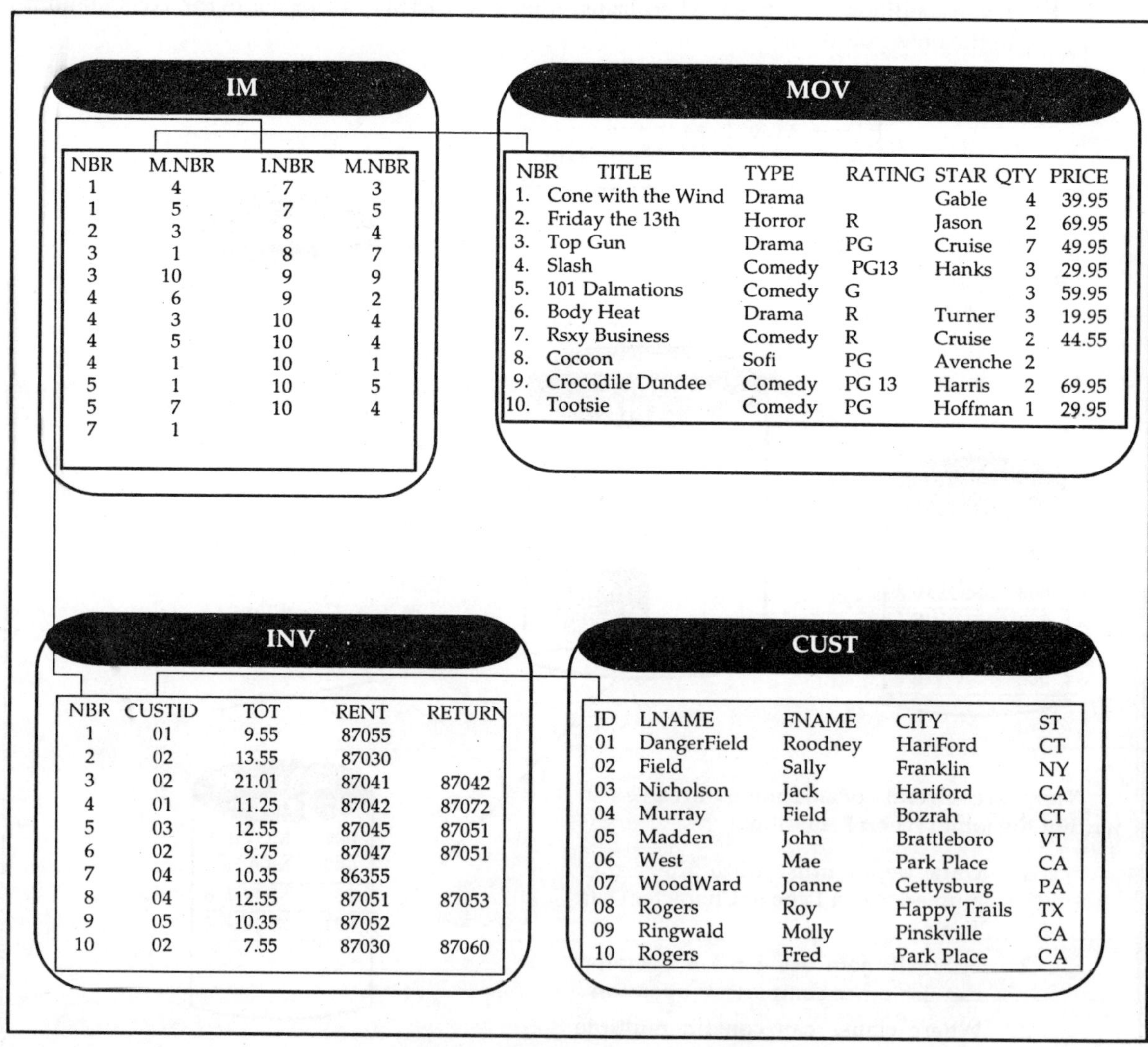

IM

NBR	M.NBR	I.NBR	M.NBR
1	4	7	3
1	5	7	5
2	3	8	4
3	1	8	7
3	10	9	9
4	6	9	2
4	3	10	4
4	5	10	4
4	1	10	1
5	1	10	5
5	7	10	4
7	1		

MOV

NBR	TITLE	TYPE	RATING	STAR	QTY	PRICE
1.	Cone with the Wind	Drama		Gable	4	39.95
2.	Friday the 13th	Horror	R	Jason	2	69.95
3.	Top Gun	Drama	PG	Cruise	7	49.95
4.	Slash	Comedy	PG13	Hanks	3	29.95
5.	101 Dalmations	Comedy	G		3	59.95
6.	Body Heat	Drama	R	Turner	3	19.95
7.	Rsxy Business	Comedy	R	Cruise	2	44.55
8.	Cocoon	Sofi	PG	Avenche	2	
9.	Crocodile Dundee	Comedy	PG 13	Harris	2	69.95
10.	Tootsie	Comedy	PG	Hoffman	1	29.95

INV

NBR	CUSTID	TOT	RENT	RETURN
1	01	9.55	87055	
2	02	13.55	87030	
3	02	21.01	87041	87042
4	01	11.25	87042	87072
5	03	12.55	87045	87051
6	02	9.75	87047	87051
7	04	10.35	86355	
8	04	12.55	87051	87053
9	05	10.35	87052	
10	02	7.55	87030	87060

CUST

ID	LNAME	FNAME	CITY	ST
01	DangerField	Roodney	HariFord	CT
02	Field	Sally	Franklin	NY
03	Nicholson	Jack	Hariford	CA
04	Murray	Field	Bozrah	CT
05	Madden	John	Brattleboro	VT
06	West	Mae	Park Place	CA
07	WoodWard	Joanne	Gettysburg	PA
08	Rogers	Roy	Happy Trails	TX
09	Ringwald	Molly	Pinskville	CA
10	Rogers	Fred	Park Place	CA

Figure 5. The Video store database.

These table-linking columns are sometimes referred to as key columns. They are described in the relational database world as being either Primary or Foreign keys, depending upon their significance to the table itself, and their significance to other tables in the database.

> *Primary Key* - the column(s) that would be considered the most important column(s) table (ID from the CUST table. NBR from the MOC and INV tables). Most often primary key fields contain unique values.
>
> *Foreign Key* — the column that stores values relating to another table's primary key column (CUSTID from the INV table is an example of a foreign key, which relates to the ID column from the CUST table).

To join tables correctly, we link one table's foreign key to another table's primary key by means of the Where clause, as in Figure 6.

6. Three Join Condition Possibilities

When you join one table with another, there are three possibilities that can unfold, depending on how the values from one table-column match the values from the other table-column. They are illustrated in Figure 7.

1. The value we are joining on appears one time in each table. In this case, one row will be created in the results table for each matching value.
2. The value we are joining on does not appear in either table. In this case, no entry is placed in the results table. This type of exception condition is sometimes important.
3. The value we are joining on appears multiple times in one or the other table. In this case, several rows will be Selected into our results table. In fact, the number of rows that is equal to the higher number of occurrences found in either table will be Selected.

Join Table I	*Primary Table II*	*Foreign Key I*	*Join Key II*	*Condition*
Cust	INV	ID	Custid	Where ID = Custid
INV	I_M	NBR	I_NBR	Where NBR = I_NBR
I_M	INV	(The primary key consists of both columns.)	NBR	Where NBR = I_NBR
I_M	Mov	NBR	Where NBR = M_NBR	
Mov	I_M	NBR	M_NBR	Where NBR = M NBR

Fig. 6. Join condition using primary and foreign keys.

7. Join Considerations

Figure 8 summarises the joining concepts.

Concept 1, the limit of joining fifteen tables in a single Select statement, would have to be considered a bit impractical, particularly in light of what we've just learned about join performance. IBM recommends a limit of no more than seven tables joined in a single statement. Four tables is even more sensible — especially if you are using medium to large-sized tables (10,000 to 100,00 rows).

```
Select LName, Custid, NBR From INV. Cust
Where Custid = ID and Custid in ('03'; '05)
```

LNAME	CUSTED	NBR
Nicholson	08	5
Madden	06	9

```
Select LName, Custid, NBR From INV. Cust
Where Custid = ID and in ('06', '07');
```

0 Rows Selected

```
Select LName, Custid, NBR From Inv. Cust
Where Custid = ID;
```

LNAME	CUSTID	NBR
Dangerfield	01	1
Dangerfield	01	4
Field	02	2
Field	02	3
Field	02	6
Field	02	10
Nicholson	03	5
Murray	04	7
Murray	04	8
Madden	05	9

Fig. 7. Join condition — three possibilities.

In Concept 2, if we are joining two tables on a column where the column name is duplicated in both tables (for instance PERSONNEL and Dept tables both referring to the Employee number column as EMPNO), we have to qualify the EMPNO column name by prefixing it with the table name and a period. This will make our column name references clear to SQL.

Concepts 3 reminds us from the three join possibilities that SQL retrieve all possible combinations of rows that satisfy the join condition. The data types for the columns in the join condition should be compatible (either both numeric or both character). NULL values never satisfy a join condition. This means that even if both rows from both tables match with NULL values in them, the rows will not be Selected.

1. May join up to 15 tables on one SELECT
2. If there are identical column names referred to in the join, those column names must be prefixed by a table name to ensure uniqueness (INV.CUST_NBR)
3. Join will retrieve all possible combinations of rows that satisfy the join condition
4. The condition after the WHERE creates the vital link between the tables that is necessary to restrict the Selection to useful rows

   Where ID = Custid
5. The Where clause may specify multiple selection criteria;

   Where ID = Custid

   And Return < 87301
6. You must have authority to access the tables you are going to join

Fig. 8 Join considerations.

8. Simple Join Exercises

Exercise 1 asks that you join the Mov and I_M tables to display movie Title and NBR and I_M columns. This a simple join, with no extra conditions. Let's do it together, step and step.

1. First check back in Section 9.5 to find the linking Columns between these two tables.
2. These two columns will make up your Where clause. Write the Where clause out here.

   Where ______________________________:
3. Now we need the Select. Which columns are we requesting?

   Select __________ . __________ . __________ . __________ . __________ .
4. We need two tables in our From statement. Separate their names with a comma:

   From __________ . __________ .

EXERCISE 1

Finally, we are ready to assemble the pieces and try it out.

1. Topic: Intermediate Select Examples
2. Exercise 1. Join the Mov and I_M tables on the movie NBR values. Display the

movie Title and NBR from the MOV table, and all of the columns from the I_M table.

3. Input Table:

MOV

NBR	TITLE	TYPE	RATING	STAR	QTY	PRICE
1	Gone with the Wind	Drama		Gable	4	39.95
2	Friday the 13th	Horror	R	Jason	2	69.95
3	Top Gun	Drama	PG	Cruise	7	49.95
4	Splash	Comedy	PG13	Hanks	3	29.95
5	101 Dalmations	Comedy	G		3	59.95
6	Body Heat	Drama	R	Turner	3	19.95
7	Risky Business	Comedy	R	Cruise	2	44.55
8	Cocoon	Scifi	PG	Ameche	2	
9	Crocodile Dundee	Comedy	PF13	Harris	2	69.95
10.	Tootsie	Comedy	PG	Hoffman	1	29.95

I_M

I_NBR	M_NBR
1	4
1	5
2	3
3	1
3	10
4	6
4	3
4	5
4	1
5	1
5	7
7	1
7	3
7	5
8	4
8	7
9	9
9	2
10	4
10	4
10	1
10	5
10	4

4. FORMAT

```
Select <columnname>, <columnname>
From <tablename>, <tablename>
Where <joincondition>:
```

5. Step 1. ______________________________

Write your answer.

____

____

____

Step 2. Enter your answer into the computer.

If you are using a computer, complete the exercise. Otherwise check your answer by looking at the answer key.

Step 3. Check your results.

6. Results Table:

TITLE	NBR	I_NBR	M_NBR
Gone with the Wind	1	3	1
Gone with the Wind	1	4	1
Gone with the Wind	1	5	1
Gone with the Wind	1	7	1
Friday the 13th	2	10	1
Top Gun	3	9	2
Top Gun	3	2	3
Top Gun	3	4	3
Splash	4	7	3
Splash	4	1	4
Splash	4	8	4
Splash	4	10	4
101 Dalmations	5	10	4
101 Dalmations	5	1	4
101 Dalmations	5	4	5
101 Dalmations	5	7	5
Top Gun	3	10	5
Top Gun	3	4	5
Splash	4	7	3
Splash	4	1	3
Splash	4	10	4
Splash	4	10	4
Splash	4	10	4
101 Dalminations	5	1	5
101 Dalminations	5	4	5
101 Dalminations	5	7	5
101 Dalminations	5	10	5
Body Heat	6	4	6
Risky Business	7	5	7
Risky Business	7	8	7
Crocodile Dundee	9	9	9
Tootsie	10	3	10

7. If your results table does not have these rows, try again or look at the answer key and execute the solution given there

   If you have trouble with this exercise, carefully review and try it again until you understand the concepts. Redo the exercise until it's clear.

EXERCISE 2

1. Topic: Intermediate Join Examples
2. Exercise 2 Join the INV and I_M tables on the invoice NBR values. Display All of the columns and All of the rows on both tables.
3. Input Table:

INV

NBR	CUSTID	TOT	RENT	RETURN
1	01	9.55	870055	
2	02	13.55	87030	
3	02	21.01	87041	87042
4	01	11.25	87042	87072
5	03	12.55	87045	87051
6	02	9.75	87047	87051
7	04	10.35	86355	
8	04	12.55	87051	87053
9	05	10.35	87052	
10	02	7.55	87030	87060

I_M

I_NBR	M_NBR
1	4
1	5
2	3
3	1
3	10
4	6
4	3
4	5
4	1
5	1
5	7
7	1
7	3
7	5
8	4
8	7
9	9
9	2
10	4
10	4
10	1
10	5
10	4

FORMAT

4. Select* From <tablename>, <tablename>;

5. Step 1. ______________________________

   Write your answer.

   ____

   ____

   ____

   Step 2. Enter your answer into the computer.

If you are using a computer, complete the exercise. Otherwise check your answer by looking at the answer key.

Step 3. Check your results.

6. Results Table:

NBR	CUSTID	TOT	RENT	RETURN	L_NBR	PM_NBR
1	01	9.55	87055		1	4
1	01	9.55	87055		1	5
2	02	13.55	87030		2	3
3	02	21.01	87041	87042	3	1
3	02	21.01	87041	87042	3	10
4	01	11.25	87042	87072	4	6
4	01	11.25	87042	87072	4	3
4	01	11.25	87042	87072	4	5
4	01	11.25	87042	87072	4	1
5	03	12.55	87045	87051	5	1
5	03	12.55	87045	87051	5	7
7	04	10.35	86355		7	1
7	04	10.35	86355		7	3
7	04	10.35	86355		7	5
8	04	12.55	87051	87053	8	1
8	04	12.55	87051	87053	8	7
9	05	10.35	87052		9	9
9	05	10.35	87052		9	2
10	02	7.55	87030	87060	10	4
10	02	7.55	87030	87060	10	4
10	02	7.55	87030	87060	10	1
10	02	7.55	87030	87060	10	5
10	02	7.55	87030	87060	10	4

7. If your results table does not have these tows, try again or look at the answer key and execute the solution give there.

EXERCISE 3

This exercise asks you to join the CUSTomer and INVoice tables, and to sort the results table. ORDER BY always comes at the end of a SELECT statement.

1. Topic: Intermediate SELECT Examples (EQUI-JOIN with ORDER BY)
2. EXERCISE 3. Join the INV and CUST tables on the customer ID values. Display the LNAME and ID columns from the CUST table, and the NBR and CUSTID columns from the INV table. Sort the output on customer ID ascending.

3. Input Table:

INV

NBR	CUSTID	TOT	RENT	RETURN
1	01	9.55	87055	
2	02	13.55	87030	
3	02	21.01	87041	87042
4	01	11.25	87042	87072
5	03	12.55	87045	87051
6	02	9.75	87047	87051
7	04	10.35	86355	
8	04	12.55	87051	87053
9	05	10.35	87052	
10	02	7.55	87030	87060

CUST

ID	LNAME	FNAME	CITY	ST
01	Dangerfield	Rodney	Hariford	CT
02	Field	Sally	Franklin	NY
03	Nicholson	Jack	Hartford	CA
04	Murray	Fred	Bozrah	CT
05	Madden	John	Bratileboro	VT
06	West	Mae	Park Place	CA
07	Woodward	Joanne	Gettysburg	PA
08	Rogers	Roy	Happy Trails	TX
09	Ringwald	Molly	Pinksville	CA
10	Rogers	Fred	Park Place	CA

FORMAT

4.
```
Select <columnname> <columnname>
From <tablename> <tablename>
Where <joincondition> Order By <columnnbr>;
```

5. Step 1. ____________________

Write your answer.

____

____

____

Step 2. Enter your answer into the computer.

If you are using a computer, complete the exercise. Otherwise check your answer by looking at the answer key.

Step 3. Check your results.

6. Results Table

LNAME	ID	NBR	CUSTID
Dangerfield	01	1	01
Dangerfield	01	1	01
Field	02	2	02
Field	02	3	02
Field	02	6	02
Field	01	10	02
Nicholson	03	5	03
Murray	04	7	04
Murray	04	8	04
Madden	05	9	05

7. If your screen does not look like this, try again or look at the answer key and execute the solution given there.

EXERCISE 4

Exercise 1 adds an additional SELECTion condition. This is no harder than the multiple conditions we tried on Chapter7. When you add extra conditions to a table join. It doesn't matter if you place them before or after the Join Condition.

Join
Condition ______________________________
Additional WHERE
Condition ______________________________
Select __________ . __________ . __________ .
From __________ . __________

1. Topic: Intermediate SELECT Examples (EQUI-JOIN with Where condition)
2. Exercise 4. Join the INV and CUST tables. Display the INV information for movies rented by Rodney Dangerfield.
3. Input Table:

INV

NBR	CUSTID	TOT	RENT	RETURN
1	01	9.55	87055	
2	02	13.55	87030	
3	02	21.01	87041	87042
4	01	11.25	87042	87072
5	03	12.55	87045	87051
6	02	9.75	87047	87051
7	04	10.35	86355	
8	04	12.55	87051	87053
9	05	10.35	87052	
10	02	7.55	87030	87060

CUST

ID	LNAME	FNAME	CITY	ST
01	Dangerfield	Rodney	Hartford	CT
02	Field	Sally	Franklin	NY
03	Nicholson	Jack	Hartford	CA
04	Murray	Fred	Bozrah	CT
05	Madden	John	Bratileboro	VT
06	West	Mae	Park Place	CA
07	Woodward	Joanne	Getiysburg	PA
08	Rogers	Roy	Happy Trails	TX
09	Ringwald	Molly	Pinksville	CA
10	Rogers	Fred	Park Place	CA

FORMAT

4.
```
Select <columnname>, <columnname>
FROM <tablename>, <tablename>
Where <joincondition> AND/OR <other condition>;
```

Hint **A short way to SELECT all columns from a table is to place a period followed by an asterick following the tablename. For example:**

Select INV. * will select all columns from the INV table.

5. Step 1. ______________________________

Write your answer.

____

____

____

Step 2. Enter your answer into the computer.

If you are using a computer, complete the exercise. Otherwise check your answer by looking at the answer key.

Step 3. Check your results.

6. Results Table:

INV.NBR	INV.CUSTID	INV.TOT	INV.RENT	INV.RETURN	ID	LNAME	FNAME
1	01	9.55	87055	99999	01	Dangerfield	Rodney
4	01	11.25	87042	87072	01	Dangerfield	Rodney

7. If your screen does not look like this, try again or look at the answer key and execute the solution given there.

EXERCISE 5

This exercise also includes an additional Where condition.

1. TOPIC. Intermediate SELECT Examples (EQUI-JOIN with WHERE condition)
2. EXERCISE 5. Join the INV and CUST tables. Display all of the last names of customers with movies to be returned.
3. Input Table.

INV

NBR	CUSTID	TOT	RENT	RETURN
1	01	9.55	87055	
2	02	13.55	87030	
3	02	21.01	87041	87042
4	01	11.25	87042	87042
5	03	12.55	87045	87051
6	02	9.75	87047	87051
7	04	10.35	86355	
8	04	12.55	87051	87053
9	05	10.35	87052	
10	02	7.55	87030	87060

CUST

ID	LNAME	FNAME	CITY	ST
01	Dangerfield	Rodney	Hartford	CT
02	Field	Sally	Franklin	NY
03	Nicholson	Jack	Hartford	CA
04	Murray	Fred	Bozrah	CT
05	Madden	John	Bratiteboro	VT
06	West	Mae	Park Place	CA
07	Woodward	Johanne	Geitysburg	PA
08	Rogers	Roy	Happy Trails	TX
09	Ringwald	Molly	Pinksville	CA
10	Rogers	Fred	Park Place	CA

FORMAT

4. Select <columnname>, <columnname>
   From <tablename>, <tablename>
   Where <joincondition> AND/OR <other condition>:

5. Step 1. ______________________________
   Write your answer.
   ____
   ____
   ____

   Step 2. Enter your answer into the computer.

   If you are using a computer, complete the exercise. Otherwise check your answer by looking at the answer key.

   Step 3. Check your results.

6 Results Table:

LName
Dangerfield
Field
Murray
Madden

7. If your screen does not look like this, try again or look at the answer key and execute the solution given there.

EXERCISE 6

The exercise requires an additional WHERE condition.

1. TOPIC: Intermediate SELECT Examples (EQUI-JOIN with WHERE condition)
2. EXERCISE 6. Join the MOV and I_M tables. Displays a list of movie information on 'PG 13' comedy films that have been rented. Remove duplicate rows.
3. Input Table:

MOV

NBR	TITLE	TYPE	RATING	STAR	QTY	PRICE
1	Gone with the Wind	Drama		Cable	4	39.95
2	Friday the 13th	Horror	R	Jason	2	69.95
3	Top Gun	Drama	PG	Cruise	7	49.95
4	Splash	Commedy	PG13	Hanks	3	29.95
5	101 Dalminations	Comedy	G		3	59.95
6	Body Heat	Drama	R	Turner	3	19.95
7	Risky Business	Comedy	R	Cruise	2	44.55
8	Cocoon	Scifi	PG	Ameche	2	
9	Crocodile Dundee	Comedy	PG 13	Harris	2	69.95
10	Tootsie	Comecy	PG	Hofman	1	29.95

I_M

I_NBR	M_NBR
1	4
1	5
2	3
3	1
3	10
4	6
4	3
4	5
4	1
5	1
5	7
7	1
7	3
7	5
8	4
8	7
9	9
9	2
10	4
10	4
10	1
10	5
10	4

FORMAT

4.
```
SELECT <columnname>, <columnname>
FROM <tablename>, <tablename>
WHERE <joincondition>
AND/OR <other condition>
```

5. Step 1. ____

   Write your answer.

   ____

   ____

   ____

   Step 2. Enter your answer into the computer.

   If you are using a computer, complete the exercise. Otherwise check your answer by looking at the answer key.

   Step 3. Check your results.

6. Results Table

MOV NBR	MOVE TITLE	MOVE TYPE	MOV RATING	MOV STAR	MOV QTY	MOV PRICE
4	Splash	Comedy	PG 13	Hanks	3	29.95
9	Crocodile Dundee	Comedy	PG13	Harris	2	69.95

7. If your screen does not look like this, try again or look at the answer key and execute the solution given there.

   ***Hint:* The fact that the movie NBR exists on the I_M Table in the M_NBR column means that the movie has been rented**

---

9. Table Joins—Interpreting SQL

1. Select Mov.* From Mov. L_M Where Star Between 'HA' and 'HZ' And NBR = M_NBR:
2. SELECT * FROM CUST, INV, INV, I_M, Mov
   WHERE CUSTID = ID And
   INV. NBR = I_NBR And
   MOV. NBR = M_NBR and
   Rating = 'R':

Use this space to write your answer.

1. ____

   ____

2. ____

   ____

11 Answer Key

There may be more than one answer to an exercise. However, the one given emphasized the chapter topic.

Exercise	1	Select Title, NBR, I_NBR from MOV, I_M Where NBR = M_NBR;
Exercise	2	Select * From INV. I_M Where I_NBR = NBR;
Exercise	3	Select LName. ID, NBR. Custid From INV, CUST Where ID = Custid Order by 4;
Exercise	4	Select INV.* ID. LName. FName From INV. Cust Where ID = Custid and LName = Dangerfield;
Exercise	5	Select LName From INV. Cust Where ID = Custid and Return is Null;
Exercise	6	Select Distinct Mov.* From Mov. I_M Where NBR = M_NBR and Type = Comedy and Rating = "PG 13"

Interpreting SQL Statements

1. Retrieve all movies that have been rented where the stars last name is between HA and HZ.
2. Display all information for customers who have rented R-rated movies. Note: this SELECT joins all four tables.

28

Software Acquisitions

LEARNING OBJECTIVES

After reading this chapter, you will be able to :

- Understand the methodolgy of evaluation and shortlisting of offers for hardware received from various vendors.
- Appreciate the considerations involved in exercising 'lease' or 'buy' options.
- Comprehend the safeguards to be provided while entering into hardware acquisition contracts.
- Understand the legal position as regards proprietorship when acquiring a software package.
- Narrate the types of risks to be guarded against in the contracts for acquisition of software packages.
- Describe the approaches to evaluation of software packages proposed to be acquired.
- Understand the merits of using computer bureau services and the safeguards to be thought of when contracting for processing services.

Hardware Acquisitions

Once a decision has been reached by an inhouse computing service, the next step is to draw up specifications of the proposed system and invite suitable vendors to tender there against.

The tender specifications are formulated within the framework of on the approved feasibility report and, besides the main technical parameters of the various units of the required hardware, they detail the objectives and scope of the project, implementation schedule, and the type of support service which the vendors will be required to provide. Vendors may also be asked to quote separately in respect of 'leasing' and 'buying' options. Additionally, the vendors may be required to provide details of infrastructure which the customer will have to arrange, and the likely cost thereof.

Tender Evaluations

There are often mismatches between the requirements as indicated by the customer and the offer as are made by individual vendors. Where the specification offered by the vendors are far below the mandatory requirements of the customer, such offers may be eliminated straightaway from the purview of short listing. Marginal shortfalls may be considered to merits. However, in the case of additional features in the offers- which could be categorised as 'desirable' — it becomes necessary to assign appropriate weights/values to such features, in order to bring all the bids on an equal footing. The additional features include quantifiable differences in:

- One-time costs as well as in the continuing running and maintenance costs.
- Equipment characteristics such as storage capacities, speeds of of various units forming part of hardware.
- In-built spare capacity as well as capability of the system to support additional peripherals.
- Support to be provided by the vendor.

Costs in the case of computer acquisitions, costs for consideration are of two types:

- One-time costs, such as cost of site preparation (space, false ceilings, special floorings, electricals, air-conditioning, etc), as also the inclusive cost of acquisition and installation of computer equipment and support facilities.
- Continuing running and maintenance costs of the entire installations.

Equipment characteristics: Bulkier/heavier equipment, obviously, needs more space and airconditioning, besides adding to the power consumption bill. On the other hand, hardware which provides higher transfer rates (that is average number of bytes passing between various functional units, per unit of time), or makes available larger storage capacity (in the CPU and/or secondary storage devices like magnetic tapes, disks, etc) or in the case of printer, if the lines printed per minute or the printed characters per line are comparatively higher, then such additional characters get entitled to weightage to the extent of their practical unity to the buying organisation. Appropriate weightage can also given to such characteristics as the availability of error detection/error correction techniques, higher mean-time-between-failures (MTBF), redundancy of components provided (to reduce chances of system failure), comparatibility with the equipment, peripherals, etc. available in the market, extra system life, relative setup and running times takes to complete a job (or a basket of jobs) by different makes/models of computers, expected trade in values, and ability of the system to run old programs(where available) without much effort.

Potential for growth: Important features under this category include:

- potentiality of the system to grow beyond the currently specified capacity by adding on certain components/sub-systems.

- potentiality of growth within a particular family of computer models. (This obviates the need for rewriting existing programs).
- capacity of the system to handle a larger variety and number of peripherals.
- ability of the system to handle additional workloads, after taken into account peak times for running the application. (This, usually, becomes possible by fine-tuning the system and/or making appropriate use of the available slack time).

Vendor Support: The aspects to be given weightage under the heading include:

- hardware maintenance facilities offered,
- help in staff-selection (by means of aptitude tests, etc.)
- training to be arranged for analysis, programmers, operatives, etc.)
- loaning of personnel if required, at specified costs for certain duration,
- assistance to be provided in the development of new application systems, conversion of existing programs (if any) to run on the offered system,
- quality and extent of docvmentation to be provided,
- back-up from the vendor's own service bureau in the case of system failure, and/ or help in arranging reciprocal backup arrangements with other organisations having a similar compute system,
- Comparative delivery periods offered by different vendors,

Lease or Buy Options

The micros (or Personal Computers) ar usually available on out-right purchase basis. The options of 'leasing' or 'buying' are actually applicable to central computer systems based on minis and for mainframes. Leasing may be offered by the vendor himself or it may be arranged through a third party which buys hardware from the vendor in the first instance. Both the 'lease' and 'buy' options have their respective merits and which one will suit a particular situation depends on consideration/evaluation of several factors.

Leasing is suitable when:

- enough liquid resources ar not available for an outright purchase,
- lease obligations are for a fairly short period (say, for three or four years),
- maintenance and service obligations on the part of the vendor are considered important,
- long-term planning for computerisation is difficult to carry out and there are lurking risks of overbuying and of technological and system obsolescence,
- residual values are not significant,
- the consideration of paying for equipment over a longer period, out of before-tax earnings are deemed more important as opposed to paying out of after-tax profits.

Disadvantages of leasing include:

- interest charges forming part of lease payments are usually higher than the lessees's regular interest rates,
- tax deductions available are often less attractive than in the case of an outright purchase,
- benefit of residual values, if substantial, goes to the vendor,
- there is less flexibility to get rid of obsolete equipment during the lease period.

Buying Computer hardware may either be bought from the vendor or an outright basis or it may be bought during or at the end of the lease period at certain pre-agreed to price. Merits of the outright purchase option include:

- flexibility of system modification at the will of the buying organisation.
- lower continuing cash outlay, as compared to leasing, (for example, cash generated by depreciation, provision is a source of funds for the organisation).
- lower cash outlay, if the system is used by the customer for a period larger than, say, five years.

Disadvantages, in contrast, include:

- high initial cost (compared to the leasing option),
- payments for maintenance agreement after the expiry of the warrantly period,
- higher overall risk in the event of buying a flawed system.

In the context of computer acquisitions, mention may also be made of two other financial options that can be availed of,when available. These are:

- **Renting** Equipment can be rented directly from the manufacturer at specified terms for specified periods. The disadvantage is higher cash outflow compared to leasing , for the same length of periods.
- **Buying used computers** Organisations having bought out hardware may outgrow their computers long before the equipment life has run out. They are, therefore, forced to unload their existing hardware.

From the customer's point of view, the dominant considerations for acquiring second-hand hardware include:

- make/model of the computer and its residual life,
- proximity of technical support for maintaining the system or assured maintenance support from the original vendor,
- bargain prices.

It is usually advantageous to buy directly from a former enduser. The latter should, however, make available for inspection his maintenance logs to the prospective customer so as to reveal/establish reliability of the system.

Final Selection of Vendor

Besides the evaluation of various technical and financial features outlines earlier, it is equally necessary to take into account the following factors in the final selection of a vendor:

- financial standing/reputation of the vendor, and the lengths of period he has been in business,
- number of similar systems installed by the vendor, and particulars of the user organisations, (users may be directly approaches to ascertain their opinion about the working/ reliability of the system),
- number of persons employed by the vendor with separate figures in respect of staff engaged on support services and staff with specialisation in the relevant application areas,
- quality of documentation,
- share of the vendor in the total market for a particular category of hardware,
- location of service centres and the number thereof.

Drawing up Computer Contracts

Vendors, usually, have their own standard forms of contract but these are often biased towards their own rights. However, after skillful negotiations it is possible to add, delete or modify certain clauses, so that the contract terms become reasonably equitable for both the sides.

The buyer must take care to safeguard his interests in respect of the following provisions in the contract.

Respective responsibilities of vendors and buyers: The contract should clearly lay down the respective responsibilities and remedies available to th e two sides in the event of non or faulty performance of the system. The remedies include special remedies, damages and specific performance. 'Special remedies' may be invoked when the vendor fails to meet delivery schedules, or is found deficient at the time of carrying out acceptance tests. Alternatives to special remedies are claims for actual, consequential and liquidated damages. 'Actual damages' compensate a party for the advantages lost in the actual bargain. 'Consequential damages' compensate the parties in respect of all foreseeable losses resulting from breach of contract. 'Liquidated damages' fix a specific amount in the event of breach of a contract condition. 'Specific performance' clauses are attracted when a system fails the acceptance tests due to deficiency in capacity. The buyer can then ask the vendor to provide additional memory or power at nil or nominal cost within a specified period.

Documentation: The customer should have the right to stop payments if adequate documentation required for the effective running of the system is withheld by the vendor.

Hardware: It is necessary that each component of the contracted hardware is identified and its performance criteria, in normal operating condition, is clearly spelled out.

Delivery and acceptance: The contract should spell out the delivery schedule and the acceptance tests/standards to be met by computer hardware during normal operating conditions throughout a specific period of use. In this connection, the vendor must accept responsibility for examining the working conditions in-which the system is to be operated. It should also be insisted that no equipment will be accepted if supplied before the scheduled date of delivery.

Right to use of equipment from other vendors: It is desirable that the customer has the right to link peripherals from other manufacturers to the CPU. However, the vendor must have protection from any damage or extra costs resulting therefrom.

Warranties: The contract would include suitable warranties, as required.

Guarantees: They are meant for assuring reliability of the system and should encompass:

- minimum hours of usable time per day,
- mean-time between-failures (MTBF),
- maximum time to repair.

Payments: The clauses covering payments to be made by the customer must clearly stipulate whether the rental/lease payments are in respect of number of hours actually used per month?shift or these are to be made at a flat monthly rate. In lease contracts, there should be an option to buy the equipment at certain stipulated prices can also as regards when that option can be exercised. The customer should have the right to assign this option to someone else.

There should be provision in the contract to protect the already negotiated prices. Also, if the vendor insists on escalation clauses, the customer should have the right to terminate the contract and recover compensation for costs incurred on preparation.

Bankruptcy There should be explicit protection to the customer in the event of the vendor becoming bankrupt. This is meant to assure access to any programs, documentation etc. relevant to the operation of the system, in case the customer has to look for another vendor.

Admittedly it is not possible to cover all the areas of problem and disputes between vendors and customers of computer hardware. The aforementioned check-lists, however, substantially cover the problems areas usually encountered.

Acquisition of Proprietary Software Packages

Barring the cases where software packages are developed by outside consultants to the spcifications of and at the expense of the user, the proprietary rights in the package remain with the original developer. This means that a software package from outside sources truly be 'bought'; it can only be licensed for use. The mode of payment for the purpose can be one or the other of the following:

- Off-the-shelf acquisition of programs stored in a cassette or a plug-in ROM module. (These modes are particularly popular in case of software to be used on PCs).
- Acquisition of the right to use a package by means of a monthly/periodical licence fee.
- One-off payment for a fixed time/perpetual use of the package.
- An initial lumpsum payment plus a regular periodical service charge.

Some software packages are also supplied by computer vendors alogwith the system and they form an integral part of computer operations. However, the vendors often charge a nominal fee for the use of such packages just to establish ownership.

Technical Aspects of Proprietary Software

When considering the acquisition of a proprietary software package, it is useful to take into account the implications, if any, of its following technical characteristics.

Memory size Amount of memory it will occupy when resident in the CPU.

Run time Some programs may require small amount of memory but much larger run times.

Adaptability Ability to mix into a multi-programming environment and in making use of the existing resources — peripherals, operating systems, utility programs, etc.

File storage File storage requirements and how efficiently it can store and retrieve data.

Modularity Adaptability to modularity and paging techniques without much degradation in processing.

Expandability Expandability refers to the built-in flexibility of the package to handle larger volumes of transactions 9made possible if the package has been designed to accommodate the expansion of master files, addition to fields, records, files, etc), besides the capability to integrate with other programs.

Reliability Significant reliability related aspects also include:

- the extent to which a package can still be used when a particular module fails,
- types of errors on the part of the user which affect performance of the packages,
- ease of recovery in the event of failure,
- capability of the package to run on more than one configuration.

Efficiency This aspect encompasses capability of the package to perform under peak load conditions. Efficiency of a package much depends on the language in which it is written and the operating system used. Where a particular package can run only on a Disk Operating System (DOS) while the installed computer system runs under a full operating system the alternatives are either to downgrade the operating system or upto upgrade the package. Both are not only costly exercises but affect efficiency of the package.

Ease of implementation implementation of an application package refers to all the associated activities and vendor support upto the point where the package meets users requirements and the user can operate it in a self-sufficient manner. Implementation of a package becomes much easier to carry out if the documentation provided by the vendors states the purpose of the package in simple and clear terms with readily understandable cross references.

Ease of use This aspect refers to the extent of effort involved in the preparation of inputs, execution of programs and interpretation of outputs. Additionally, the package should have the capability to run on different hardware configurations and under different operating systems.

Vendor support This is critically important in such areas as documentation, software modification/ enhancement/maintenance as well as education of the user personnel of several levels— clerical, technical, operational and managerial.Using flowcharts and other appropriate tools, the documentation should comprchensively describe the system logic, inputs, outputs, files, the instruction to be followed by the operators, etc.

Other aspects relating to documentation are date of delivery, number of copies to be provided by the vendor and the user's right to make more copies.

Security This refers to the inbuilt capability of the package to prevent unauthorised access to software and data and to maintain integrity of the system.

Risks and Benefits

Acquisition of proprietory software carries with it certain potential risks so far as the buyer is concerned:

These are:

- non-performance including failure to meet specifications it such matters as using more hardware resources than anticipated, taking more run time than expected, and the like,
- excessive costs of modification or integration to meet user requirements,
- the vendor discontinuing his business resulting loss of his support,
- infringement of copyright on the part of the vendor which, at some stage, might land the buyer in difficulties.

Such risk, however, can be substantially minimised by inclusion of the following clauses in the contract for licensing software.

- right to terminate the contract if the package fails to provide the agreed to level of performance,
- vendor to provide assistance to carrying out the requisite modification etc. within a specified period and at reasonable, agreed to, rates,
- right to continuous use of the package in case the developer discontinue his business with a further right to modify the package without penalties, charges or obligations,
- comprehensive indemnifications to the user in the event of any copyright infringement on the part of the vendor.

The risks and their coverage apart, it is by now well recognised that acquisition of right type of software packages affords many advantages. For example:

- A good acquired package makes it possible to run the computer system in a matter of days as opposed to a custom-made package which may take months to develop, undergo tests, etc. There is no risk of delays due to programmers quitting in midstream,
- An acquired package usually costs only a fraction of what it would cost to develop it inhouse or by engaging an outside consultant.
- Packages offered by established/reputed software houses are usually reliable and conform to the standards stated in the associated documentation,
- Acquired packages can be subjected to comprehensive performance tests, before taking the decision to buy.

Mention may also be made of certain drawbacks:

- It is not altogether easy, particularly, for a first time computer user, to draw up a comprehensive evaluation criteria covering all the conditions/contingencies in which the package may have to function. so, a package selected on the basis of inadequate or faulty criteria may fail to perform in certain eventualities.
- Extensive modifications in the package, if and when required, may lead to dilution of vendor support, for obvious reasons.

Approaches to Software Evaluation

These include benchmarking, drawing upon the experience of other users and referring to reports independence software research organisations.

- **Benchmarking** Benchmark is the name given to a sample program specially designed to evaluate the comparative performance of hardware or software. As regards evaluation of software benchmarking is largely concerned with validation of vendor's claims a respect of (a) minimum hardware configuration needed to operate the package, and (b) time required to execute a program in ideal conditions and how the own performance of the package nd that of other program under execution is affected, when running in a multi-programming mode.

- **Experience of other users** Vendors usually provide a list of other users. More often than not such a list contains names of only satisfied users. More weightage should be given to the opinion independently sought from the existing user whose configuration and operational environment closely resembles one's own.
- **Reports of independent research organisation** Many research organisations lime Datapro carry out these days evaluation of various proprietary software projects offered by software houses. These evaluations are objective and comprehensive covering such areas as reliability, efficiency case of use, user rating/satisfaction and many others. Their reports are published at regular intervals. Such evaluations can well be relied upon by the prospective buyer of software package.

Computer Bureau Services

It will be useful at this stage to consider also the technical and economic issues involved in using externally available computer bureau services as an alternative to setting up an inhouse computer system or expanding the existing one.

Typically, the processing power, storage capacities, technical expertise and specialised software packages as made available by a bureau are much larger in scale than those provided in an average inhouse computer centre. Availing of bureau services is particularly useful in situations where the organisation happens to be the first time computer user and must acquire sufficient experience and confidence before thinking in terms of inhouse facilities. However, there are also certain risks involved in using bureau services. These are as follows:

- As the data is stored and processed at the bureau premises there is risk of breach of security.
- In order to protect its business interests in unscrupulous bureau may wish to withhold programs developed at the user's cost when the user wants to set up inhouse facilities or shift the processing work to another bureau.
- There was competing claims on computer time from the several clients of the bureau. A particular user organistion's interest may suffer as a result thereof.

It is therefore essential for the user organisation's to protect its own interest by incorporating suitable provisions in the processing contracts. The main aspects to be covered include the following:

- The user organisation should have a continuous and absolute right of access to its own data stored at bureau's premises.

- The user organisation should have absolute proprietary right in the programs developed at its cost.
- In the case of destruction of data due to bureau's negligence, the costs involved in reconstruction should be the responsibility of the bureau's.
- In the case of loss resulting from breach of confidentiality of data and/or program attributable to the bureau, the latter should carry the responsibility of making good the loss to the user organisation.
- The bureau should undertake the responsibility of supplying the processed data according to predefined schedule unless there are delays on the part of the user in supplying the required inputs. As regards occasional reports to be supplied on request, the contract should explicitly state the response times.
- The basis of billing to the user should be clearly defined in the contract. The usual bases of billing are as under, which may be used in conjunction, as appropriate.
    - ❑ computer time used for actual processing,
    - ❑ fixed monthly charges plus a charge based on activity items, for example the number of employees whose payroll is processed,
    - ❑ data storage charges per thousand characters per month,
    - ❑ connect time, that is the time when the terminal and the user's end is hooked upto the computer,
    - ❑ terminal charges, maintenance etc. on a monthly basis,
    - ❑ modem charges, etc.,
    - ❑ charges for using the proprietary software of the bureau.
- A processing contract should not be for lengthy periods and it should be possible to terminate it a a short notice of, say 30 to 90 days.
- There should be a price adjustment formula, applicable when the contract comes up for renewal.
- The contract should have provisions to protect the interest of the user organisation in the event the bureau discontinues its business during the contracted period.

SELF-TEST

1. True of False?
    (a) While evaluating offers of hardware made by different vendors, full weightage should be given to each additional or support characteristics of the offered hardware.
    (b) In the long run, 'buying' is a better option than 'leasing' hardware.
    (c) Benchmarking should be carried out when buying second-hand hardware.

(d) When contracting for hardware purchase, the buyer must accept the terms contained in the vendor's standard form of contract.

2. Match the following:

(i)	Benchmark	(a)	Ability of a package to accept expansion of master files, additions to fields and records.
(ii)	Service Bureau		
(iii)	User rating of	(b)	Sample program used for evaluating different computers and their software.
(iv)	Expandability of software package	(c)	A computer install- action which processes data of other organisations at its own premises, for a charge.
(v)	Plug-in ROM module.	(d)	A hardware semi-conductor component with software stored in it.
		(e)	Evaluation of software carried out by computer research organisation on the basis of grading obtained from specific users.

3. The evaluation of a vendor must include:
   (a) Market reputation of the vendor as regards technical and maintenance support provided.
   (b) Cost of offered hardware.
   (c) Running cost of equipment.
   (d) Additional features of the offered hardware.
   (e) Financial viability of the vendor.
4. Which of the following are relevant cost considerations in acquiring a software package:
   (a) Leas or buy options.
   (b) Current system compatibility.
   (c) Guarantees and warranties available.
   (d) Maintenance arrangements available.
   (e) Confidentiality of software package.
5. Which of the following conditions are generally included when inviting tenders for hardware:
   (a) Cost of site-preparation.
   (b) Cost of air-conditioning.
   (c) Delivery schedules.

(d) Vendor support for system design programming and training of user's staff.

Connectability of CPU to peripherals of other vendors.

6. Which of the following is the most important consideration in the contractor licensing a software package.?
   (a) The operator's ability to run the package.
   (b) After-sale support from the vendor.
   (c) Periodical licensing fees/one-off payment for software package.
   (d) Vendor's right to lease software package.
7. True or false?
   (a) A software package bought against an one-off payment becomes property of the buyer in perpetuity.
   (b) If a bought or leased package uses more hardware facility than what is specified, it becomes obligatory on the part of the vendor to take back his software package.
   (c) Installation of package is deemed to have taken place only when the user can operate it in a self-sufficient manner.
   (d) Modification to bought-out software can be carried out only by the original developer.
   (e) The proprietory rights in a software package developed by a consultant remain with him even thought it is developed to the specification to and at the cost of the buyer.

KEY TO SELF-TESTS

Chapter 1

1. a; b; e; h; i; j; l; m are true
2. b; c
3. a; b
4. All
5. a; b; c
6. d
7. a; b

Chapter 2

1. a; c; d
2. d

3. a
4. a
5. c
6. b
7. c
8. (i)(c); (ii)(a)
9. b
10. a; e; f
11. 1 X 2 = 2
    1 X 2 + 0 = 2
    2 X 2 + 1 = 5
    5 X 2 + 1 = 11
    11 X 2 + 1 = 23
12. 1 0 1 0 0
    Step 1(-) 1 1 0 0 0
    Step II 1 0 1 0 0
    Step II 0 1 1 0 1
    = 13 decimal
13. 0010 0000 0111
14. None
15. e
16. c
17. c
18. c

Chapter 3

1. c
2. a; b; d
3. c
4. a
5. a; b
6 (i) (d,l,m); (ii) (j.k,l); (iii) (c,e,i); (iv) (b,g.h); (v) (a, f)
7. d,e,f,g;h

Chapter 4

1. (i)(c); (ii)(e); (iii)(a); (iv)(b); (v)(d)
2. b
3. i(c); ii(a); iii(b); iv(d)
4. (a)
5. (c)
6. b; d; e; f; j

Chapter 5

1. i(c); ii(b, d, e, f); iii(a)
2. a (ALU); b and c (Control); d (Primary Storage)
3. (a) and (e) are true
4. i(b, d); ii(a); iii(d, f); iv(c); v(e)
5. i(b); ii(a); iii(d, f) iv(c); v(e)
6. (d)
7. (b)
8. (a)
9. i(c); ii(a); iii(b)
10. (a)
11. (a)
12. (a)
13. (a)
14. (f)
15. (c)
16. (a); (b); (c); (d); (f)
17. (g), (h) and (j) are false
18. (b)
19. i(a); ii(b); iii(d)

Chapter 6

1. f; e
2. a; b
3. (true) is false
4. b; c
5. i(b); ii(a); iii(c)
6. a and c are false

7. b
8. a
9. c
10. c
11. (a) true; (b) false; (c) true, (d) true; (e) false; (f) false; (g) false.

Chapter 7

1. a; b
2. b
3. a

   c
4. i(b); ii(a); iii(d); iv(c); v(f); vi(e); vii(h); viii(g); ix(i); x(l); xi(d); xii(k)
5. i(c); ii(d); iii(a); iv(e); v(b); vi(g); vii(f); viii(j); ix(h); ix(l); x(i)
6. a; c; d
7. c; d; e
8. a
9. c
10. All are true

Chapter 8

1. i(c, d, e, f); ii(a, b)
2. c, h, j are false
3. d
4. d
5. b
6. b
7. a
8. b

Chapter 9

1. d
2. d
3. d
4. d
5. a
6. d
7. i(c); ii(b); iii(a).

29

The Unix "Operating" System

The UNIX revolution must be one of the finest things that has happened to the computing industry in recent times. It has a large number of outstanding and diverse concepts, developed and perfected over a period of time. It simplifies a lot of things and yet has phenomenal power. It has practically everything an operating system should have, and several features which operating systems never had. Its richness and elegance go beyond the commands and tools that constitute it, while simplicity permeates the entire system.

However, UNIX also makes many demands of the user. It requires a different type of commitment to understand the subject, even when the user is an experienced computer professional. It introduces certain concepts not known to the computing community before, and uses numerous symbols whose meanings are anything but obvious. It achieves unusual tasks with a few keystrokes, but it takes time to devise a sequence of them for a specific task. It doesn't tell you whether you are right or wrong, and doesn't warn you of the consequences of your actions. What makes matters worse is that the documentation available today, even though vastly improved, is still quite cryptic. That is probably the reason why it still remains a subject which is largely unappreciated and little understood.

Kernighan and Pike (*The UNIX Programming Environment*, Prentice-Hall) lament that "as the UNIX system has spread, the fraction of its users who are skilled in its application has decreased" People have been using the system as they would use any operating system, and writing comprehensive programs which have already been written before. Beginners with some experience in MSDOS think of UNIX in terms of MSDOS, quite oblivious of the fact that UNIX has much more to offer. This certainly is not an encouraging trend, and serious efforts need to be made both by the designers, teachers, as well as users, to see that they are not going to support a product simply because it is the only universally portable operating system in use.

Even though it is usual for a beginner to feel overwhelmed by the sheer weight of the system, that doesn't, however, in any way imply that UNIX is unconquerable. The most common problem faced by him (even when he is an experienced computer professional) is in not knowing where to begin, or how much to learn. The system unfortunately wasn't conceived with the novice in mind. It has an unusual history which probably is responsible for most of its apparent incoherence. But if you are willing to put in some *guided* effort, then you will gradually see the story unfolding with indisputable clarity and simplicity. Focus your attention on the essentials and ignore the frills, at least initially.

It is a widely acknowledged fact that, irrespective of what the textbooks may preach (including this one !), a personal interaction with the system has most definite advantages. In this opening chapter, you will first learn to play around with the UNIX system a little, for a first-hand "feel". After you have grasped some of the fundamental features in this introductory session, you should know something about the evolution and philosophy behind the system. This knowledge is necessary because, in many instances, you will find the system behaving in an awkward manner. You shouldn't be baffled by such responses if you are aware of the design considerations that have led to such behaviour. The introductory session is drawn up first because the concepts are presented with reference to it. Some of these concepts may seem abstract, but you shouldn't be deterred if you have not understood them initially. Absorb as much as you can, think for a while, and then move on to the other chapters.

A BRIEF SESSION

The UNIX system can be used only by those persons who maintain an "account" with the computer

ystem. This lis

of accounts is maintained separately in the computer. You can't simply sit down at ny terminal and start banging away if your name doesn't feature in the list. That will be oth inadvisable and an impossible thing to do.Ask the administrator of the system to open an account for you. Once that is done, and you have been allotted

terminal, be sure to start only when you see the following message on the screen:log n:The **"login:"** message can be preceded by one or two words, depending on the machine you a e using, but t

eword

"login" should definitely appear on the terminal. In case it doesn't, it probably eans that the previous user at this terminal has not terminated his session, and some im ortant work could be going on. You shouldn't disturb his work but rather consult the *syst m administrator.*When the system prompts you with the above message, it expects a resp nse, from you. Curiously enough, you can say that, the **"login:"** message indicates that the previous user is "logged out", i.e, has terminated his session. You are now expected to enter a special *user name* or *account,* which has been allotted to you by your system administrator. This user account is maintained by the system to check for illegal responses. So, if "kumar" happens to be your user name, enter the following at the prompt:

login: **kumar** <*Enter*>

If you make mistakes while typing the user name, most UNIX systems won't permit backspacing to wipe out errors; so enter your name carefully (SCO XENIX is more permissive). If you still make mistakes, simply press the <*Enter*> key one or two times till the **"login:"** message reappears on the screen. Be sure to terminate your response with the <*Enter*> key to make the system "see" the input that you have entered. The user name is also referred to as the *user-id* or *login name,* and you will often see these terms used interchangeably. You should also use only lowercase letters for the login name, .and avoid using special characters which can create problems.

If a password has been allotted to you, the system will flash the following message: password:

If you know your password, then key it in at this prompt. To wipe out errors, backspacing is not permitted at this stage either (SCO XENIX excepted again). Use the same technique of pressing <*Enter*> a couple of times till the **"login** t" message is displayed. The password won't be echoed to the terminal as you enter it for obvious reasons; unauthorised users are not expected to have knowledge of your password. If you enter an incorrect password, then the system will respond with the message:

login incorrect
login:

To minimise chances of breach of security, the system doesn't indicate whether the error message was due to an incorrect login name or an incorrect password. In either case, you will have to reenter the user name and the password. On some systems you will be permitted to reenter your password a fixed number of times before you get it right. MSDOS users should immediately notice the security restrictions imposed by the UNIX system, though this aspect shouldn't be unfamiliar to users migrating from similar time-sharing environments.

If you have a password allotted, and have still managed to forget it, then contact your system administrator. Key in the correct password, followed by <*Enter*> and then, depending on the installation, you may get the following message:

Welcome to XENIX System V
for personal computers
Brought to you by
The Santa Cruz Operation

Terminal type is ansi
You have mail
$_

This message was obtained on the terminal of an AT-80286 machine running XENIX, a "derivative" of UNIX. The $ (currency symbol) following the message is the system prompt, which indicates to the user that some user is *logged in,* and that the system is ready to accept any commands from him. The cursor is positioned immediately after the $ prompt (shown by the underscore character), waiting to accept input. On some systems you may see a different prompt—the % or #, for instance. You can even choose your own prompt by making appropriate settings in a startup file. Knowledge of the type of terminal is often important because some programs require to know that. The message **"You have mail"** is really an electronic mail feature by which messages are sent to users of the system by other users, as well as by the system administrator. In this case, it is a system generated message meant for those users who have been allotted a user account.

Now that you have successfully made an entry into the system, you have free access to most of the wonderful things that UNIX offers. You can enter a sequence of characters, using your keyboard, and expect the system to interpret them as *commands.* Whether the command is legitimate or not depends on its presence in a predetermined list. However, no damage is usually done even if the command is not acknowledged by the machine. You can start your first meaningful dialogue with the system by changing the password, using a command named **passwd:**

5 passwd *<Enter>*
Old Password: *<Enter>*
Ncw Password; *<Enter>*
Reenter Password: *<Enter>*
$_

When you enter the word **passwd** (note the spelling), followed by the *<Enter>* key, the system prompts you for the old password, which you have to key in at this prompt. It checks first whether you have entered a valid password, and if you have, it then prompts you twice for the new password. Enter the new password twice as required, using the password naming rules applicable for your system. As expected, the characters that you key in are not echoed to the terminal; so you must type carefully and slowly. Illegitimate passwords are simply rejected by the system, and you will be required to enter the **passwd** command again.

Ex 1.1: Enter the sequence cat /etc/passwd. You will find a line pertaining to you. Change your password and observe the line again. Do you notice any difference?

The password framing rules depend on the brand of UNIX being used. On one system on an AT-80386, a password is required to be at least six characters long, of which at least two must be numeric. Use a mix of uppercase and lowercase alphabets, as well as numbers;to make the password unmeaningful to others. This will prevent unauthorised users from intruding into your "territory" by pure guessing. If they still manage to do that owing to your negligence, then be assured that they can cause irreparable damage to your system!

If you enter a valid password, then the $ prompt will be returned, indicating that the job has been performed. Next time you log in, remember that you will need to enter the new password to gain entry into the system. Since you are expected to be the custodian of your password name, remember it as long as you don't change it again. If you still forget it, then rush to your system administrator.

A word here about the system administrator. He is a very important person, and is responsible for the proper management of the entire setup. He allocates the user accounts, maintains the file systems, takes backups, manages the disk space, besides performing several other important functions. The efficiency of the system will, to a great extent, be determined by the effectiveness of the system administrator. He is the person to be contacted in case of a genuine problem.

passwd is, in UNIX jargon, called a *command,* a UNIX command. Like **passwd,** there are several such commands in the system. Another command, **tput** clears the screen:

$ **tput clear** <*Enter*>

<...... .*Screen clears* ......>.

$_

There are two words this time. Here, **tput** is the command name, and **clear** is its *argument.* When a command is used with an argument, it implies that there can be at least two possible values of the argument (usually more). In other words, **tput** can be used with other words (or arguments) as well. When the **tput** command is used with the clear argument, the resultant action is to clear the screen.

Once the screen clears and the $ prompt reappears, you can enter your third command:

$ **pwd** <*Enter*>

/usr/kumar

$-The **pwd** command helps you ascertain your bearings with reference to the file syst

m, kumar was

signed a u

er

account by the system administrator, and whenever a user logs in using the login nam "kumar", UNIX "places" him in a *directory* named after his login name, in this case kum r. This directory is really a sub-directory' under a "higher" directory, named **usr**. The / preceding the word **usr** indicates the absolute point of reference in the UNIX file system. Thi reference point is known as *root.* The **pwd** command, like **CD** of MSDOS, generates the complete pathname of the current directory, except that the \ (backslash) there is replaced here by a / (frontslash).

You can list out the names of the files available in this directory, using the **ls** command:

$ ls *<Enter>*

README

chap01chap02chap03helpdir progs$_The **ls** command displays a list of six files which a

e available in this directory. Three of the files actually contain the chapters of this textbook. Notice the files are arranged alphabetically, with uppercase having precedence over lower.

Since the files containing the first three chapters have similar filenames, UNIX lets you use a special short-hand notation (*) to access them:

$ ls chap* *<Enter>*

chap01

chap02

chap03

$_

You can see the contents of the file **README** by using the **cat** command (similar to the **TYPE** command of MSDOS):

$ **cat README** *<Enter>*

Remember to terminate every command with the <Enter> key

The completion of every command is indicated by the $ prompt

$_

The file **README** contains a fairly friendly and helpful message which you will do well to remember. But what does the file **progs** contain? Use the cat command again to find out:

$ **cat progs**

&A^G.^E.A..H^A..Adept.hP^Adept.qQ^Aemp.hR^Aemp.q$_

The prompt doesn't appear in a separate line this time. Moreover, what you see on the terminal could also be quite different from the one above, but it at least indicates that **progs** is no ordinary file. It could be a directory, and the next command **(cd)** shows that it is so:

$ **cd progs**

$_

The cd (change directory) command changes your current directory, and the silent return, of the prompt confirms that **progs** in indeed a directory. This should be quite obvious to MSDOS users,

Ex 1.2. What do you think an ls command will disclose at this stage?

When you logged in to the system, you were greeted with the message **"You have mail".** It is a good idea to see the "mailbox" with the **mail** command:

$ **mail** <*Enter*>

From root Thu Dec 20 15:52:26 1990

To: kumar

Subject: A hearty welcome

Date: Thu Dec 20 15:52:26 1990

The system administrator welcomes you to the UNIX club

You must use this command every time you are notified.

that some mail has arrived — Bye

?

Try the command on your system to view the messages that the system has sent you. You can see that the prompt has changed to a ?. This is the prompt used by the **mail** command, and like it, many commands have prompts of their own, quite distinct from the system prompt ($). You have the option here of entering any **mail** "sub-command", or you can simply press the <*Enter*> key a couple of times till you have exhausted reading all mail. After you have finished, simply enter

q <*Enter*>

at this **?** prompt to return you to the **$** prompt.

1. The <*Enter*> Key

You have had your first interaction with the system after logging in. You must have noticed that every command is terminated by hitting the <*Enter*> key. On some machines, this key can have the name <*Return*>. It is a feature of computers in general, and UNIX in particular, that the text the user types at the terminal remains hidden from the system until the <*Enter*> key is pressed. First-time users often fail to appreciate this point because there is no "<*Enter*> key" in the human information system. Humans register speech or text, as it is being spoken or read, in a continuous manner. In this respect, this key resembles the shutter of a camera; nothing gets into the film until the shutter is pressed. Since the requirement is obvious, henceforth, the explicit mention of this key will be avoided, except in unobvious circumstances.

When the <*Enter*> key is pressed, it shoots out the character with the ASCII octal value 12 (decimal value 10.) to the system. This is also known as the *newline* character, and is the universal character used by UNIX systems to terminate a command, or a line of text. This character is also generated by using the key sequence <*Control-j*>. (Keep pressed the key marked **<Control>** and then the key marked **j**.) When you see some text output on the screen, the system prepends a *CR (carriage return)* character to it, though it is not preserved in the text.

You can try out some more UNIX commands, to find out today's date for example:

$ date

Thu Dec 20 16:32:33 EST 1990

$_

The **date** command displays the date and time to the nearest second. MSDOS users should notice that the invocation of this command doesn't prompt you for changing the date. It is a security feature of UNIX that the facility of changing the date rests only with the system administrator (though he uses the same command to do that !).

You can also find out the people who are presently using the system:

$ who

kumar	tty01	Dec 20 16:17
Sharma	tty02	Dec 20 16:25

$_

There are currently two users, namely kumar and Sharma. The terminal names, as well as the date and time they logged in, are also indicated. Observe that the output of the command doesn't include any headers to indicate what the various columns mean. Generally the output generated by UNIX commands are curt, and sometimes quite incomprehensible. This is an extremely important feature of the system, and is in great measure responsible for the unfriendly image that it has acquired. You will yourself discover, while going through the pages of this text, that it is actually a blessing in disguise.

UNIX has simple symbols (also called *operators*) for creating and storing information in files. Instead of viewing the output of the **who** command on the terminal, you can save the information in a file **user.lst** by using a special symbol, > (the right chevron character on your keyboard):

$ who > user.lst

$_

You see nothing on the terminal except the return of the prompt. In the UNIX system, there is a mechanism of *redirecting* any output, normally coming to the terminal, to a disk file; a > does that easily. In this case, it stored the output of the **who** command in the file **user.lst.** You can verify this by finding out whether the file **user.lst** actually contains the output of the **who** command. The **cat** command, used with a filename, displays the file's contents:

```
$ cat user.lst
kumar       tty0l     Dec 20 16:17
Sharma      tty02     Dec 20 16:25
$_
```

Here you have a glimpse of the UNIX magic. The system looked up its "log book" for details of the current users, and then, using the operator >, it created and opened the file **user.lst** to write the output of the **who** command to it—all with only a single line of code. The complex and mundane task of file handling is taken care of by the system.

Ex 1.3: Enter the sequence > user.lst and find out what happens. Repeat the process by removing the space after the > symbol. Does it make any difference?

How many lines are there in the file? The **wc** command answers this question:

```
$ we user.lst
2 10 74 user.lst
$_
```

Observe once again the brevity that typically characterises UNIX; it merely echoes three numbers along with the filename. You have to have the manual or this text in front of you to know that the file **user.lst** contains 2 lines, 10 words and 74 characters.

Now, you should see something which is often hailed as the finest feature of the system. Previously, you used the **who** command to find out the current users of the system, and then the > symbol to save the output in the file **user.lst.** You then counted the number of lines, words and characters of this file using the **wc** command. In this way you could count the number of persons who are currently using the system. It would be a splendid idea if you could count the number of users directly, without using the intermediate file. UNIX does indeed offer such a feature of using two commands in a *piped* manner:

```
$ who I wc
2   10   74
$_
```

See how you can arrive at the same result, without using the intermediate file **user.lst,** by simply connecting the output of the **who** command to the input of the **wc** command. The special symbol I (known as a *pipe*) performs the job of connecting the two. If you can connect a number of UNIX commands in this way, then you can perform difficult tasks quite easily.

Ex 1.4: Try connecting the other commands with the pipe (I) Do they all work?

The system also features a programming facility. You can assign a value to a variable at the prompt:

$ x-5

$_

and then evaluate the value of this variable by using the **echo** command:

$ **echo $x**

5

$_

Ex 1.5: Attempt the assignment by providing a space on either end of the -.

So far, what you have seen is only a small fragment of the UNIX giant, though you have already been exposed to some of its key features. All these commands and features will be considered in some detail in the subsequent chapters, and it is a good idea to suspend the session for the time being. You should use the **exit** command to do that:

$ **exit**

login:

Alternatively, you can use <*Control-d*> (generated by pressing the <Control> key and the character d on the keyboard) to quit the session. The **"login:"** message confirms that the session has been terminated, thus making it available for the next user.

THE BACKGROUND

UNIX had a modest beginning at AT&T Bell Laboratories in the late sixties. That was when AT&T withdrew its team from the MULTICS project, in which General Electric and MIT were also active participants. Some of the people who participated in that project then began work on the development of a computing environment for the staff of the Computing Science Research Group of Bell Laboratories, to pursue "programming research". Ken Thompson and Dennis Ritchie then designed and built a system, based on a design made out by Rudd Canaday. Even though the MULTICS system had a number of limitations and had to be finally abandoned, much of the present UNIX system owes its origin to MULTICS.

Strangely enough, the immediate motivation towards development of this operating system-seems to have been a space travel game, which Thompson had developed for the PDP-7. The .game supposedly showed the planetary bodies in heavenly motion, along with a spacecraft which could be landed in any one of them. The motion of the spacecraft was jerky and slow on this time-sharing system. Thompson then approached the management for a DEC-10, an expensive time-sharing system then introduced by Digital Equipment Corporation.

Fortunately the request was declined, leaving T & R (Thompson and Ritchie) with no option but to design an operating system for a standby PDP-7. A multitasking system supporting two users was the result of their work. This new system had an elegant file system, a command interpreter and a set of utilities. A member of the team, Brian Kemighan, suggested the name UNICS (then jokingly referred to as the Uniplexed Information and Computing System) for this operating system, which was obviously a pun on MULTICS. In 1970, UNICS finally became the name by which it is known today—UNIX.

Operating systems have always, i.e. till UNIX came on the scene, been designed with a particular machine in mind. Similarly, computers were also built for a specific operating system. They were invariably written in assembler, which understood and accessed the hardware well, and had good speed. This was imperative in those days when hardware was expensive and human labour comparatively cheap. Consequently, it wasn't considered prudent to invest resources in improvement of the environment of the software designer. It was obvious to T & R that development of a general operating system running on more than one type of hardware would imply use of a high-level language with consequent sacrifice of speed. But with hardware prices tumbling and labour cost spiralling, the question then was this—was it worth doing that?

It was here that T & R made what can be regarded as one of the most important decisions in recent times. Speed can be traded off against utility and portability. They reasoned that it didn't matter if the machine performed somewhat slowly, if it could offer portability and productive tools to offset the loss in efficiency. Consciously and deliberately, they rejected the idea of finalising the UNIX code in assembler, because they thought that it would be repeating the same story all over again. Instead, portability was foremost in the minds of these two persons, and they were willing to sacrifice some speed if that saved development time. UNIX had to be ported to any hardware.

Originally written in assembler, UNIX was rewritten in 1973 in C, which was principally authored by Ritchie. C incidentally is based on the interpretive B language developed by Thompson. Writing the system in C made it possible to maintain it and move it to different hardware platforms. However, speed still suffered. This deficiency has been rectified to a great extend today, With improvements in hardware that are taking place at an accelerated pace, the sluggishness of the system has been greatly minimised.

There have been contributions from other quarters also. By virtue of an anti-trust decree, AT&T was prohibited from selling UNIX-based products, even though the product was in some demand externally. Finally, AT&T went in for a liberal licensing agreement, which made the source code available to universities, industry and the government at a nominal cost, without any support or warranty. Development of UNIX started in a big way outside Bell Labs.

Ken Thompson's sabbatical at the University of California, Berkeley in 1975 was the prime mover of the second stream of development of the UNIX system there. The Computer Science Department at Berkeley emerged as the most notable external contributor, with their BSD (Berkeley Software Distribution) versions. Among Berkeley's notable achievements that are found today in practically every system are the **ex** and **vi** editors, the **more** utility and the C shell.

Using the BSD system as a development platform, another UNIX variant, the SunOS from Sun Microsystems emerged. Sun, the **ex vi** editors and the C shell owe their origin to William Joy. Sun's major contribution is the Network File System.

Microsoft Corporation, in collaboration with SCO (The Santa Cruz Operation) produced what certainly is the largest selling UNIX flavour—XENIX. Today, XENIX is available on a vast range of machines, using chips of the Intel family (the 8086, 80286, 80386 and 80486 microprocessors), as well as the Motorola family (the 68000 series), With some utilities borrowed from the BSD system, XENIX has now been merged with UNIX. It is no longer a separate system. However, SCO now offers UNIX as a separate product (. SCO-UNIX).

In 1983, AT&T introduced System V, which is still widely used, and incorporates the major enhancements made by these vendors. In the same year, UNIX received its most coveted reward yet— the blessings of Big Blue. IBM offered UNIX on the PC.

Since then, the UNIX system has evolved through constant upgradations and enhancements to become the most popular operating environment after MSDOS. And while MSDOS restricts its operations to personal computers, UNIX has been ported to a wide variety of machines, ranging from super-micros to mainframes. The UNIX system is still in a state of sustained growth, with an increasing number of people falling prey to its mysterious charm.

In 1990, AT&T introduced System V Release 4, which unifies the three main variants of the system along with AT&T's own. The result is a single and versatile system that takes into account the requirements specified by various standards committees and industry. The most popular commands from the BSD system, XENIX and the SunOS, have now been merged with the AT&T set. Some of the older commands have also been enhanced to provide even more power. In this book, the Release 4 enhancements will be pointed out separately, as considered necessary.

THE UNIX PHILOSOPHY

But why is UNIX really so popular? There are many reasons, and even if you are able to find them, it will be difficult to quantify the extent of their influence. Instead, it will be more meaningful to understand the philosophy behind its conception, and highlight the important aspects of the system.

UNIX has a number of features, mostly good and some bad, but it is necessary to know at least some of them. It is indeed unique, a product of several talented people who combined many ideas and cast them in a simple and easy-to-understand structure. In the words of T & R, "the success of UNIX lies not so much in new inventions but rather in the full exploitation of a carefully selected set of fertile ideas, and especially in showing that they can be keys to the implementation of a small and yet powerful operating system."

1. The Two Illusions

From that "carefully selected set", Kaare Christian (*The UNIX Operating System*, John

Wiley) detects two powerful concepts—"files have places and processes have life" The first assumes that files are situated in space, which makes it easy to locate them with reference to a predetermined place. Moreover, you can be "placed" at a specific location in the.'file system, and you can also "move" from one place to another. This real life-model makes the UNIX file system easily comprehensible.

The second concept treats the processes as life-like and this enables us to understand them with reference to time. It is appropriate to treat processes in the same way as mortals. Processes have parents, children and grandchildren, and are born, even reborn and die. Like files, processes also follow a separate hierarchical tree structure, and because a process is simply the time image of an executable file, you can access and control it with the greatest of ease.

2. Kernel and Shell

The entire UNIX system is supported by a handful of essentially simple concepts, Foremost amongst them is the division of labour between two agencies, one interacting with the user, and the other with the machine's hardware. This is achieved by two abstract constituents—the kernel and the shell. The relationship between the two is depicted in Figure 1.

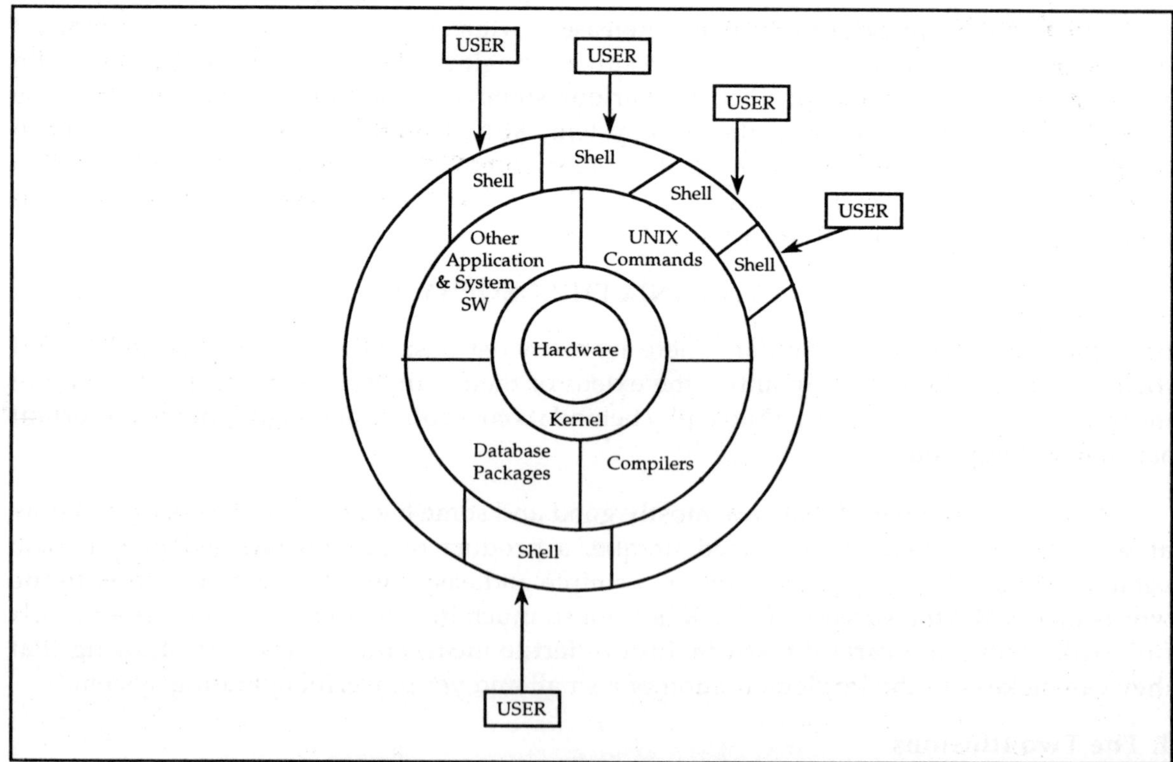

Fig. 1. The Structure of the UNIX System

The kernel is the heart of the system—a collection of programs mostly written in C, which communicate with the hardware directly. There is only one kernel for any system. It is that part of the UNIX system that is loaded into memory when the system is booted. It manages the system resources, allocates time between users and processes, decides process priorities and performs all the other tasks which you wouldn't like to bother about. Because the kernel isolates itself from the user programs, and these programs are independent of the hardware they use, it is easy to move them across different systems. Programs, therefore, must not have knowledge of the devices they use. The kernel, in traditional parlance, is often called *the* operating system.

Ex 1.6: Change your directory to / (root) and locate the kernel (the file named unix or xenix)

The shell, on the other hand, is the "sleeping beauty." Technically another UNIX command, it is the interpreter of user requests. Computers don't have any inherent capability of translating commands into action. An interpreter is required, and that job in the UNIX system is handled by the shell. It takes a command from the user deciphers it and by exchanging information, communicates with the kernel to see that the command is executed. It is actually the interface between the user and the kernel, which effectively insulates the user from the knowledge of kernel functions. The shell is the agency which lakes care of the features.of redirection, using the > and I symbols. It also has a programming capability of its own.

Ex 1.7; Change your directory to /bin and locate the shell (the file named sh).

3. Small is Beautiful

Generally, designers have not attempted to develop tools which can solve a variety of programming problems. Instead, they have adopted Schumacher's philosophy—"small is beautiful", and developed a large number of commands (a few hundreds of them), each of which performed one simple job only. You used cat to display the contents of a file, **pwd** to indicate the present working directory, and **wc** to count the number of lines, words, characters, and so on. You even combined two of them (**who I wc**) to count the number of users in the system. It was the belief of the designers that all complex problems can be handled by stringing together a couple of these simple commands.

The reason for adopting such an approach is simple. They considered a complex task to be a sum total of a number of simple ones. While these tools are meant to be used as building blocks, what gave the system its power and flexibility was the interrelationships that can be built up by connecting a couple of these tools. In the early 70's, pipes were introduced, an idea originally suggested by Doug McIlroy, and later developed by Thompson. This made it possible to connect a couple of commands, with one command taking input from another. The commands that can be connected in this way are called *filters,* because they filter or manipulate the data in different ways. You have already seen how two commands (**who** and **wc**) were used with the / (pipe) to count the number of users in the system. No separate command was designed to perform the job.

Pipes and filters form the central feature of the UNIX philosophy. Most UNIX tools today are designed with the requirement that the output of one tool be used as the input of another. That is why the architects of the UNIX system had to make sure that commands didn't throw out excessive verbiage and clutter the output. That is also the reason why UNIX programs are not interactive. If the output of the **who** command contained column headers, or if it prompted the user for specific information, then it would have made little sense as input to the we command. By interconnecting a couple of tools in this way, you can have an enormous number of combinations of their usage. That is why it is better to have a command handling a specialised function rather than have one which tries to solve all problems itself. Though UNIX started with this concept, it was somewhat forgotten when tools were added to the system later.

4. The Featureless File

Apart from the illusory effect that the system produces of a file having absolute coordinates, UNIX doesn't really care to know the type of file that you are using. All files are alike in the UNIX system, and it considers even directories and devices as members of the file system. A file to UNIX is simply an array of bytes, and its size is simply equal to the number of bytes that you put into it. It can contain virtually anything; text, object code or a directory structure. Unlike other operating systems, you don't need to have a predefined structure of a file to work with it. However, applications (especially database packages) use a certain structure for the data files, but UNIX imposes no such restriction.The UNIX "Operating" System 15.

In UNIX the dominant file type is text, where lines are delimited by the newline character. The system features a host of tools which are meant to be used with such files, though some of them can very well work with other types of files. When you change a password, the information is stored (though in an encrypted manner) in a text file **/etc/ passwd.** You can schedule a number of tasks by making suitable entries in another text file (called a *crontab*). Text files can be easily modified with an editor, and if you edit them, you can acquire total control over the behaviour of the system. A typical text file contains a series of bytes, sometimes with a suitable delimiter to separate fields. UNIX encourages you to organise your information in this way, if you wish to use its text manipulation capabilities.

UNIX demolishes, once and for all, the idea of fixed length records. On its own, ii doesn't require that records have a fixed length, nor does it need to know the character count of each. Almost all the text manipulation tools also work with files which have variable record lengths. Though the concept of a *record* is virtually absent in the operating system, for ease of understanding, the term will continue to be used in this text interchangeably with *line*.

5. Pattern Matching

The system was designed to see that a minimum number of keystrokes achieve the maximum amount of work. That is why UNIX commands are seldom more than four characters long. But it is the pattern matching feature of UNIX that makes it so attractive to the programmer. You listed the chapters of the text by using the Is command with an unusual argument (**chap***), instead of specifying all the filenames explicitly. The * is a special character used by the system to indicate that the expression can match a number of filenames. If you choose your filenames carefully, then you can use a simple expression to access a whole lot of them.

The * (known as a *metacharacter*) is not the only special character used by the UNIX system; there are several others. UNIX features elaborate pattern matching schemes, using several characters from this metacharacter set. The matching is not confined to filenames only. Some of the most advanced and useful tools also use a special expression called a *regular expression,* which is framed with characters from this set. When you use a single expression to match a number of similar patterns, you can catch, them all in one shot. This book emphasises heavily the importance of regular expressions, and shows you how you can perform complex pattern matching tasks using them.

Ex 1.8: Try listing out all single and double character filenames in your directory with the arguments? and??, respectively.

6. Portability

Till UNIX appeared on the scene, operating systems were written in assembly language, which used less memory, and executed instructions faster than those written in other languages. UNIX exploded the notion that machine efficiency was more important than human productivity. That is why it was written in a high-level language, which freed it from a particular computer design and its underlying architecture. UNIX introduced the idea of moving an entire operating system with its file system, utilities and application programs to a totally different machine.

UNIX is highly portable ; it is available on a variety of hardware, ranging from the 8088-based IBM PC to the Cray 2. This was one of the objectives of the designers—to design an operating system which would take care of the expensive investments made by organisations in software development. Experienced users will surely agree that the policy of hardware vendors to down the customer to one specific type of hardware is more of a handicap than a blessing. This was happening in pre-UNIX days, but now, once software has been developed on any UNIX system, it can be easily ported to any other UNIX machine with minimum modifications. And because the source code is always available, the hardware vendor usually performs these modifications with no difficulty.

7. Open Systems

The system from the very beginning had an open architecture—one could add to the tool kit by simply writing a program and storing the executable in a separate area in the file system. A separate device can also be added by creating a file for it. This is possible because everything in UNIX is treated as a file; whether it is a source program, an executable, a floppy device, printer or terminal. Modification of the system is easy because the source code is always available. Moreover, with the vast amount of information available on the subject in the form of books, magazines, courses, etc., UNIX can be used more efficiently.

8. Programming Facility

UNIX is highly programmable ; ,it was designed for a programmer, not a casual end user. To appreciate and exploit UNIX fully, one *must* be a programmer. An MSDOS user who is not a programmer will certainly find the transition quite overwhelming.

The UNIX shell has all the necessary ingredients like control structures, loops and variables which establish it as a programming language in its own right. Though the language is somewhat difficult to learn, it has phenomenal power. The shell programming language simplifies a number of things which are simply impossible to conceive in other languages. It can be combined easily with the commands and other programs in such ways that it may sometimes appear that the two are inseparable. Proficient UNIX programmers seldom take recourse to any other language for text manipulation problems.

9. Multi-user

The who command that you tried out in the brief session suggests that UNIX is a multi-user system, which means that more than one user can be using the system at any lime. There can be up to a few hundred users sharing the system resources, based on the concept of time sharing, with each user allotted a time slice without his being aware of it. In fact, it will appear to the user that the system was completely dedicated to him. You will also have noticed that all memory and disk space allocation was done automatically by the system without your knowledge or intervention.

10. Multi-tasking

While it is possible for several users to run their respective jobs (also called *processes*) at the same time, UNIX even permits a user to run more than one job al a time. You counted the number of lines, characters and words with the **wc** program, and wailed for the **$** prompt to appear to enter your next command. You might Just as well have relegated the job to the background, by simply affixing an **&** (ampersand) to the **wc** command, and then run, say, the **date** command in the foreground:

```
$ wc user.lst > user.knt &
456
$_
$ date
Thu Dec 20 17:52:33 EST 1990
$_
```

This feature, called *multi-tasking,* is an important feature of the operating system, and permits a user to perform less urgent jobs in the background, while doing the more important ones in the foreground (It wasn't really done here). This involves a considerable amount of work for the process management system, anti yet the user doesn't really have to bother about it.

11. The Tool Kit

By one definition, UNIX is a collection of tools, which lets you dispense with programming work for many applications. These applications range from such mundane tasks as copying or deleting a file, to somewhat sophisticated database operations that can be performed by using the tools in combination. The architects of the system were probably not aware that, by adding a rich set of filtering tools to the tool kit, they had created an environment for developing applications, using the features of the UNIX system alone. The power of these fillers is simply mind-boggling, and by combining them, seemingly impossible tasks can be made to look easy. Unfortunately, this point is not appreciated to the fullest extent by most users, and it is most common to find a programmer writing a program in COBOL or even in C, for which a readymade tool is available in the UNIX tool kit.

You will towards the end of the journey eventually use these lools and their apparent interrelationships to build sophisticated applications. You will establish the power of the UNIX system in developing a relational database application without writing a single line of code in any high-level language ! To enable you to use these tools effectively, and with optimum efficiency, is the main purpose of this book.

12. System Calls and Libraries

UNIX is written in C. Though there are a couple of hundred commands handling specialised functions, they all do that by using a handful, of functions, called *system calls.* All library functions and utilities are written in terms of them. While there are several brands of UNIX available in the world, they all have one thing in common ; all use the same system calls. If an operating system used different system calls, then it wouldn't be UNIX.

System calls form the infrastructure of the kernel where they are defined and implemented. Since the kernel is the memory-resident portion of the UNIX system, interacting through system calls represents an efficient means of communication with the system. When a user wishes to write to a file, he uses the **write( )** system call without going into the details of programming that achieve this write operation. When a brand of UNIX is ported to another machine, it is only the implementation part of the system calls that needs to be reprogrammed, not the system calls themselves.

The much talked about "device independence" of most UNIX commands can be attributed to the same code these commands use to access devices and files. This is possible because the system calls also do that. The **open( )** system call is used to open both a device as well as an ordinary file. This made it possible to have a conceptually clean file system and a powerful tool kit. The same system calls are available to every C programmer who wants to develop tools of his own.

13. The User Interface

UNIX has a pretty weak user interface. This must be an anachronism in today's world of user-friendly interfaces where pop-up menus and windows provide attractive front-ends (with a mouse to boot). The Mackintosh or WINDOWS user simply selects an option to get a thing done; very little keying in of text is required. He doesn't have to bother about syntax or options ; the system takes care of that. Though UNIX does provide menu-based shells and windowing facilities, it simply doesn't have any of the frills that Apple and MSDOS users have taken for granted.

These interfaces shield us from knowledge of the operating system, the file system and all the tools. The Mackintosh can do that because FINDER doesn't have too many functions anyway. But UNIX has, and it is in your interest to know as much about the features of the operating system as possible. Because UNIX can often dispense with the need to write a comprehensive C program by combining a couple of tools, you shouldn't fall prey to attractive front-ends, which mar your understanding of the system and can sometimes affect your productivity.

Nevertheless, if UNIX is to survive, the interface certainly needs to be improved upon. The most common argument cited against introducing interfaces is that UNIX is meant for the intelligent programmer. This argument doesn't hold good any more because it is now a fully commercial product, which is being used by different users with varied backgrounds and aptitudes.

Release 4 does indeed take a step forward in this direction. Apart from the facility of running multiple shell sessions, it now features a menu-based interface (FACE), which suppresses the usual command line. The latest release also features a graphical interface, which lets you Start up multiple applications in different windows, with facilities to cut and paste data. UNIX systems today also provide a special menu-oriented tool for the system administrator. An efficient administrator, however, must go beyond the interface, and be fully aware of the internal functions of the system.

14. Documentation

UNIX documentation admittedly is one of its weakest points. It is extremely uneven, sometimes ephemeral, and at other times lucid. There is no denying the fact that some of the most important aspects of the system have been, at least to the beginner, treated miserably in the manuals. Since UNIX was written by programmers for programmers, quite often the manual assumes a thorough knowledge of most of the system. It is quite possible for a user to be misled into thinking that a particular feature is not available with a command because it wasn't specifically mentioned in the section. The manuals are good reading material only aller you have sufficiently mastered the system.

It is unfortunate that the important aspects of the system still remain Incomprehensible to most users. Most UNIX systems are used in the same way as MSDOS—a handful of commands used in isolation. Admittedly, there was no way that a user could broach the subject with confidence. Until recently, the knowledge base for this subject was frugal, and genuine support was impossible to obtain. This is the principal reason why there is a surfeit of textbooks available on this subject today. All attempt to compensate for the deficiency of the UNIX documentation. With this enormous base of text material available on this subject, and the scope of getting oneself enlightened through training courses and seminars, UNIX has become easier to tame today than it was even five years ago.

With the goal of building a comfortable relationship with the machine, T & R naturally had the programmer in mind when designing the system. Instead of designing a system for others, they designed the system for themselves. This, they thought, would enable the system to maintain itself. If designers are forced to use the system themselves, then they quickly become aware of the deficiencies, and are forced to correct them before doing anything else. This they could afford to do because UNIX wasn't developed as a commercial product, and the project didn't have any predefined objective. It had a lot of time in correcting and refining itself before it could be commercialised. T & R acknowledge this fact in these words: "We have not been faced with the need to satisfy someone else's requirements, and for this freedom we are grateful."

ON-LINE HELP FACILITY—THE MAN COMMAND

A criticism often levelled against the UNIX system is the terse syntax of the commands which makes them difficult to use. Moreover, the system is also said to be unfriendly as it fails to acknowledge the execution of a command (successful or otherwise) with a suitable message. You will see how often the prompt returns without even indicating whether the task has been performed. Files are overwritten or removed without even warning the user ! These deficiencies were justified by projecting UNIX as being exclusively designed for programmers, who wouldn't be interested in lengthy messages from the system. With UNIX now available in practically every type of industry, this unfriendly image has been somewhat rectified in Release 4.

There are cases, however, when some help will be required, since there a quite a number of such commands (varying from around 200 to 400) and the syntax of some of them can be extremely confusing, even to the expert. UNIX offers an on-line help facility with the **man** command. For example, for help on the command **wc**, you simply have to enter

$ man **wc**
WC(l)   UNIX 5.3   WC(1)
NAME
wc - word count
SYNOPSIS
wc [-Iwc] [names]

Description

We counts lines, words and characters in the named files, or in the standard, input if no names appear. It also keeps a total count for all named files. A word is a maximal String of characters delimited by spaces, tabs, or new-lines.

The options 1, w, and c may be used in any combination to specify that a subset of lines, words, and characters are to be reported. The default is -Iwc.

When names are specified in the command line, they will be printed along with the counts.

Example
wc filea fileb filec

reports the number of lines, words, and characters in each of the files.

$_

The entire contents of Section 1 of the UNIX manual pertaining to the **wc** command are dumped on the screen. In every case, the command synopsis (or syntax) is listed with a brief description, and a suitable example or two. This facility is indeed quite helpful as the user can obtain the correct syntax of the command, and also have a fair idea about its objectives as well. The limitations of the command are quite often specified explicitly, an indication of the honesty and integrity of the designers.

The UNIX manual is structured in such a way that all the commands that you normally use are found in Section 1. Occasional references to other sections can also be reflected together, saving the user from the hassle of consulting too many volumes, with the added disadvantage of searching out the command from each one of them. AT&T has divided the manual into eight sections, which are shown in Table 1.

TABLE 1

Organisation of UNIX Manuals

Section	Description
1	Commands
2	System calls
3	Subroutines
4	Special files
5	File formats
6	Games
7	Miscellaneous facilties
8	Maintenance programs & procedures

Vendors don't often organise the documentation in this way, though the online manual is seldom tampered with. Thus, to look for assistance on the **vi** command (the full-screen editor) from Section 1 of the manual, use the command

$ man 1 vi

The output will be a number of pages of documentation on the **vi** editor, selected from Section 1 of the documentation, **man** can also be invoked with other options, but a detailed treatment beyond what has been mentioned already is simply not necessary. Since **man** also happens to be a UNIX command like **who** or **wc,** for help on the **man** command, simply enter

$ man man

The **man** facility occupies 2 to 3 megabytes of disk space, so it is quite possible that the installation you may be working on may not have **man** installed. In such a case, you will have to consult the system manual. Alternatively, you can try the **help** command, which provides some assistance, though not to the extent envisaged in man. (Note that even **help** may not be available on your system.)

SOME USEFUL TIPS

There are certain things which **man** won't tell you. For instance, if the display from a command is scrolling too fast for you to see on the terminal, you can halt the output temporarily, by pressing *<Control-s>*, and resume scrolling, by pressing *<Control-q>*,

If you make mistakes in typing, you can use the backspace key for erasing, or *<Control-b>* If you want to kill the line that you have entered without executing it, use *<Control-u>*, If you want a premature termination of a command, press *<Control-c>or* the <Del>key. If your *<Enter>* key doesn't work, you can use *<Control-j>* or *<Control-m>* However, remember that these functions are system dependent, and it is quite possible that some of the keys may not work in quite the same way as mentioned here. If you have problems, then seek the assistance of the system administrator. (He will solve them by using the **stty** command.)

UNIX provides a full-duplex terminal, which means that you can type your command at any time, and feel satisfied that the system will interpret it. When you run a long program, the **$** prompt won't appear till the program execution is complete. Subsequent commands can be entered at the keyboard (as many commands as you wish) without waiting for the prompt. There is a type-ahead buffer which stores all these commands, and passes them on for execution after the previous program has completed its run. If you type correctly, then simply don't bother even if the output from the previous program garbles the display !

If you have a terminal which behaves in an erratic manner (especially when editing a file with a full-screen editor), then use the command **stty sane** to restore sanity. If you still have other problems that you can't tackle this way, then contact your system administrator.

REVIEW

You now have a "feel" of what the UNIX system is all about—a collection of files, processes and tools, something more than what an operating system is expected to be. It is mostly written in C, which lets you move the entire system, with all its files and utilities, to a totally different hardware. There can be several users and several processes, all using the system concurrently. Management of disk space, memory, files and processes are all kept outside the purview of the user, and handled by the kernel. The. shell acts as a go-between, allowing the user to remain ignorant of the hardware details, as well as the intricate processes that run in any UNIX system.

UNIX has a number of commands in its arsenal, each command handling a specialised function. It also uses special symbols to create files and facilitate communication between two commands. For this reason, the output of a typical command is brief, without labels or headers. Since several commands produce a multi-columnar output, the UNIX manual or a suitable text should always be kept as reference while using the machine. Because the system was designed by programmers for programmers, it assumes that the user is well conversant with the features' of the system. That is why UNIX allows a user a good deal of freedom without even warning him.

UNIX is indifferent to the type of file you use. Its liberal definition of a file includes devices as well as directories. It doesn't insist on fixed length records, and a file can contain virtually anything that you put into it. However, it does treat text files specially, and has several tools which manipulate them. Because it always has an open structure, you can enhance the power of the system by adding a file representing a tool or a device.

UNIX has a large number of important and abstract concepts. It is not a system which you can master by simply sitting at a terminal and trying out the commands from the manual. You don't learn concepts that way, and the manual doesn't provide them. A good deal of reading, supported by adequate hands-on sessions, is necessary before you can start feeling confident. Many people use UNIX in the same way as MSDOS. Don't make the mistake of doing that. Don't write a program which is available in the system. It doesn't pay to reinvent the wheel.

Glossary of Key Computer Terms

Access Time: The clapsed time between transfer of information from a backing storage to the main memory. Such a measurement is important in a feasibility study.

Accounting Checks: Refers to control on input data that is based on such accounting principles as control totals, cross totals or hash data.

Accumulator: A register or storage location in which the results of an arithmetic or logic operation are formed.

Acoustic Coupler: A device is a data communications system that converts electrical data signals to/from tones for transmission over a telephone line, using a conventional telephone headset.

Activity Ratio: A measurement of file activity. It is computed as the relationship of records use to the total number of records in the file. Synonymous with *hit rate*.

Address: A location in a computer system that can be referred to in a program. The location may be in the main memory, in a terminal, in a peripheral device or any other physical item in a computer system.

Algorithm: (1) A set of sell-defined rules for solving a problem in a finite number of operations. (2) In the context of encryption, this is the set of mathematical operations used to transform data to or from a ciphered form. Most techniques use both an algorithm and a keyword to achieve this.

Analog Computer: A computer in which data is represented in the form of continuously physical quantities such as pressure, temperature revolutions, speed or sound, or voltage. Used in scientific operations and manufacturing for controlling the operation.

ANSI (American National Standard Institute): The name of the U.S.A. standards-forming body, headquartered in NY City, See ASCII.

Append: To add more records at the end of a file.

Applications Software: A program (or group of programs) which processes data for a user. Written for or by a user it tells the computer how to do a specific job. Examples are: payroll programs and inventory control programs. The software does the productive work and usually represents the single biggest user investment in data processing.

Archive: A procedure for transferring data from an on-line storage medium or memory area, to an off-lone storage medium.

Arithmetic-Logic Unit (ALU): In a computer system, that section of the CPU, which contains the circuits for carrying out arithmetic operation and logical comparisons.

Array: A table of one or more dimension stored in the computer memory in which individual locations are addressed by coordinate positions instead of by their unique data names.

Array Processor: Also called parallel processor or multiprocessor, it is a special-purpose processor (or attachment to another processor), designed for fast mathematical computations when data is structured in the form of arrays (matrices) or vectors.

Artificial Intelligence: The capability of a computer to perform functions that are normally associated with human intelligence, such as reasoning, learning and self-improvement.

ASCII (American National Standard Code for Information Interchange): A standard code, composed of 7-bit coded characters (8-bit including partly check) established by the American National Standard Institute, designed for information systems and other associated equipment. The ASCII set encompasses both control and graphic characters.

Assembly Language: A machine-oriented programming language, referred as a low-level language. It uses nemonics codes which closely correspond-one-to-one correspondence - to the specific instruction set of a particular computer system. Programs written in assembly language (source code) are converted into a machine-readable form by an Assembler prior to execution. Assembly language may provide such facilities as the use of micro-instruction.

Asynchronous Computer: A digital computer in which each operation starts as a result of a signal generated by the completion of the previous operation. In contrast, in a *synchronous computer* all operations are timed to synchronise with a master clock.

Audio Response Unit (ARU): A device that links a computer system to a telephone net work to provide audible responses to enquiries made from touch-tone telephone sets. Responses can be in the form of human speech (*see voice response unit*) or other tones and sounds.

Audit Trail: Historic data and information available for examination in order to prove the origin, flow and destination of data within as well as the correctness and integrity with which the prescribed security procedures have been followed.

Authentication: The process of ensuring that information has originated from an authorised source. It may employ an algorithm (which remains fixed) or a keyword (which is usually changed periodically).

Automated Clearing House (ACH): A computerised facility operated to process electronic transactions such as interbank payments of funds and other paperless transactions.

Automated Office: A generic term referring to the merger of computers, office electronic devices and telecommunications technology in an office environment.

Back-end Processor: The computer that serves as an interface between a larger CPU and database stored on direct access storage devices, like magnetic disks.

Background Processing: In multi-programming the automatic execution of lower priority (background) computer programs during periods when the system resources are not required to process high priority (foreground) programs.

Backup: Alternate programs of equipment used in case the original is incapacitated.

Backup Copy: A copy of a master file kept for reference in case the original file is destroyed or gets corrupted. It is also required when master files are updated as the previous versions of changed records get over written.

Bandwidth: The range of frequencies assigned to a communications channel or system. The difference between the highest and lowest frequencies of a band, is expressed in terms of hertz.

Bar Code: A set of parallel lines of varied thickness and space on products sold in super markets. The lines represent alphanumeric characters which can be recognised and interpreted by an optical scanner. The lines represented by bars is known as Universal Product Code.

Bar Graph: Data when displayed as a set of evenly spaced bars, each bar representing a value in the range.

BASIC: Beginners All Purposes Symbolic Instruction Code. A high-level interactive programming language frequently used with personal computers and in time-sharing environments.

Batch Processing: A technology in which a number of similar items or transactions to be processed are grouped (batched) for processing as a single unit. Contrasted with *real-time processing* in which transactions are dealt with as they arise.

Baud: (Rhymes with 'codes') It is the standard unit for expressing transmission capabilities of line terminals, interface equipment etc. (Roughly equal to bits per second).

Benchmark: A set of test problems designed to compare the relative performance of different computer systems or sub-systems.

Binary: Pertaining to pair as in the binary notation system in which only the digits 0 to 1 are used.

Binary Coded Decimal: **it refers to a decimal notation in which the individual decimal digits are represented by a binary group code in the 8-4-2-1 coded decimal notation. For example number 23 is represented in the following manner:

8	4	2	1	8	4	2	1
0	0	0	0 = 2	0	0	1	1 = 3

Binary Digit: Either of the character 0 or 1. Abbreviated as *bit*.

Binary Number System: A number system with a base, or radix, of 2.

Bit Transfer Rate: The number of bits transferred per unit time, usually expressed in bits per second (bps).

Block: Related records, characters, or digits that are grouped and handled as a unit during data storage and transfer operations.

Blocking Factor: The number of logical records of a given size-contained in a single physical record, such as, a block.

Booting: A technique for loading a program into a computer's memory in which the program's initial instructions direct the loading of the rest of program.

Bootstrap: A technique by which sequence of initial instruction (usually from read-only memory) is used to load or "pull" (bootstrap) the rest of the program into the computer memory.

Bottom-up Design: A systems analysis technique characterised by initiation at the detail level and construction in successive level of greater generality.

Branch: An instruction that transfers program control to one or more alternative paths in the program under certain conditions.

Branch Instruction: An instruction in a program that controls branching. Synonymous with *decision instruction.*

Buffer: A storage device used to compensate for the difference in the rates of flow of data from one device to another e.g. from one Input/Output (I/O) device to CPU.

Bug: A program defect or error.

Bus: A path or channel for transmitting data, usually, between a computer and peripheral equipment.

Byte: Synonymous with character. Each byte consists of a combination of eight binary digits (bits).

Cache Memory: A high speed, buffer type memory set aside in some computers for temporarily storing very active data and instructions, during processing. It is filled in from the main memory, the process being automatic. Since cache memory is faster than the main memory, processing gets speeded up.

CAD/CAM: Computer-Aided Design/Computer-Aided Manufacturing.

Canned Programs: Program written by an outside supplier and provided to a user in a machine-readable form.

CASE Acronym for computer-aided software (or systems) engineering. A computerised methods of software development which incorporates structured approach to system design, creation of data dictionaries and writing of actual application programs.

Cell: In a spreadsheet, the space created by the intersection of a vertical column and a horizontal row.

Central Processing Unit: (CPU) The component of a computer system with circuitry to control the interpretation and execution of instruction. It includes primary storage, arithmetic-logic and control sections.

Chaining: A system of storing records in which each record belonging to a group of records is connected to the field for other record by means of a chain. The chain is formed by using a field in record to contain the physical medium address of the next record in the logical sequence.

Channel: In data communications, a path for electrical transmission between two or more points. Also called a circuit, facility, line, link, or path. In a computer, it is the hardware device along which data transfers take place within the CPU and the peripherals.

Character: An individual letter, numeral, or special character. In computers, characters are made up of a number of bits. Synonymous with *byte.*

Character Recognition: The facilities or operations involved in the machine interpretation of graphic characters, e.g. MICR, OCR.

Check Digit: A digit added to each number in a coding system which allows for detection of errors in the recording of the code numbers. Through the use of the check digit and a pre-determined mathematical formula, recording errors such as digit reversal can be noted. See also *parity bit.*

Checkpoint/Restart Facility: A facility for restarting execution of a program, at some point other than the beginning, after the program was terminated due to a program or system failure. In teleprocessing, a facility that records the status of the teleprocessing network all designated intervals or following certain events.

Chief Programmer Team: The organisation of a programming project designed to promote a structured and hierarchical approach to programming.

Chip: A thin, small piece of semiconductor material on which integrated circuits have been formed. Scope of the term also includes associated packaging and connecting pins.

Coaxial Cable: A cable consisting of one conductor, copper tube or wire, surrounded by a sort of shield made of a separate electricity insulated wire.

Compatibility: The capability of computer hardware which enables it to accept and process data prepared by another make/model of computer without conversion or code modification.

COBOL: (Common Business Oriented Language). A high level language developed for business data processing applications.

CODASYL: A Conference on Data Systems Language. This group developed COBOL in 1960 and later developed database facilities and associated languages - DML (Data Manipulation Language) and DDL (Data Description Language).

Coding: Writing a list of instructions that cause a computer to perform specified operations.

COM (Computer-Output-Microfilm): Normal printed output of a computer reduced to one of available microforms by a special output device that takes the place of the line printer.

Command: A signal (for group of signals) which causes a computer to execute an operation or series of operations.

Compile: To prepare a machine language program from a high-level, symbolic language program by generating more than one machine instruction for each symbolic statement, as well as performing the function of an assembler.

Compiler: A program that accepts instructions in high-level language and converts each instruction into a multitude of machine language instructions, from which the computer can run the jobs. Also called language processor. A typical compiler can also perform such functions as lexical scan (to eliminate redundancies) arithmetic scan (to convert arithmetic expressions to a form suitable for computations), insertion of default options, optimisation and simplification of text to produce an improved parsed version and the like.

Computer: A device that can perform a sequence of automatic and/or logic operations and produce useful results, without human intervention, except in preparing the device and, possibly, initiating the operations. It performs operations under the direction of a detailed step-by-step stored program of instructions. Unless otherwise specified, the term connotes a digital computer.

Concentrator: A device that matches a larger number of input channels with a fewer number of output channels. The input channels are usually low speed asynchronous, and the output channel(s) is high speed, synchronous.

Conditional Transfer: An instruction that may cause a departure from the sequence of instructions being followed, depending upon the result of an operation, the contents of a register, or the setting of an indicator.

Configuration: A particular group of interconnected functions units that form a computer system or sub-system.

Console: A panel in a computer used for communication between the operator or maintenance engineer and the computer. CRT terminals or a typewriter consoles are the most common.

Control Panel: The top three lines of a spreadsheet in Lotus 1-2-3 that displays all addresses, cell contents, program prompts and command menu.

Control Program: An operating system support program that monitors the excertion of other programs.

Conversion: The process of changing from one method of data processing in another or from one computer system to another.

Counter: A device (e.g. a register) used to represent the number of occurrences of an event.

CPS: Characters per second.

CPU (Central Processing Unit): That part of the computer which decodes instructions and controls the hardware used to execute them.

Cursor: A position indicator employed on a VDU screen to indicate a character to be corrected or a position in which data is to be entered.

Cybernetics: The comparative study which explores the internal workings of both people and machines and their interaction with each other.

Cycles Per Second: (1) Hertz (2) The number of times per second that some multiple step operation is performed.

Cylinder: The tracts on a disk which can be assessed without repositioning the read/write heads (also known as *seek area*).

Daisy Wheel: An interchangeable element used on electronic typewriters and printers attached to word processors. It is a rotatable wheel with type slugs at the end of 'spoke'- type bars to produce a fully formed character.

DASD: Direct access storage device.

Data: Facts, the raw material of information.

Data Capture: Functions performed by a terminal or computer in capturing information relating to a transaction. Information captured is stored and can be accessed to provide audit trails, printed statements, etc.

Data Definition Language: The language used to describe the schemas, subschemas, and storage schemes in a database management system.

Data Dictionary: A program that lists and describes all data elements residing in a database.

Data Integrity: A performance measure based on the rate of undetected errors.

Data Item: The smallest unit of named data in a program. It may consist of any number of bits or bytes, and is often referred to as a field or data element.

Data Management System: The programs in an operating system that provide access to data, perform, or monitor storage of data, and control I/O devices.

Data Manipulation: Any combination of the following operations; classifying, merging, computing, moving and editing.

Data Preparation: Translating data collected manually to become computer input using, for example key-to-floppy.

Data Processing System: A network of machine components capable of accepting information, processing it according to a plan and producing the desired results.

Data Transfer Rate: Refers to the measurement of speed at which data may be read from or written to the device from the lowest to the highest speed and density available.

Database: A non-redundant collection of interrelated data items processable by one or more applications. Non-redundant means that individual data elements appear only once (or at least less frequently than a normal file organisations) in the database. Interrelated means that the files are constructed with an ordered and planned relationship that allows data elements to be tied together, even though they may not necessarily be in the same physical record. Processable by one or more applications means that data is shared and used by several different sub-systems.

Database Administrator (DBA): The individual charged with the responsibility for the proper administration and control of the corporate database and its use.

Database Machine: The hardware component, usually a special purpose mini-computer, of a database management system that performs functions normally executed by software and the host computer. See also *back-end processor*.

Database Management System: A software program that provides a systematic approach to storing, updating, and retrieval of information stored as data items, usually in the form of records in a file, where many users access common data bank.

Database Structure: The field, record, and interrecord relationship that define collectively the format in which data is stored.

Default Drive: The letter appearing in the Disk Operating System (DOS) prompts that indicates which drive the DOS will be using.

Default Settings: Settings assumed by the program when no other setting is specified.

Deblocking: The process of separating blocked data into individual logical records.

Debug: The process of detection, location and elimination of errors in software.

Decision Support System: A program tailored to management needs and designed to aid decision-making process.

Decision Table: A matrix of contingencies that are to be considered with the actions to be taken. Sometimes used in place of flowcharts for program documentation.

Decision Tree: An approach towards identifying risks and probabilities in a problem situation involving uncertainty, or chance events, by sketching in the form of a 'tree' various courses that might be undertaken. The expected value of each alternative is the sum of various possible outcomes weighed by their probability of occurring.

Degradation factor: A measure of the loss in performance that results from reconfiguration of a data processing system; for example, a slow down in run time due to a reduction in the number of central processing units.

Density: The number of bits in single linear track measured per unit of length of the recording medium.

Desktop Computer: A personal computer used for business tasks or located in a corporate environment.

Diagnostics: Error messages printed by a computer to indicate system problems and improper program instructions.

Digital Computer: A computer that solves problems by operating on discrete data representing variables by performing arithmetic and logical processes from a stored program on these data. Contrast with *analog computer*.

Digital Data: Information represented by a code-comprising a sequence of discrete elements.

Digitise: To convert to, or express in a digital form, data that was expressed originally in analog form.

Direct Access: Pertaining to storage devices in which the time required to retrieve data is independent of the physical location of the data.

Direct Access Storage Device (DASD): A basic type of storage medium that allows data to be accessed by positioning the medium or accessing mechanism directly at the storage location. The time required for such access is independent of the location of the data most recently accessed. Synonymous with *random access*. File organisations on a DASD can be sequential, direct, or indexed sequential. Contrast with *serial or sequential access*.

Disk: A physical means of information storage in which data is encoded on the magnetic recording surfaces of a single or pack of disks mounted on a central vertical spindle.

Diskette: A floppy disk. A low cost magnetic medium used for I/O and secondary storage purposes.

Distributed Database: One logical database that has been divided among physical locations within a distributed information system.

Distributed Processing: A data processing arrangement in which processing is performed in two or more computers, but in which all or most of stored data accessed resides in one processor.

Documentation: The preparation of documents, during system analysis and subsequent programming, that describes such things as the system, the programs prepared and the changes made therein at later dates.

DOS/VS: Disk Operating System/Virtual Storage.

Dot Prompt: A dBase III Plus prompt, represented by a dot that allows direct entry of commands.

Dot Matrix Printer: A type of printer in which each character is formed by a grid or matrix pattern of dots.

Doubled Density: The storage of information on a diskette in such a manner that the capacity becomes twice that of a standard diskette. This is accomplished by either doubling the number of tracks per inch, doubling the serial bit density, or a combination of both.

Double Sided Diskette: A type of diskette that utilise both of its sides for the storage of information. A double sided diskette can be loaded into a floppy disk drive with a dual read/write head assembly, or used on standard single head drive, takenout, flipped, and reinserted for read/record operations on both sides.

Dumb Terminal: A device, such as VDU, which is linked to the computer and does not incorporate any of its own processing capability; in contrast to *intelligent terminal.*

Dump: To transfer the contents of specified internal storage locations on to another, usually more permanent, storage medium. It is done for a specific purpose such as to allow use of storage for other purpose to safeguard against faults or errors, and to facilitate debugging. Also referred to as *core dump, tape dump* or *disk dump.*

Duplex: Simultaneous two-way independent transmission in both directions. Also referred to as *full duplex.*

Dynamic Memory: Semiconductor memory characterised by high density, but requiring periodic refresh of stored data.

EAROM (Electrically Alterable Read Only Memory): A specialised random access read memory with a special, show write cycle and a much faster read cycle, used with microprocessors and microcomputers.

EBCDIC (Extended Binary Coded Decimal Interchange Code): A coded character set comprising 8-bit coded characters, developed by IBM and a de facto industry standard.

Echo Check: An error control technique wherein the receiving terminal or computer returns the original message to the sender to verify that the message was received correctly.

Edit: To arrange data in accordance with a specified format. Editing includes insertion of constant characters such as page numbers and decimal points into computer output, modification or addition of data, deletion of unwanted data, format, code conversion, and application of standard processes like zero suppression.

Editor: Software that permits the review and editing of a program or text.

Electronic: A term applied to devices, circuits and systems in which transistors and other semi-conductor devices or valves are used to control electric current, etc.

Electronic Funds Transfer (EFT): A generic term referring to a cashless approach used to pay for goods and services. Electronic signals between computers are often used to adjust the accounts of the parties involved in the transactions.

Electronic Mail: A generic term used to describe the transmission of message by the use of computer systems and communications facilities.

Emulator: A stored logic device or program that permits one computer to execute the machine instruction of another computer of a different design.

Encryption: Process of transforming plain text or data to cipher text for the purpose of privacy or security. The process employs an algorithm (which remains fixed) and a keyword (which is usually changed periodically).

Ergonomics: The study of the interaction between people and machines.

Error Message: Output from a computer indicating what has gone wrong and where.

Ethernet: A medium speed (10 MBps) means of transmitting data in Local Area Network, based on coaxial cable.

Error Rate: The ratio of data incorrectly received to the total amount of data transmitted.

Execution Time: For a computer system, it refers to the time at which an object program actually performs the instructions coded in the procedure division, using the actual data provided. As regards the arithmetic-logic unit portion of the CPU, the term refers to the time during which an instruction is decoded and performed.

Executive Routine: A segment of the operating system that controls the execution of other portions of the operating system. Synonymous with *supervisory routine.*

Exchangeable Disk: A magnetic disk that an operator can install on a drive and remove when required. In contrast are non-removable or fixed disks employing, what is referred to as , *Winchester* technology.

Expert System: A software application that contains, and is able to use, data on a specific field of knowledge, as for example, in medical diagnoses.

Express Mail: In Local Area Networks, an electronic message sent to the recipient's 'electronic main box' that displays a message on the PC screen that mail is waiting. Simultaneously the PC keyboard get locked and remains so until the recipient acknowledges the messages on the screen.

External DOS Command: A DOS command that requires the DOS diskette to be in the drive when the command is used. This is necessary as program statement to carry out the command must be read from the diskette and loaded into ROM.

Facsimile (FAX): A system of telecommunication to transmit images which are reproduced at the receiving terminal as hard copy. The original image is scanned and converted to an electrical signal, and the electrical signal is subsequently converted to a replica of the original image at the other end.

Fallback: A procedure or facility that assures continued operation, although often in degraded mode, when failures occur.

Families of Computers: A series of computer models of the same logical design, but of different speeds and configuration rules, designed to enable the user to start with a less powerful model and migrate successively to more powerful models without having to change associated software and hardware elements.

Fetch: To access data or instructions from a file in memory.

Fibre optic Cable: A data transmission medium made of very thin threads of glass that can transmit large volumes of data at the speed of light.

Field: A logical grouping of numbers or characters that carry information (e.g. an account number, customer name, account balance, etc). Same as *data item.*

File: A collection of related records treated as a unit.

File Activity: In a file or a database, the number of records updated or processed during a processing cycle.

File Extension: One, two or three characters added to a file name following the period (.) sign, to certain files, as created.

File Maintenance: The activity of keeping a file up-to-date by adding, changing or deleting data.

File Organisation: A method by which records of a file can be accessed. The most common organisations are 'serial' 'sequential', 'indexed sequential', 'direct' or 'random'. A 'standard file' or organisation is one for which the manufactures can provide the necessary software for access.

File Server: The central computer that controls the transfer of data between PCs to the printers and electronic mail. Also referred to as Control Unit.

File Structure: The method of organising physical and logical records to optimise data access.

File Volatility: In a file or a database the rate at which records are added or deleted.

Firmware: Program instructions stored in a read only memory. The read-only memory converts the extended user-specific instructions to the basic instruction of the computer. See *microcode.*

Fixed and Exchangeable Disk Storage: (FEDS) A magnetic disk unit in which some disks are fixed and other are operator exchangeable.

Fixed-length Record: A record having the same length as all other record with which it is logically or physically associated. Contrast with *variable-length record.*

Flag: An indicator that an equipment or a program has reached a certain condition.

Flops: Acronym for floating point operations per second. A measure of processor performance sometimes used for comparison of various computer models.

Flowchart: A systems analysis or programming tool that uses symbols to represent operations, data, and equipment, and that defines the major phases of the processing as well as the various data media used. Flowcharts also enable the designer to conceptualise the procedure necessary and to visualise each step and item on a program.

Foreground Processing: High priority processing, usually for realtime activities, which is automatically given precedence, by means of interrupts, over lower priority 'background' processing.

Format: (1) A contraction meaning the FORm of MATerial designating the pre-determined arrangements of characters of data for input/output. (2) A display of numeric values in a spreadsheet.

Frame: A group of bit positions extending across magnetic tape or paper tape. The bit positions which can contain one character.

Formula: In spreadsheets, a mathematical expression that yields numeric values based on the relationships between two or more cells in the spreadsheets.

FORTRAN: (FORmula TRANslator), A high-level language used to perform mathematical computations.

Frequency: An expression of how often a periodic (repetitions) wave form or signal regenerates itself at a given amplitude. It is usually expressed in hertz (Hz) or cycles per second.

Front-end Processor: A dedicated communications computer at the 'front-end' of a host computer. It may perform line control, message handling, code conversion, error control, and applications functions such as control and operation of special purpose terminals. See also *Communications controller*.

Full Duplex: The use of two different sets of frequencies by the originating and answering stations, which enable communications to occur in both directions at one time.

Garbage-in Garbage-out (GIGO): A warning that incorrect input will produce incorrect output.

Gate: An electronic circuit in a microprocessor having several input channels to determine one output channel.

General-purpose Computer: A computer designed to solve a large variety of problem, e.g. a stored program computer which may be adapted to a large class of applications.

Generalised Sort-Merge Program: A program that is designed to sort or merge many types of records in a variety of formats.

Generation: The designation of computers according to their lineage. Each new generation is characterised by a change in the basic technology, such as the progression from vacuum tubes to transactions, and from transistors to integrated circuits.

Generation of File: In batch processing, when file of data is updated, the new file created is knows as new generation. In magnetic tape files it is usual to retain at least three generations as a security precaution against loss or damage to the current generation. The three generation are knows as the Grandfather, Father and Son.

Graphics: The use of the computer for drawing lines under complete program control. Also refers to the attachment of a vector scope and light pen on-line to the computer, enabling the user and the computer to interact and jointly draw pictures on the face of the vector scope.

Half Duplex: A circuit designed for transmission alternatively in either direction but not in both directions simultaneously. Contrast with *duplex*.

Hard Copy: Machine output in a permanent visually readable form; for example printed reports, listings, documents, and summaries.

Hardware: Physical computer equipments.

Hardwired: A processing system employing wired circuitry to implement system functions. This type of equipment is usually cheaper than software programmed systems but is less flexible.

Hash Total: An arithmetic total of data used for checking the accuracy of one or more corresponding fields of a file, such as job numbers, invoicing serial numbers, etc, that ordinarily would not be summed to see that all transactions have been processed. When the hash totals agree, the data is considered verified.

Header-Record: A record containing common, constant, or identifying information for a group of records that follow.

Hertz: A unit of frequency equal to one cycle per second. Abbreviated *Hz.*

Heuristic: A directed trial and error approach.

Hexadecimal: Pertaining to a number system with a base of 16; valid digits range from 0 through F, where Frepresents the highest units position (15). Synonymous with *hex.*

High-level Languages: Programming methods that allow the programmer to express operation in a less direct form, that is closer to the normal human language representation of the procedures that the computer is to perform. Such languages are usually problem-oriented or procedure-oriented as distinguished from machine-oriented and/or mnemonic languages. Common examples are Cobol (for business applications), Fortran (for mathematical work), and Basic (a simple, easy-to-use language).

HIPO Charts: (Hierarchy-plus-Input-Process-Output Charts), Charts used in the analysis, and programming of computer applications.

Host Computer: The main or controlling computer in a multiple computer network operation that normally provides high-level services, such as computation, database access, or special programs or programming languages for other computers in the network.

Housekeeping: Routine procedures carried out at intervals in a computer installation necessary, for example, to ensure that data remains efficiently organised and unwanted data and software are purged or archived.

Hybrid Computer: A data processing device using both analog and discrete data representation.

Hypertext: A rather recent development in the field of DBMS. Hypertext software makes it possible for the users to organise and access information in such a manner that any file, graphics, text, digital information, etc. can be directly connected to, any other file, graphics, text, etc. guided by the user's own mental association with any word; phase, piece of information that can be used as the key.

Impact Printer: A printer that forms characters by physically striking a ribbon and paper.

Indexed Sequential Organisation: A file organisation used on direct access storage devices in which records are arranged in logical sequence by key. Indexes to these keys permit direct access to individual records.

Information: It is the meaning derived from raw data that has been arranged and displayed in such a way that it can be related to that which is previously known.

Information Centre: A group established within an organisation to provide hardware facilities, technical support, and education to the user community. The information centre usually is organised separately from the MIS department and operates as liaison between MIS and users.

Ink Jet Printer: A non-impact printing system in which the print head moves across the surface of the copy paper, shooting a stream of tiny, electrostatically charged ink drops at the page, placing them precisely to from individual print characters.

Input: Data entered into a computer system for storage or processing.

Input Device: A device such as a VDU, teletypewriter, etc. which converts data from the form in which it has been received into electronic signals that can be interpreted by the computer.

Input/Output Control System (IOCS): It is a set of programs used in an operating system to handle all input and output work such as opening files, closing files, backspacing tape, moving tape forward when a bad spot is encountered, etc, IOCS is used on all backing storage devices. The programmer's source instructions (macro instructions) call in the IOCS instructions.

Instruction: a statement to the computer that specifies an operation to be performed by the system and the values or locations of all operands. An instruction is usually made up of an operation code and one or more operands.

Instructions Per Second: A measurement of the power of the processor. It is usually measured in terms of millions or thousands of instructions per second - MIPs or KIPs.

Instruction Set: The set of instructions which a computer data processing system is capable of performing.

Instruction Time: The position of a CPU cycle during which an instruction is fetched and decoded.

Integrated Software: Any software package that combines several applications, for example, LOTUS 1-2-3 which combines spreadsheets, graphics and database functions built on common data.

Intelligent Terminal: A terminal with some logical capability: a remote device that is capable of performing some editing or other function upon input and/or output data. See *dumb terminal.*

Interactive Operation: An on-line operation also referred as conversational mode in which the user presents problem to computer, gets results etc.

Job: A unit of work of the computing system from the standpoint of installation accounting and/or operating system control. A job consists of one or more steps or programs. Usually includes all necessary computer programs, linkages, files, and instructions to the operating system.

Job Control Language (JCL): A programming language used to code job control statements, for supplying information to the operating system and the operators about the program, e.g. name of user, how much memory is required, estimated run time, priority, tapes, required, other programs, etc., so that the operating system can carry out the required tasks without operator intervention.

Justification: To position characters of text so that left or right margins are aligned. Also, to order digits so that the least significant or most significant is always at the left or right margin.

K: The symbol for two, raised to the tenth power (kilo), equal to 1.024.

Kernel: An OS master program for the overall management of a computer system. Synonymous with *monitor* and *supervisor*. Central piece of UNIX OS which starts up an inter active program for each user, referred to as the *shell.*

Key-Data Entry Devices: A keyboard equipped devices used to prepare data so that the computer can accept it. Include key-to-tape key-to-disk units, etc.

Key Expression: The fields used to determine the order of records in an index file.

Label: One or more characters used to identify a program statement or a data item.

Laser: A device which transmits an extremely narrow and coherent beam of electromagnetic energy in the visible light spectrum.

Latency: Refers to time between an address interpretation and the start of the actual transfer. Latency includes the delay associated with access to storage devices.

Legend: A brief description of symbols used in a graph to represent data ranges.

Letter Quality Printer: A printer that generates output of a quality that matches the output available from a standard office typewriter.

Library: A collection of organisation information. In electronic data processing, a program library is a collection of available computer programs and routines. The libraries used by an organisation are known as its *data bank.*

Library Routine: A tested routine maintained in a library of programs.

Light Emitting Diode (LED): A diode which glows when supplied with an electric current.

LightPen: A tool for VDU terminal operators that causes the computer to change or modify the display on the cathode ray tube. The pen's response to light from the display is transmitted to the computer which, in turn, relates the computer action to the section of the image being displayed. In this way, the operator can delete or add text, maintain tighter control over the program and choose alternative courses of action.

Line Graph: Data represented in a graph as a set of points along a line.

Line Printer: The computer output peripheral that prints an entire line of characters as a unit. Suitable for high printing speed.

Linkage Editor: The language processor in the operating system that prepares the output of language translatators for execution. It combines separately produced modules; resolves cross references among them, replaces, deletes and adds control sections, and produces an executable load module.

Liquid Crystal Display (LCD): A graphic display on a terminal screen using an electro luminescent technology to form symbols or shapes.

List: A data structure in which each item of data can contain pointers to other items. Any data structure can be represented in this way, which allows the structure to be independent of the storage of the items.

Local Area Network (LAN): A system for linking terminals, programs, storage, and graphic devices at multiple workstations over relatively small geographic areas of rapid communications.

Location: Part of the main memory in which an instruction or item can be stored and which is usually identified by an address.

Logical File: It is a complete set of records for a specific application or purpose. It may occupy only a part of a physical file or may extend over more than one physical file, e.g. an inventory file which is a logical file containing a record for each item in inventory may require one or more reels of magnetic tape.

Logical Record: The record of data created as a single, logical data unit by the application procedure; data values which share a common context. Contrasted with *physical record.*

Login: The sign-on procedure used to access the communication network.

Loop: A sequences of computer instructions that repeats itself until a pre-determined count or other test is satisfied.

Low-level Language: A programming language in which instructions have a one-to-one relationship with machine code.

LSI (Large-scale Integration): Refers to a chip with more than 100,000 transistors.

Machine Cycle: The basic operating cycle of a CPU during which a single instruction is fetched, decoded, and executed.

Machine Language: A binary language all digital computers must use. All other programming languages must be compiled or translated ultimately into binary language before entering the processor. Binary language is used directly by a machine.

Macro: A programming language, (usually, assembly language) that generates more than one absolute language instruction. Synonymous with *macro call.*

Magnetic Disk: a flat circular platter with a magnetic surface on which data can be stored in the form of magnetized spots. Data is arranged in concentric tracks sound the disks and is accessible to reading and writing heads on an arm which can be moved to the desired track as the disk rotates.

Magnetic Ink Character Recognition (MICR): Machine recognition of characters printed with magnetic ink. The MICR code consists of a set of 10 numeric symbols and four special symbols standardised as font E 13B in the USA and the UK. There is also a continent standard called CMC 7 font. It consists of numeric characters, alphabets and five special characters each represented by seven vertical bars.

Magnetic Tape: Flexible plastic tape often 0.5 inch wide with seven or nine channels or horizontal, rows, that extend the length of the tape. One side is uniformly coated with magnetic material on which data is stored. It is used for registering television images, or computer data. Magnetic tape is a 'sequential' medium with a very low cost per bit.

Main Memory: The primary storage facilities forming an integral physical part of the computer and directly controlled by the computer. In such internal facilities, all data is automatically accessible to the computer. See *internal storage.*

Mainframe: A large-scale computer, usually the primary processor for an organisation.

Maintenance Programming: The act of changing and modifying existing programs to meet changing conditions.

Management Information System (MIS): A data processing system that is designed to furnish management supervisory personnel with current information to aid in the performance of management functions. Data is recorded and processed for operational purposes, problems are isolated and referred to upper management for decision-making and information is fed back to reflect progress in achieving major objectives.

Mark Sense: A method of automated input in which marks made on a document with an electrically conducive pencil are interpreted by a sensing device and transmitted to a storage medium or processor.

Master File: A main reference file of information used in a computer system. It provides information to be used by the program and can be updated and maintained to reflect the results of the processing operation.

Mean-time-between-failure (MTBF): The average time the system or a component of the system works without faulting.

Media: The vehicles by which information is stored or transmitted, classified as source, input and output, for example a floppy disk.

Medium Scale Integration (MST): Usually less than 100 circuits on a single chip of semiconductor. Widely used in third generation systems.

Memory: The circuitry and devices that accept and hold binary numbers and are capable of storing data as well as programs. Memory must allow rapid access to information. Various types are: Disk, drum, semiconductor, magnetic core, change-coupled devices, bubble domain, etc.

Memory Dump: A listing of the contents of a storage device, or selected parts of it.

Memory Management: The allocation of main memory space on a multi-programming system.

Menu: A choice of program options provided by the computer to the user on a display screen.

Menu Dialogue: One form of man/machine communication where the user is offered to menu specifying a variety of options. Once the user has chosen one item on the menu, say, by pressing the number on the keyboard corresponding to the menu number of the chosen option, the system will respond with the appropriate action.

Merge: An operation combining two or more files of data into one in a pre-determined sequence.

Message Switching: A communication process which enables one or more transactions or related information to be routed to its destination on a shared network.

Metal Oxide Semiconductor (MOS): A common material and method for making integrated circuits.

MICR Reader/Sorter: A document handler that permits both the reading of MICR encoded documents and the sorting of those documents on digits selected either at the unit console (off-line) or by the computer program (on-line).

Microcode: Low-level language programs imbedded in the architecture of a computer, usually in ROM, and executed automatically. Synonymous with *firmware.*

Microcomputer: A computer system that has a microprocessor as its processor unit, and also includes storage and input/output facilities in the basic unit, all off which may or may not be on a single chip.

Microfirm: A roll of photographic film, small in size, but when developed and projected onto a screen, produces a legible copy of the items or form photographed. See *COM-Computer-Output-Microfirm.*

Microfiche: A rectangular transparency approximately four inches by six inches containing multiple rows of greatly reduced page images of reports, catalogue, rate books, etc. Data reductions range from 13 up to several hundred times smaller than the original.

Microprocessor: The central unit of microcomputer that contains the logical elements for manipulating data and performing arithmetical or logical operations on it. A single chip may contain RAM, ROM, and PROM memories, clocks, and interfaces for memory and I/O devices.

Microsecond: One-million of a second.

Micro-to-Mainframe Link: Software created linkages between PCs and mainframe computers by which the mainframe computer can respond to the queries made by the user from his PC.

Milli-second: One-thousand of a second.

Minicomputer: A small to medium size programmable general purpose computer typically used for dedicated applications. Usually it is a parallel binary system with 8,16,18,24 or 36 bit word length incorporating semiconductor or magnetic core memory offering from 4K words to 64K words or storage and a cycle time of 0.2 to 8 microseconds or less.

Mnemonic: A term applied to something that assists human memory. Thus a mnemonic term is often an abbreviation designed to help programmers to remember instructions, e.g., ART for arithmetic operation or MPY for multiply.

Model: An approximate mathematical representation that simulates the behaviour of a process device or concept so as to attain an increased understanding of the system.

Modem: Contraction of MODulator/DEModulator; a conversion device installed in parts or each end of an analog communications line. The modem at the transmitting end converts digital signals from a computer or terminal into analog signals for transmission purposes, whole the modem at the destination converts the signal into digital form for the receiving device.

Modulation: Application of information on a carrier signal by varying one or more of the signal's basic characteristics (frequency, amplitude, or phase); the conversion of a signal from its original format (e.g. digital) to analog format.

Module: A program unit that is discrete and identifiable with respect to combining with other units, and loading.

Monitor: (1) A software or hardware tool that is used to supervise, control, or verify the operations of a system. (2) The output device that displays messages on the screen for temporary viewing by the user.

Mouse: A mall pointing input device used with PCs. It rolls on a flat surface and this movement guides the cursor on the display screen. The buttons on its top. A combination of the movement of the mouse and the pressing of button on the mouse, selects the menu item and causes the PC to perform the required operation.

Multiplexer: A hardware device that allows handling of multiple low speed signals over single high-speed channel.

Multiprocessing: A hardware and software architecture which allows more than one processor to work on different parts of a program at the same time.

Multiprocessor: A computer network consisting of two or more central processors under a common control.

Multiprogramming: The ability of a computer a run more than one program simultaneously within the same computer. The facility depends on the operating system available.

Multitasking: An IBM term for multithreading. Refers to the concurrent execution of one main task and one or more subtasks in the same partition.

Multithreading: A program construction technique which allows more than one logical path through the program to be executed simultaneously.

Multi-level Sort: In dBase III Plus, a sorted file in which records are organised by the first specified keyfield and within that by a second specified keyfield.

Multi-user: A computer that can support several work-stations working simultaneously.

Nanosecond: One-thousand millionth (billionth) of a second (10^9 second).

Narrowband Channels: Sub-voice grade channels characterised by a speed range of 100 to 200 bits per second.

Network: A number of computer terminals and/or computer processors linked together by telecommunications lines.

Networking: Connecting geographically separated computers together over transmission lines. In teleprocessing, a number of communications lines connecting a computer with remote terminals. In general communication applications, the interconnection of multiple communication channels, multiple terminals, and/or computers (nodes). See also *multi-processing.*

Network Data Structure: A method of organising a database, with linkage external to the physical organisation.

Nibble: Popular name for four bits, or half a byte.

Node: Any station, terminal, terminal installation communications computer, or communications computer installation in a computer network.

Non-volatile Storage: A storage medium that retains its contents in the absence of power.

Non-impact Printer: A printer that creates images on paper without physical impact between the print head and paper, for example, Laser and Thermal printers.

Number Cruncher: An application involving many complex calculations but, relatively, little input and output.

Object Program or Code: The final result of a language transaction, ready to be loaded into the computer.

OCR (Optical Character Recognition): A process of light-sensitive recognition by machines of printed or written characters from an output device, that serves as direct input to a computer system. This permits capturing input data at the entry source, by passing additional processing operations. Contrast with *MICR.*

OEM (Original Equipment Manufacturer): Organisations that develop entire customised computer systems. Often OEMs buy components from different hardware and software vendors and package a complete system for retail.

Off-line: Pertaining to those peripherals or operations that are part of a system but are not directly controlled by the central processor.

On-line: Peripherals providing immediate access to computer files for data entry or enquiry purposes. The peripherals are attached to and controlled by the central processor.

On-line Processing: A general data processing term concerning access to computers, in which the input data enters the computer directly from the point of origin or in which output data is transmitted directly to where it is used. The process usually requires random access storage.

Open System: Refers to PCs, having multifunction boards with ports built into them to add on compatible devices, like printers, graphic devices, etc.

Operand: The part of a computer instruction that tells the computer where the data to be processed is stored.

Operating System: The specialised software that controls and monitors the execution of all other programs that reside in the computer processor, including application programs and other system software. It is usually supplied by the computer vendor.

Optical Disk: An emerging storage medium that employs laser technology, and is characterised by extremely high capacity. Also see *videodisk.*

Optical Mark Reading: Input method which automatically recognises whether or not a mark (such as diagonal line) is placed in a particular position on a form. Useful to record, for example, meter reading.

Output: Data of text produced from a computer storage or processing system in any form, e.g. screen display, telecommunications message, printed report, magnetic tape, etc.

Overflow Area: A physical area of external storage in which data not contained initially in the external prime data area is stored.

Overlay: A technique by which a program that exceeds allotted main memory storage can be loaded in segments.

Packaged Software: Software purchased from third parties designed to meet the needs of several organisations.

Packet Switching: A data communication technique in which a message is broken into smaller units called packets, which may be individually addressed and routed through the network, possibly using several different routes. The receiving end node ascertains that all packets are received in the proper sequence before forwarding the complete message to the addressee.

Paging: In virtual storage systems, the process of transferring pages between real storage and external page storage. If a page is not transferred from auxiliary storage until it is actually needed, then paging is said to be done by demand.

Parallel Processing: Processing of more than one program at the same time by more than one processor. To be distinguished from multi-programming in which only one processor is active but processes more than one program at a time.

Parity Check: A method of checking the accuracy of binary data after the data has been transferred to or from storage. The number of I-bits in a binary character is controlled by the addition or delection of a parity bit.

Password: A unique word or string of characters that a program, computer operator, or user must supply to meet security requirements, before gaining access to the system. The password confidential, as opposed to the user identification.

Patch: To modify a program in a rough or expedient way; often to the object version of the already complied program.

Peripherals: The input, output and backing storage devices.

Personal Computer: A small computer or intelligent terminal whose main applications are for personal rather than corporate problem solving.

Personal Identification Device: A card badge device normally used a connection with a personal identification number (PIN), which, when introduced into a terminal, uniquely identified the user to the access control system.

Physical File: It is a physical unit such as a magnetic tape or a disk.

Physical Record: The block of data stored between two gaps in a storage medium. It may contain several logical records. This is the minimum amount of data which can be transferred at one time between the processor and the secondary storage media.

Pie Chart: A graph that compares parts with the whole with values in the data range shown as a wedge or pie of a circle.

Picosecond: One trillionth of a second. One thousandth of a nanosecond.

Picture File: A file used to print graphs. It contains definition of the graph and carries a fie extension 'PIC'.

Pipeline: Configuration of a processor based on the division of an operation into a sequence of sub-operations that are executed independently.

Pixels: The picture elements consisting of individual dots that form an image on the PC screen.

Plug-compatible: A computer or other device supplied by a vendor that interfaces to another vendor's system; or which can substitute for another vendor's equipment and run the same programs without modification.

Point of Sale Terminal (POS): A device used at super markets that (a) immediately updates sales and inventory records at a central CPU, and (b) producing a printed sale transaction receipt.

Polling: A centrally controlled method of permitting terminals on a multi-terminal line to transmit without contending for the line. The polling device contracts terminals according to the order specified by the user.

Port: A point of attachment between an interface device (controller or other peripheral) and a channel or an interface device and a controller.

Portability: The ability to move a program from one computer to another. High-level languages ease portability.

Printed Circuit Board (PCB): An insulated board onto which a metal coating is applied, then etched away, leaving paths of circuits. Also called PC boards, boards, cards, PC cards.

Print Formating: In word processing the ability of the system to print the textual matter created by means of text editing with certain formating commands, like text justification, page numbering, centering, inserting heading, etc.

Problem-oriented Language: A source language suited to describing procedural steps that is designed for convenience of program specification in a general problem area rather than for easy conversion to machine instruction code. The components of such a language may bear little resemblance to machine instructions. POLs are generally machine independent (Fortran, Basic, Cobol, PL/I, etc.)

Procedure-oriented Language: A high-level programming language whose instruction set is used to model business and scientific procedures. See *Problem-oriented Language.*

Processing: To employ a systematic sequence to operations in produce a specified result by performing operations on data.

Process Control: Pertaining to systems whose purpose is to provide automation of continuous operations, and characterised by in-line adjustments to regulate an operation, this is contrasted with numerical control, which provides automation of discrete operations.

Program: A set of sequenced instructions to cause a computer to perform particular operations.

Program Dump: An object program and the contents of its data storage areas 'frozen' all a specific point during its execution and displayed in alphanumeric form.

Programming Language: Any language in which computer processing instructions (programs) are written. Most programming languages are high-level languages that must be translated into executable machine language.

PROM(Programmable Read Only Memory): A control memory in which the stored information can be altered, but not as easily as in ordinary memory. In some PROMs, the contents may be erased by prolonged (minutes) application of ultraviolet light, and then rewritten. A core-memory version is called EAROM (Electricity Alterable ROM).

Prompt: A question or other indication that the computer is waiting for a response from the user.

Protocol: The set of rules that govern the exchange of signals among the entities in a data communications network.

Prototyping: Developing a low cost system with key features often using high level languages and paying little attention to technical design efficiency, in order to test user behaviour with the system to improve design features as also estimates of benefits.

Pseudocode: English-like description of the processing steps in a computer program.

Pulldown Menu: A list of options on the screen when menu is opened.

Query Language: A high-level program language that allows a terminal operator to engage in a dialogue with a computer without having to write a program.

RAM (Random-Access-Memory): A storage technique in which the time required to obtain data is independent or the location. There is no difference in the time required to operate to or from any address. Core memories are RAMs; however, the term is usually used with respect to semiconductor memories.

Random Access: Pertaining to a storage device where data or blocks of data can be read in any particular order (e.g. disk). Random access devices to not have to be read from the beginning to find a specific address as is necessary with paper tape and magnetic tape. See *direct-access storage device.*

Range Checks: Tests against pre-determined maximum ad minimum acceptable values of data. Useful for detecting large errors in interest rates and value data; but not generally so useful when applied to transaction values.

Raster Scan: The technique of generating images on a display screen by focussing on electron beam on a phosphor quoted screen. Used in VDUs.

Ratio Tests: Tests of relationship between numerical quantities such as average balance and interest paid. Often not a definite indication of error but useful for high unusual ratios for further investigation.

Read-only Memory (ROM): A memory that cannot be altered during normal computer use.

Information is permanently stored and can be read from any locations at high speed, but can never be altered.

Real time: The processing of transactions as they occur rather than batching them. Pertaining to an application in which response to input is fast enough to effect subsequent inputs and/or guide the process, and in which records are updated immediately. On-line processing is used for fore real-time systems; however, not all on-line processing is real-time. An on-line system may be shared by many users; then response time is not always immediate.

Reasonableness Check: A control procedure used to ensure that the value of a data element or output is consistent with an expected value.

Record: A collection of related items of data (fields) treated as a unit.

Record Format: The specific form established for a data record; a specification which includes the data item names, sequences of data-items, numbers of data symbols, required to represent data item values, and the type of symbols to be found in a record.

Register: Location in the ALU used for special functions such the accumulator, instruction decoder, etc.

Regular Mail: In LAN, a message that is distributed to the recipient's electronic mail box.

Relational Database: A method of organising a database to permit association of information contained in separate records by placing data associated with each key in separate tables.

Relative Cell Address: In spreadsheets, the adjustment of the cell address to reflect its new location, when copied or moved.

Remote Batch: A method of entering job into the computer from a remote terminal in a conversational mode, for processing later in a batch processing mode.

Remote Job Entry: (1) Input and output capabilities at a distance from the main computer service but close to the user (2) A remote job entry terminal with its own processor and memory which can act as stand-alone system for some local applications when not communicating with the main computer.

Report Program Generator (RPG): A processing program that can be used to generate object programs that produce reports. RPG has powerful and relatively simple input/output file manipulation (including table look-up), but is relatively limited in algorithmic capabilities.

Resolution: For a CRT screen, the visual clarity of a display resulting from the number of dots per square inch in a particular screen matrix.

Response Time: Time taken for the computer to reply to a user request.

Rotational Delay: The time required for a particular record stored on a rotating secondary memory device to be positioned under the read/write head.

Run: The single and continuous execution of a program by a computer or a given set of data.

Schema: The logical description of a database, including the definition of the name and data type of each field making up each record and the definition of the relationships that link files.

Scrolling: A function on a CRT terminal that allows the operator to move the display horizontically or vertically in order to view pervious or subsequent screens.

Security: The general subject of making sure the computerised data and program files of the company cannot be accessed, obtained, or modified by unauthorised personnel, and can't be destroyed by the computer on its programs. Security is implemented by special software, special hardware, and the computer's operating procedure.

Seek Time: The time that is needed to position the access mechanism of a direct access storage device at a specified position. See also access time.

Semiconductor: A substance like silicon that allows the flow of electronic current.

Sequential Access: The facility to obtain data form, or to enter data into, a storage device in such a way that the process depends on the location of that data and on a reference to data previously accessed or stored. Synonymous with serial access. Contrast with *direct access* and *random access.*

Sequential Data Set: A data set whose records are organised on the basis of their successive physical positions, such as on magnetic tape.

Sequential Processing: Batch processing.

Serial Access: Access to information in storage by searching sequentially through the storage medium, e.g. on magnetic tape and microfilm. Contrast with *direct* and *random access.*

Shared Hardware Resources: In LAN, resources like printer shared by all PCs.

Simplex Circuit: A communication line used in one direction only or in either direction but not at the same time.

Simulation: The use of programming techniques alone to duplicate operation of one computing system on another computing system. In computer programming, the technique of setting up a routine for one computer to make it operate as nearly as possible like some other computer. Contrast with *emulation.*

Smart Terminal: Intelligent terminal.

Software: A term coined to contrast computer programs with the 'iron' or hardware of a computer system. Software programs are stored sets of instructions that govern the operation of a computer system and make the hardware run. The processor programs, library routine, manuals, and other service programs supplied by a computer manufacturer to facilitate the use of a computer. In addition, it may refer to other programs specially developed to fit the users needs. All the documents associated with a computer.

Source Data Automation (SDA): The capturing of data for machine entry, as a key-product of producing a required documents such as a purchase order, job order, or other source document. The by-product then serves as input for a computer.

Source Document: An original document of some type whose data is to be convened into machine readable form.

Source Program: A computer program written in symbolic language which will be converted into an absolute language object program using a process or program.

Special-purpose Computer: A computer that is designed to handle a restricted class of problems.

Specifications: A precise and detailed statement of hardware and/or system requirements.

Speech Recognition: The capability of an electronic device to accept an operator's voice as input and convert the analog waveforms into a digital representations.

Spooling: Simultaneous Peripheral Operations On-Line. The transfer of data to temporary backing storage. The data is subsequently processed or output.

Spreadsheet: A grid of vertical column and horizontal rows used to enter and manipulate data.

Stacked Bar Graph: A graph that displays data values as bars stacked one upon the other.

Star Network: A computer network with peripheral nodes all connected to one or more computers as a centrally located facility. Same as *centralised network.*

Status Line: Bottom line in the display screen that displays documents number, page line, etc. as well as position of the cursor.

Storage Media: The physical units upon which data is recorded, e.g. magnetic tape, magnetic disk, floppy disks, etc.

Streamer: A magnetic tape unit designed specifically to support a fixed disk (Winchester) magnetic disk system by holding files and transferring them rapidly to and from the disk, when required. The unit typically uses one half inch tape recorded at 1600 characters per inch and incorporates a microprocessor to calculate the tape diameter on each reel and to control reel speeds accordingly to maintain constant tape tension.

String: A connected sequence of characters of bits that is treated as a single data item.

Structured Design: A program or system development procedure that involves modularisation into logical functional units using top-down methods.

Structured Programming: A systematic technique of program design. It assumes the disciplined use of a few basic coding structures and the use of top-down concept to decompose main functions into lower level components for modular cooling purposes.

Structured Walk-through: A formalised technique whereby one programmer describes the step-by-step functioning of his or her program to other programmers.

Sub-routine: Program segments that performs specific functions. By creating the required function as a sub-routine, the statements associated with that function may be coded once and executed at many different points in a program.

Sub-schema: The logical description of a subset of the database. See also *schema.*

Supercomputer: Any computer characterised by very high processing speed and power and usually referring to a special purpose computer that performs in a scientific environment.

Supervisor: The part of an operating system that coordinates the use of resources and maintains the flow of CPU operations, rather than processing data to produce results.

Synchronous Computer: A computer in which all operations and events are controlled by equally spaced pulses from a clock. Contrasted with *asynchronous computer.*

Syntax Error: A system response to a mistake in instruction; such as a transposition of characters of omission of a character or words.

Systems: An organised collection of parts or procedures, united by regulated interaction and interconnected to perform a function.

System Analysis: Complete analysis of all activity phases of an organisation to determine precisely what must be accomplished and how to accomplish it, and development of detailed procedure for all collection, manipulation, and evaluation of data associated with its operation.

Systems and Support Software: The variety of software including assemblers, compilers, subroutine libraries, operating systems, application programs, etc. usually provided by the computer vendor free or at low cost.

Table Look-up: The process of using a table of data stored in main memory during the running of the program to obtain a function value.

Tape Drive: A mechanism for controlling the movement of magnetic tape past a reading or writing head.

Teleconferencing: The use of interactive audio, audiographic, video, or computer systems for electronic group communications.

Teleprocessing: The processing of data that is received from or sent to remote locations by way of telecommunication lines. Such systems are essential to hook up remote terminals or connect geographically separated computers. See also *telecommunications.*

Teletext: A generic name for the broadcast of messages and graphics as part of a television signals using the blank space or unused portion of the signal.

Terminal: A device equipped with a keyboard (or other input device) and an output device (e.g. display or printer) that is connected to a computer system for the input and/or output of data. A terminal may be simple as a telephone, or as complex as a small computer. Terminals are generally used for on-line systems.

Test Data: A set of special inputs designed to test a particular program or a group of programs to reveal errors, if any. The term applies to data used with benchmarking programs.

Test Data Generator: Software for forming test data files holding desired or randomly generated values in nominated fields of nominated records. Most effective if controlled by the record data definitions used in application programs so that fields can be identified by the same symbolic names and test data can be recomplied in the same manner as programs, upon a change of field or record format.

Text Editing: Specific flexible editing facilities designed into a computer program to permit the original keyboarding of textual copy, without regard for the eventual format or medium for publication. Once the copy has been placed in computer storage, it can be edited and justified into any required column width only any specified type font, by specifying the format required.

The Assistant: A menu method of entering dBase III Plus commands.

Time-sharing: A method of operation in which the resources of a computer facility are shared by several users via terminals for different purposes at (apprarently) the same time. Although the computer actually services each user in sequence its high speed makes it appear that all handled simultaneously.

Time Slice: An interval of time on the central processing unit allocated for use in performing a task. Once the interval has expired. CPU time is allocated to another task; thus a task cannot monopolise CPU time beyond a fixed limit. In systems with time-sharing, a segments of time allocated to a terminal job.

Top-down Design: System planning characterised by examination first of the major function, and then its subfunctions, until the system's scope and details are fully understood.

Track: A channel on a direct-access device that contains data which can be read by a single reading head without changing its position. It may refer to the track on a disk which rotates under a read head, or the track on a magnetic stripe that is passed by a fixed read head.

Trailer Label: Information written after a file has been processed indicating how many logical records make up the file, what is the batch total, and so on.

Transfer Rate: The average number of data units (characters, bytes, words and blocks) passing between functional units, per unit time. The terms is used with respect to local transfers as well as transfers over communication links.

Transaction File: A file containing update transactions to be processed against a master file. Synonymous with *detail file.*

Transaction Processing (TP) Processing in which the programs to be executed are selected from a (remote) terminal which also supplies, some of, or all of, input parameters, and in which results are returned to the terminal upon completion of processing. Such processing is on-line and also, usually, real time. Opposite of *batch processing.*

Tree Structure: In a database, a hierarchic level by-level arrangement in which a parent data item can have one or more child data items, but which does not allow a child data item to have more than one parent.

Turn-around Document: A customer bill or other document, all or part of which is returned to the sender. Usually, the returned position (stub) contains machine-readable data prepared by the sender's computer system.

Turn-around Time: The elapsed time between submission of a job to a computing center and the return of results. In communications, the actual time required to reverse the direction of transmission from send to receive or vice versa when using a half duplex circuit.

User-Friendly: A term applied terminal-type computer equipment that is easy to operate and has good error recovery facilities.

Utility Program: A program, usually supplied by a computer manufacturer, that is able to perform routine housekeeping, sorting or error correction functions on any file. Some are used for copying files while others for changing their contents. Some of these are very powerful and could be used to bypass access control and amend accounting data fraudulently, leaving no trace.

Validation: The programmed checking of data or results to ensure that they pass pre-defined standards.

Value Added Carriers: A class of communications common carrier authorised to lease raw communication trunks from the transmission carriers, augment these facilities with computerised switching, and provide enhanced or 'value-added' communications service.

Value Added Carriers: A class of communications common carrier authorised to lease raw communication trunks from the transmission carriers, augment these facilities with computerised switching, and provide enhanced or 'value-added' communication service.

Variable-Length Record: A record having a length independent of the length of other records with which it is logically or physically associated.

Verification: An attempt to find errors by executing a program in a test or simulated environment.

Video Disk: A rigid, random access storage medium for analog or digital data written/read by a laser. See *optical disk.*

Videotex: Generic term describing a computer based system that facilitates the electronic distribution of information and services from their providers to their consumers. The information takes the form of screens full of alphanumeric text and/or graphics. One-way videotex is called viewdata. Videotex is also commonly used synonymously with viewdata to denote a two-way interactive system.

Viewdata: Two-way interactive videotex. Videotex by itself and viewdata are commonly, and thus confusingly, used interchangeably to refer to the two-way interactive form of videotex.

Virtual Machine: An operating system capability which makes available machine's resources to user, as required solely for his purposes, although other users may be accessing the same machine in different ways.

Virtual Memory: Synonymous with *virtual storage.* It is an operating system facility which enables a program to run in a machine larger than the size of the main memory available to it. The operating system stores bits of the program on backing storage 'swapping' it into the main store, when it is needed, without affecting the program's operation.

Visual Display Unit: A TV-like display screen and associated keyboard.

Voice Print: A technique for verifying an individual's identify by the pattern produced by his or her voice.

Voice-grade Channel: A device used on a telephone circuit to permit the presence of telephone currents to effect a desired control. Such a device is used in most echo suppressors.

Volatile Storage: A semiconductor for storage device that loses its contents when electrical power is removed.

Volume: A recording medium that is mounted or dismounted as a unit, for example a reel of magnetic tape, a disk pack, a data cell.

VLSI: Very Large Scale Integration.

Wand: A device attached to a point of sale unit to read for coded and other tags on goods.

What...If Analysis: A technique of evaluating the effect of changing certain values in the spreadsheet to see what effect they have on other values in the spreadsheet.

Wideband: A communicating channel having handwidth characterised data transmission speeds of 10,000 to 500,000 bits per second.

Winchester Disk: A rigid (hard), non-removable, magnetic oxide coated random access storage medium scaled in a filtered enclosure along with the read/write heads and the head actuator. Very close head-to-disk clearance tolerances allow cry dense data storage.

Window: Program controlled division of the display screen into several sections each to show the current status of several programs running simultaneously.

Word: A group of characters occupying one storage location in a computer. It is treated by the computer circuits as an entity, by the control and as an instruction, and by the arithmetic unit as a quantity.

Word Length: The number is bits in a word. Longer word lengths increase efficiency and accuracy, but add complexity and cost. Word length determines the number of memory locations that can be directly accessed, using single word address.

Word Processing: The application of any computer system to the manipulation of textural information.

Work File: In sorting, an intermediate file used for temporary storage of data.

Work Station: A VDU terminal at which a certain type of business related work is performed, e.g order entry or invoicing. It is usually a local terminal rather than a remote terminal.

Zone Bits: Used in different combination with numeric bits to represent alphanumeric characters.

Index

□□□